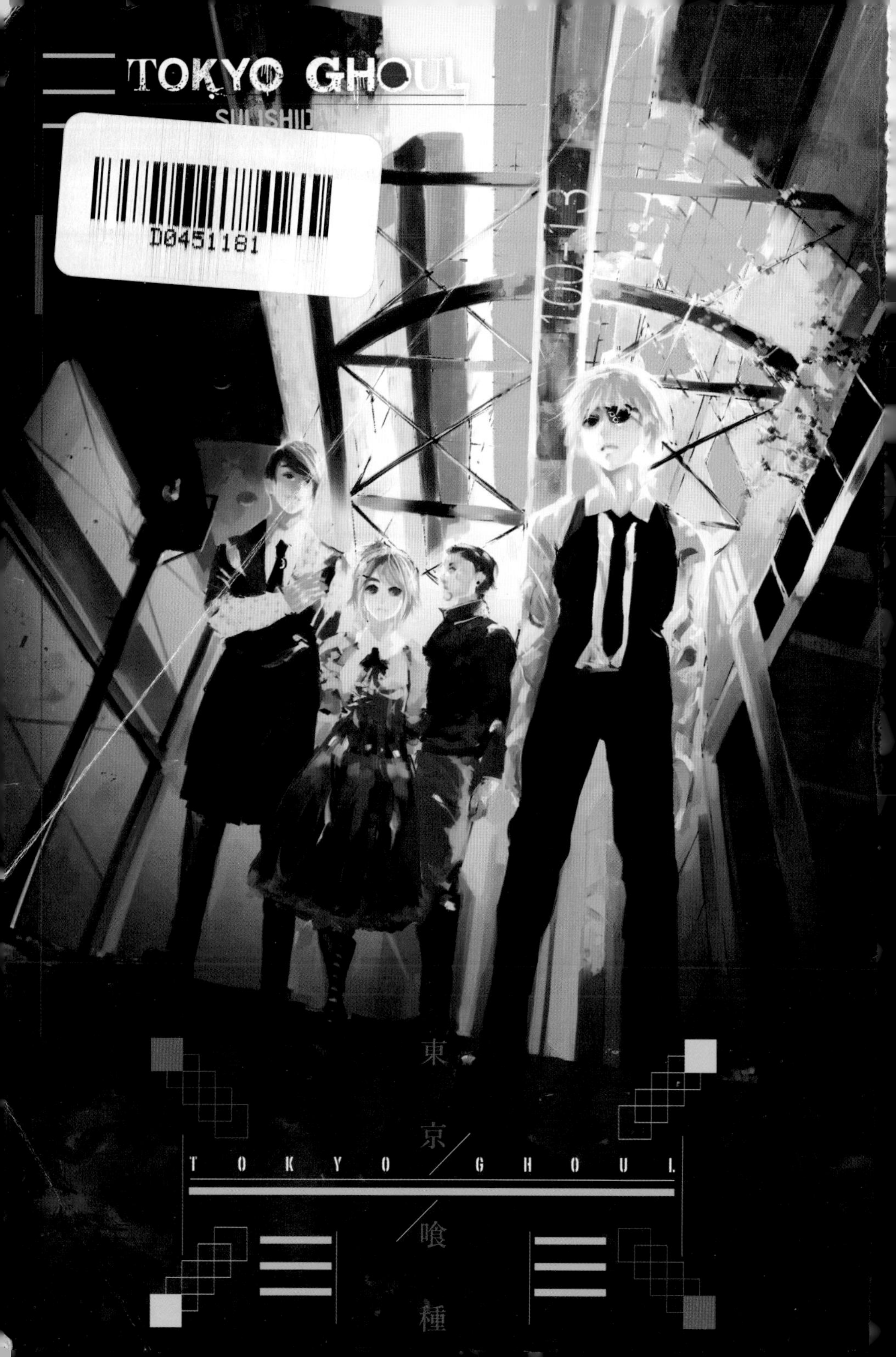
TOKYO GHOUL
東京喰種
TOKYO GHOUL

SUI ISHIDA was born in Fukuoka, Japan. He is the author of ***Tokyo Ghoul*** and several ***Tokyo Ghoul*** one-shots, including one that won him second place in the *Weekly Young Jump* 113th Grand Prix award in 2010. ***Tokyo Ghoul*** began serialization in *Weekly Young Jump* in 2011 and was adapted into an anime series in 2014.

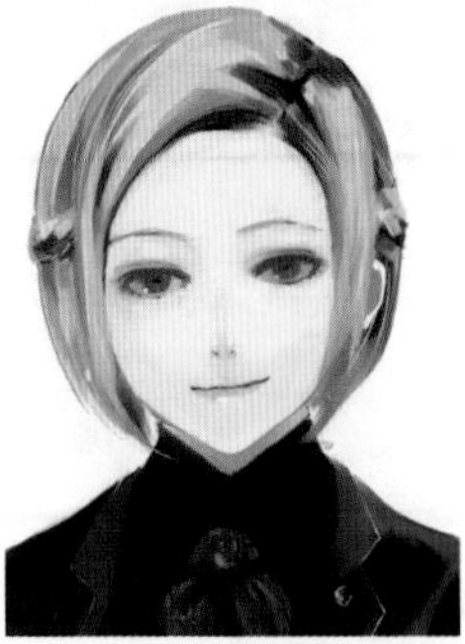

AKIRA MADO

真戸 暁（マド アキラ）

BORN June 6th Gemini

Ghoul Investigator Training Academy Graduate
(Head of the Class)

BLOOD-TYPE: A

Size: 164 cm 49 kg FEET 23.0 CM

Likes: MAKING QUINQUES, puzzle-solving, cats
Respect: Parents, Kisho Arima
Quinque: Prototype 1: Bikaku
A prototype ordered during her Academy days. Damaged from wear and tear.
Prototype 2: Bikaku
A prototype ordered upon appointment to Rank 2 Investigator. Equipped with a shape-changing feature, but damaged from improper adjustment by the engineer.

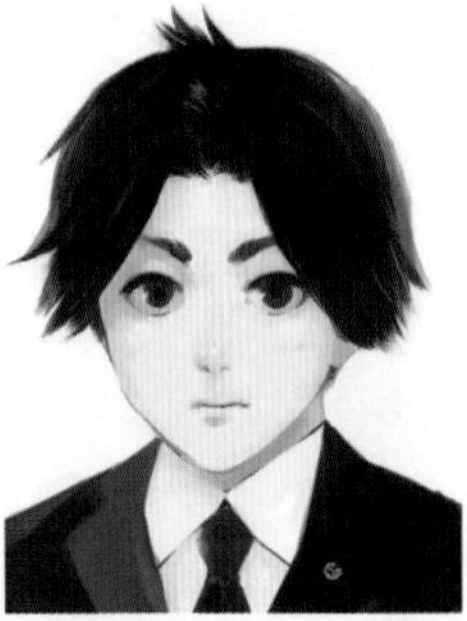

SEIDO TAKIZAWA

滝澤 政道（タキザワ セイドウ）

BORN September 10th Virgo

Ghoul Investigator Training Academy Graduate
(2nd in Class)
CCG Main Office Rank 2 Investigator

BLOOD-TYPE: A

Size: 171.5 cm 67 kg FEET 26.0 cm

Likes: Sports spectating, cop shows, dogs
Respect: Kisho Arima, Kotaro Amon
Quinque: Dohi: Ukaku
Given to him from Investigator Hoji. A Quinque made from a Chinese Ghoul's Kagune.

東京喰種

TOKYO GHOUL

9

TOKYO GHOUL

SUI ISHIDA

TOKYO GHOUL

sui ishida

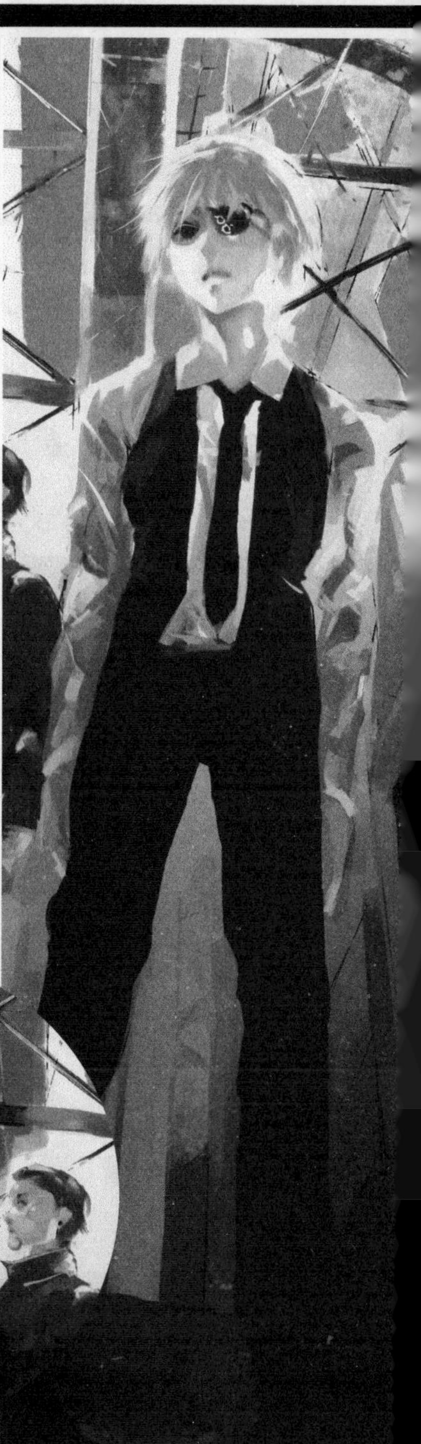

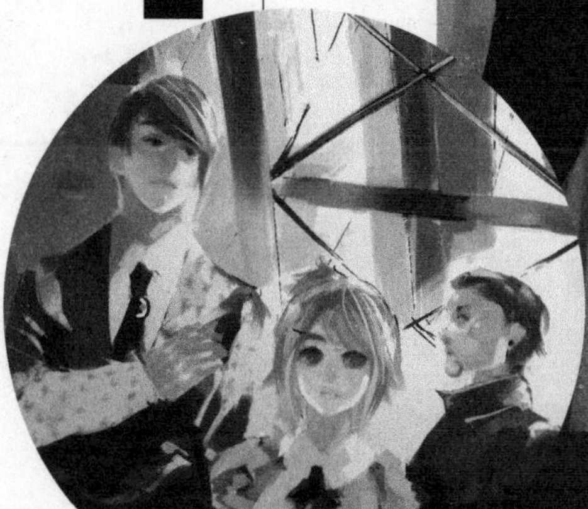

TOKYO GHOUL

TOKYO GHOUL SO FAR

喰 GHOULS 種

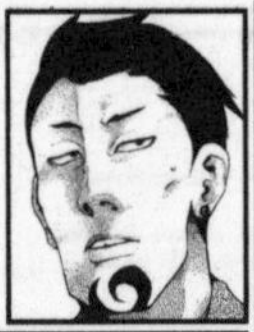

KAZUICHI BANJO

Former leader of the 11th Ward who admires Rize. Former member of the Aogiri Tree, but joins Kaneki after the fall of the 11th Ward.

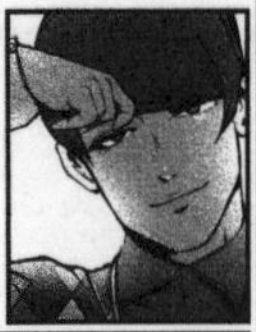

SHU TSUKIYAMA

A Gourmet who seeks the taste of the unknown. Obsessed with Kaneki who is a half-Ghoul.

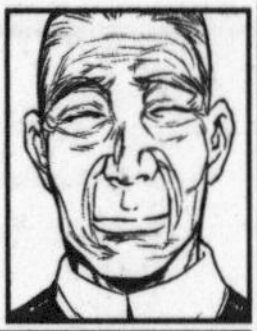

YOSHIMURA

The owner of Anteiku. Guides Kaneki so he can live as a Ghoul. Often works with Yomo. Shrouded in mystery.

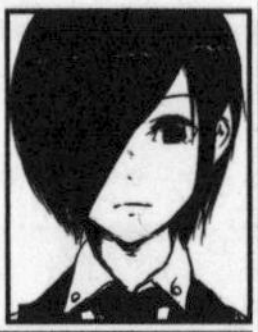

TOUKA KIRISHIMA

A conflicted heroine with two sides, rage and kindness. Ayato's older sister. Lives with the conflict of longing to be human. Hated investigators in the past…?

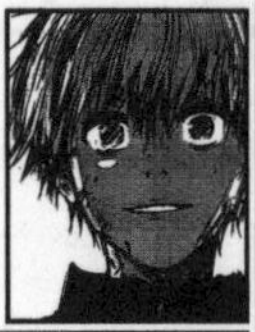

KEN KANEKI

An ordinary young man with a fondness for literature who meets with an accident, has Rize's organs transplanted into him and becomes a half-Ghoul. Struggling to find his place in the world. After being abducted by the Aogiri Tree and enduring Yamori's torture, the Ghoul inside him awakens.

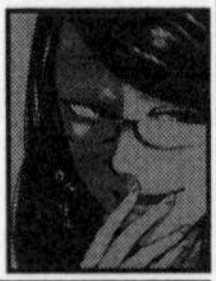

RIZE KAMISHIRO
DECEASED

Freewheeling Binge Eater who despised boredom. Previously lived in the 11th Ward. Met Kaneki in the 20th Ward and then had an accident. There are rumors she used an alias to hide her true identity.

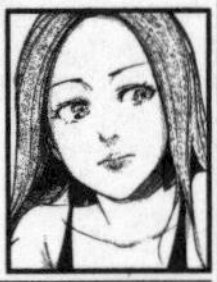

ITORI

Owner of Helter Skelter, a bar in the 14th Ward. Places the utmost importance on information.

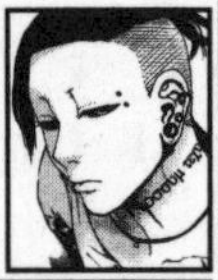

UTA

Owner of HySy Artmask Studio, a mask shop in the 4th Ward. Has a troubled history with Yomo.

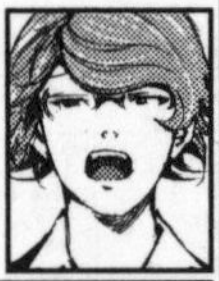

NISHIKI NISHIO

Studious. Adept at blending in with humans. Eats *taiyaki* with no problem. Has a human girlfriend and has a compassionate side to him.

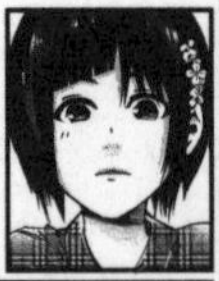

HINAMI FUEGUCHI

An orphan whose parents were killed by the CCG. Displays tremendous Ghoul power when she is awakened. But now…?!

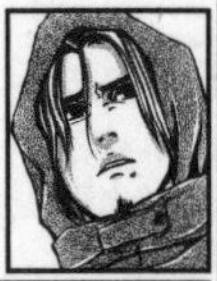

RENJI YOMO

Does not appear out in the open that often. Taciturn and unfriendly, but is trusted by many. Frequently works with Yoshimura. Concerned about Kaneki's condition.

[GHOUL]

A creature that appears human yet consumes humans. The top of the food chain. Finds anything other than humans and coffee unpleasant. Releases a highly lethal natural weapon unique to Ghouls, known as Kagune, from their bodies to prey on humans. Can be cannibalistic. Only sustains damage from Kagune or Quinques that are made from Kagune.

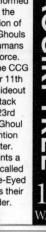

AOGIRI TREE 11TH WARD

A group of Ghouls formed with the ambition of ruling Ghouls and humans with force. Lures the CCG to their 11th Ward hideout to attack the 23rd Ward Ghoul Detention Center. Appoints a Ghoul called the One-Eyed King as their leader.

ONE-EYED KING

The head of Aogiri Tree. His true identity is shrouded in mystery.

NICO

Yamori's former partner. Has a keen sense of smell. Actually is not a member of Aogiri. Possibly a member of the Clown Mask group…?!

YAMORI [DECEASED]

Possessed unrivaled combat skills. Feared as the 13th Ward's Jason for his brutal nature. Confined and tortured Kaneki, but was eventually defeated.

AYATO KIRISHIMA

Touka's younger brother. Even more hot-blooded than his sister. Recruited by Aogiri because of it. Has disdain for his sister and the 20th Ward.

ETO

Origin unknown. Often seen with Tatara.

NORO

Direct subordinate of the One-Eyed King. Silent and mysterious.

TATARA

Direct subordinate of the One-Eyed King. Boasts high combat capabilities, but…?!

 HUMANS

CCG GHOUL INVESTIGATORS

A government agency founded by Tsuneyoshi Washu. Develops Ghoul extermination specialists at the Academy to maintain peace in the wards. Its principal functions are the development and evolution of Quinques, and the eradication of Ghouls from Tokyo.

KUREO MADO [DECEASED]

An investigator with an unusual obsession with Quinques. Loathed Ghouls who killed his family and eventually lost his life.

KISHO ARIMA (SPECIAL INVESTIGATOR)

Personally recruited by Chairman Washu and joined the CCG under special dispensation. Accomplished many distinguished achievements and climbed up the ranks with exceptional speed.

ITSUKI MARUDE (SPECIAL INVESTIGATOR)

Biding his time for a promotion. Has an aversion to Quinques.

SEIDO TAKIZAWA (RANK 2 INVESTIGATOR)

Joined the Bureau the same year as Juzo. Respects Amon and Arima.

JUZO SUZUYA (RANK 3 INVESTIGATOR)

An eccentric who joined the CCG under special dispensation. Enjoys killing and longs for exceptionally lethal Quinques.

YUKINORI SHINO-HARA (SPECIAL INVESTIGATOR)

Ex-Academy instructor. A onetime colleague of Mado and Amon's drill instructor. Appears easygoing, but…

KOTARO AMON (RANK 1 INVESTIGATOR)

An investigator with a very strong sense of justice determined to eradicate Ghouls. Dedicated to avenging Mado's loss through his ongoing battle with Kaneki.

Summary

Kaneki, an average college student, is fated to live as a Ghoul when Rize's organs are transplanted into him. While questioning and struggling with the existence of creatures that take human lives to survive, he searches for how the world should be. One day while at Anteiku, he is abducted by the Aogiri Tree organization. While being held captive and viciously tortured by Yamori, he accepts that he is a Ghoul. He escapes from Aogiri Tree with help from members of Anteiku. The CCG finally brings down Aogiri Tree's 11th Ward hideout, bringing the three-way battle to a close. However…

東京喰種

TOKYO GHOUL

TOKYO GHOUL

SUI ISHIDA

CONTENTS

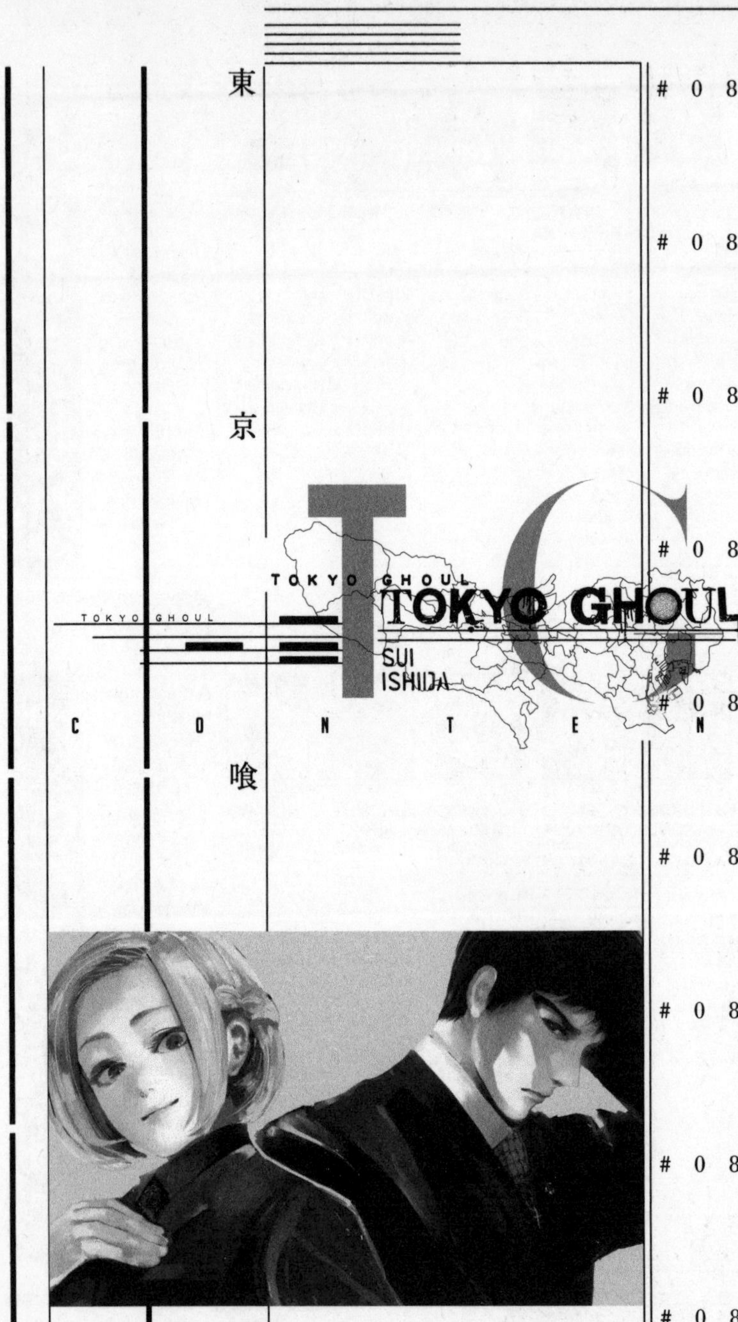

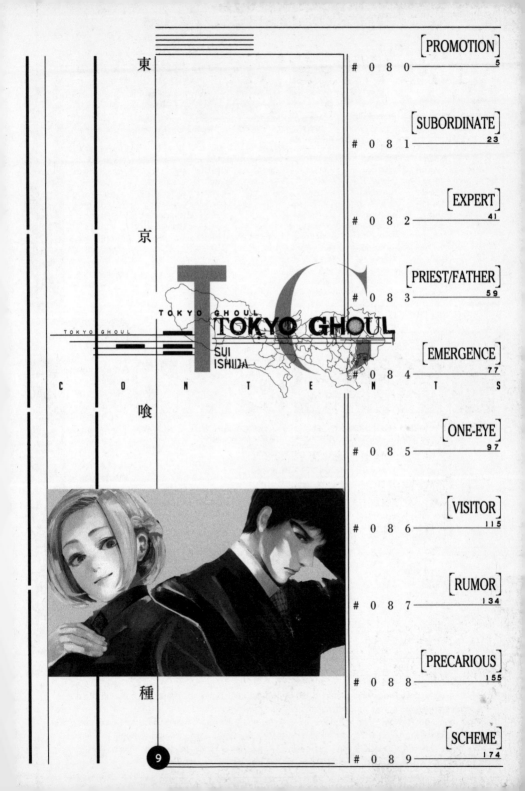

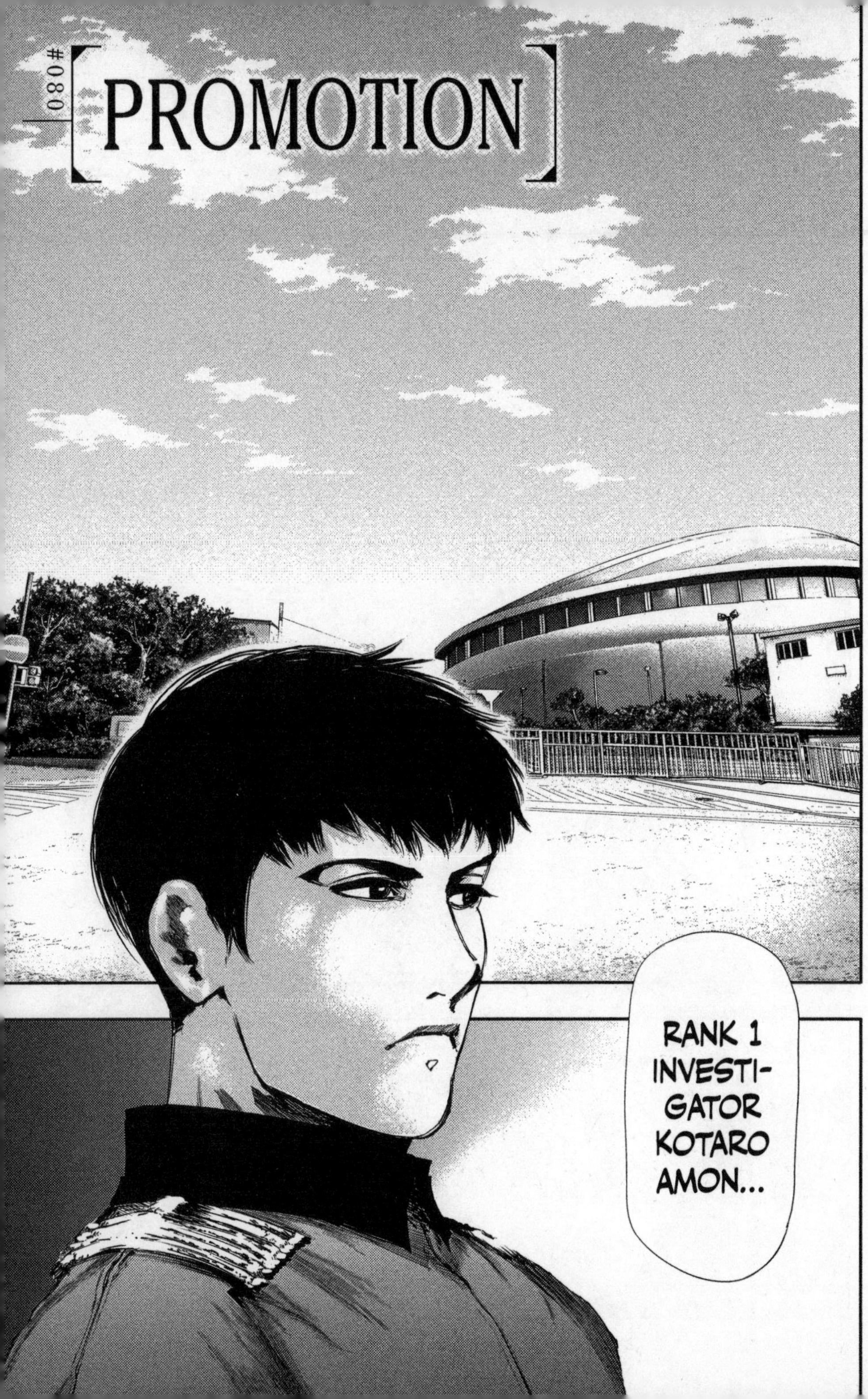
#080
PROMOTION
RANK 1 INVESTI-GATOR KOTARO AMON...

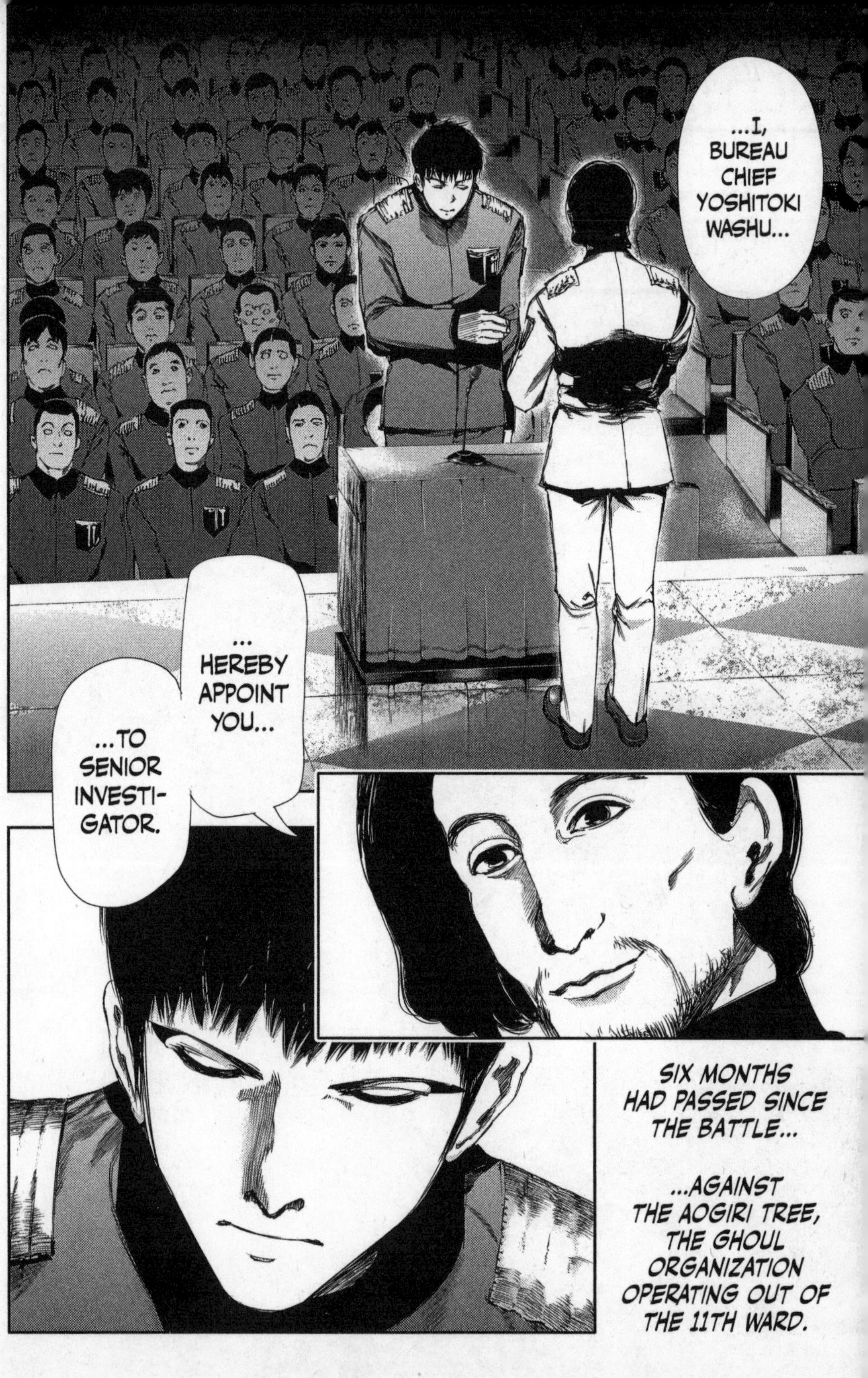
...I, BUREAU CHIEF YOSHITOKI WASHU...
... HEREBY APPOINT YOU...
...TO SENIOR INVESTI-GATOR.
SIX MONTHS HAD PASSED SINCE THE BATTLE...
...AGAINST THE AOGIRI TREE, THE GHOUL ORGANIZATION OPERATING OUT OF THE 11TH WARD.

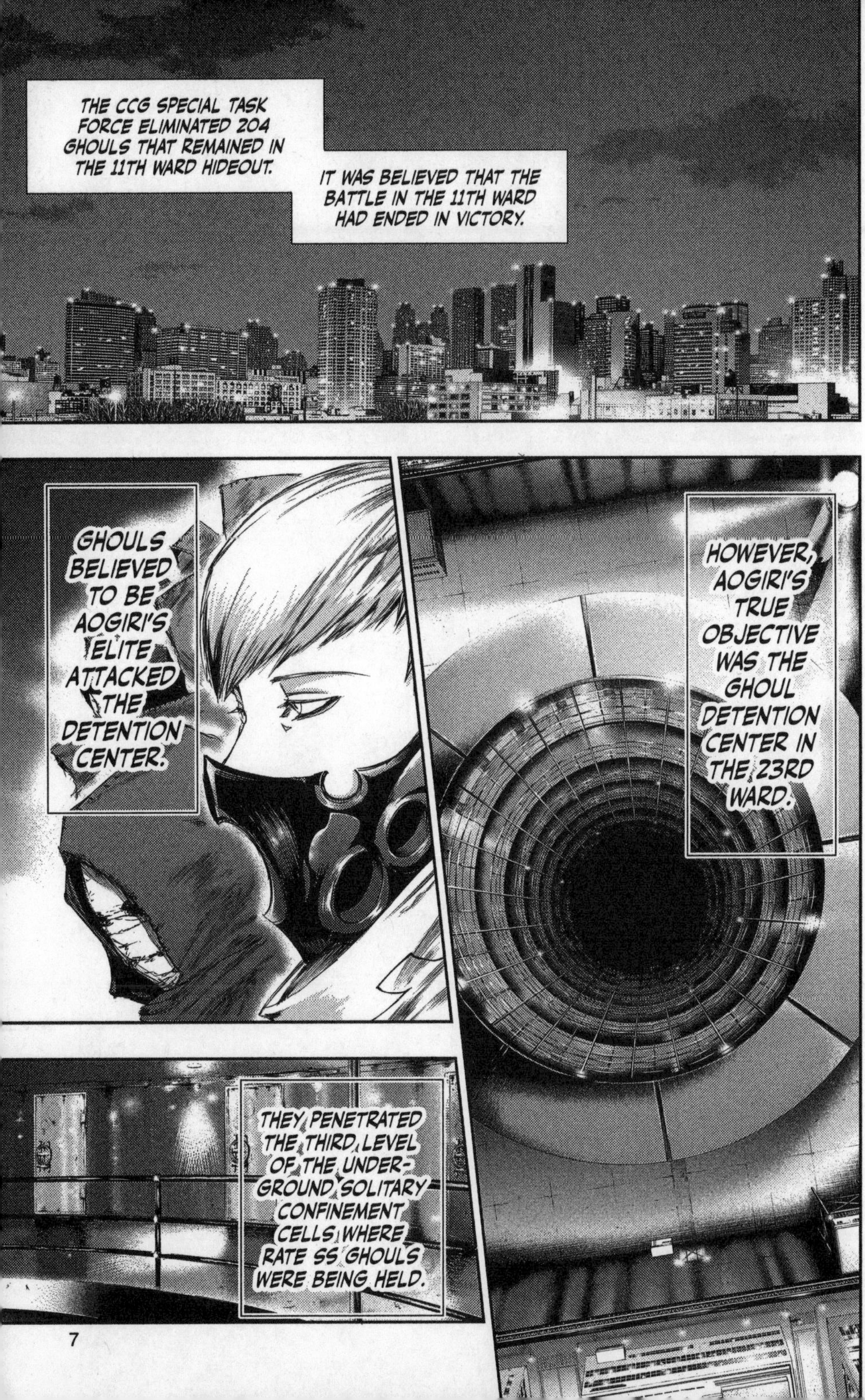
THE CCG SPECIAL TASK FORCE ELIMINATED 204 GHOULS THAT REMAINED IN THE 11TH WARD HIDEOUT.
IT WAS BELIEVED THAT THE BATTLE IN THE 11TH WARD HAD ENDED IN VICTORY.
HOWEVER, AOGIRI'S TRUE OBJECTIVE WAS THE GHOUL DETENTION CENTER IN THE 23RD WARD.
GHOULS BELIEVED TO BE AOGIRI'S ELITE ATTACKED THE DETENTION CENTER.
THEY PENETRATED THE THIRD LEVEL OF THE UNDER-GROUND SOLITARY CONFINEMENT CELLS WHERE RATE SS GHOULS WERE BEING HELD.

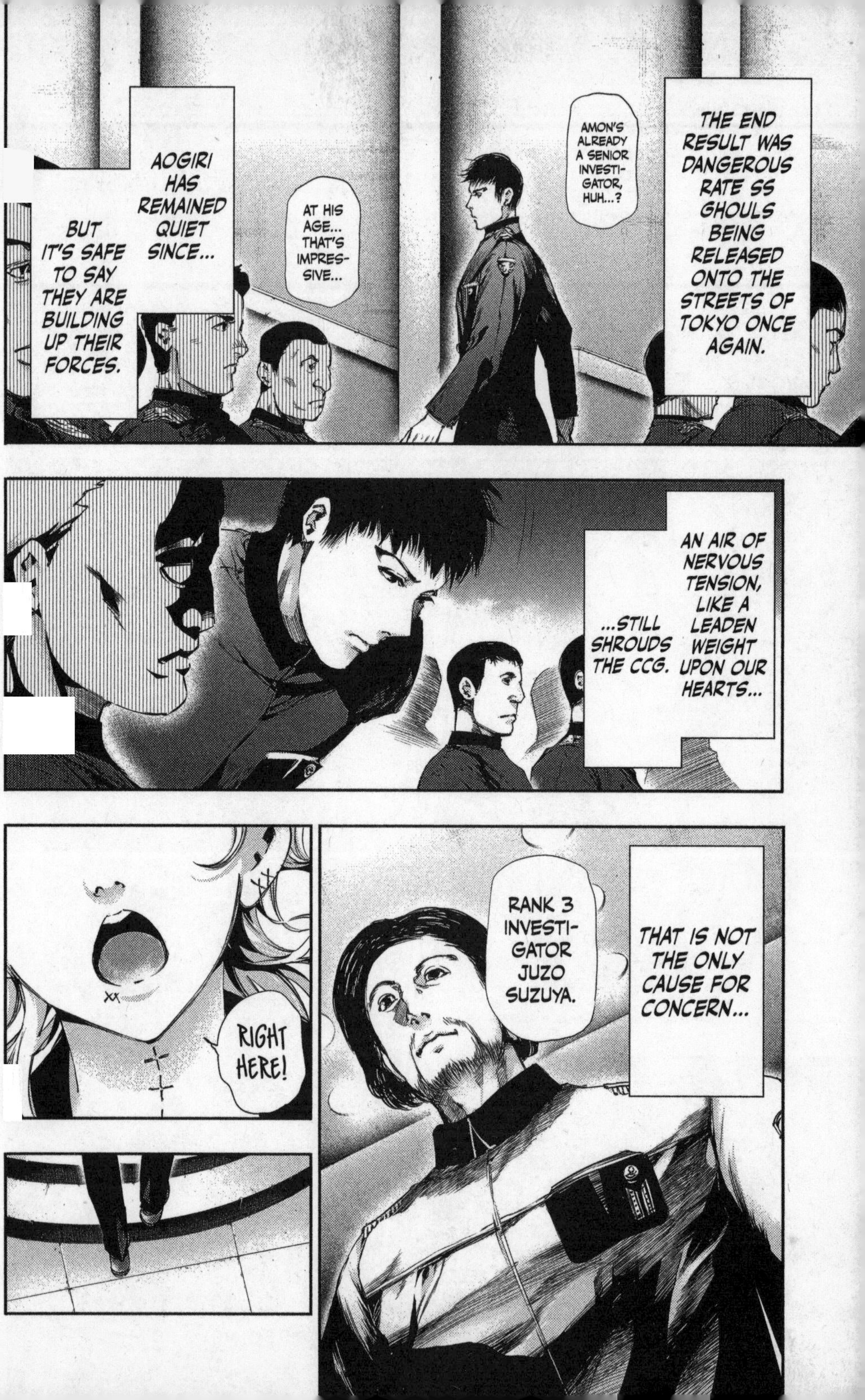
THE END RESULT WAS DANGEROUS RATE SS GHOULS BEING RELEASED ONTO THE STREETS OF TOKYO ONCE AGAIN.
AMON'S ALREADY A SENIOR INVESTI-GATOR, HUH...?
AT HIS AGE... THAT'S IMPRES-SIVE...
AOGIRI HAS REMAINED QUIET SINCE...
BUT IT'S SAFE TO SAY THEY ARE BUILDING UP THEIR FORCES.
AN AIR OF NERVOUS TENSION, LIKE A LEADEN WEIGHT UPON OUR HEARTS...
...STILL SHROUDS THE CCG.
THAT IS NOT THE ONLY CAUSE FOR CONCERN...
RANK 3 INVESTI-GATOR JUZO SUZUYA.
RIGHT HERE!

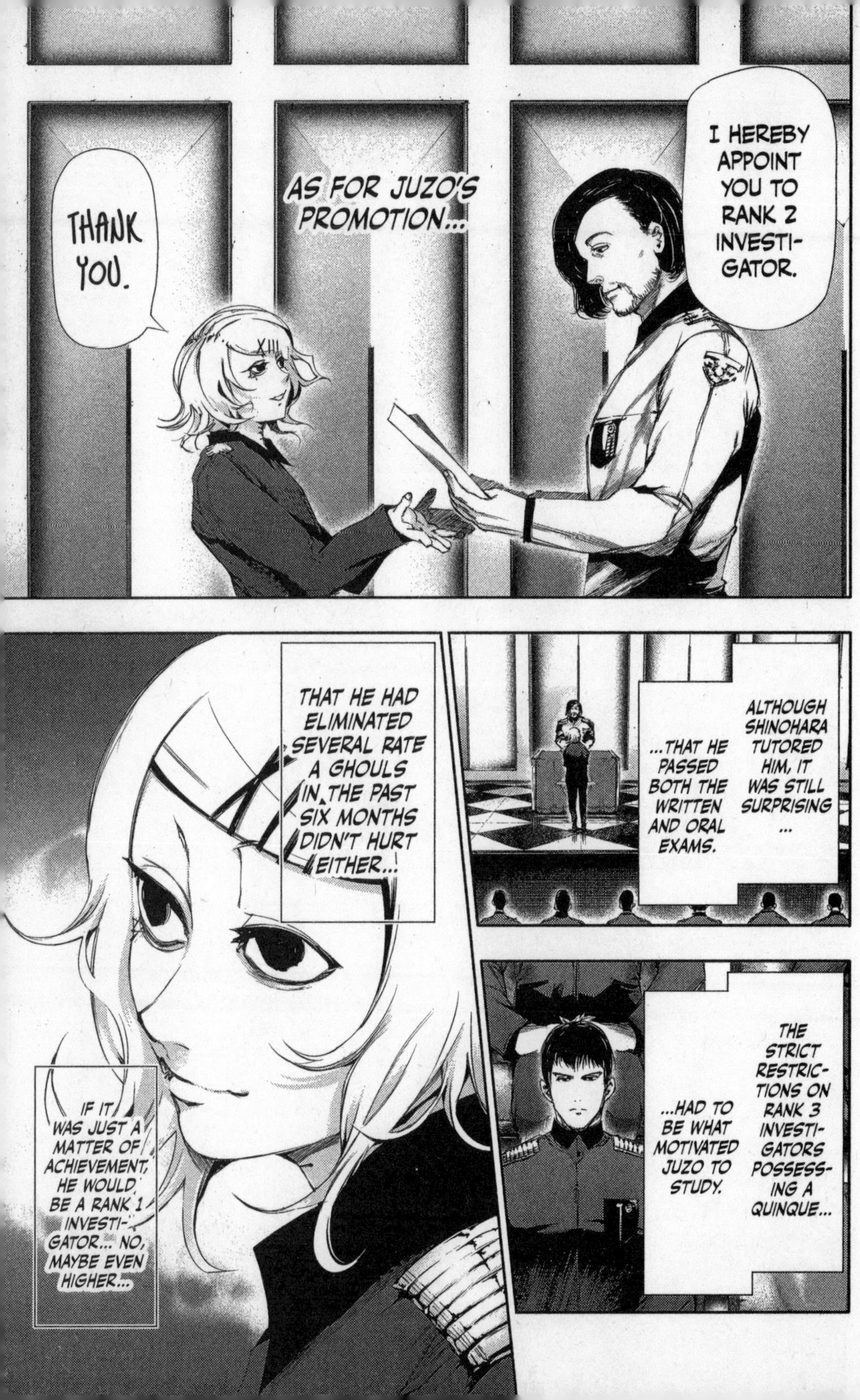
I HEREBY APPOINT YOU TO RANK 2 INVESTIGATOR.
AS FOR JUZO'S PROMOTION...
THANK YOU.
ALTHOUGH SHINOHARA TUTORED HIM, IT WAS STILL SURPRISING...
...THAT HE PASSED BOTH THE WRITTEN AND ORAL EXAMS.
THE STRICT RESTRICTIONS ON RANK 3 INVESTIGATORS POSSESSING A QUINQUE...
...HAD TO BE WHAT MOTIVATED JUZO TO STUDY.
THAT HE HAD ELIMINATED SEVERAL RATE A GHOULS IN THE PAST SIX MONTHS DIDN'T HURT EITHER...
IF IT WAS JUST A MATTER OF ACHIEVEMENT, HE WOULD BE A RANK 1 INVESTIGATOR... NO, MAYBE EVEN HIGHER...

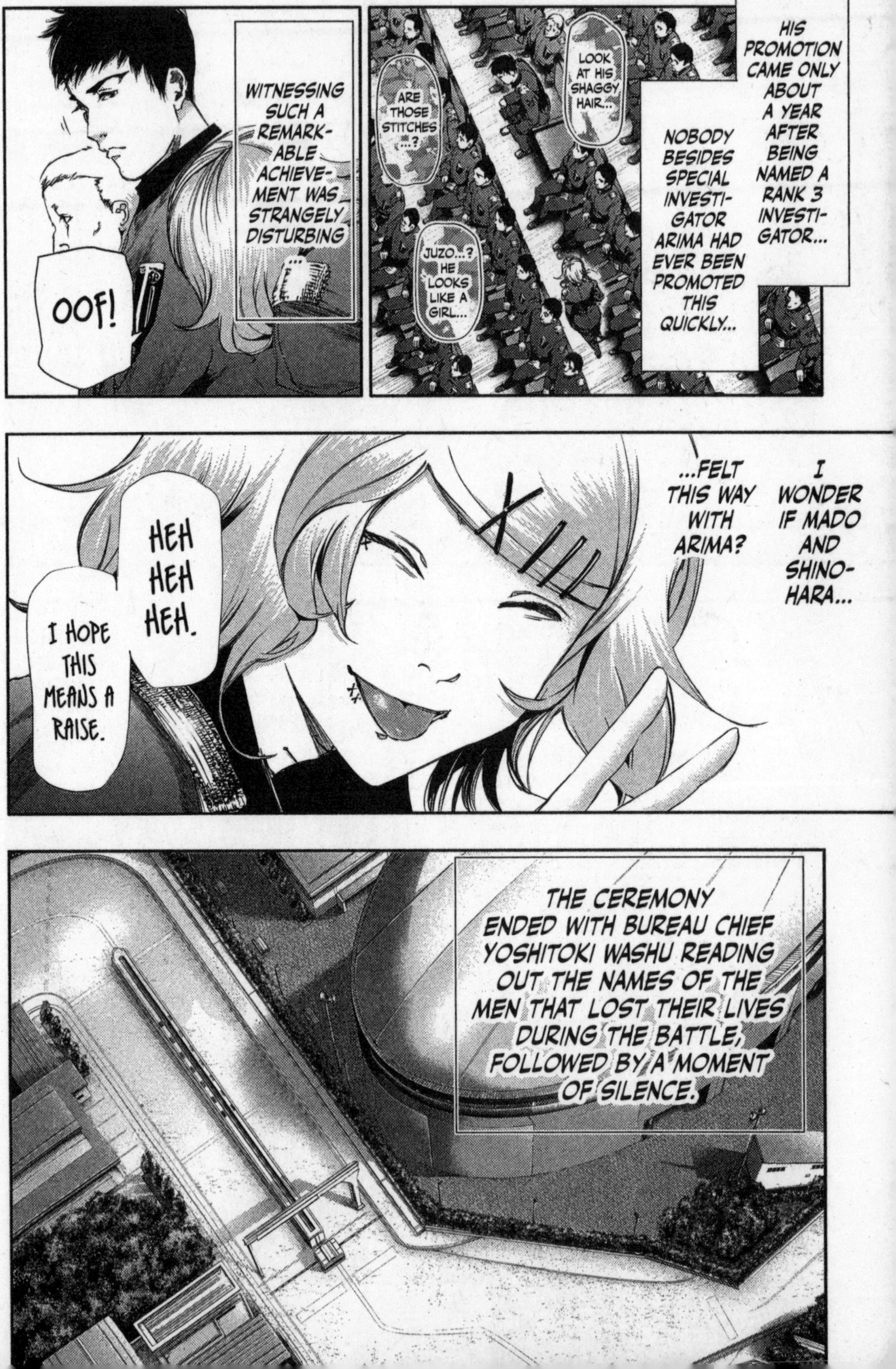
HIS PROMOTION CAME ONLY ABOUT A YEAR AFTER BEING NAMED A RANK 3 INVESTIGATOR...
NOBODY BESIDES SPECIAL INVESTIGATOR ARIMA HAD EVER BEEN PROMOTED THIS QUICKLY...
LOOK AT HIS SHAGGY HAIR...
ARE THOSE STITCHES ...?
JUZO...? HE LOOKS LIKE A GIRL...
WITNESSING SUCH A REMARKABLE ACHIEVEMENT WAS STRANGELY DISTURBING
...
OOF!
I WONDER IF MADO AND SHINOHARA...
...FELT THIS WAY WITH ARIMA?
HEH HEH HEH.
I HOPE THIS MEANS A RAISE.
THE CEREMONY ENDED WITH BUREAU CHIEF YOSHITOKI WASHU READING OUT THE NAMES OF THE MEN THAT LOST THEIR LIVES DURING THE BATTLE, FOLLOWED BY A MOMENT OF SILENCE.

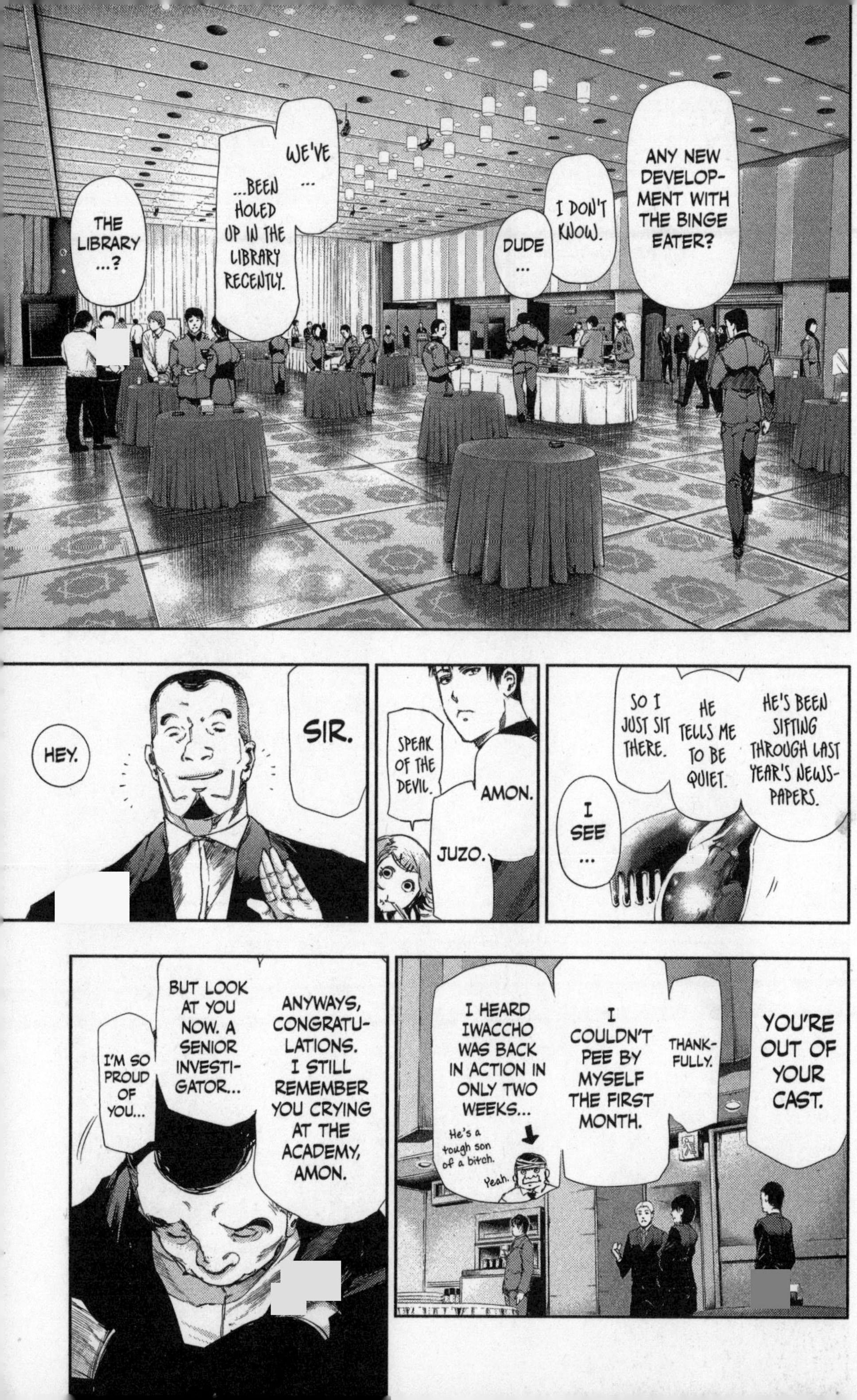
ANY NEW DEVELOPMENT WITH THE BINGE EATER?
I DON'T KNOW.
DUDE ...
WE'VE ...
...BEEN HOLED UP IN THE LIBRARY RECENTLY.
THE LIBRARY ...?
HE'S BEEN SIFTING THROUGH LAST YEAR'S NEWSPAPERS.
HE TELLS ME TO BE QUIET.
SO I JUST SIT THERE.
I SEE ...
AMON.
JUZO.
SPEAK OF THE DEVIL.
SIR.
HEY.
YOU'RE OUT OF YOUR CAST.
THANKFULLY.
I COULDN'T PEE BY MYSELF THE FIRST MONTH.
I HEARD IWACCHO WAS BACK IN ACTION IN ONLY TWO WEEKS...
He's a tough son of a bitch.
Yeah.
ANYWAYS, CONGRATULATIONS. I STILL REMEMBER YOU CRYING AT THE ACADEMY, AMON.
BUT LOOK AT YOU NOW. A SENIOR INVESTIGATOR...
I'M SO PROUD OF YOU...

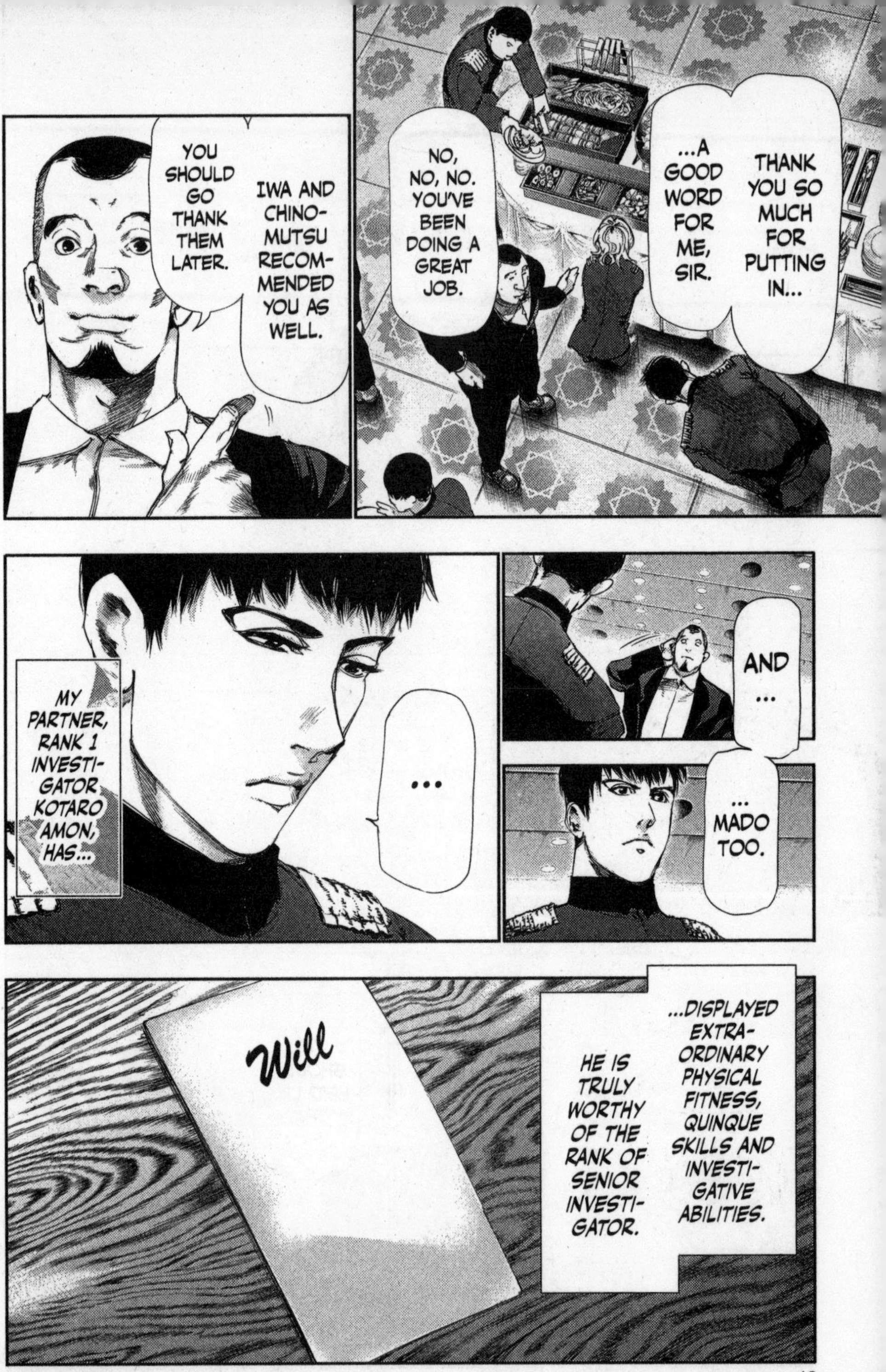
THANK YOU SO MUCH FOR PUTTING IN...
...A GOOD WORD FOR ME, SIR.
NO, NO, NO. YOU'VE BEEN DOING A GREAT JOB.
IWA AND CHINO-MUTSU RECOMMENDED YOU AS WELL.
YOU SHOULD GO THANK THEM LATER.
AND ...
... MADO TOO.
...
MY PARTNER, RANK 1 INVESTIGATOR KOTARO AMON, HAS...
...DISPLAYED EXTRAORDINARY PHYSICAL FITNESS, QUINQUE SKILLS AND INVESTIGATIVE ABILITIES.
HE IS TRULY WORTHY OF THE RANK OF SENIOR INVESTIGATOR.
Will

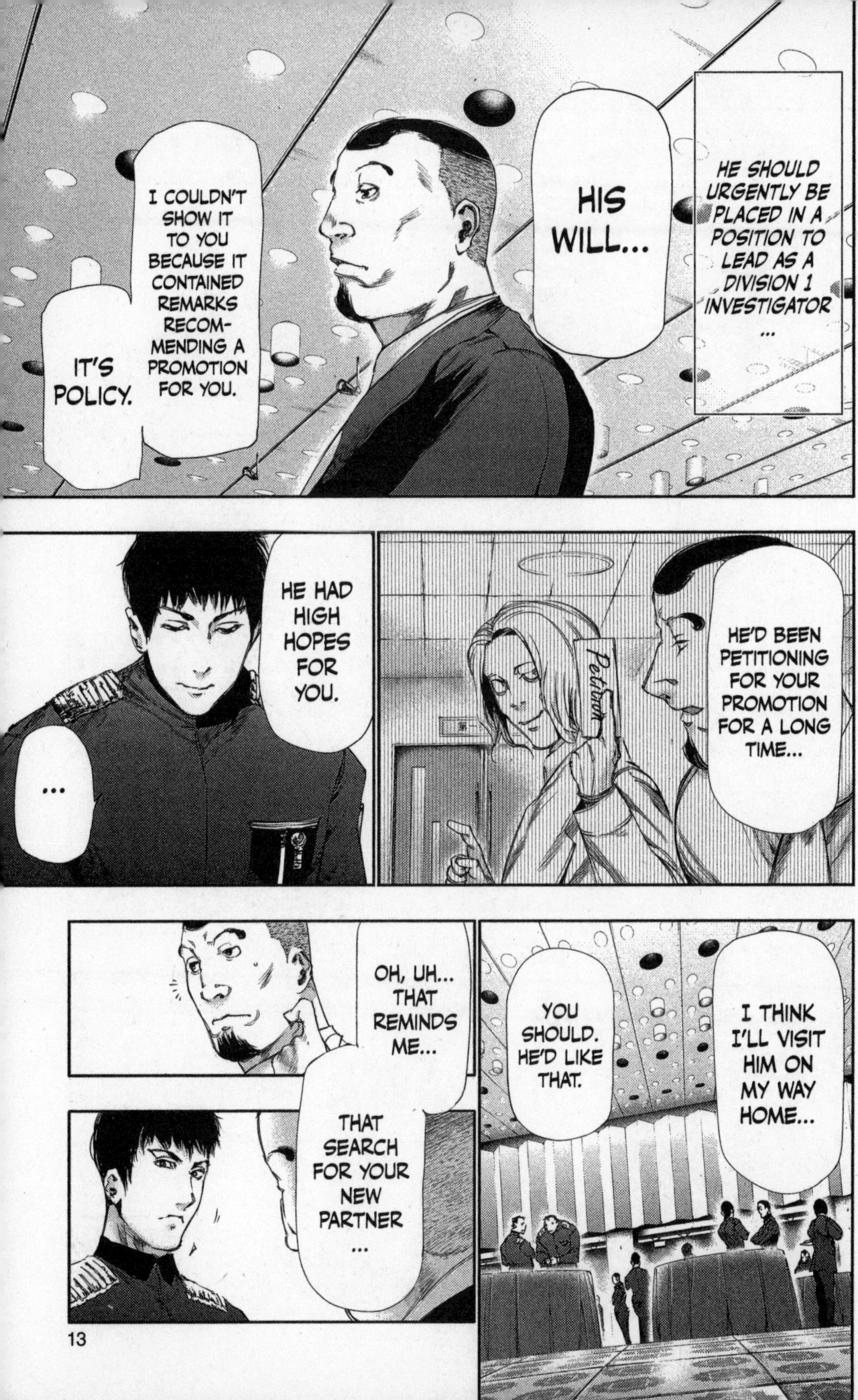
HE SHOULD URGENTLY BE PLACED IN A POSITION TO LEAD AS A DIVISION 1 INVESTIGATOR ...
HIS WILL...
I COULDN'T SHOW IT TO YOU BECAUSE IT CONTAINED REMARKS RECOM-MENDING A PROMOTION FOR YOU.
IT'S POLICY.
HE'D BEEN PETITIONING FOR YOUR PROMOTION FOR A LONG TIME...
Petition
HE HAD HIGH HOPES FOR YOU.
...
I THINK I'LL VISIT HIM ON MY WAY HOME...
YOU SHOULD. HE'D LIKE THAT.
OH, UH... THAT REMINDS ME...
THAT SEARCH FOR YOUR NEW PARTNER ...

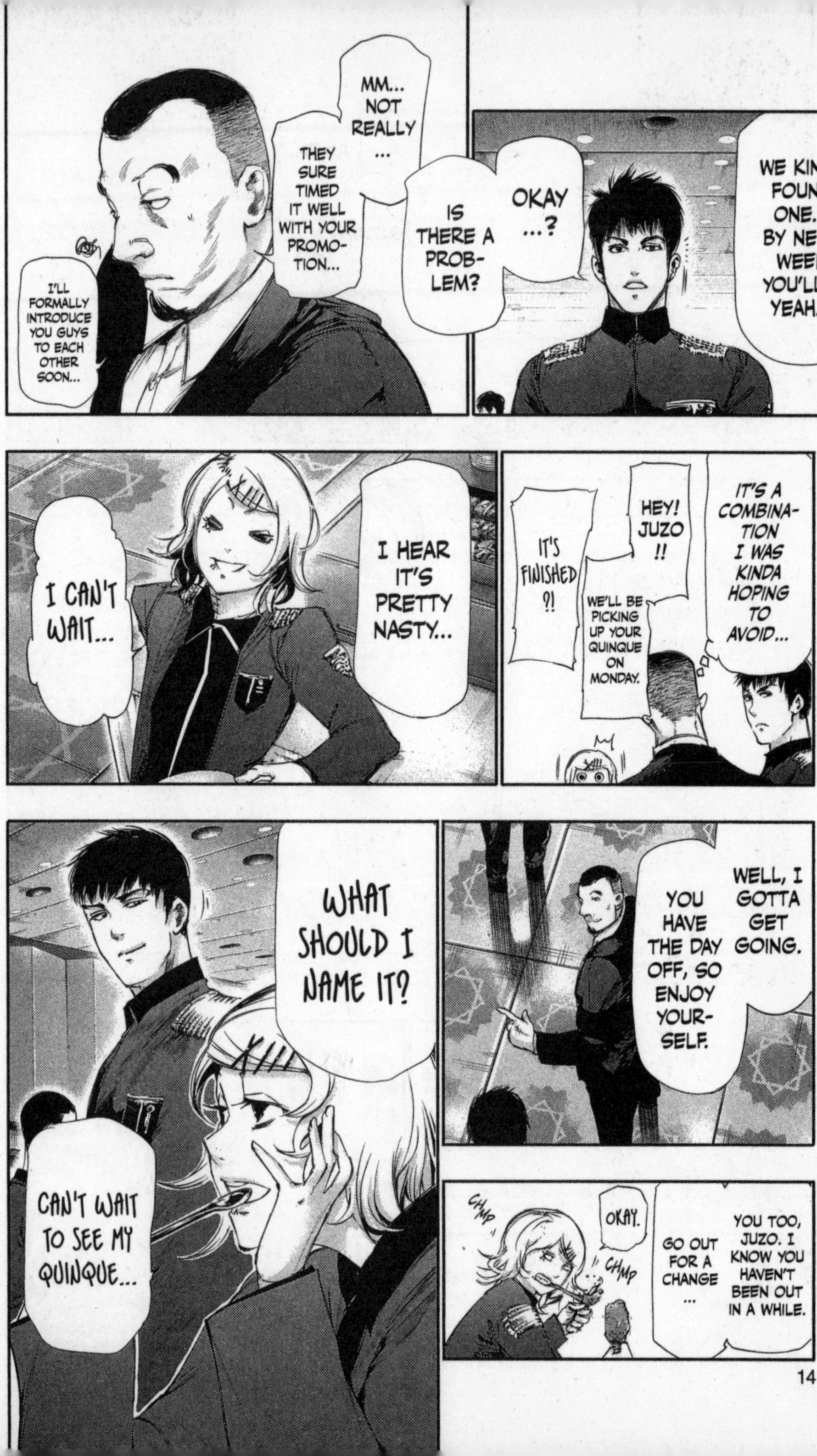

WE KINDA FOUND ONE... BY NEXT WEEK YOU'LL... YEAH...
OKAY ...?
IS THERE A PROB-LEM?
MM... NOT REALLY ...
THEY SURE TIMED IT WELL WITH YOUR PROMO-TION...
I'LL FORMALLY INTRODUCE YOU GUYS TO EACH OTHER SOON...
IT'S A COMBINA-TION I WAS KINDA HOPING TO AVOID...
HEY! JUZO !!
WE'LL BE PICKING UP YOUR QUINQUE ON MONDAY.
IT'S FINISHED ?!
I HEAR IT'S PRETTY NASTY...
I CAN'T WAIT...
WELL, I GOTTA GET GOING.
YOU HAVE THE DAY OFF, SO ENJOY YOUR-SELF.
YOU TOO, JUZO. I KNOW YOU HAVEN'T BEEN OUT IN A WHILE.
GO OUT FOR A CHANGE ...
OKAY.
CHMP
CHMP
WHAT SHOULD I NAME IT?
CAN'T WAIT TO SEE MY QUINQUE...

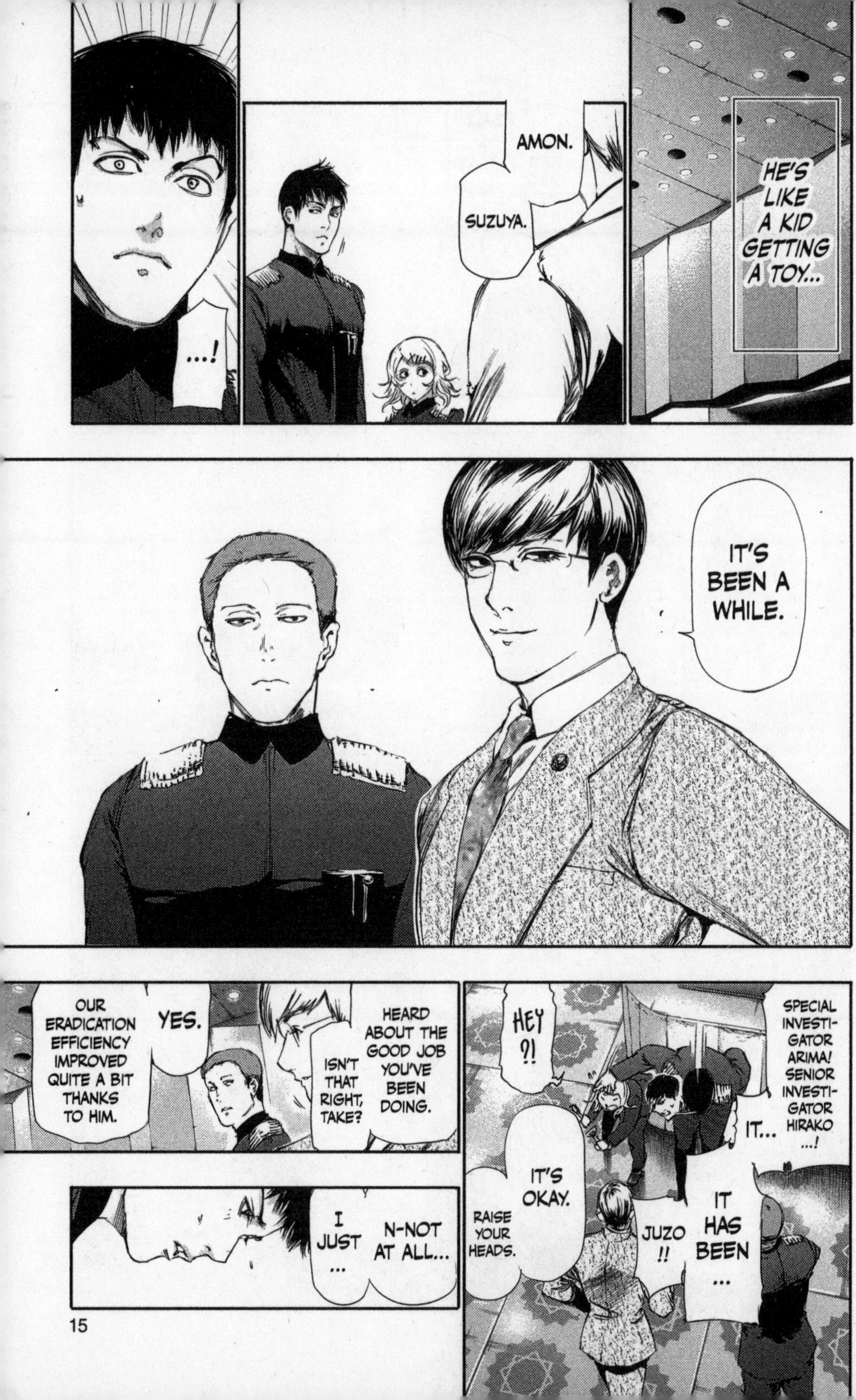
HE'S LIKE A KID GETTING A TOY...
AMON.
SUZUYA.
...!
IT'S BEEN A WHILE.
SPECIAL INVESTIGATOR ARIMA! SENIOR INVESTIGATOR HIRAKO ...!
IT...
HEY ?!
IT HAS BEEN ...
JUZO !!
IT'S OKAY.
RAISE YOUR HEADS.
HEARD ABOUT THE GOOD JOB YOU'VE BEEN DOING.
ISN'T THAT RIGHT, TAKE?
YES.
OUR ERADICATION EFFICIENCY IMPROVED QUITE A BIT THANKS TO HIM.
N-NOT AT ALL...
I JUST ...

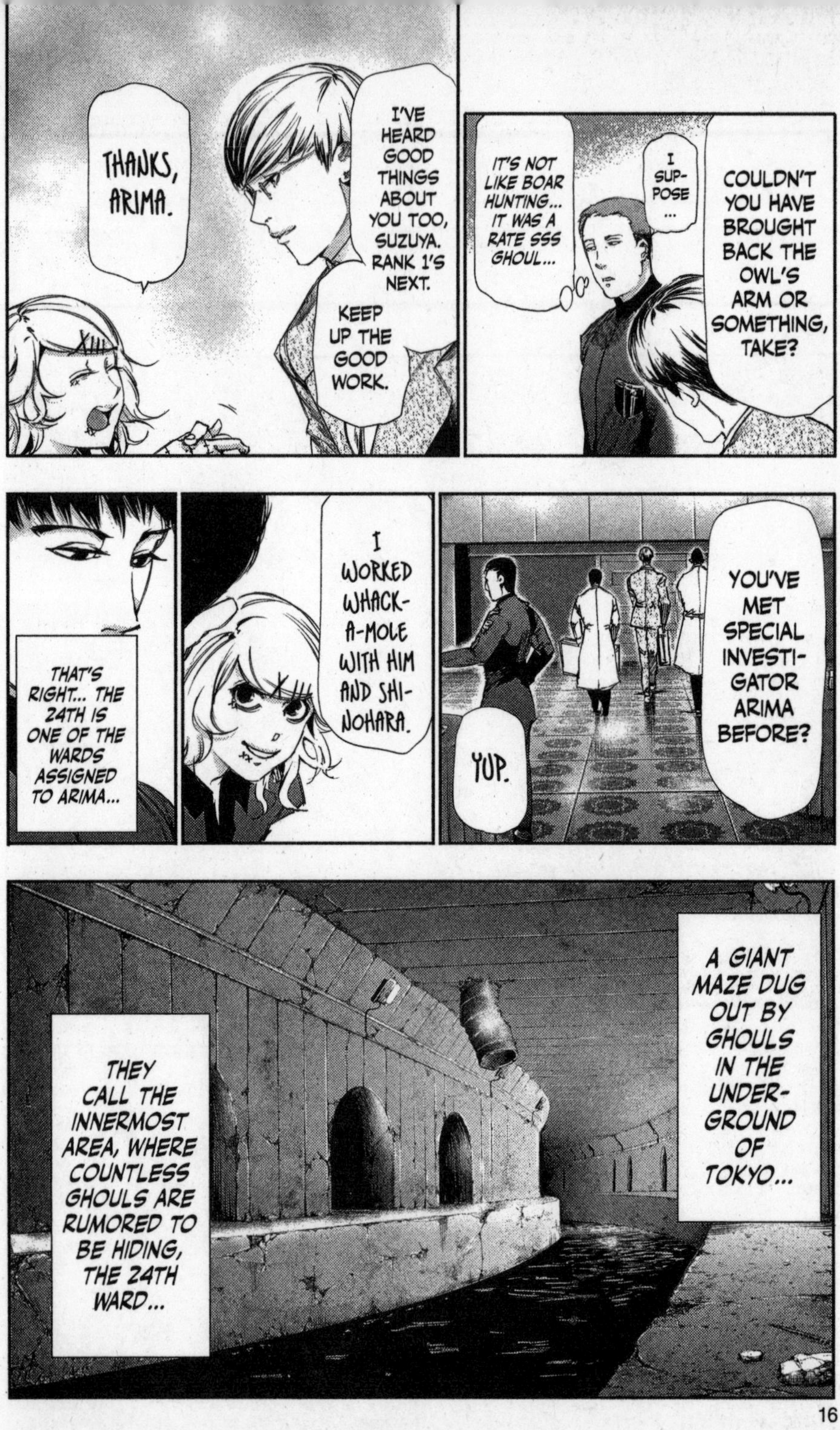
COULDN'T YOU HAVE BROUGHT BACK THE OWL'S ARM OR SOMETHING, TAKE?
I SUPPOSE...
IT'S NOT LIKE BOAR HUNTING... IT WAS A RATE SSS GHOUL...
I'VE HEARD GOOD THINGS ABOUT YOU TOO, SUZUYA. RANK 1'S NEXT.
KEEP UP THE GOOD WORK.
THANKS, ARIMA.
YOU'VE MET SPECIAL INVESTIGATOR ARIMA BEFORE?
YUP.
I WORKED WHACK-A-MOLE WITH HIM AND SHINOHARA.
THAT'S RIGHT... THE 24TH IS ONE OF THE WARDS ASSIGNED TO ARIMA...
A GIANT MAZE DUG OUT BY GHOULS IN THE UNDERGROUND OF TOKYO...
THEY CALL THE INNERMOST AREA, WHERE COUNTLESS GHOULS ARE RUMORED TO BE HIDING, THE 24TH WARD...

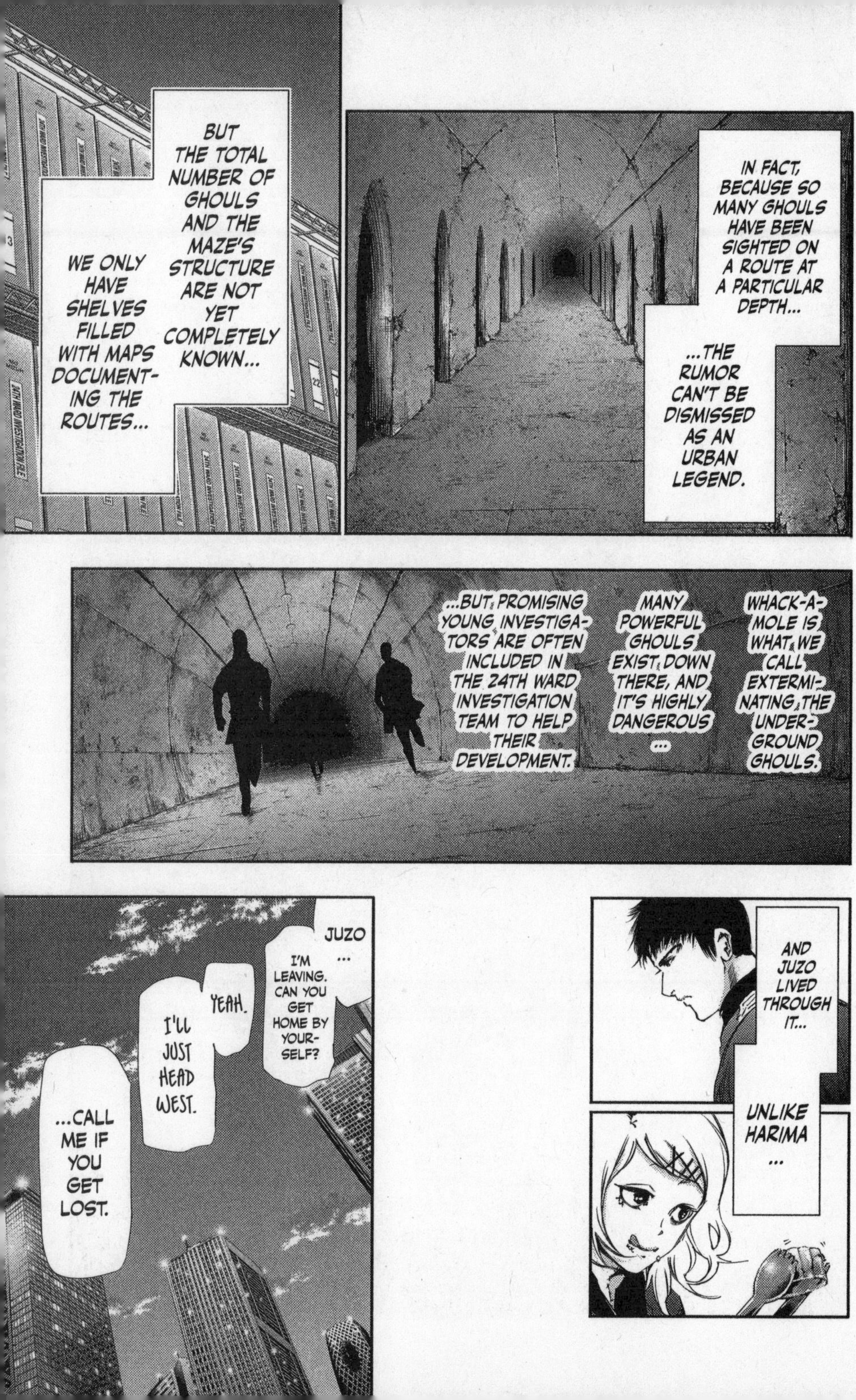
IN FACT, BECAUSE SO MANY GHOULS HAVE BEEN SIGHTED ON A ROUTE AT A PARTICULAR DEPTH...
...THE RUMOR CAN'T BE DISMISSED AS AN URBAN LEGEND.
BUT THE TOTAL NUMBER OF GHOULS AND THE MAZE'S STRUCTURE ARE NOT YET COMPLETELY KNOWN...
WE ONLY HAVE SHELVES FILLED WITH MAPS DOCUMENTING THE ROUTES...
WHACK-A-MOLE IS WHAT WE CALL EXTERMINATING THE UNDERGROUND GHOULS.
MANY POWERFUL GHOULS EXIST DOWN THERE, AND IT'S HIGHLY DANGEROUS...
...BUT PROMISING YOUNG INVESTIGATORS ARE OFTEN INCLUDED IN THE 24TH WARD INVESTIGATION TEAM TO HELP THEIR DEVELOPMENT.
AND JUZO LIVED THROUGH IT...
UNLIKE HARIMA...
JUZO...
I'M LEAVING. CAN YOU GET HOME BY YOURSELF?
YEAH.
I'LL JUST HEAD WEST.
...CALL ME IF YOU GET LOST.

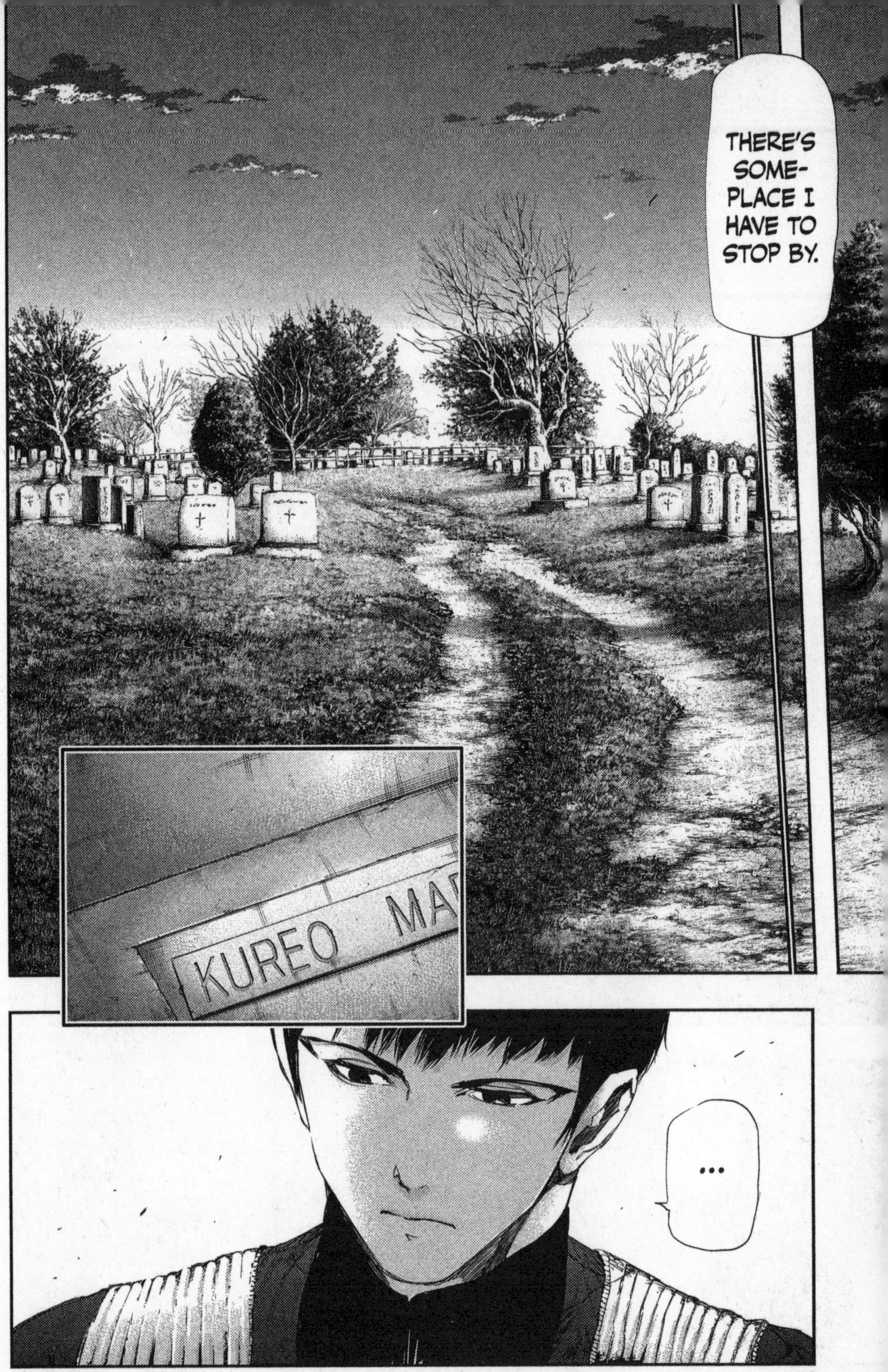
THERE'S SOME-PLACE I HAVE TO STOP BY.
KUREO MA
...

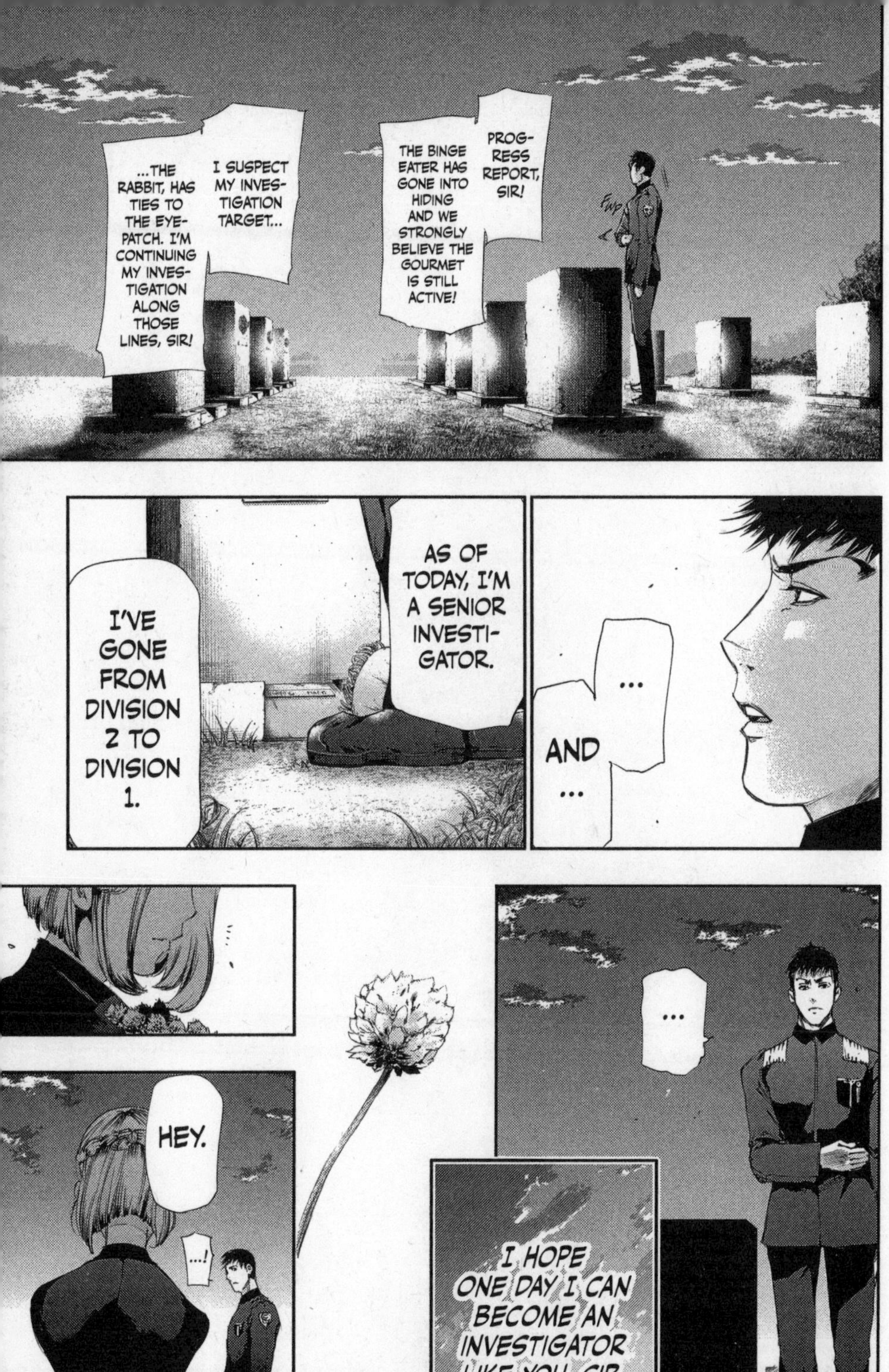
PROG-RESS REPORT, SIR!
FWP
THE BINGE EATER HAS GONE INTO HIDING AND WE STRONGLY BELIEVE THE GOURMET IS STILL ACTIVE!
I SUSPECT MY INVES-TIGATION TARGET...
...THE RABBIT, HAS TIES TO THE EYE-PATCH. I'M CONTINUING MY INVES-TIGATION ALONG THOSE LINES, SIR!
...
AND ...
AS OF TODAY, I'M A SENIOR INVESTI-GATOR.
I'VE GONE FROM DIVISION 2 TO DIVISION 1.
...
I HOPE ONE DAY I CAN BECOME AN INVESTIGATOR LIKE YOU, SIR.
...
HEY.
...!

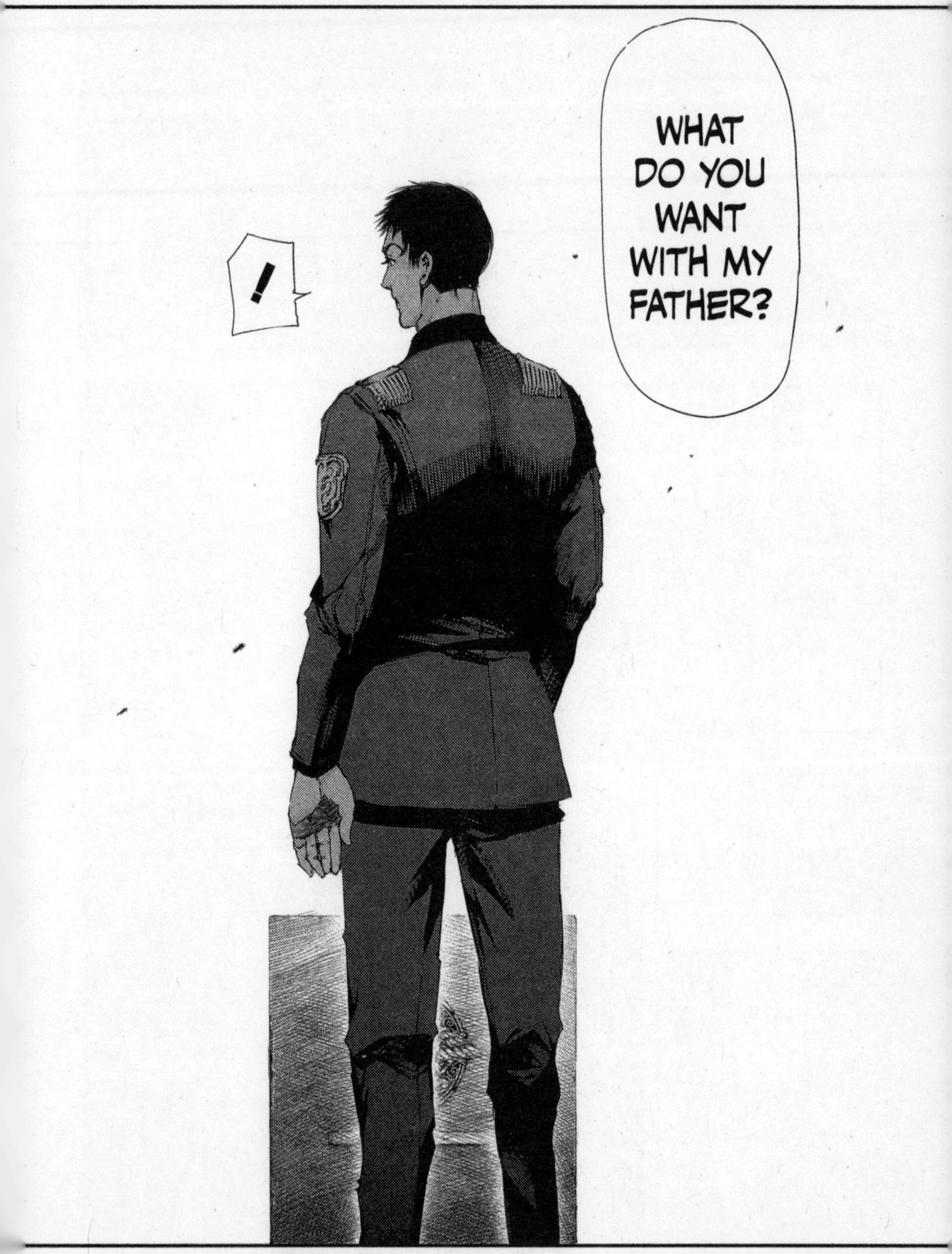
WHAT DO YOU WANT WITH MY FATHER?
!

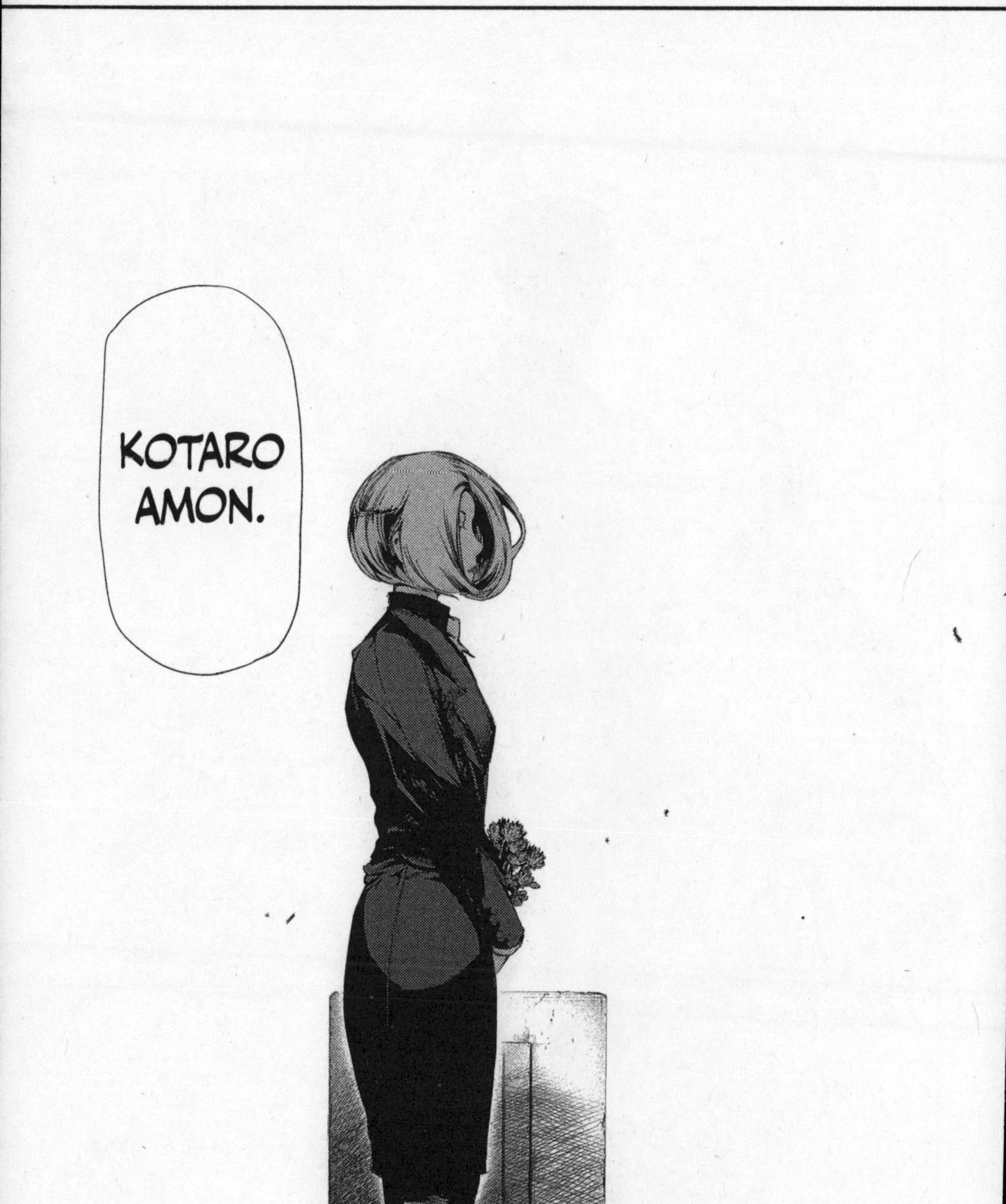
KOTARO AMON.

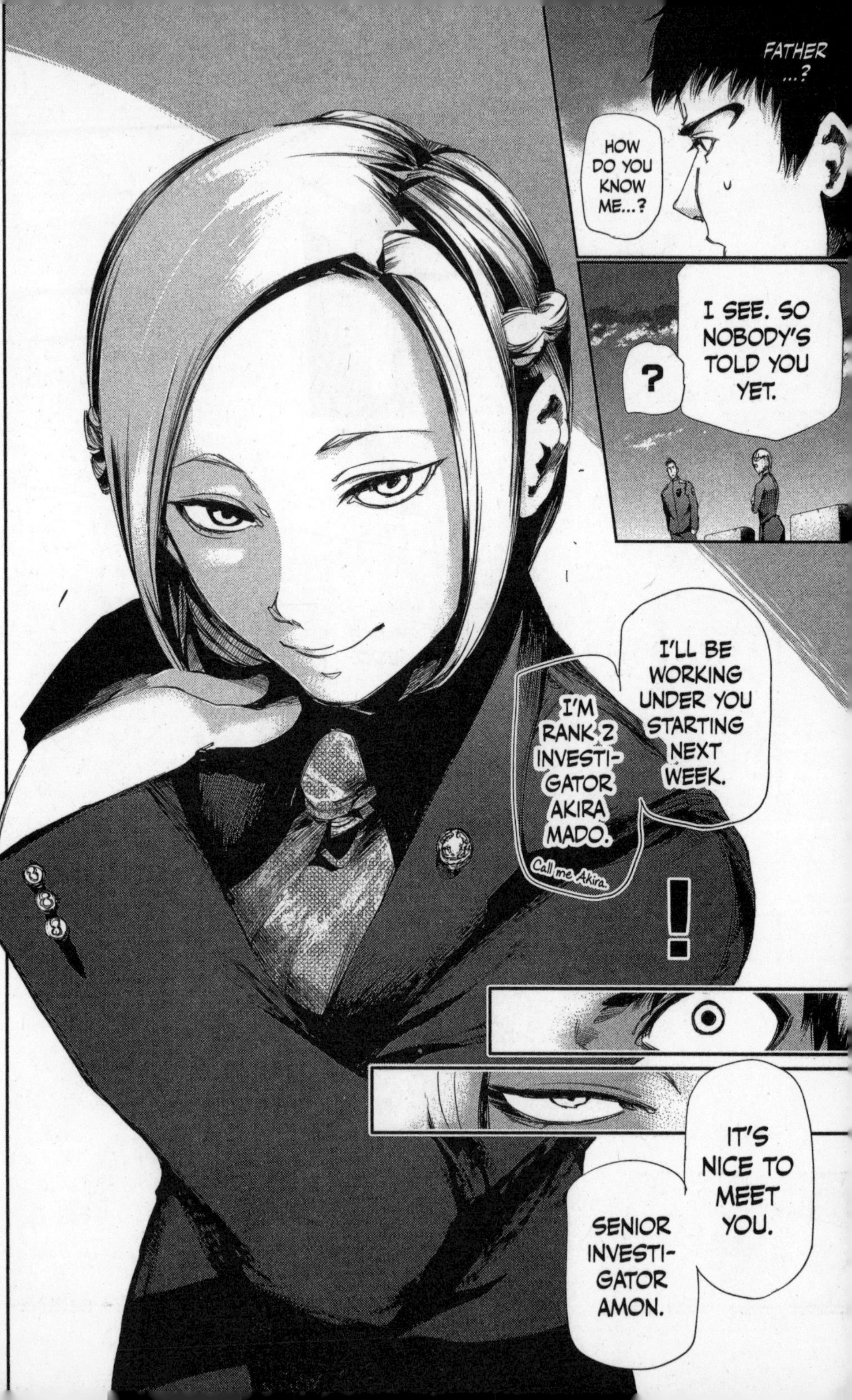
FATHER ...?
HOW DO YOU KNOW ME...?
I SEE. SO NOBODY'S TOLD YOU YET.
?
I'LL BE WORKING UNDER YOU STARTING NEXT WEEK.
I'M RANK 2 INVESTIGATOR AKIRA MADO.
Call me Akira.
!
IT'S NICE TO MEET YOU.
SENIOR INVESTIGATOR AMON.

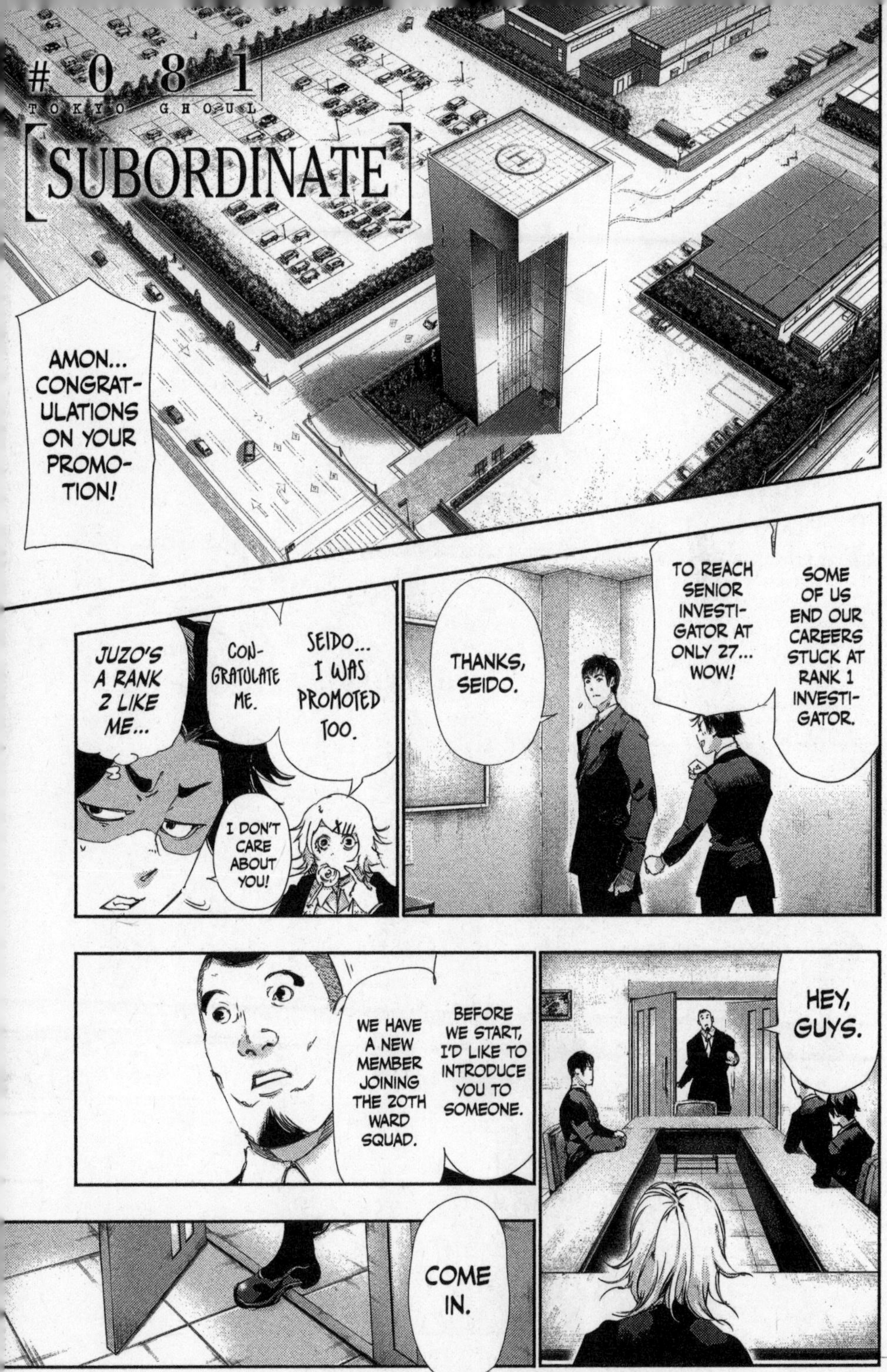

#081
TOKYO GHOUL
[SUBORDINATE]
AMON... CONGRAT-ULATIONS ON YOUR PROMO-TION!
SOME OF US END OUR CAREERS STUCK AT RANK 1 INVESTI-GATOR.
TO REACH SENIOR INVESTI-GATOR AT ONLY 27... WOW!
THANKS, SEIDO.
SEIDO... I WAS PROMOTED TOO.
CON-GRATULATE ME.
JUZO'S A RANK 2 LIKE ME...
I DON'T CARE ABOUT YOU!
HEY, GUYS.
BEFORE WE START, I'D LIKE TO INTRODUCE YOU TO SOMEONE.
WE HAVE A NEW MEMBER JOINING THE 20TH WARD SQUAD.
COME IN.

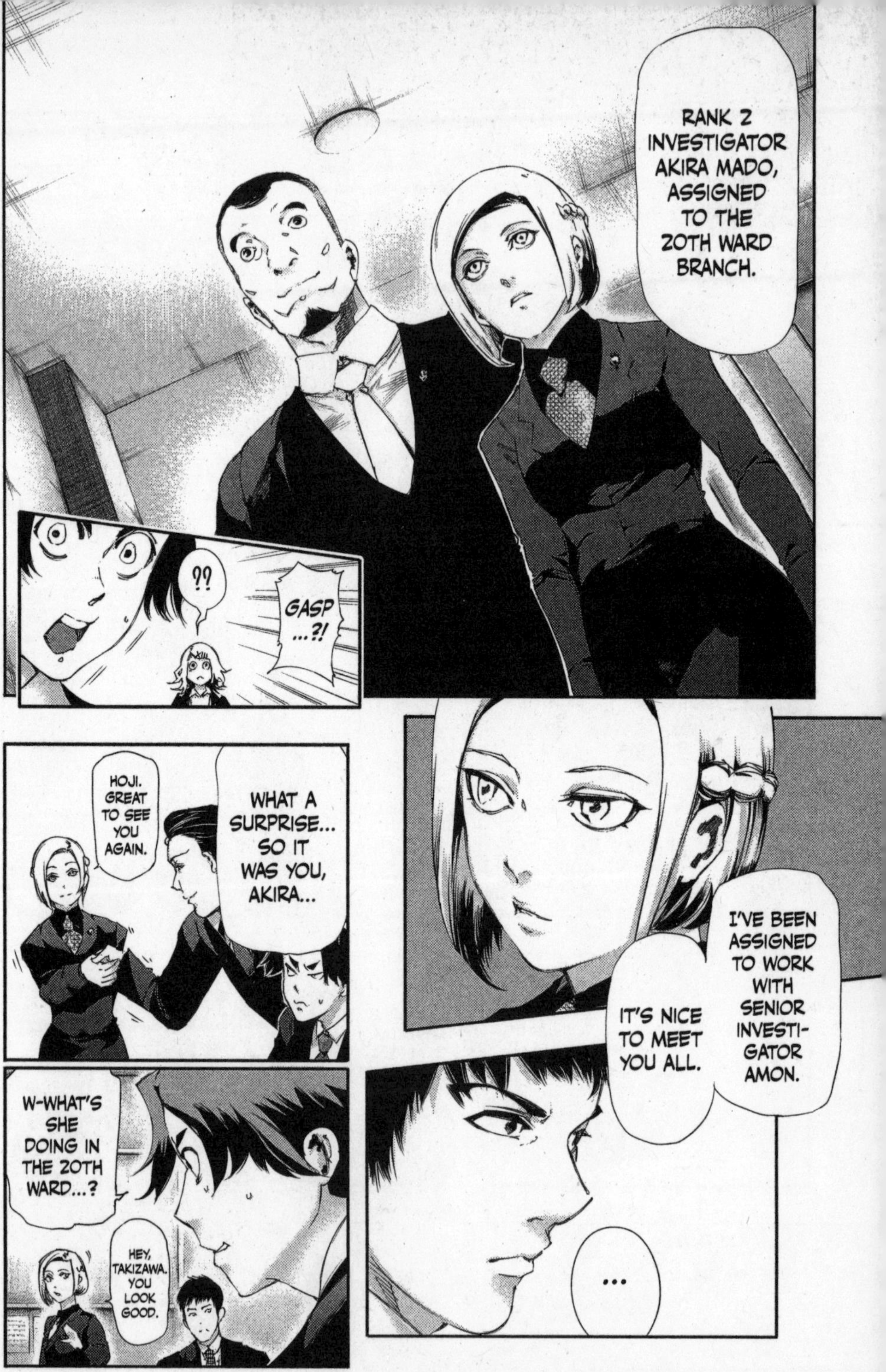
RANK 2 INVESTIGATOR AKIRA MADO, ASSIGNED TO THE 20TH WARD BRANCH.
GASP ...?!
??
I'VE BEEN ASSIGNED TO WORK WITH SENIOR INVESTI-GATOR AMON.
IT'S NICE TO MEET YOU ALL.
WHAT A SURPRISE... SO IT WAS YOU, AKIRA...
HOJI. GREAT TO SEE YOU AGAIN.
...
W-WHAT'S SHE DOING IN THE 20TH WARD...?
HEY, TAKIZAWA. YOU LOOK GOOD.

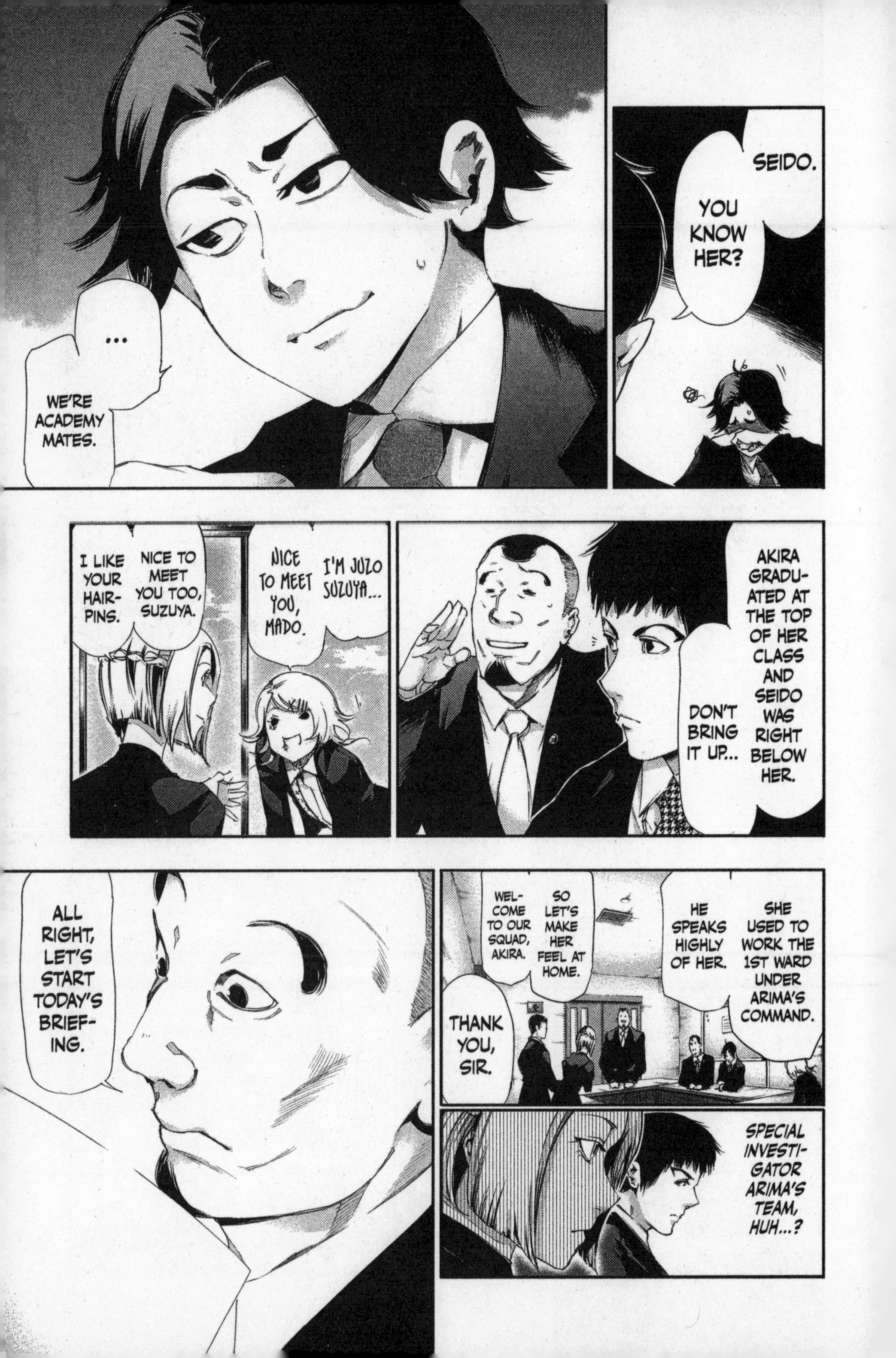
SEIDO.
YOU KNOW HER?
...
WE'RE ACADEMY MATES.
AKIRA GRADUATED AT THE TOP OF HER CLASS AND SEIDO WAS RIGHT BELOW HER.
DON'T BRING IT UP...
I'M JUZO SUZUYA...
NICE TO MEET YOU, MADO.
NICE TO MEET YOU TOO, SUZUYA.
I LIKE YOUR HAIRPINS.
SHE USED TO WORK THE 1ST WARD UNDER ARIMA'S COMMAND.
HE SPEAKS HIGHLY OF HER.
SO LET'S MAKE HER FEEL AT HOME.
WELCOME TO OUR SQUAD, AKIRA.
THANK YOU, SIR.
SPECIAL INVESTIGATOR ARIMA'S TEAM, HUH...?
ALL RIGHT, LET'S START TODAY'S BRIEFING.

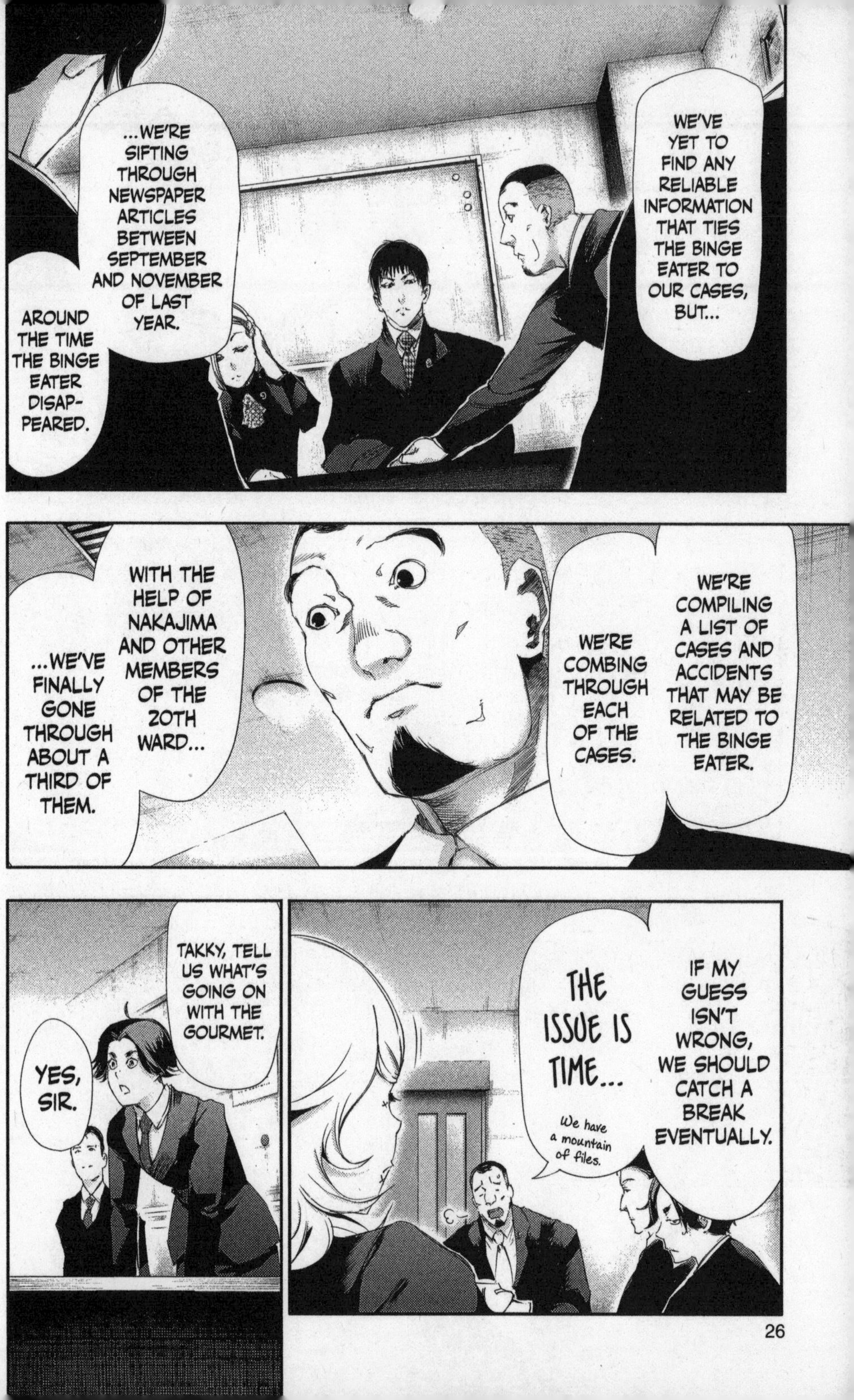
WE'VE YET TO FIND ANY RELIABLE INFORMATION THAT TIES THE BINGE EATER TO OUR CASES, BUT...
...WE'RE SIFTING THROUGH NEWSPAPER ARTICLES BETWEEN SEPTEMBER AND NOVEMBER OF LAST YEAR.
AROUND THE TIME THE BINGE EATER DISAPPEARED.
WE'RE COMPILING A LIST OF CASES AND ACCIDENTS THAT MAY BE RELATED TO THE BINGE EATER.
WE'RE COMBING THROUGH EACH OF THE CASES.
WITH THE HELP OF NAKAJIMA AND OTHER MEMBERS OF THE 20TH WARD...
...WE'VE FINALLY GONE THROUGH ABOUT A THIRD OF THEM.
IF MY GUESS ISN'T WRONG, WE SHOULD CATCH A BREAK EVENTUALLY.
THE ISSUE IS TIME...
We have a mountain of files.
TAKKY, TELL US WHAT'S GOING ON WITH THE GOURMET.
YES, SIR.

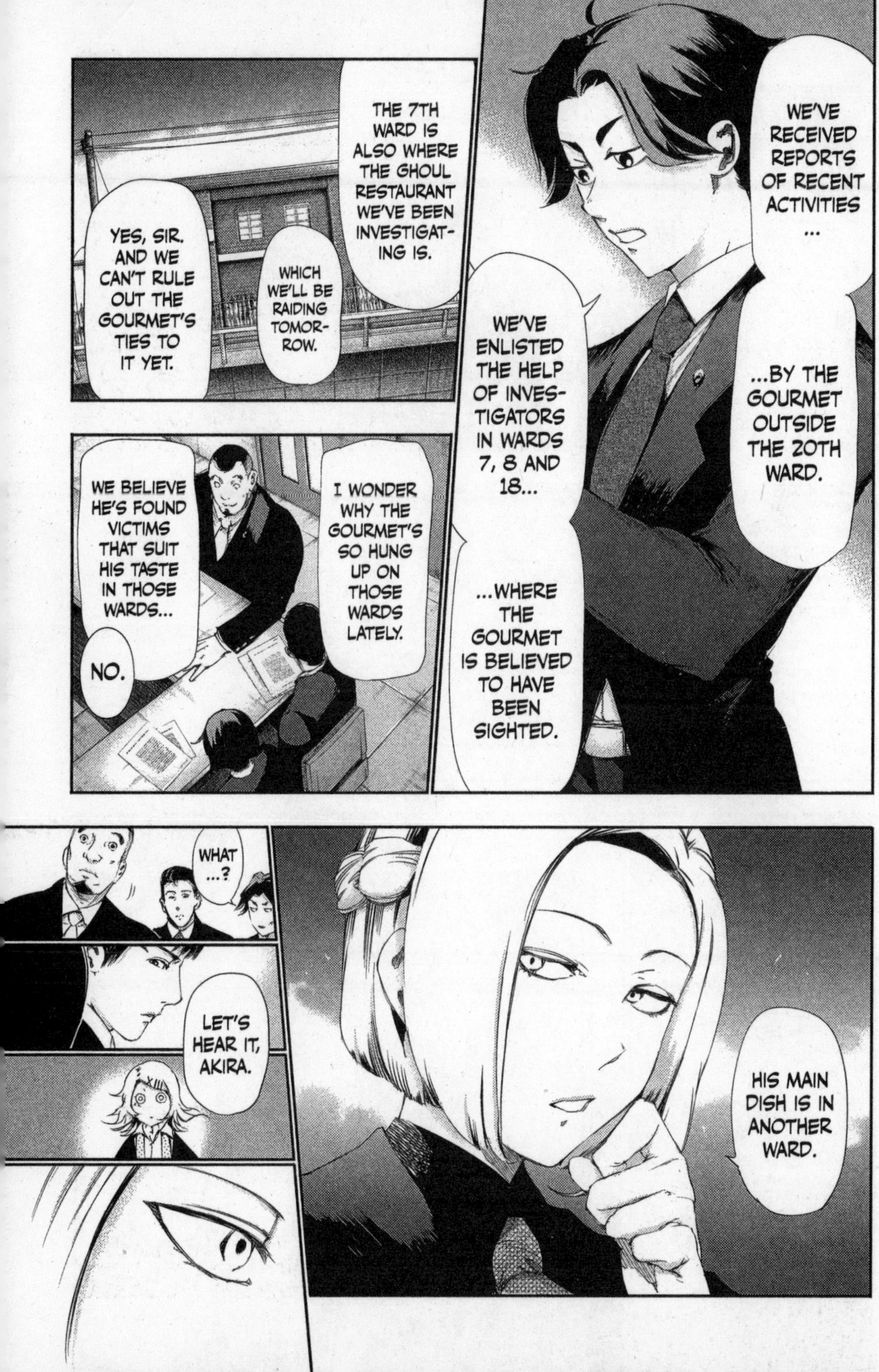
WE'VE RECEIVED REPORTS OF RECENT ACTIVITIES ...
...BY THE GOURMET OUTSIDE THE 20TH WARD.
WE'VE ENLISTED THE HELP OF INVESTIGATORS IN WARDS 7, 8 AND 18...
...WHERE THE GOURMET IS BELIEVED TO HAVE BEEN SIGHTED.
THE 7TH WARD IS ALSO WHERE THE GHOUL RESTAURANT WE'VE BEEN INVESTIGATING IS.
WHICH WE'LL BE RAIDING TOMORROW.
YES, SIR. AND WE CAN'T RULE OUT THE GOURMET'S TIES TO IT YET.
I WONDER WHY THE GOURMET'S SO HUNG UP ON THOSE WARDS LATELY.
WE BELIEVE HE'S FOUND VICTIMS THAT SUIT HIS TASTE IN THOSE WARDS...
NO.
HIS MAIN DISH IS IN ANOTHER WARD.
WHAT ...?
LET'S HEAR IT, AKIRA.

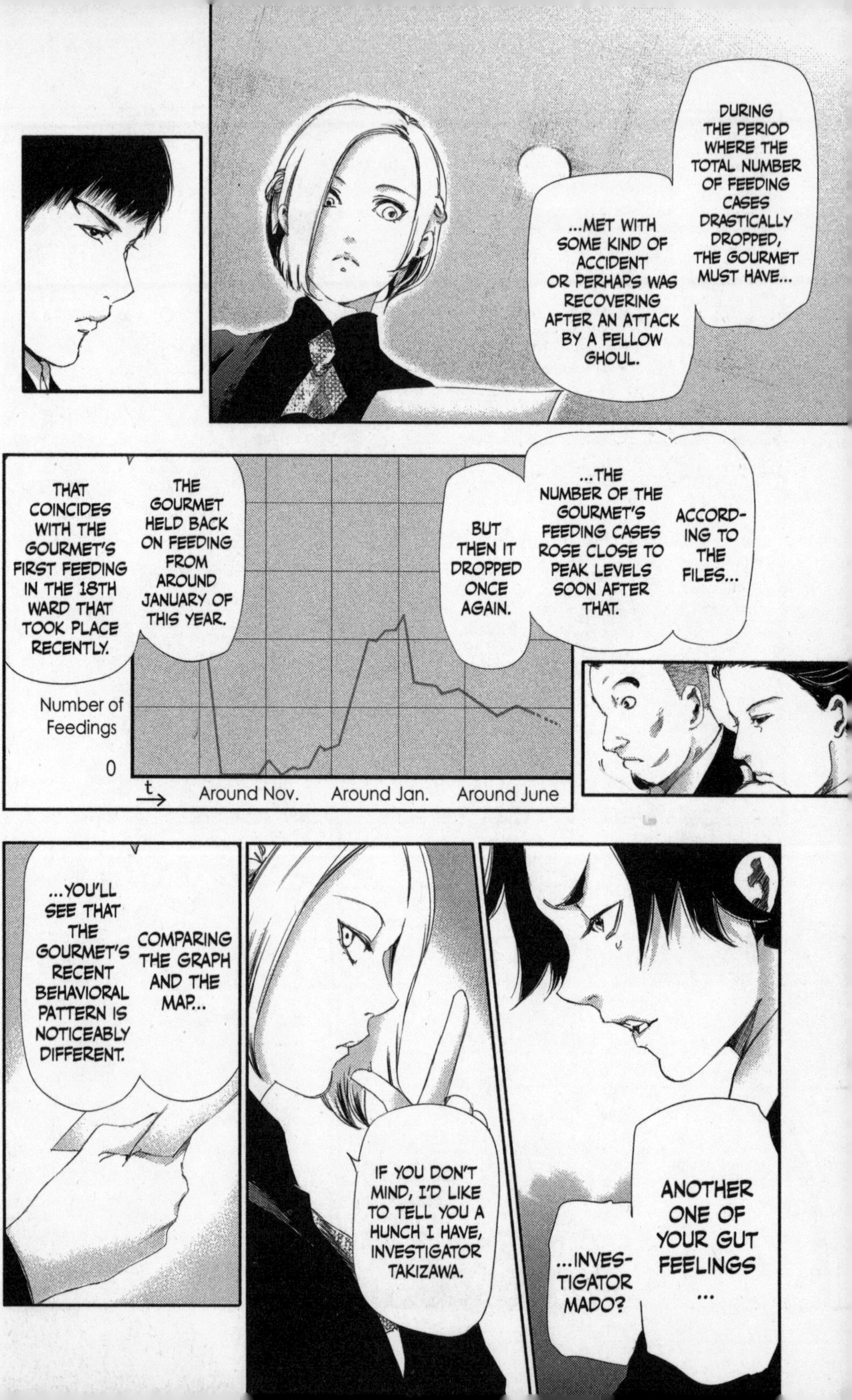

DURING THE PERIOD WHERE THE TOTAL NUMBER OF FEEDING CASES DRASTICALLY DROPPED, THE GOURMET MUST HAVE...
...MET WITH SOME KIND OF ACCIDENT OR PERHAPS WAS RECOVERING AFTER AN ATTACK BY A FELLOW GHOUL.
ACCORD-ING TO THE FILES...
...THE NUMBER OF THE GOURMET'S FEEDING CASES ROSE CLOSE TO PEAK LEVELS SOON AFTER THAT.
BUT THEN IT DROPPED ONCE AGAIN.
THE GOURMET HELD BACK ON FEEDING FROM AROUND JANUARY OF THIS YEAR.
THAT COINCIDES WITH THE GOURMET'S FIRST FEEDING IN THE 18TH WARD THAT TOOK PLACE RECENTLY.
Number of Feedings
0
t
Around Nov.
Around Jan.
Around June
ANOTHER ONE OF YOUR GUT FEELINGS ...
...INVES-TIGATOR MADO?
IF YOU DON'T MIND, I'D LIKE TO TELL YOU A HUNCH I HAVE, INVESTIGATOR TAKIZAWA.
COMPARING THE GRAPH AND THE MAP...
...YOU'LL SEE THAT THE GOURMET'S RECENT BEHAVIORAL PATTERN IS NOTICEABLY DIFFERENT.

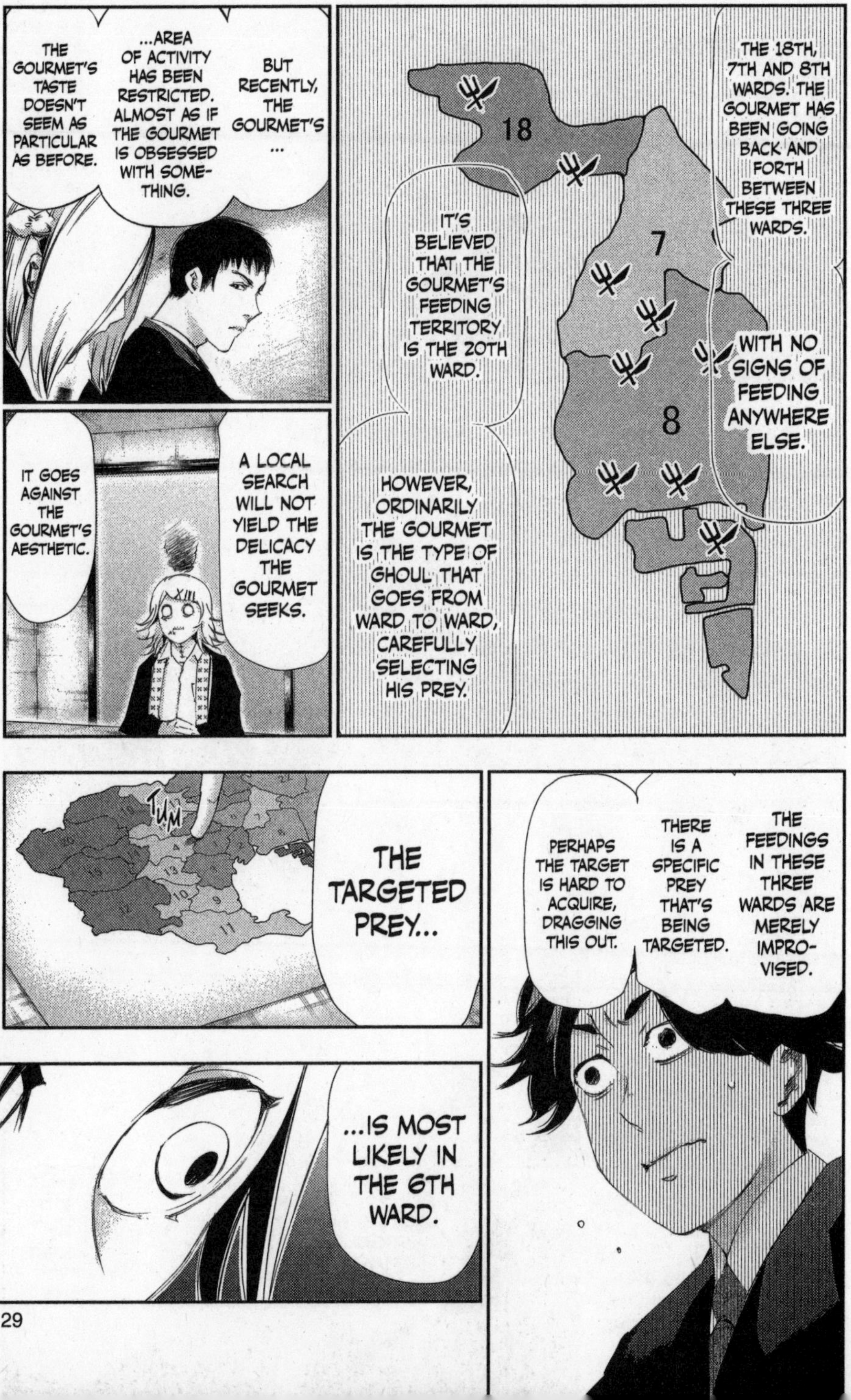
THE 18TH, 7TH AND 8TH WARDS. THE GOURMET HAS BEEN GOING BACK AND FORTH BETWEEN THESE THREE WARDS.
18
7
8
WITH NO SIGNS OF FEEDING ANYWHERE ELSE.
IT'S BELIEVED THAT THE GOURMET'S FEEDING TERRITORY IS THE 20TH WARD.
HOWEVER, ORDINARILY THE GOURMET IS THE TYPE OF GHOUL THAT GOES FROM WARD TO WARD, CAREFULLY SELECTING HIS PREY.
BUT RECENTLY, THE GOURMET'S ...
...AREA OF ACTIVITY HAS BEEN RESTRICTED. ALMOST AS IF THE GOURMET IS OBSESSED WITH SOME-THING.
THE GOURMET'S TASTE DOESN'T SEEM AS PARTICULAR AS BEFORE.
A LOCAL SEARCH WILL NOT YIELD THE DELICACY THE GOURMET SEEKS.
IT GOES AGAINST THE GOURMET'S AESTHETIC.
THE FEEDINGS IN THESE THREE WARDS ARE MERELY IMPRO-VISED.
THERE IS A SPECIFIC PREY THAT'S BEING TARGETED.
PERHAPS THE TARGET IS HARD TO ACQUIRE, DRAGGING THIS OUT.
TUM
THE TARGETED PREY...
...IS MOST LIKELY IN THE 6TH WARD.

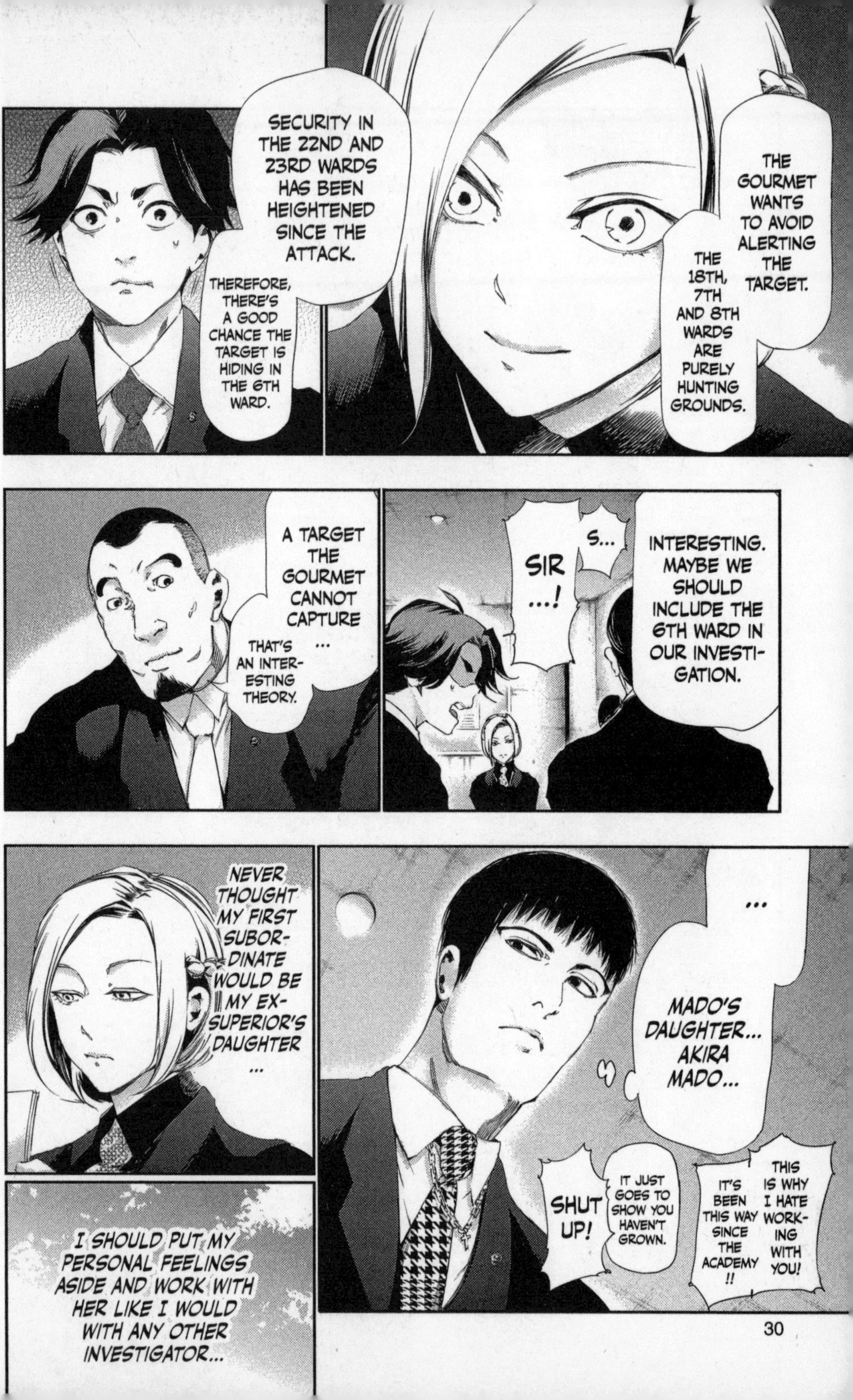
THE GOURMET WANTS TO AVOID ALERTING THE TARGET.
THE 18TH, 7TH AND 8TH WARDS ARE PURELY HUNTING GROUNDS.
SECURITY IN THE 22ND AND 23RD WARDS HAS BEEN HEIGHTENED SINCE THE ATTACK.
THEREFORE, THERE'S A GOOD CHANCE THE TARGET IS HIDING IN THE 6TH WARD.
INTERESTING. MAYBE WE SHOULD INCLUDE THE 6TH WARD IN OUR INVESTI-GATION.
S...
SIR ...!
A TARGET THE GOURMET CANNOT CAPTURE ...
THAT'S AN INTER-ESTING THEORY.
...
MADO'S DAUGHTER... AKIRA MADO...
THIS IS WHY I HATE WORK-ING WITH YOU!
IT'S BEEN THIS WAY SINCE THE ACADEMY !!
IT JUST GOES TO SHOW YOU HAVEN'T GROWN.
SHUT UP!
NEVER THOUGHT MY FIRST SUBOR-DINATE WOULD BE MY EX-SUPERIOR'S DAUGHTER ...
I SHOULD PUT MY PERSONAL FEELINGS ASIDE AND WORK WITH HER LIKE I WOULD WITH ANY OTHER INVESTIGATOR...

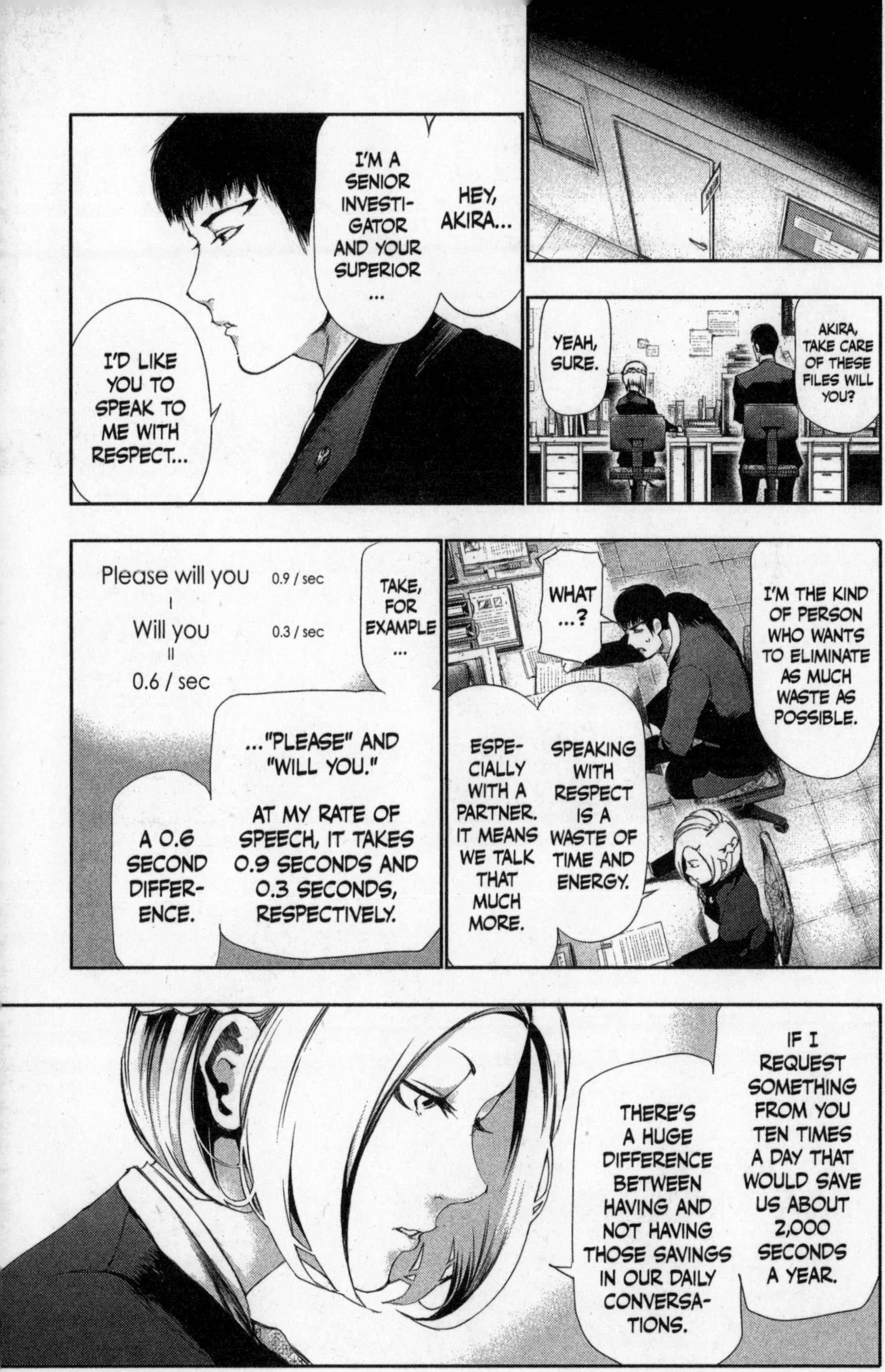
AKIRA, TAKE CARE OF THESE FILES WILL YOU?
YEAH, SURE.
HEY, AKIRA...
I'M A SENIOR INVESTIGATOR AND YOUR SUPERIOR...
I'D LIKE YOU TO SPEAK TO ME WITH RESPECT...
I'M THE KIND OF PERSON WHO WANTS TO ELIMINATE AS MUCH WASTE AS POSSIBLE.
WHAT...?
SPEAKING WITH RESPECT IS A WASTE OF TIME AND ENERGY.
ESPECIALLY WITH A PARTNER. IT MEANS WE TALK THAT MUCH MORE.
TAKE, FOR EXAMPLE...
Please will you 0.9 / sec
Will you 0.3 / sec
0.6 / sec
..."PLEASE" AND "WILL YOU."
AT MY RATE OF SPEECH, IT TAKES 0.9 SECONDS AND 0.3 SECONDS, RESPECTIVELY.
A 0.6 SECOND DIFFERENCE.
IF I REQUEST SOMETHING FROM YOU TEN TIMES A DAY THAT WOULD SAVE US ABOUT 2,000 SECONDS A YEAR.
THERE'S A HUGE DIFFERENCE BETWEEN HAVING AND NOT HAVING THOSE SAVINGS IN OUR DAILY CONVERSATIONS.

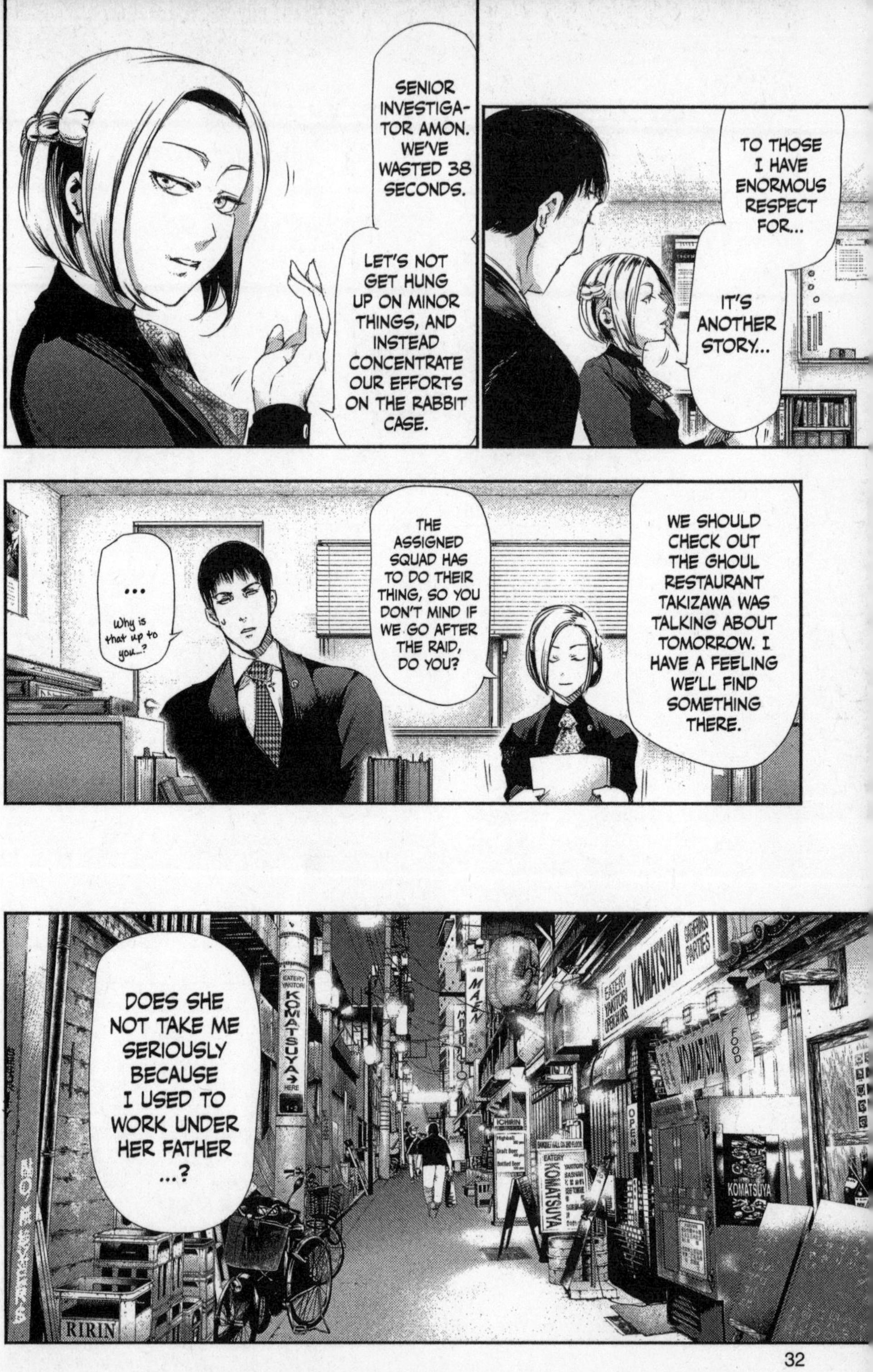
TO THOSE I HAVE ENORMOUS RESPECT FOR...
IT'S ANOTHER STORY...
SENIOR INVESTIGATOR AMON. WE'VE WASTED 38 SECONDS.
LET'S NOT GET HUNG UP ON MINOR THINGS, AND INSTEAD CONCENTRATE OUR EFFORTS ON THE RABBIT CASE.
WE SHOULD CHECK OUT THE GHOUL RESTAURANT TAKIZAWA WAS TALKING ABOUT TOMORROW. I HAVE A FEELING WE'LL FIND SOMETHING THERE.
THE ASSIGNED SQUAD HAS TO DO THEIR THING, SO YOU DON'T MIND IF WE GO AFTER THE RAID, DO YOU?
...
Why is that up to you...?
KOMATSUYA
FOOD
OPEN
EATERY KOMATSUYA
EATERY YAKITORI KOMATSUYA HERE
RIRIN
DOES SHE NOT TAKE ME SERIOUSLY BECAUSE I USED TO WORK UNDER HER FATHER ...?

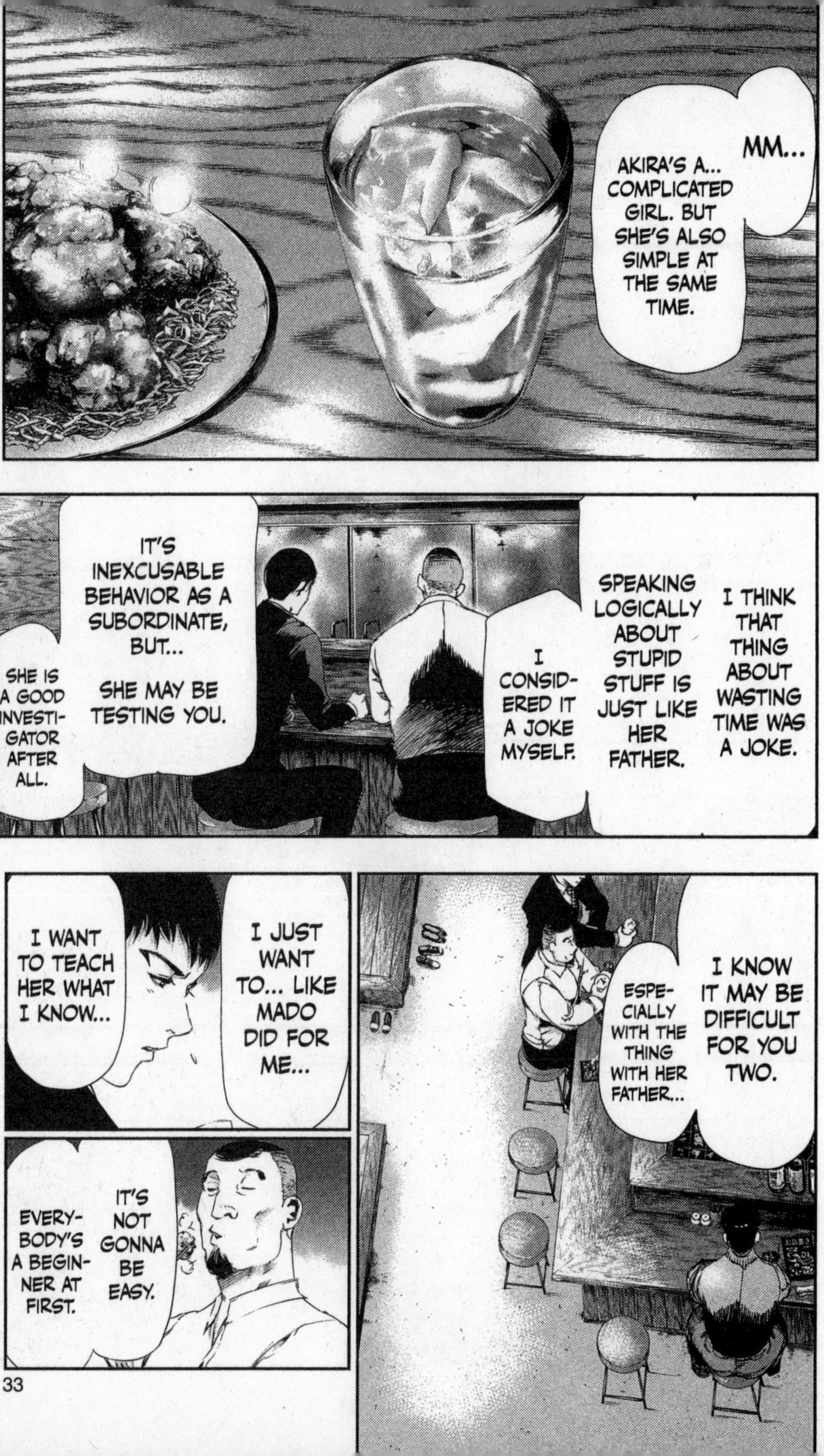
MM...
AKIRA'S A... COMPLICATED GIRL. BUT SHE'S ALSO SIMPLE AT THE SAME TIME.
I THINK THAT THING ABOUT WASTING TIME WAS A JOKE.
SPEAKING LOGICALLY ABOUT STUPID STUFF IS JUST LIKE HER FATHER.
I CONSIDERED IT A JOKE MYSELF.
IT'S INEXCUSABLE BEHAVIOR AS A SUBORDINATE, BUT...
SHE MAY BE TESTING YOU.
SHE IS A GOOD INVESTIGATOR AFTER ALL.
I KNOW IT MAY BE DIFFICULT FOR YOU TWO.
ESPECIALLY WITH THE THING WITH HER FATHER...
I JUST WANT TO... LIKE MADO DID FOR ME...
I WANT TO TEACH HER WHAT I KNOW...
IT'S NOT GONNA BE EASY.
EVERYBODY'S A BEGINNER AT FIRST.

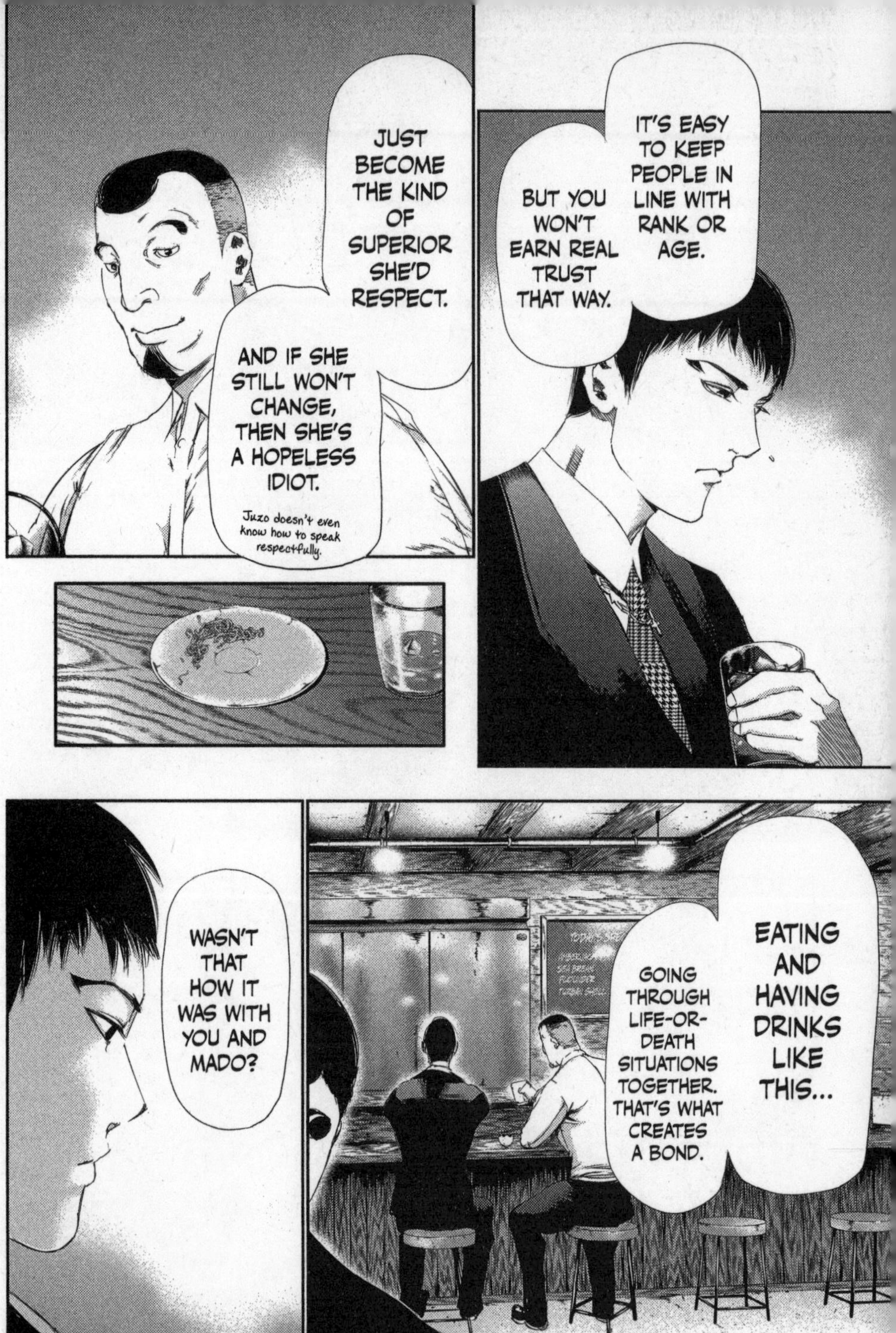
IT'S EASY TO KEEP PEOPLE IN LINE WITH RANK OR AGE.
BUT YOU WON'T EARN REAL TRUST THAT WAY.
JUST BECOME THE KIND OF SUPERIOR SHE'D RESPECT.
AND IF SHE STILL WON'T CHANGE, THEN SHE'S A HOPELESS IDIOT.
Juzo doesn't even know how to speak respectfully.
EATING AND HAVING DRINKS LIKE THIS...
GOING THROUGH LIFE-OR-DEATH SITUATIONS TOGETHER. THAT'S WHAT CREATES A BOND.
WASN'T THAT HOW IT WAS WITH YOU AND MADO?

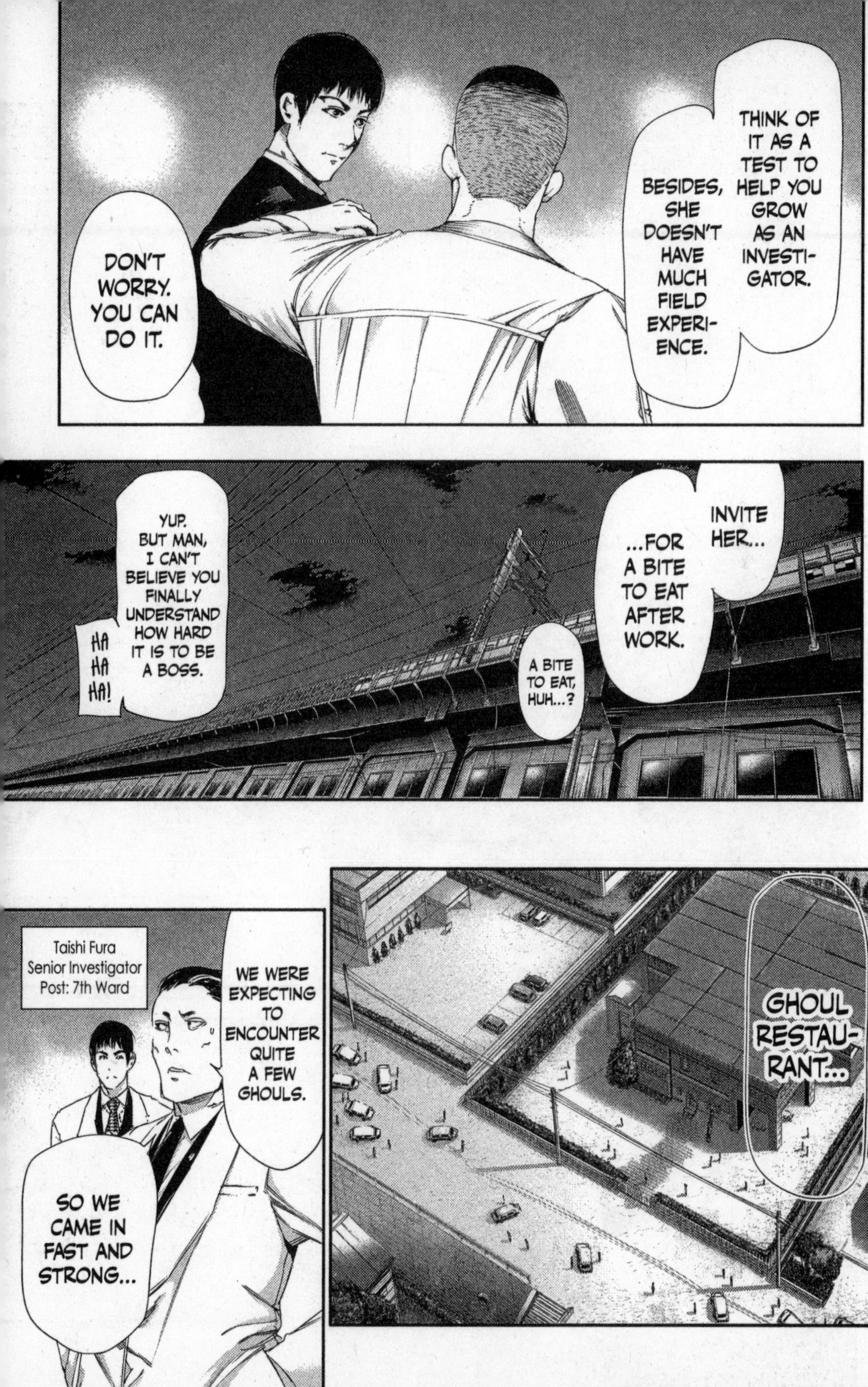
THINK OF IT AS A TEST TO HELP YOU GROW AS AN INVESTIGATOR.
BESIDES, SHE DOESN'T HAVE MUCH FIELD EXPERIENCE.
DON'T WORRY. YOU CAN DO IT.
INVITE HER...
...FOR A BITE TO EAT AFTER WORK.
A BITE TO EAT, HUH...?
YUP. BUT MAN, I CAN'T BELIEVE YOU FINALLY UNDERSTAND HOW HARD IT IS TO BE A BOSS.
HA HA HA!
GHOUL RESTAURANT...
Taishi Fura Senior Investigator Post: 7th Ward
WE WERE EXPECTING TO ENCOUNTER QUITE A FEW GHOULS.
SO WE CAME IN FAST AND STRONG...

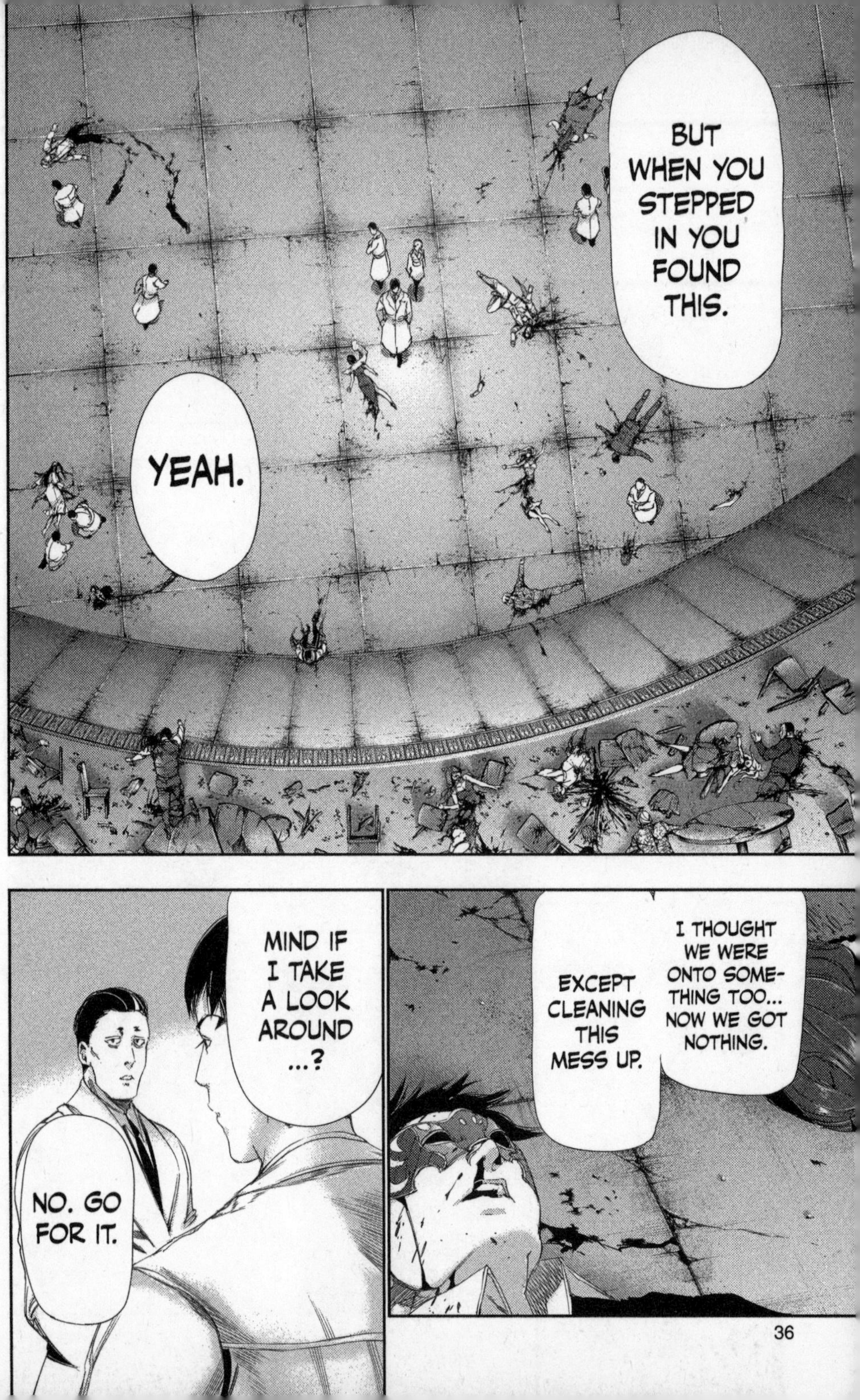
BUT WHEN YOU STEPPED IN YOU FOUND THIS.
YEAH.
I THOUGHT WE WERE ONTO SOME-THING TOO... NOW WE GOT NOTHING.
EXCEPT CLEANING THIS MESS UP.
MIND IF I TAKE A LOOK AROUND ...?
NO. GO FOR IT.

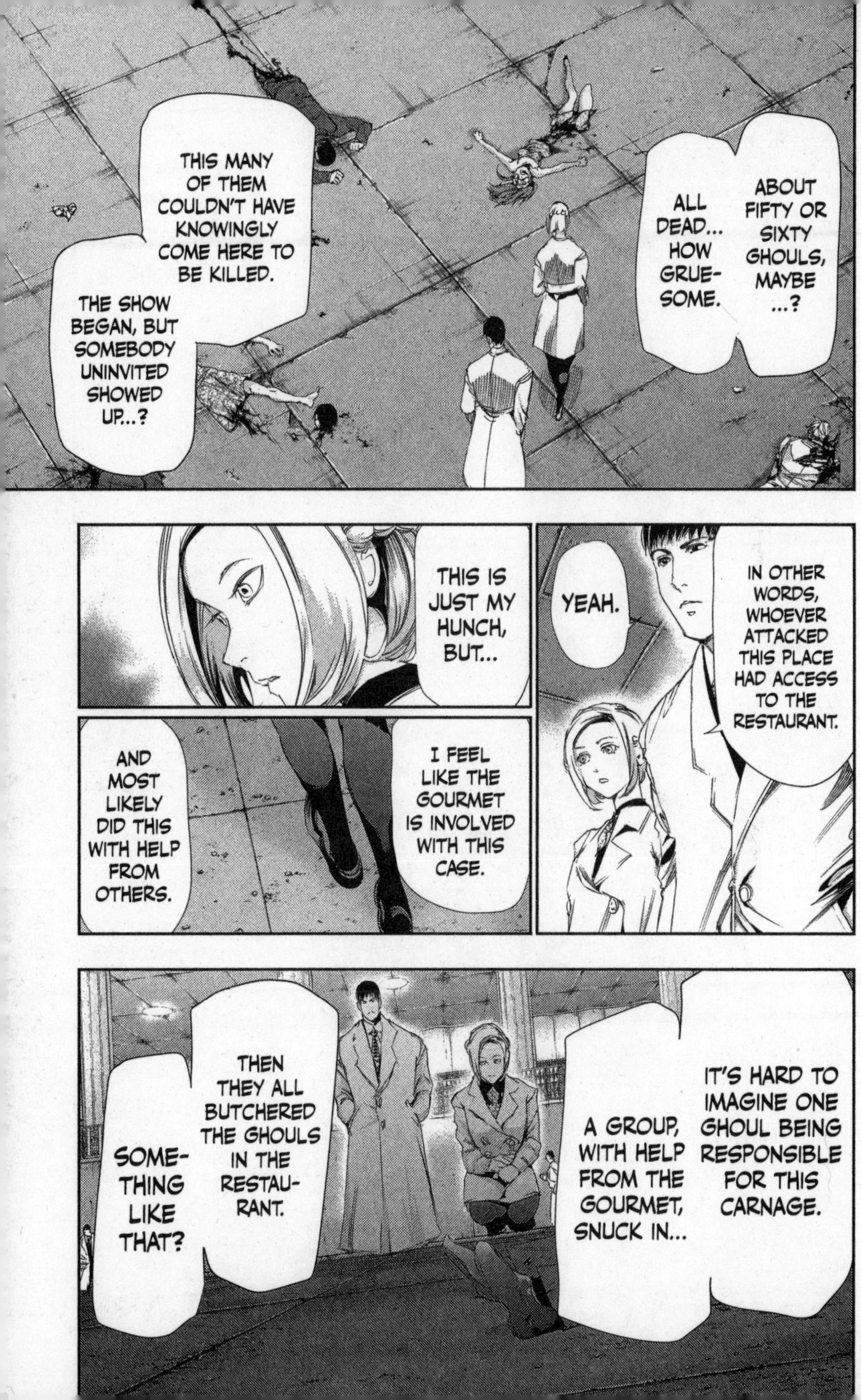
ABOUT FIFTY OR SIXTY GHOULS, MAYBE ...?
ALL DEAD... HOW GRUESOME.
THIS MANY OF THEM COULDN'T HAVE KNOWINGLY COME HERE TO BE KILLED.
THE SHOW BEGAN, BUT SOMEBODY UNINVITED SHOWED UP...?
IN OTHER WORDS, WHOEVER ATTACKED THIS PLACE HAD ACCESS TO THE RESTAURANT.
YEAH.
THIS IS JUST MY HUNCH, BUT...
I FEEL LIKE THE GOURMET IS INVOLVED WITH THIS CASE.
AND MOST LIKELY DID THIS WITH HELP FROM OTHERS.
IT'S HARD TO IMAGINE ONE GHOUL BEING RESPONSIBLE FOR THIS CARNAGE.
A GROUP, WITH HELP FROM THE GOURMET, SNUCK IN...
THEN THEY ALL BUTCHERED THE GHOULS IN THE RESTAURANT.
SOMETHING LIKE THAT?

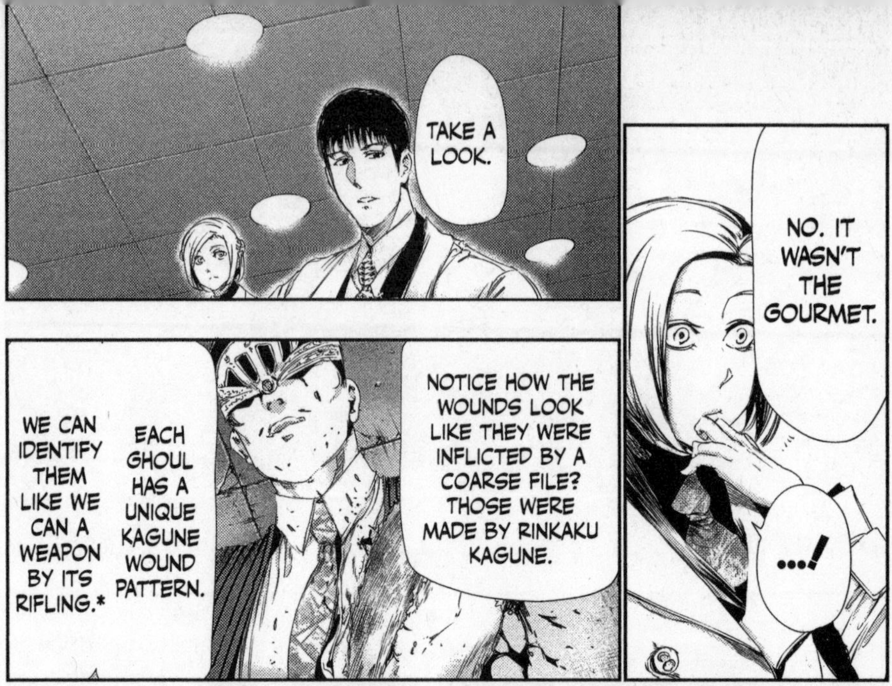
NO. IT WASN'T THE GOURMET.
...!
TAKE A LOOK.
NOTICE HOW THE WOUNDS LOOK LIKE THEY WERE INFLICTED BY A COARSE FILE? THOSE WERE MADE BY RINKAKU KAGUNE.
EACH GHOUL HAS A UNIQUE KAGUNE WOUND PATTERN.
WE CAN IDENTIFY THEM LIKE WE CAN A WEAPON BY ITS RIFLING.*

*Spiral grooves in the barrel of a firearm. Like fingerprints, each firearm has a unique groove making it possible to identify.

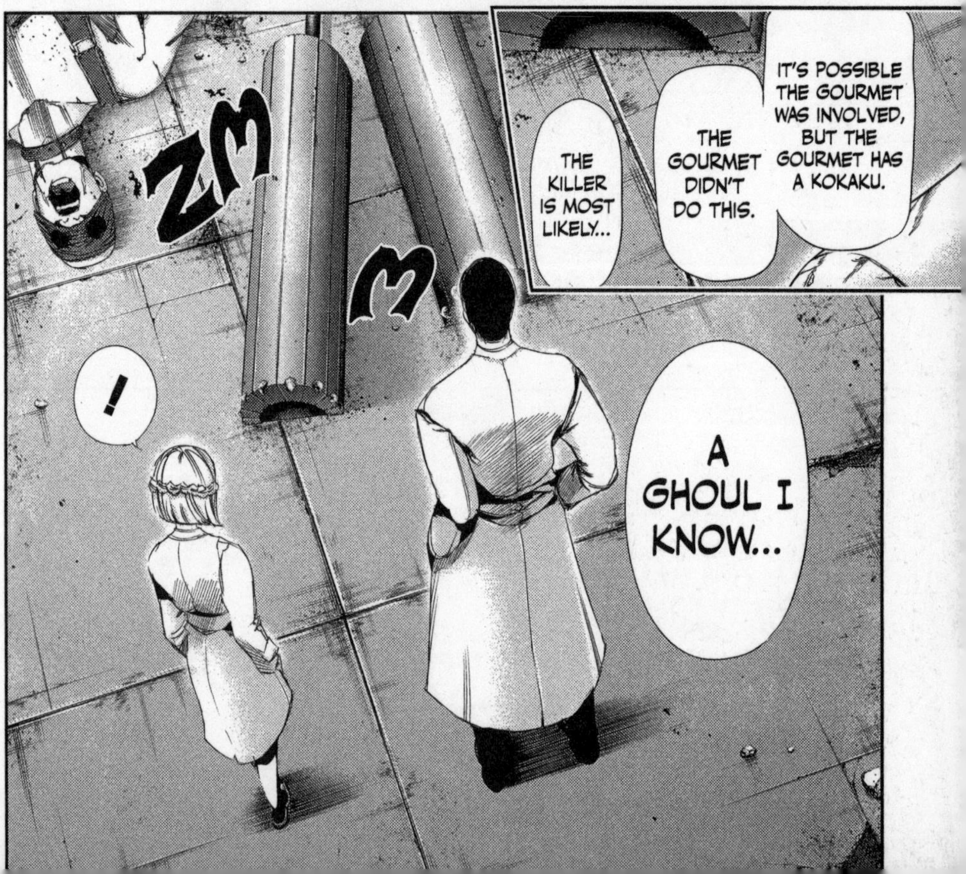
IT'S POSSIBLE THE GOURMET WAS INVOLVED, BUT THE GOURMET HAS A KOKAKU.
THE GOURMET DIDN'T DO THIS.
THE KILLER IS MOST LIKELY...
A GHOUL I KNOW...
ZMM
!

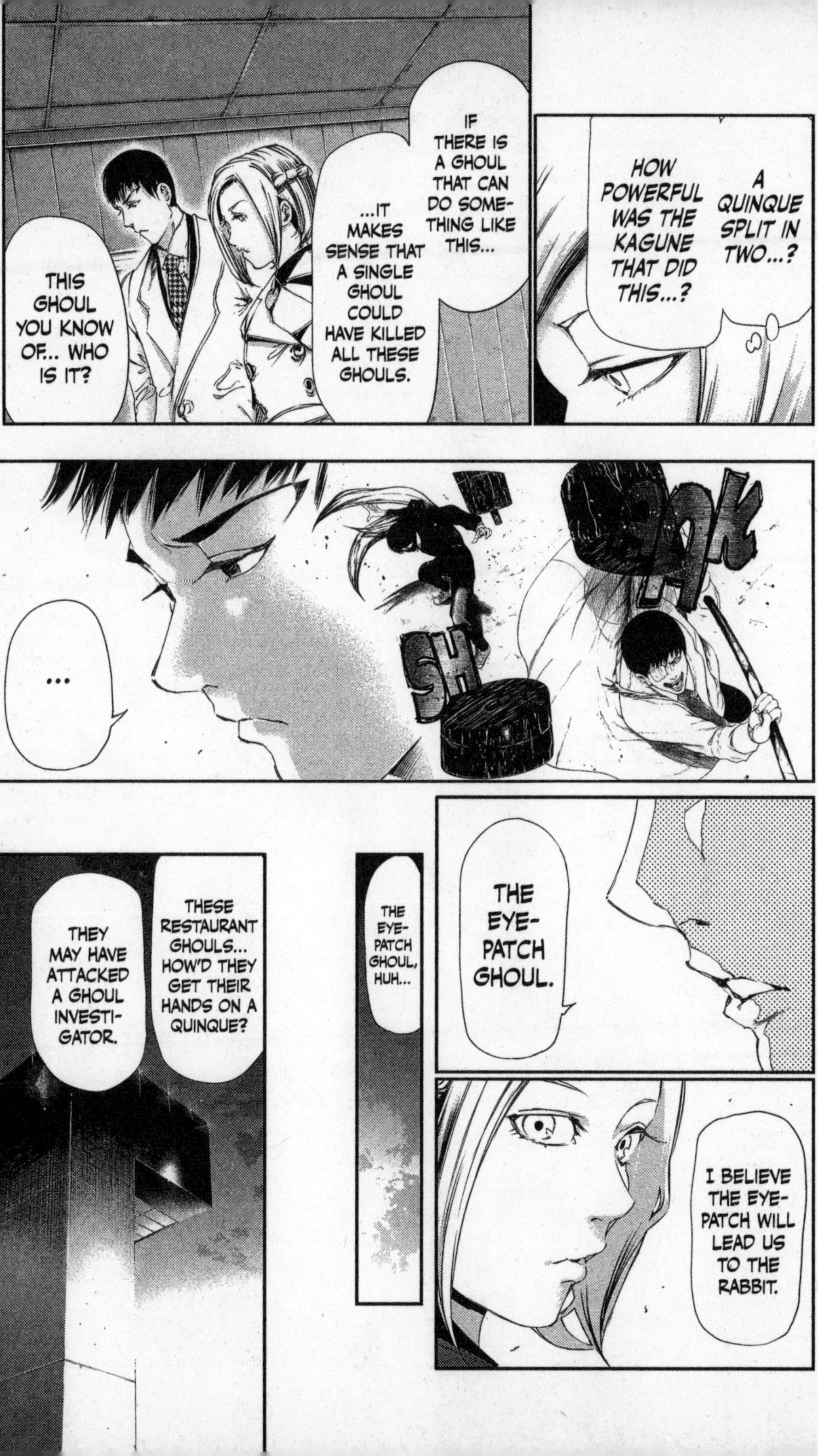
A QUINQUE SPLIT IN TWO...?
HOW POWERFUL WAS THE KAGUNE THAT DID THIS...?
IF THERE IS A GHOUL THAT CAN DO SOMETHING LIKE THIS...
...IT MAKES SENSE THAT A SINGLE GHOUL COULD HAVE KILLED ALL THESE GHOULS.
THIS GHOUL YOU KNOW OF... WHO IS IT?
...
THE EYE-PATCH GHOUL.
I BELIEVE THE EYE-PATCH WILL LEAD US TO THE RABBIT.
THE EYE-PATCH GHOUL, HUH...
THESE RESTAURANT GHOULS... HOW'D THEY GET THEIR HANDS ON A QUINQUE?
THEY MAY HAVE ATTACKED A GHOUL INVESTIGATOR.

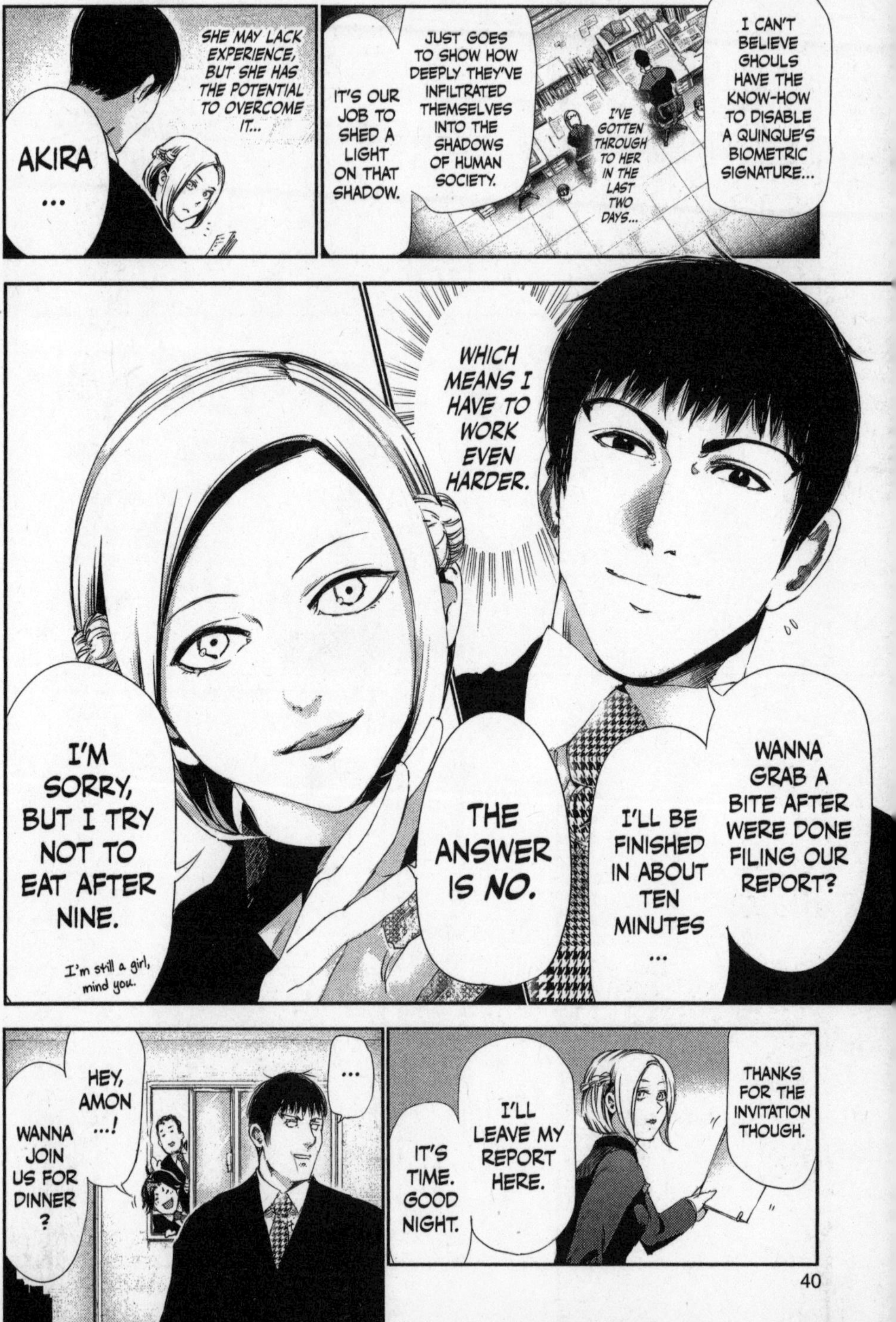
I CAN'T BELIEVE GHOULS HAVE THE KNOW-HOW TO DISABLE A QUINQUE'S BIOMETRIC SIGNATURE...
I'VE GOTTEN THROUGH TO HER IN THE LAST TWO DAYS...
JUST GOES TO SHOW HOW DEEPLY THEY'VE INFILTRATED THEMSELVES INTO THE SHADOWS OF HUMAN SOCIETY.
IT'S OUR JOB TO SHED A LIGHT ON THAT SHADOW.
SHE MAY LACK EXPERIENCE, BUT SHE HAS THE POTENTIAL TO OVERCOME IT...
AKIRA ...
WHICH MEANS I HAVE TO WORK EVEN HARDER.
WANNA GRAB A BITE AFTER WERE DONE FILING OUR REPORT?
I'LL BE FINISHED IN ABOUT TEN MINUTES ...
THE ANSWER IS *NO.*
I'M SORRY, BUT I TRY NOT TO EAT AFTER NINE.
I'm still a girl, mind you.
THANKS FOR THE INVITATION THOUGH.
I'LL LEAVE MY REPORT HERE.
IT'S TIME. GOOD NIGHT.
...
HEY, AMON ...!
WANNA JOIN US FOR DINNER ?

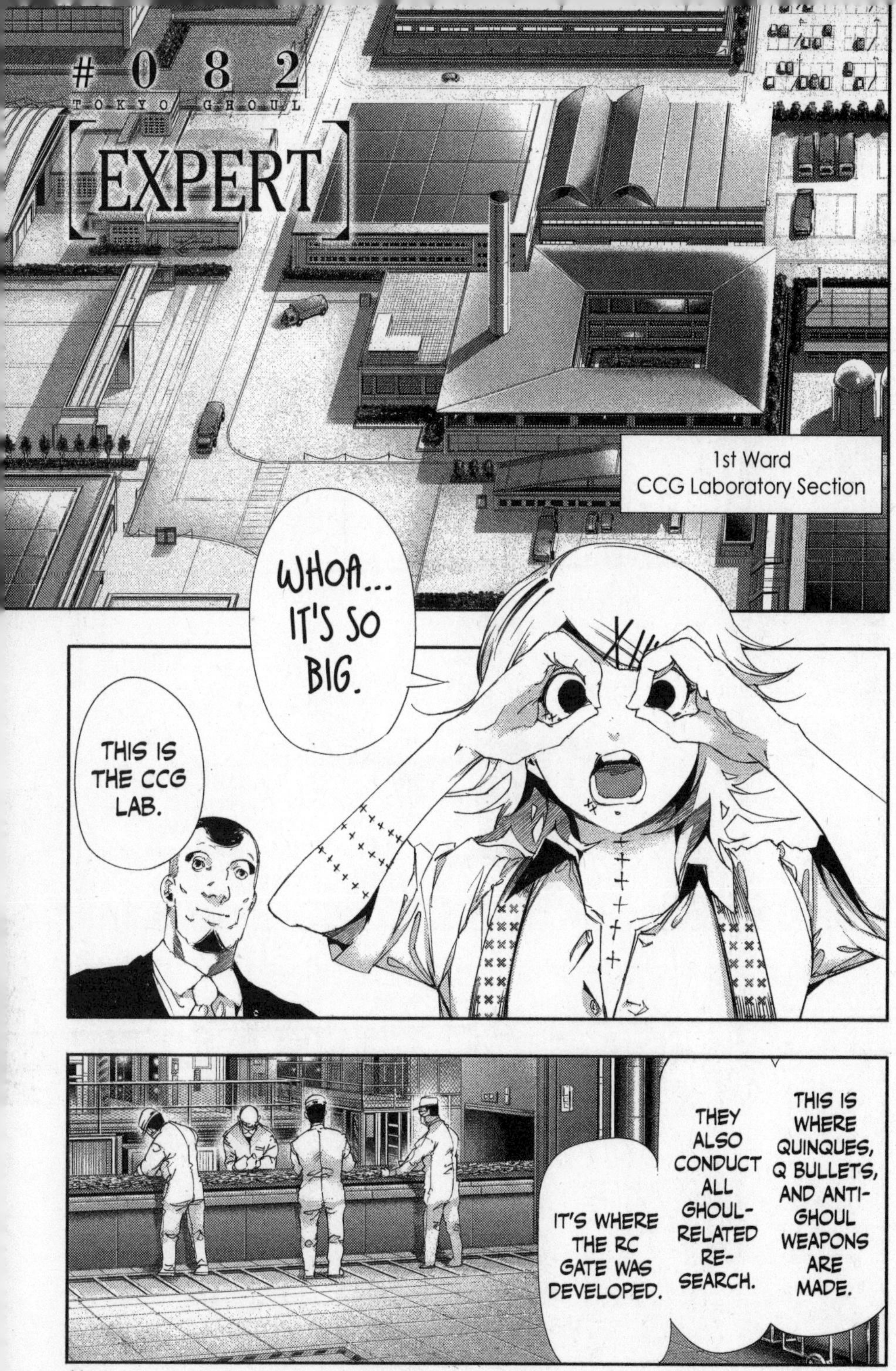

#082
TOKYO GHOUL
[EXPERT]
1st Ward CCG Laboratory Section
WHOA... IT'S SO BIG.
THIS IS THE CCG LAB.
THIS IS WHERE QUINQUES, Q BULLETS, AND ANTI-GHOUL WEAPONS ARE MADE.
THEY ALSO CONDUCT ALL GHOUL-RELATED RE-SEARCH.
IT'S WHERE THE RC GATE WAS DEVELOPED.

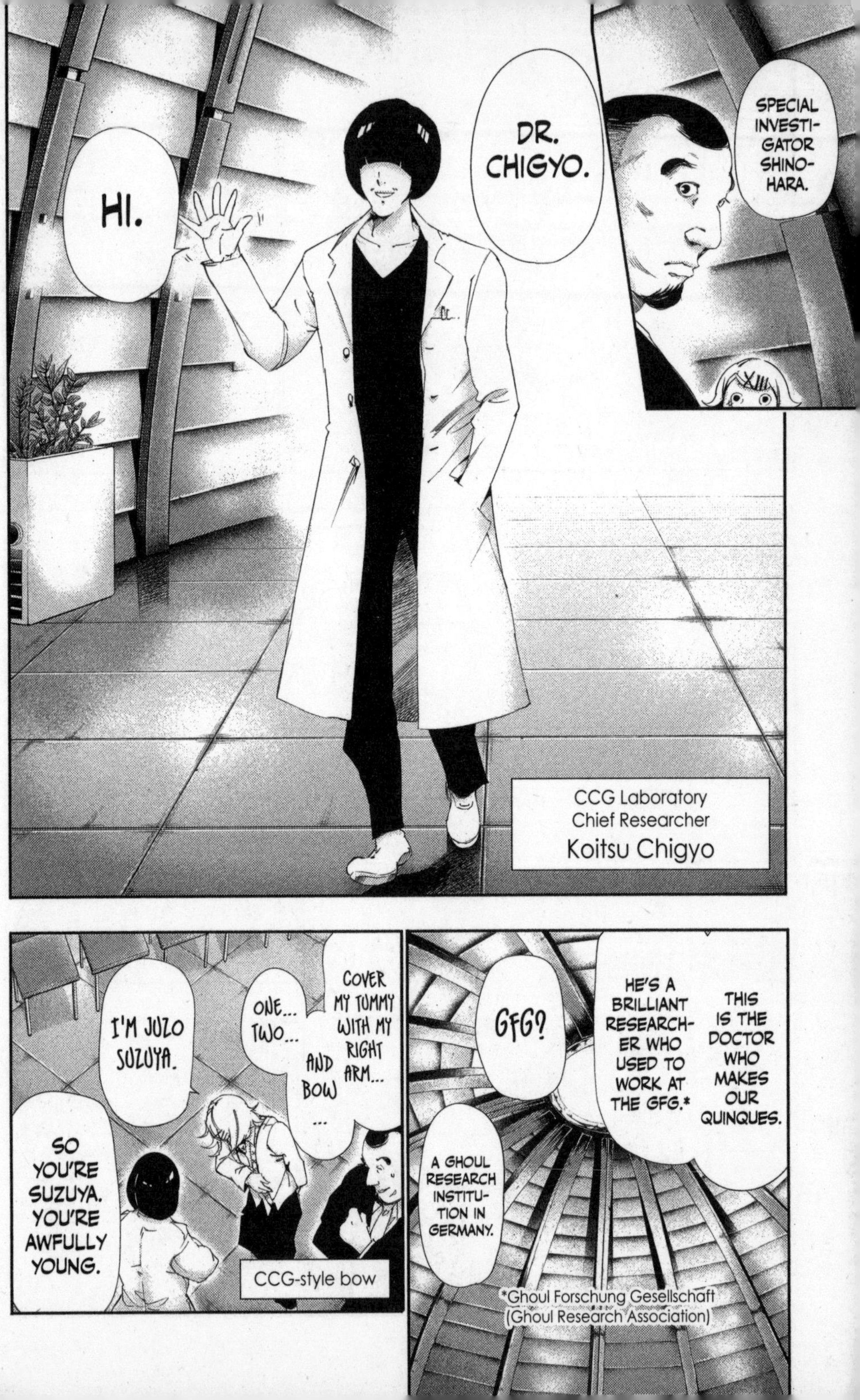
SPECIAL INVESTIGATOR SHINOHARA.
DR. CHIGYO.
HI.
CCG Laboratory Chief Researcher Koitsu Chigyo
THIS IS THE DOCTOR WHO MAKES OUR QUINQUES.
HE'S A BRILLIANT RESEARCHER WHO USED TO WORK AT THE GFG.*
GFG?
A GHOUL RESEARCH INSTITUTION IN GERMANY.
*Ghoul Forschung Gesellschaft (Ghoul Research Association)
COVER MY TUMMY WITH MY RIGHT ARM...
ONE... TWO...
AND BOW ...
I'M JUZO SUZUYA.
SO YOU'RE SUZUYA. YOU'RE AWFULLY YOUNG.
CCG-style bow

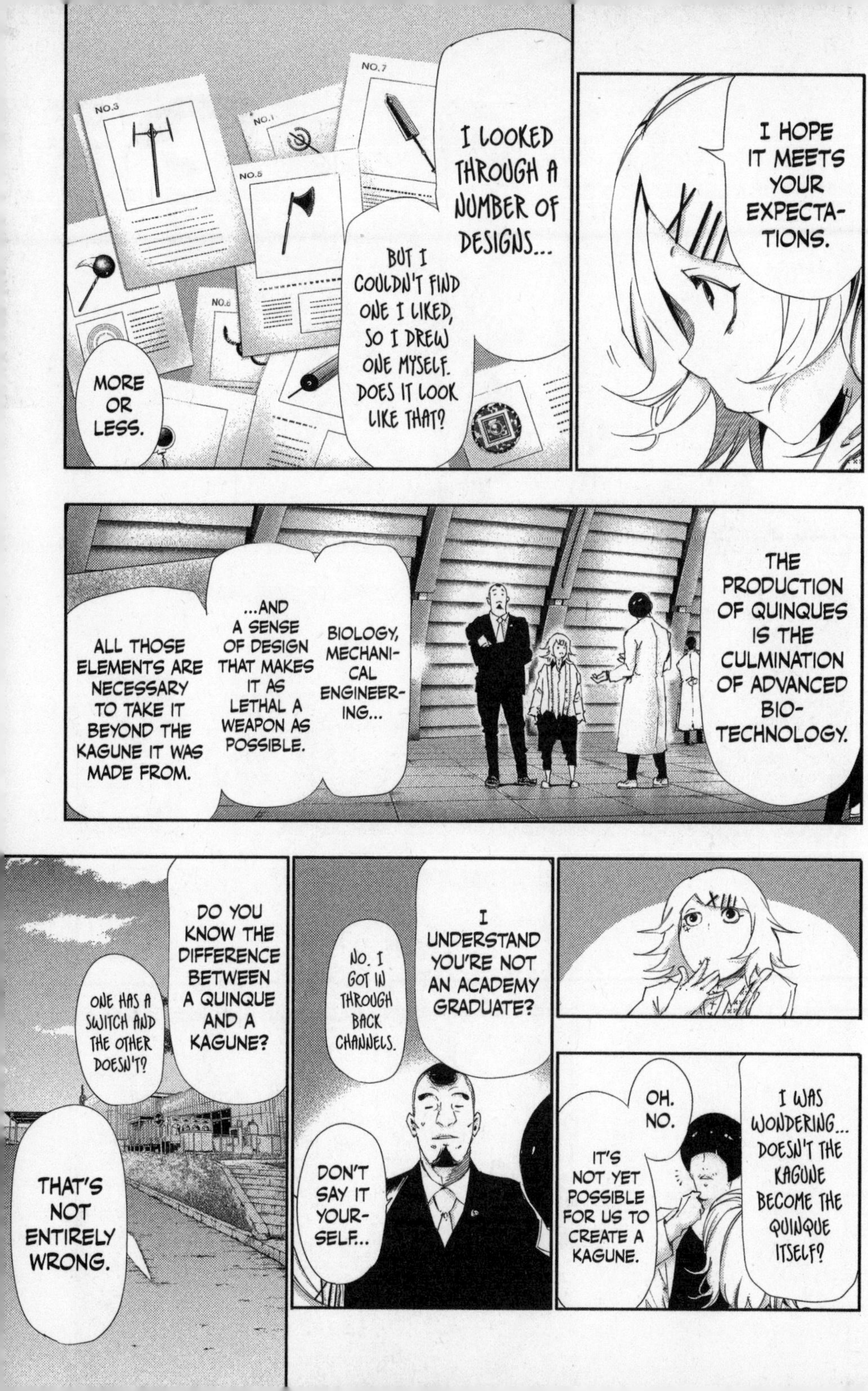
I HOPE IT MEETS YOUR EXPECTATIONS.
NO.7
NO.3
NO.1
NO.5
NO.6
I LOOKED THROUGH A NUMBER OF DESIGNS...
BUT I COULDN'T FIND ONE I LIKED, SO I DREW ONE MYSELF. DOES IT LOOK LIKE THAT?
MORE OR LESS.
THE PRODUCTION OF QUINQUES IS THE CULMINATION OF ADVANCED BIO-TECHNOLOGY.
BIOLOGY, MECHANICAL ENGINEERING...
...AND A SENSE OF DESIGN THAT MAKES IT AS LETHAL A WEAPON AS POSSIBLE.
ALL THOSE ELEMENTS ARE NECESSARY TO TAKE IT BEYOND THE KAGUNE IT WAS MADE FROM.
I WAS WONDERING... DOESN'T THE KAGUNE BECOME THE QUINQUE ITSELF?
OH. NO.
IT'S NOT YET POSSIBLE FOR US TO CREATE A KAGUNE.
I UNDERSTAND YOU'RE NOT AN ACADEMY GRADUATE?
NO. I GOT IN THROUGH BACK CHANNELS.
DON'T SAY IT YOURSELF...
DO YOU KNOW THE DIFFERENCE BETWEEN A QUINQUE AND A KAGUNE?
ONE HAS A SWITCH AND THE OTHER DOESN'T?
THAT'S NOT ENTIRELY WRONG.

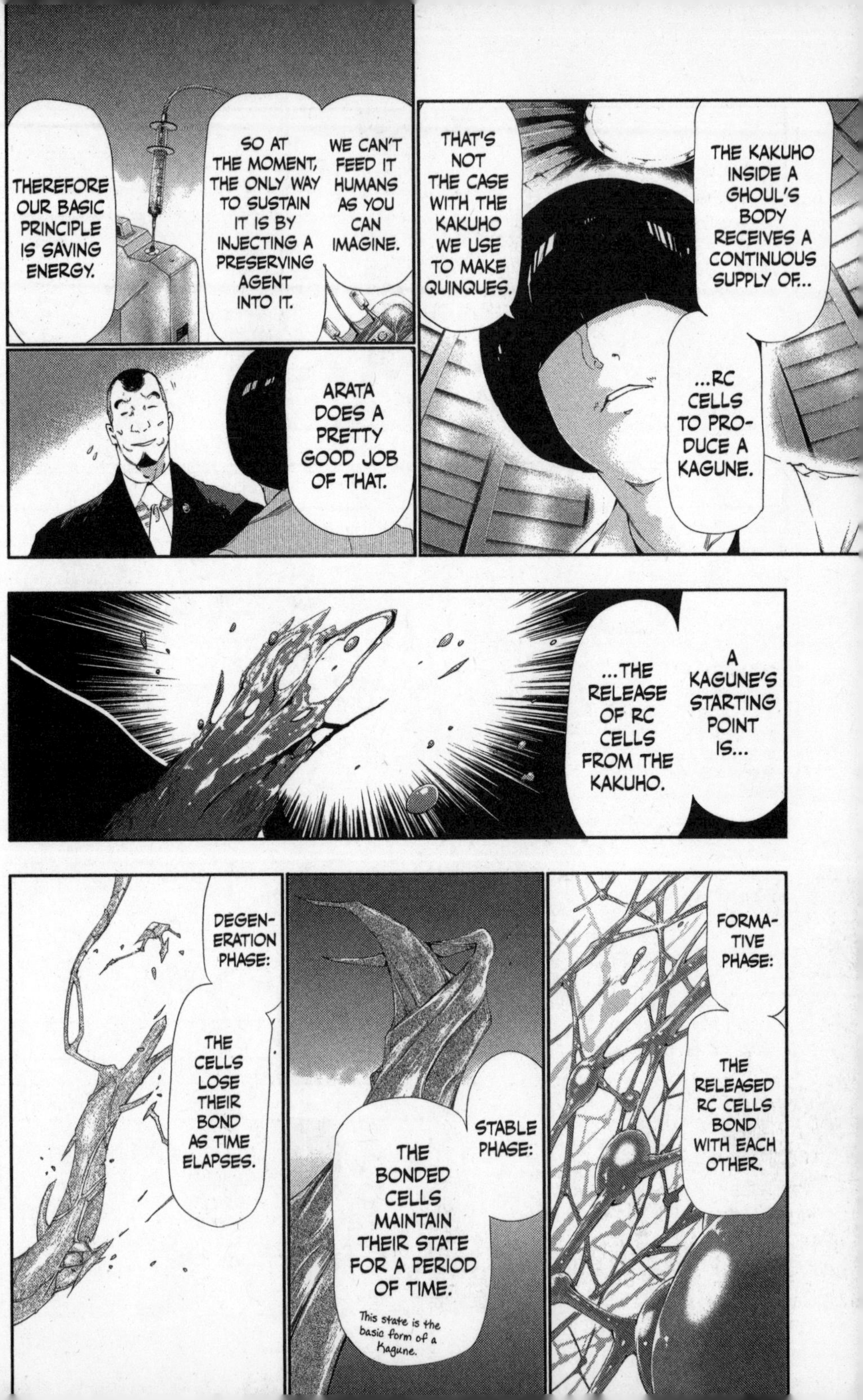
THE KAKUHO INSIDE A GHOUL'S BODY RECEIVES A CONTINUOUS SUPPLY OF...
...RC CELLS TO PRODUCE A KAGUNE.
THAT'S NOT THE CASE WITH THE KAKUHO WE USE TO MAKE QUINQUES.
WE CAN'T FEED IT HUMANS AS YOU CAN IMAGINE.
SO AT THE MOMENT, THE ONLY WAY TO SUSTAIN IT IS BY INJECTING A PRESERVING AGENT INTO IT.
THEREFORE OUR BASIC PRINCIPLE IS SAVING ENERGY.
ARATA DOES A PRETTY GOOD JOB OF THAT.
A KAGUNE'S STARTING POINT IS...
...THE RELEASE OF RC CELLS FROM THE KAKUHO.
FORMATIVE PHASE:
THE RELEASED RC CELLS BOND WITH EACH OTHER.
STABLE PHASE:
THE BONDED CELLS MAINTAIN THEIR STATE FOR A PERIOD OF TIME.
This state is the basic form of a Kagune.
DEGENERATION PHASE:
THE CELLS LOSE THEIR BOND AS TIME ELAPSES.

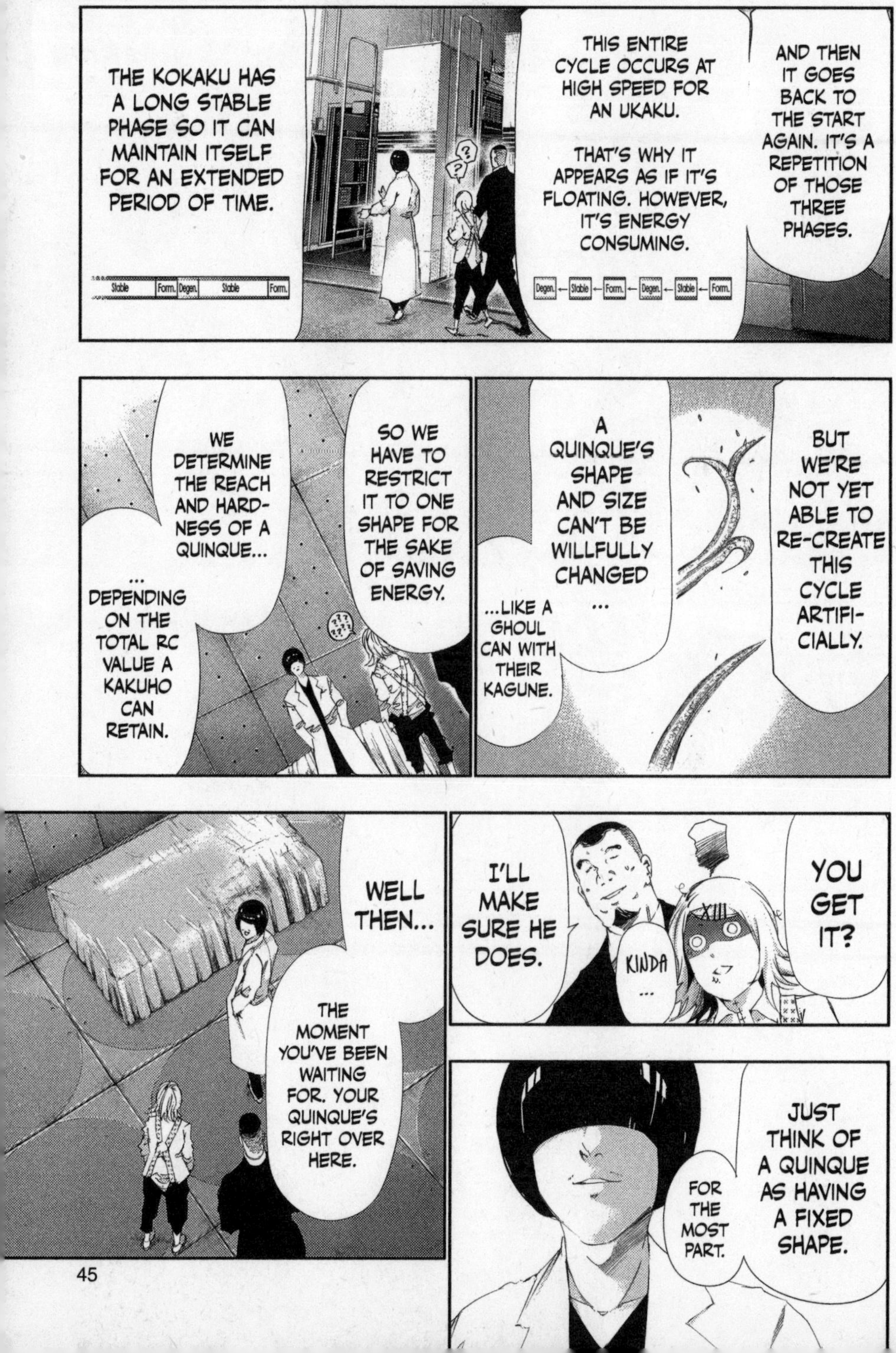
AND THEN IT GOES BACK TO THE START AGAIN. IT'S A REPETITION OF THOSE THREE PHASES.
THIS ENTIRE CYCLE OCCURS AT HIGH SPEED FOR AN UKAKU.
THAT'S WHY IT APPEARS AS IF IT'S FLOATING. HOWEVER, IT'S ENERGY CONSUMING.
Degen. ← Stable ← Form. ← Degen. ← Stable ← Form.
THE KOKAKU HAS A LONG STABLE PHASE SO IT CAN MAINTAIN ITSELF FOR AN EXTENDED PERIOD OF TIME.
Stable Form. Degen. Stable Form.
BUT WE'RE NOT YET ABLE TO RE-CREATE THIS CYCLE ARTIFICIALLY.
A QUINQUE'S SHAPE AND SIZE CAN'T BE WILLFULLY CHANGED...
...LIKE A GHOUL CAN WITH THEIR KAGUNE.
SO WE HAVE TO RESTRICT IT TO ONE SHAPE FOR THE SAKE OF SAVING ENERGY.
WE DETERMINE THE REACH AND HARD-NESS OF A QUINQUE...
...DEPENDING ON THE TOTAL RC VALUE A KAKUHO CAN RETAIN.
YOU GET IT?
I'LL MAKE SURE HE DOES.
KINDA...
JUST THINK OF A QUINQUE AS HAVING A FIXED SHAPE.
FOR THE MOST PART.
WELL THEN...
THE MOMENT YOU'VE BEEN WAITING FOR. YOUR QUINQUE'S RIGHT OVER HERE.

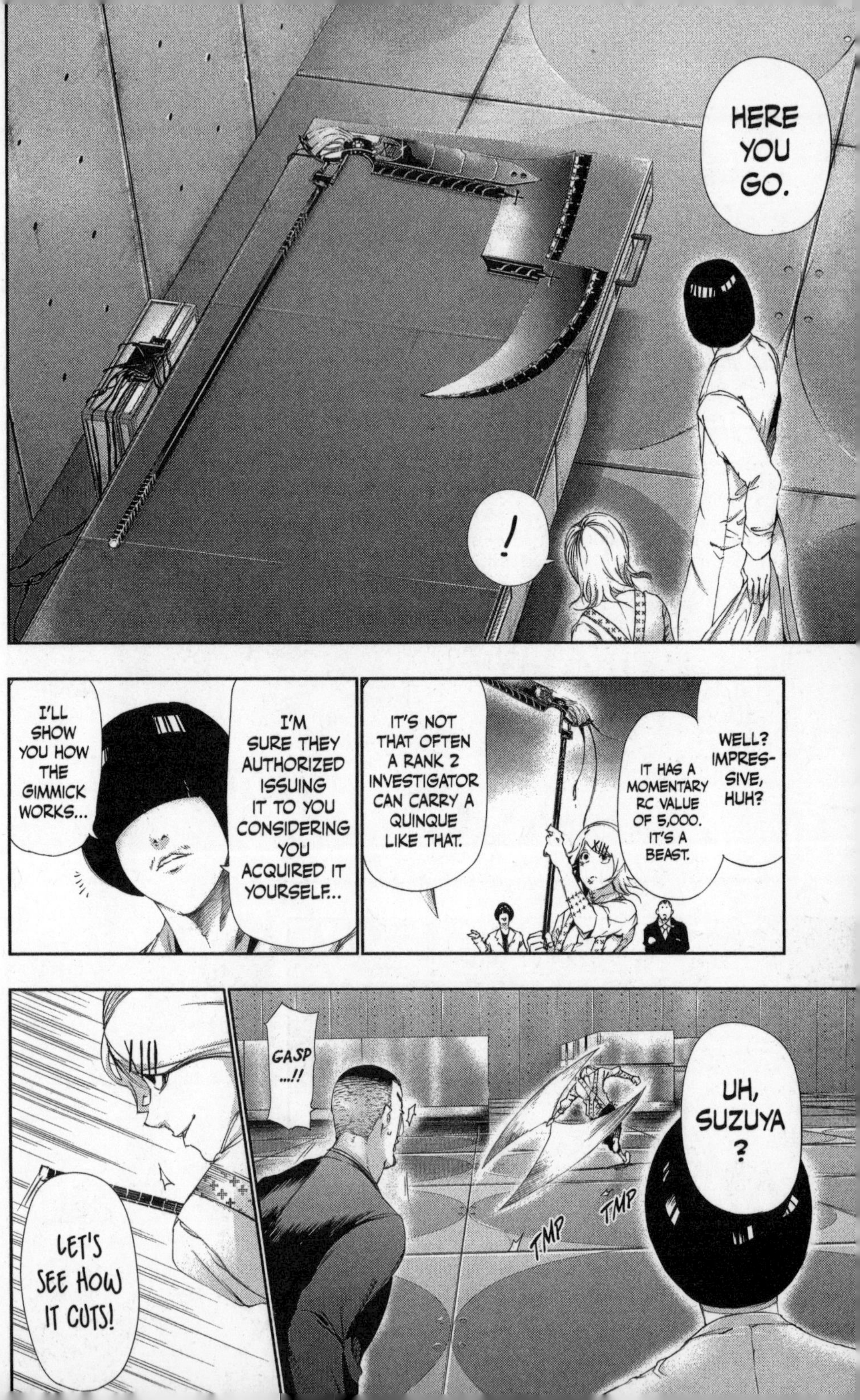
HERE YOU GO.
!
WELL? IMPRES-SIVE, HUH?
IT HAS A MOMENTARY RC VALUE OF 5,000. IT'S A BEAST.
IT'S NOT THAT OFTEN A RANK 2 INVESTIGATOR CAN CARRY A QUINQUE LIKE THAT.
I'M SURE THEY AUTHORIZED ISSUING IT TO YOU CONSIDERING YOU ACQUIRED IT YOURSELF...
I'LL SHOW YOU HOW THE GIMMICK WORKS...
UH, SUZUYA?
TMP
TMP
GASP ...!!
LET'S SEE HOW IT CUTS!

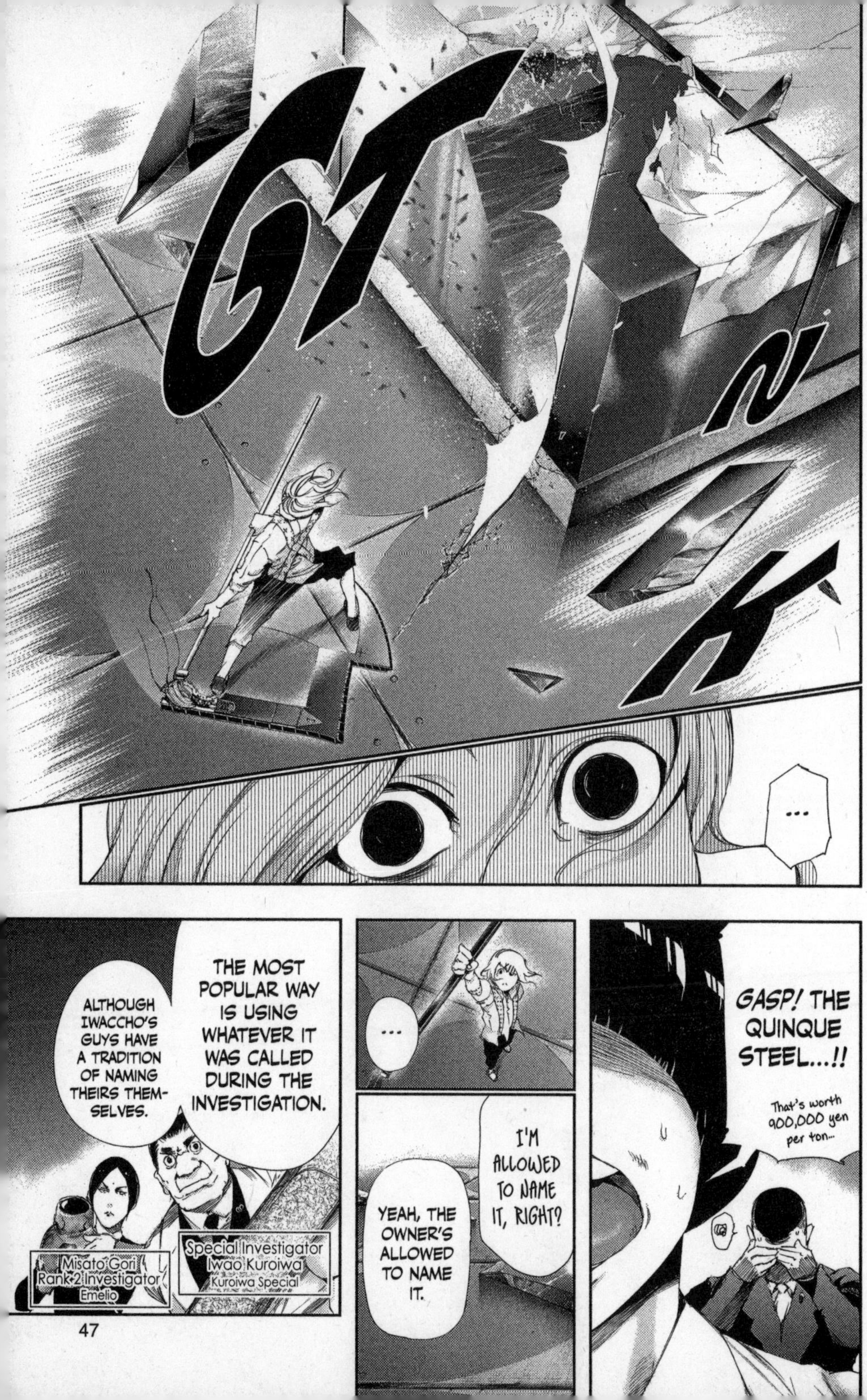
GTNK
...
GASP! THE QUINQUE STEEL...!!
That's worth 900,000 yen per ton...
...
I'M ALLOWED TO NAME IT, RIGHT?
YEAH, THE OWNER'S ALLOWED TO NAME IT.
THE MOST POPULAR WAY IS USING WHATEVER IT WAS CALLED DURING THE INVESTIGATION.
ALTHOUGH IWACCHO'S GUYS HAVE A TRADITION OF NAMING THEIRS THEM-SELVES.
Special Investigator Iwao Kuroiwa Kuroiwa Special
Misato Gori Rank 2 Investigator Emelio

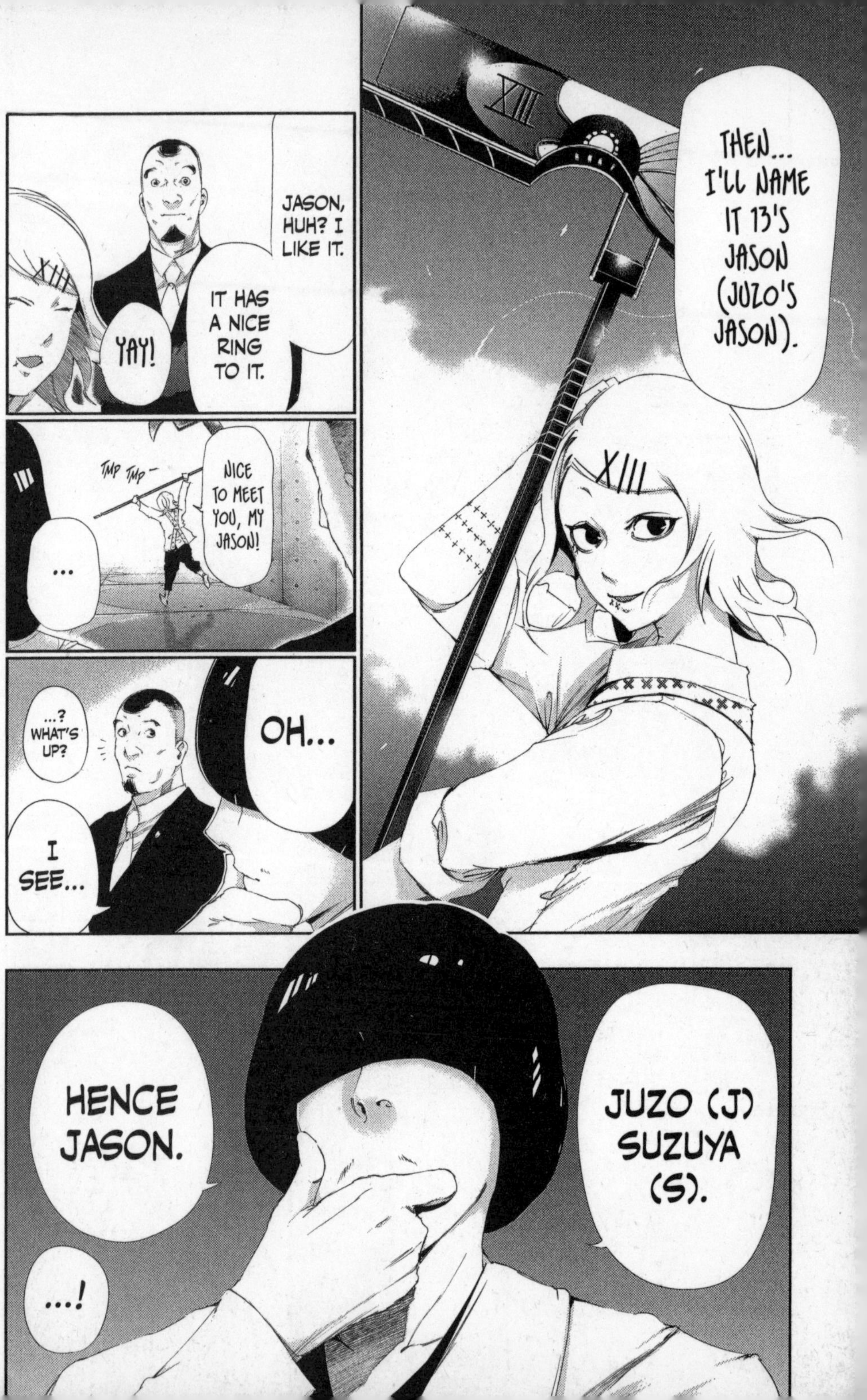
THEN... I'LL NAME IT 13'S JASON (JUZO'S JASON).
JASON, HUH? I LIKE IT.
IT HAS A NICE RING TO IT.
YAY!
NICE TO MEET YOU, MY JASON!
TMP TMP
...
OH...
...? WHAT'S UP?
I SEE...
JUZO (J) SUZUYA (S).
HENCE JASON.
...!

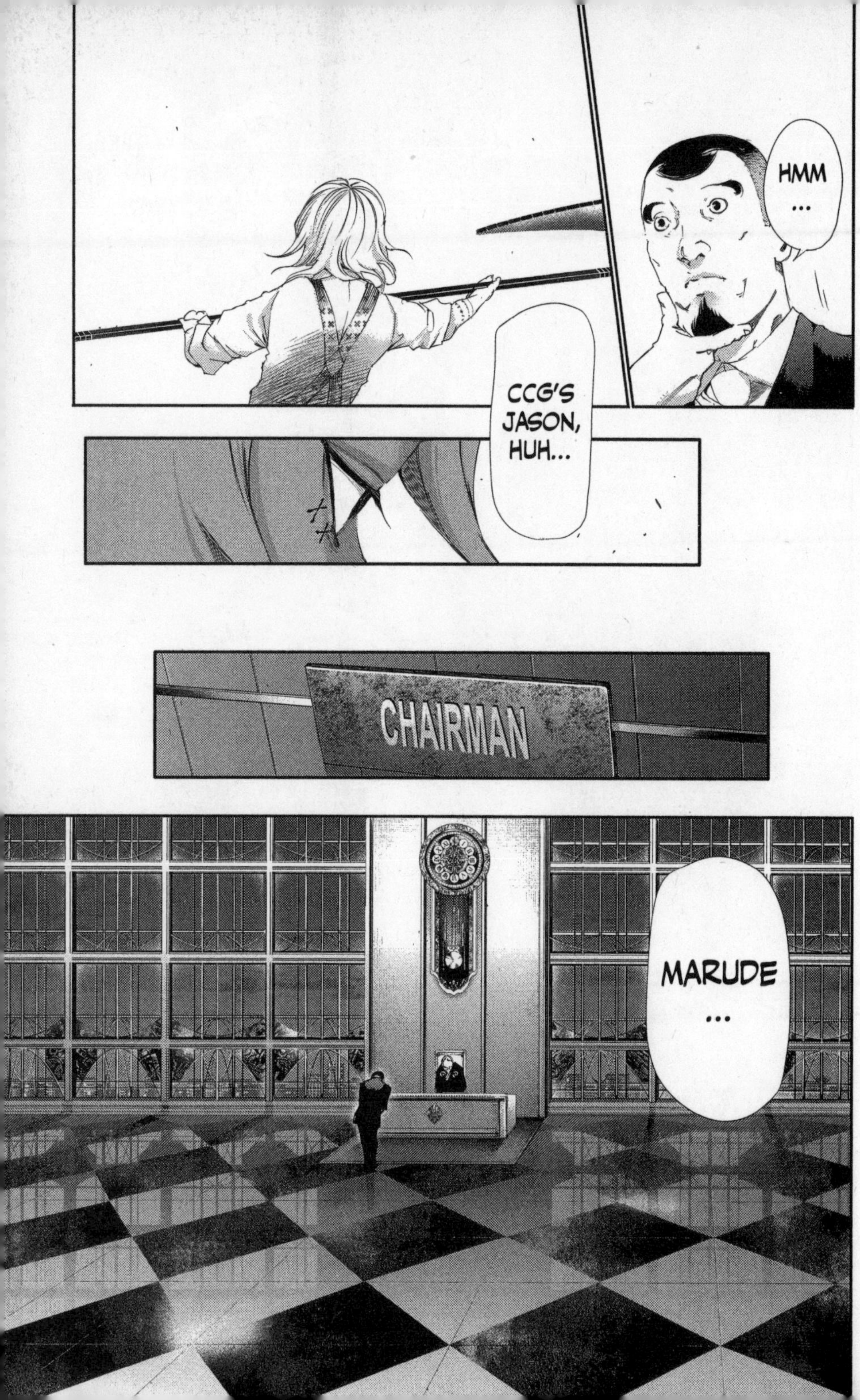
HMM ...
CCG'S JASON, HUH...
CHAIRMAN
MARUDE ...

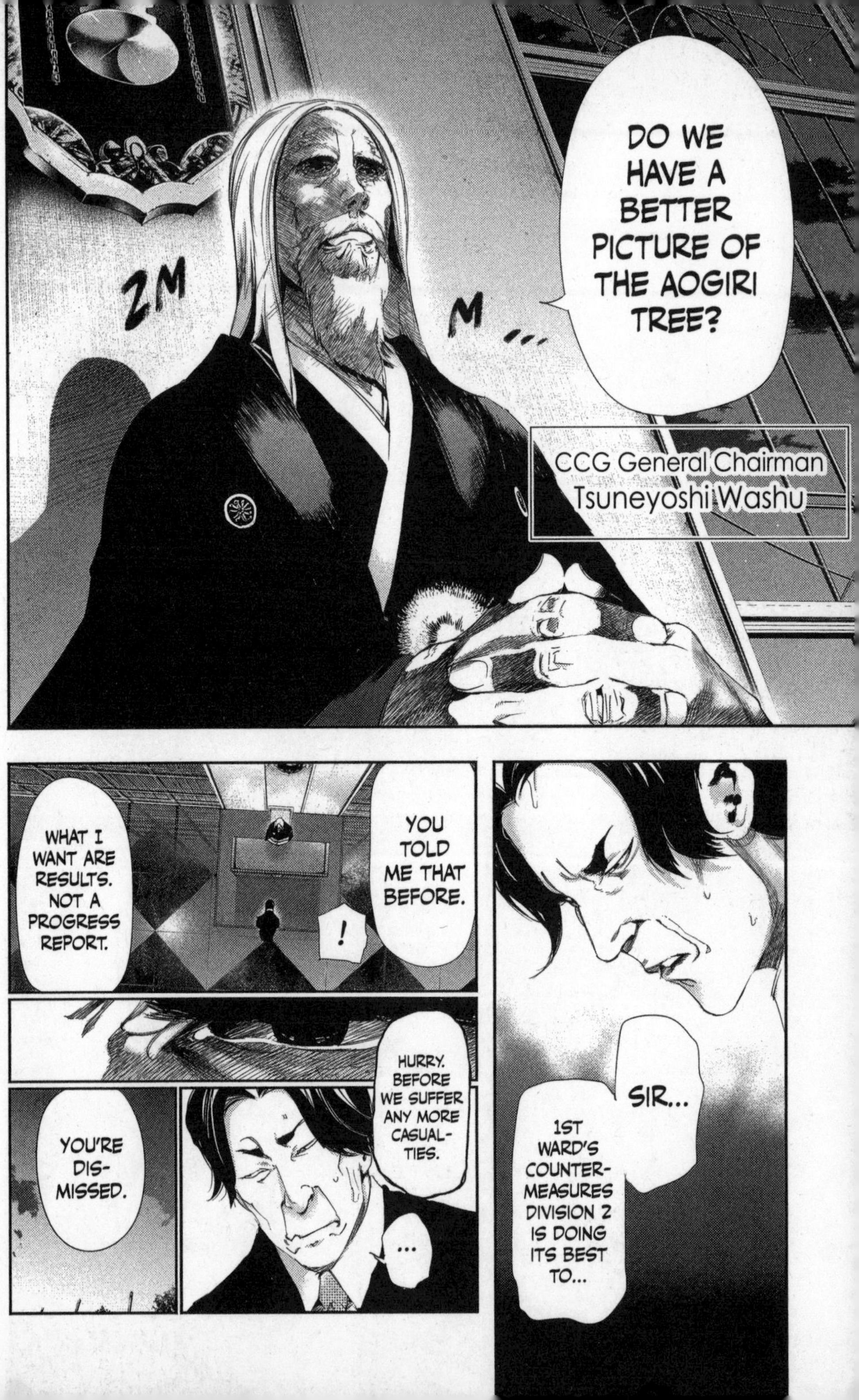
DO WE HAVE A BETTER PICTURE OF THE AOGIRI TREE?
CCG General Chairman Tsuneyoshi Washu
ZM M...
SIR...
1ST WARD'S COUNTER-MEASURES DIVISION 2 IS DOING ITS BEST TO...
YOU TOLD ME THAT BEFORE.
!
WHAT I WANT ARE RESULTS. NOT A PROGRESS REPORT.
HURRY. BEFORE WE SUFFER ANY MORE CASUAL-TIES.
...
YOU'RE DIS-MISSED.

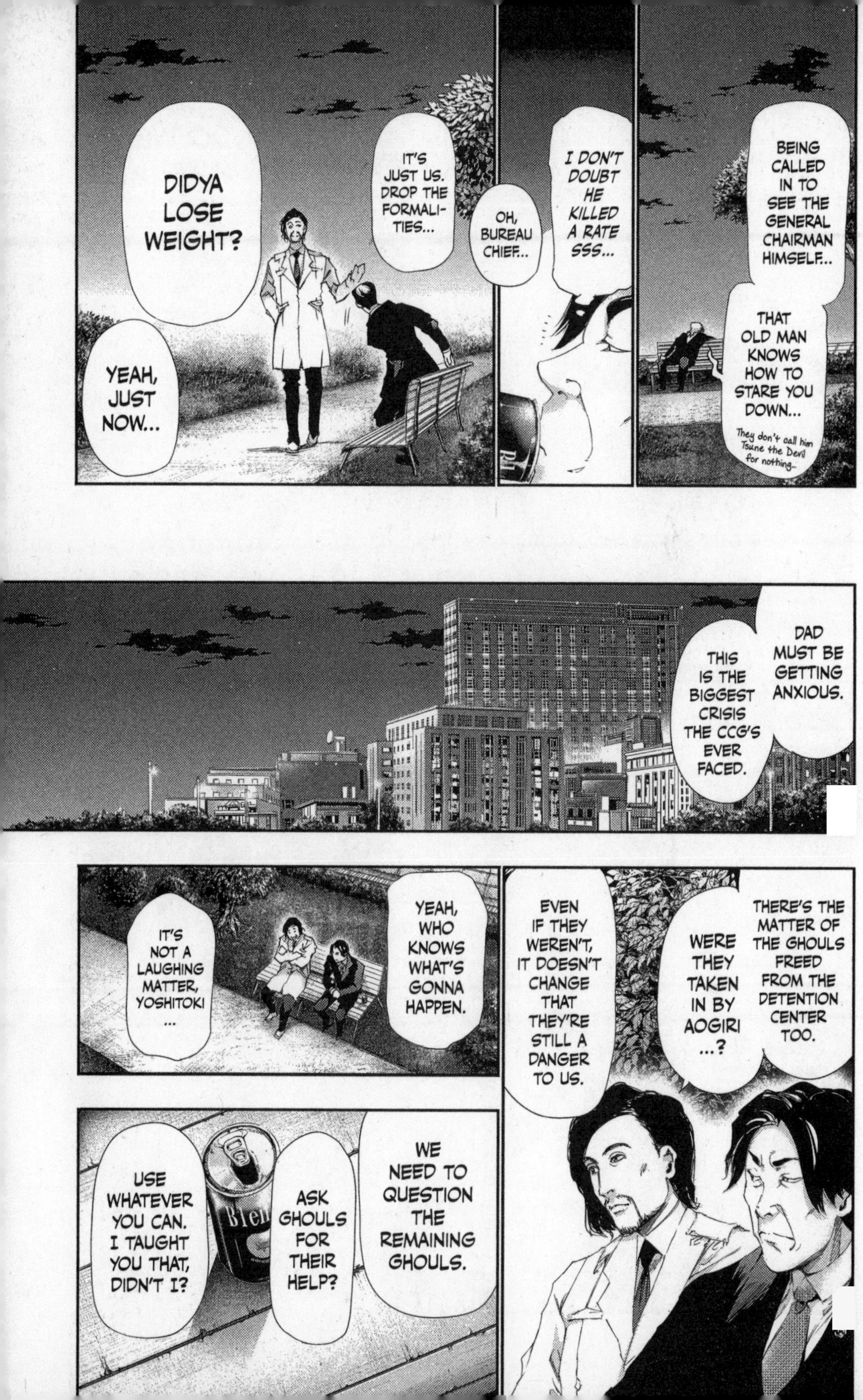
BEING CALLED IN TO SEE THE GENERAL CHAIRMAN HIMSELF...
THAT OLD MAN KNOWS HOW TO STARE YOU DOWN...
They don't call him Tsune the Devil for nothing...
I DON'T DOUBT HE KILLED A RATE SSS...
OH, BUREAU CHIEF...
IT'S JUST US. DROP THE FORMALI-TIES...
DIDYA LOSE WEIGHT?
YEAH, JUST NOW...
DAD MUST BE GETTING ANXIOUS.
THIS IS THE BIGGEST CRISIS THE CCG'S EVER FACED.
THERE'S THE MATTER OF THE GHOULS FREED FROM THE DETENTION CENTER TOO.
WERE THEY TAKEN IN BY AOGIRI ...?
EVEN IF THEY WEREN'T, IT DOESN'T CHANGE THAT THEY'RE STILL A DANGER TO US.
YEAH, WHO KNOWS WHAT'S GONNA HAPPEN.
IT'S NOT A LAUGHING MATTER, YOSHITOKI ...
WE NEED TO QUESTION THE REMAINING GHOULS.
ASK GHOULS FOR THEIR HELP?
USE WHATEVER YOU CAN. I TAUGHT YOU THAT, DIDN'T I?

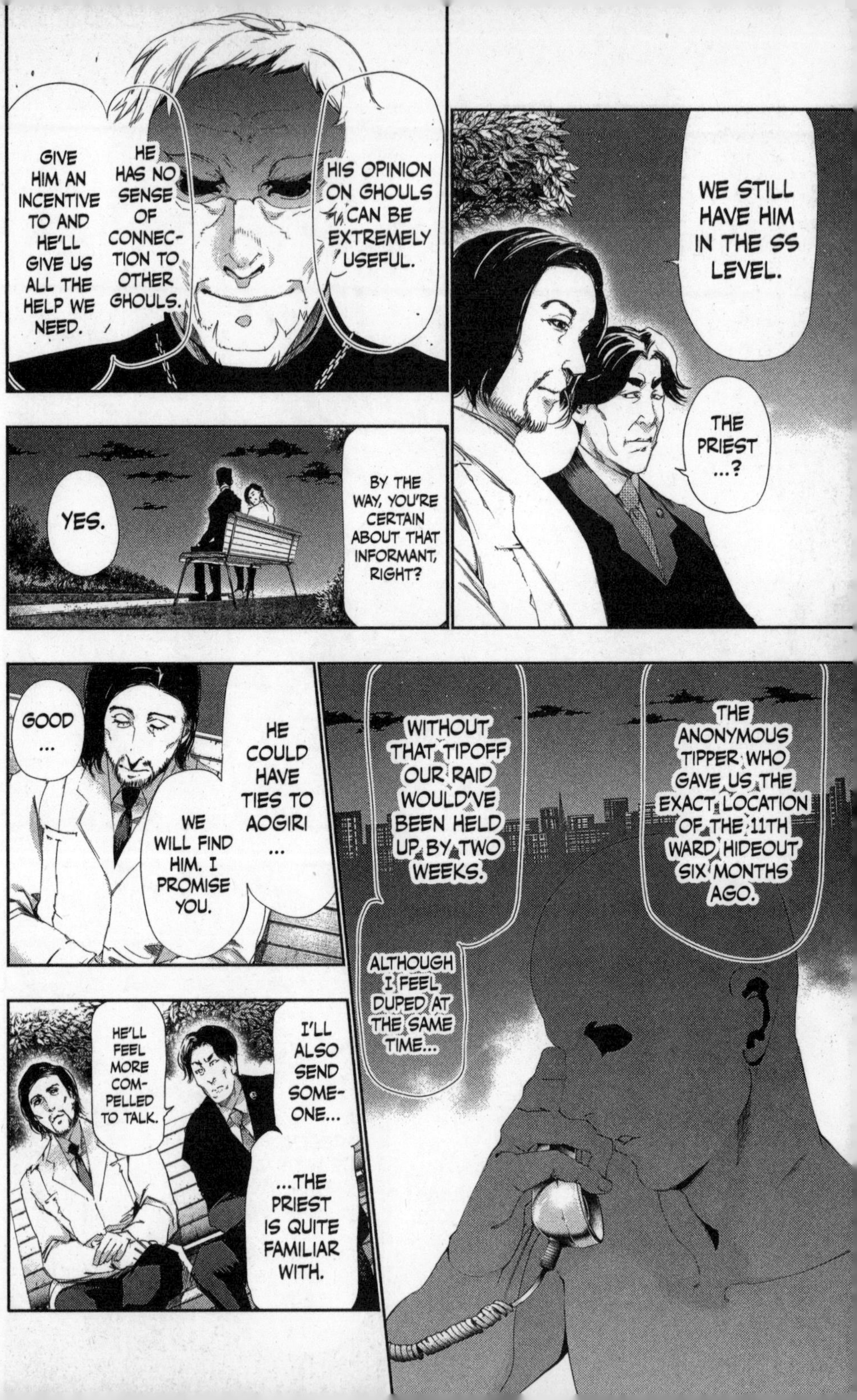
WE STILL HAVE HIM IN THE SS LEVEL.
THE PRIEST ...?
HIS OPINION ON GHOULS CAN BE EXTREMELY USEFUL.
HE HAS NO SENSE OF CONNECTION TO OTHER GHOULS.
GIVE HIM AN INCENTIVE TO AND HE'LL GIVE US ALL THE HELP WE NEED.
BY THE WAY, YOU'RE CERTAIN ABOUT THAT INFORMANT, RIGHT?
YES.
THE ANONYMOUS TIPPER WHO GAVE US THE EXACT LOCATION OF THE 11TH WARD HIDEOUT SIX MONTHS AGO.
WITHOUT THAT TIPOFF OUR RAID WOULD'VE BEEN HELD UP BY TWO WEEKS.
ALTHOUGH I FEEL DUPED AT THE SAME TIME...
HE COULD HAVE TIES TO AOGIRI ...
WE WILL FIND HIM. I PROMISE YOU.
GOOD ...
I'LL ALSO SEND SOMEONE...
...THE PRIEST IS QUITE FAMILIAR WITH.
HE'LL FEEL MORE COMPELLED TO TALK.

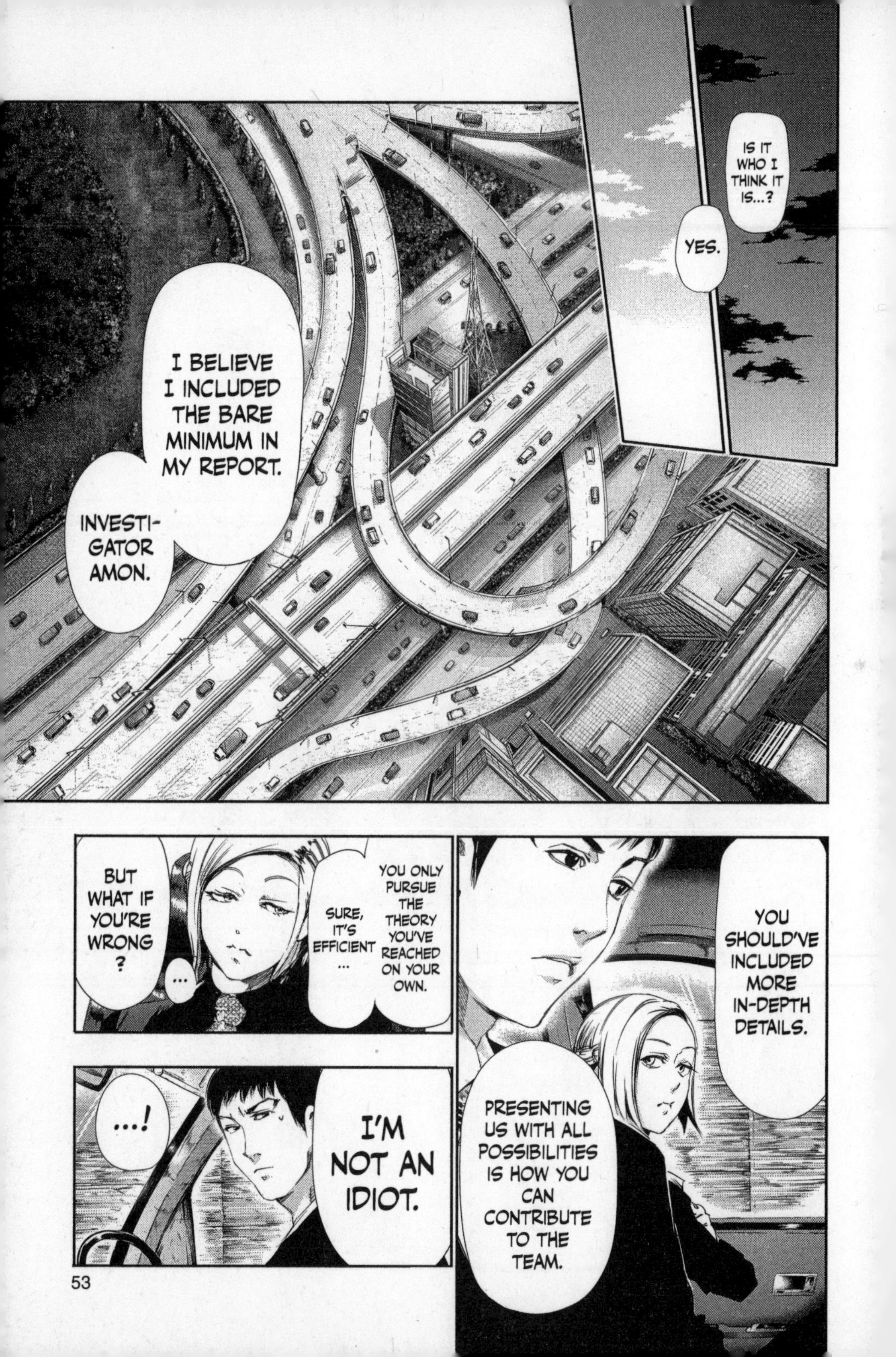

IS IT WHO I THINK IT IS...?
YES.
I BELIEVE I INCLUDED THE BARE MINIMUM IN MY REPORT.
INVESTI-GATOR AMON.
YOU SHOULD'VE INCLUDED MORE IN-DEPTH DETAILS.
PRESENTING US WITH ALL POSSIBILITIES IS HOW YOU CAN CONTRIBUTE TO THE TEAM.
YOU ONLY PURSUE THE THEORY YOU'VE REACHED ON YOUR OWN.
SURE, IT'S EFFICIENT...
BUT WHAT IF YOU'RE WRONG?
...
I'M NOT AN IDIOT.
...!

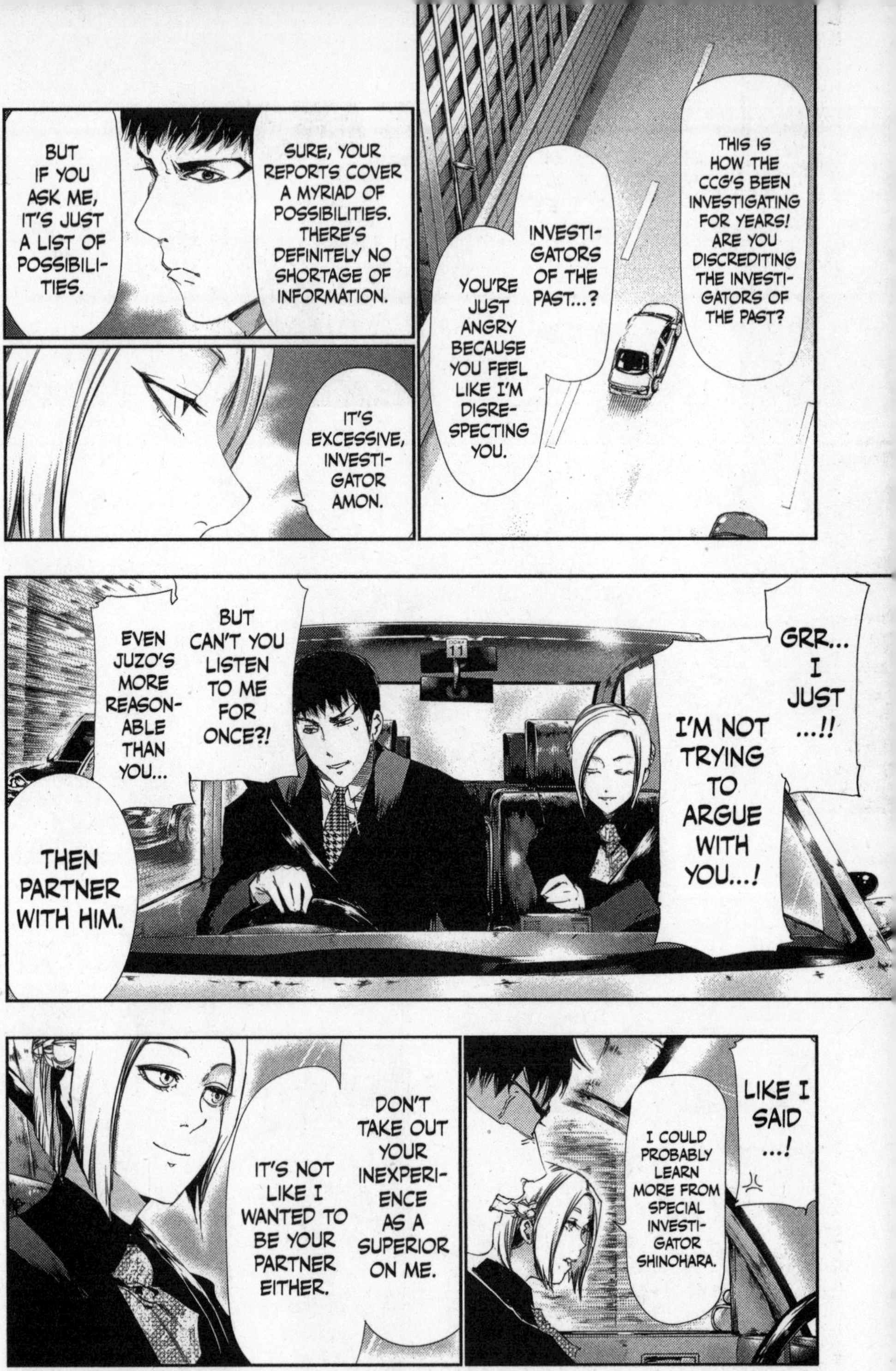
THIS IS HOW THE CCG'S BEEN INVESTIGATING FOR YEARS! ARE YOU DISCREDITING THE INVESTIGATORS OF THE PAST?
INVESTIGATORS OF THE PAST...?
YOU'RE JUST ANGRY BECAUSE YOU FEEL LIKE I'M DISRESPECTING YOU.
SURE, YOUR REPORTS COVER A MYRIAD OF POSSIBILITIES. THERE'S DEFINITELY NO SHORTAGE OF INFORMATION.
BUT IF YOU ASK ME, IT'S JUST A LIST OF POSSIBILITIES.
IT'S EXCESSIVE, INVESTIGATOR AMON.
GRR... I JUST ...!!
I'M NOT TRYING TO ARGUE WITH YOU...!
BUT CAN'T YOU LISTEN TO ME FOR ONCE?!
EVEN JUZO'S MORE REASONABLE THAN YOU...
THEN PARTNER WITH HIM.
LIKE I SAID ...!
I COULD PROBABLY LEARN MORE FROM SPECIAL INVESTIGATOR SHINOHARA.
DON'T TAKE OUT YOUR INEXPERIENCE AS A SUPERIOR ON ME.
IT'S NOT LIKE I WANTED TO BE YOUR PARTNER EITHER.

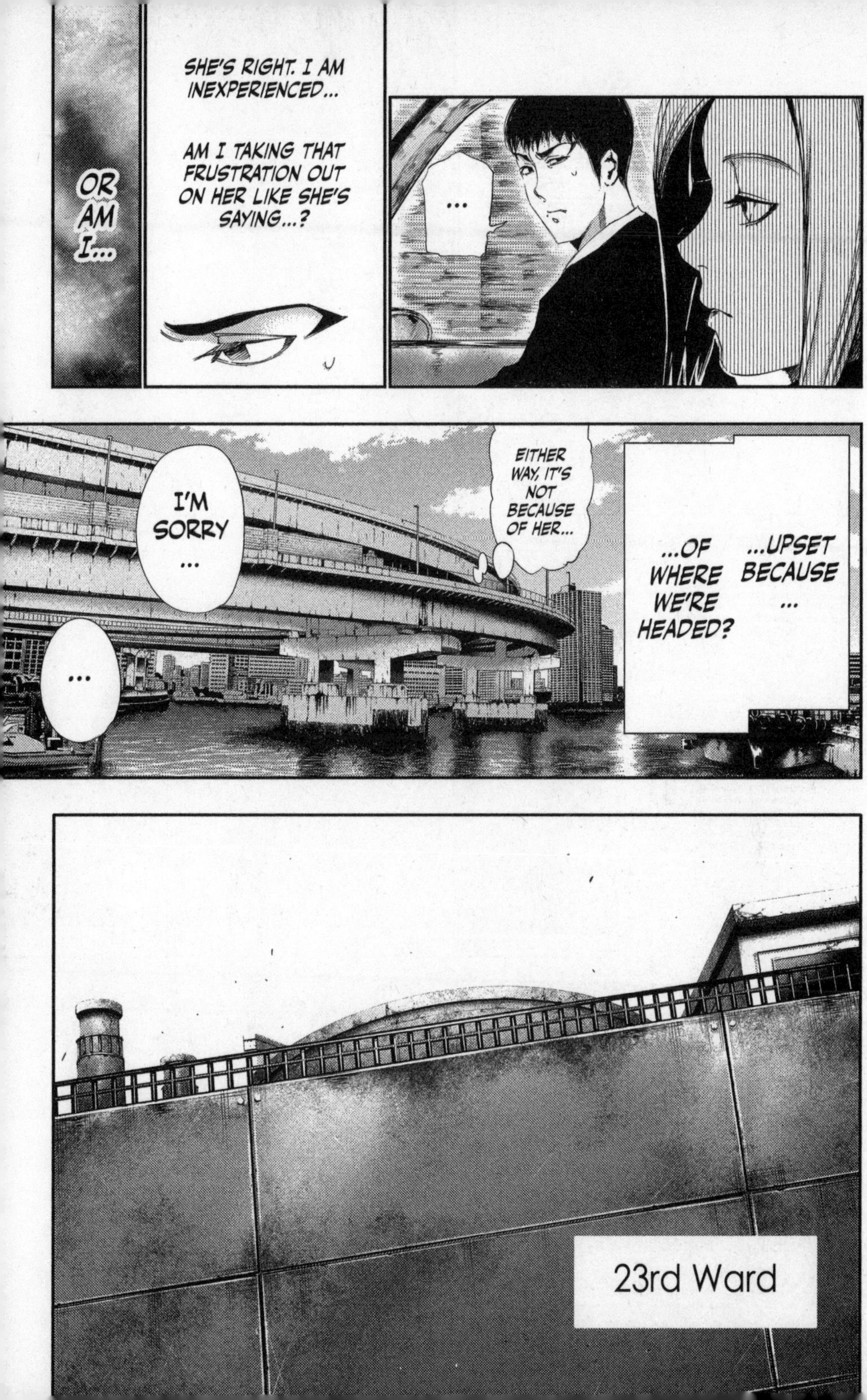
...
SHE'S RIGHT. I AM INEXPERIENCED...
AM I TAKING THAT FRUSTRATION OUT ON HER LIKE SHE'S SAYING...?
OR AM I...
...UPSET BECAUSE ...
...OF WHERE WE'RE HEADED?
EITHER WAY, IT'S NOT BECAUSE OF HER...
I'M SORRY ...
...
23rd Ward

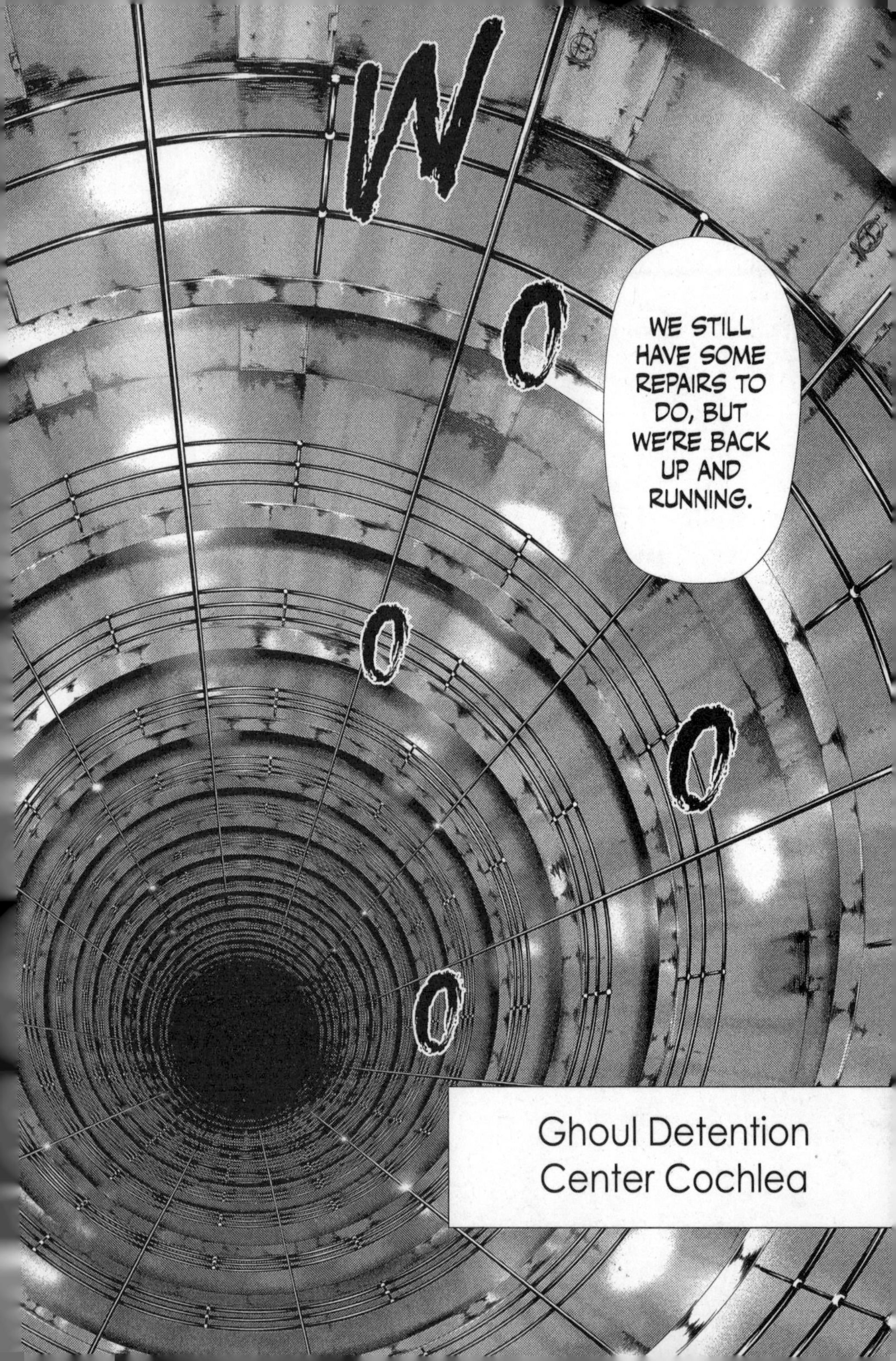
WOOOO
WE STILL HAVE SOME REPAIRS TO DO, BUT WE'RE BACK UP AND RUNNING.
Ghoul Detention Center Cochlea

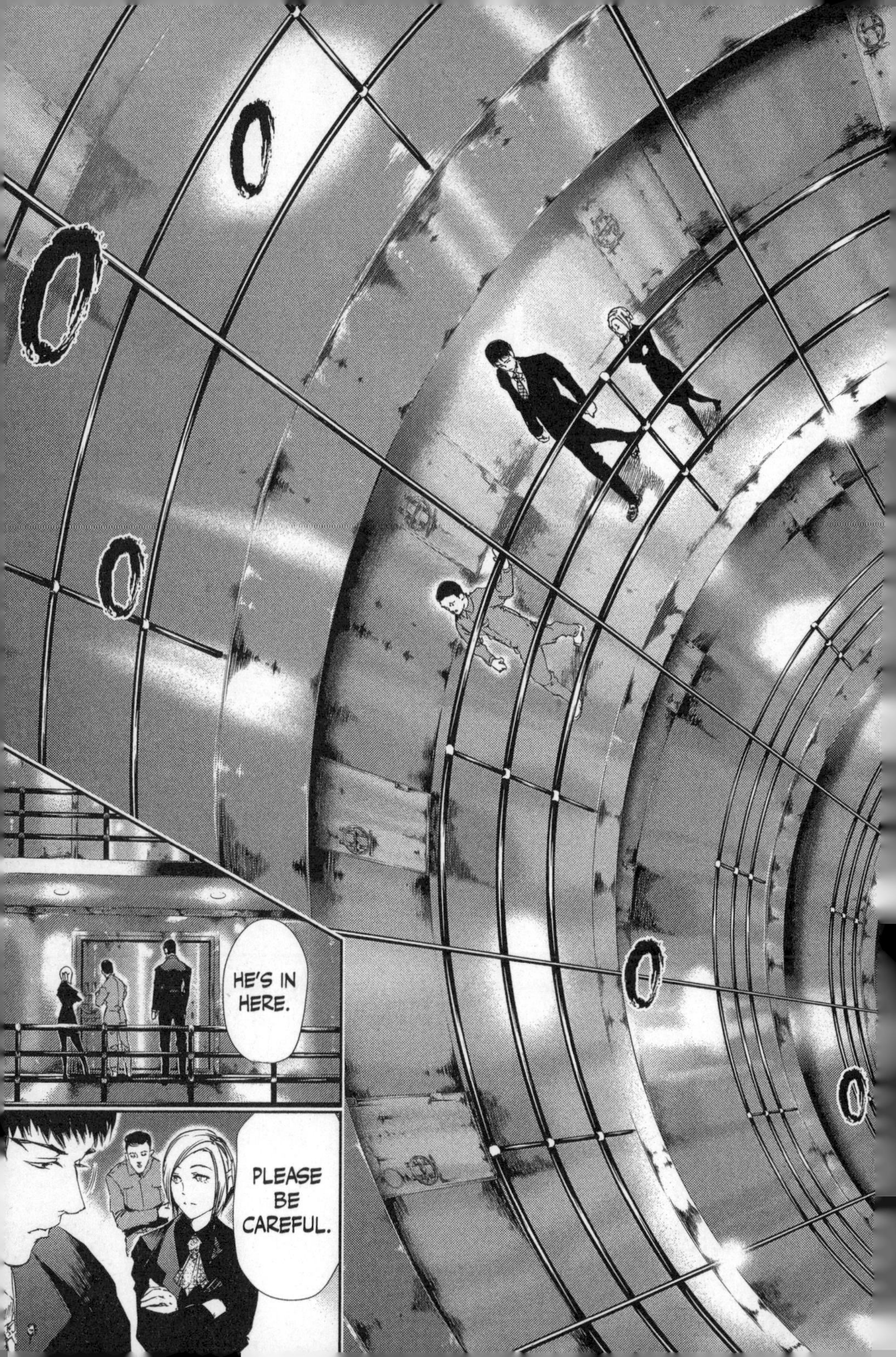
HE'S IN HERE.
PLEASE BE CAREFUL.

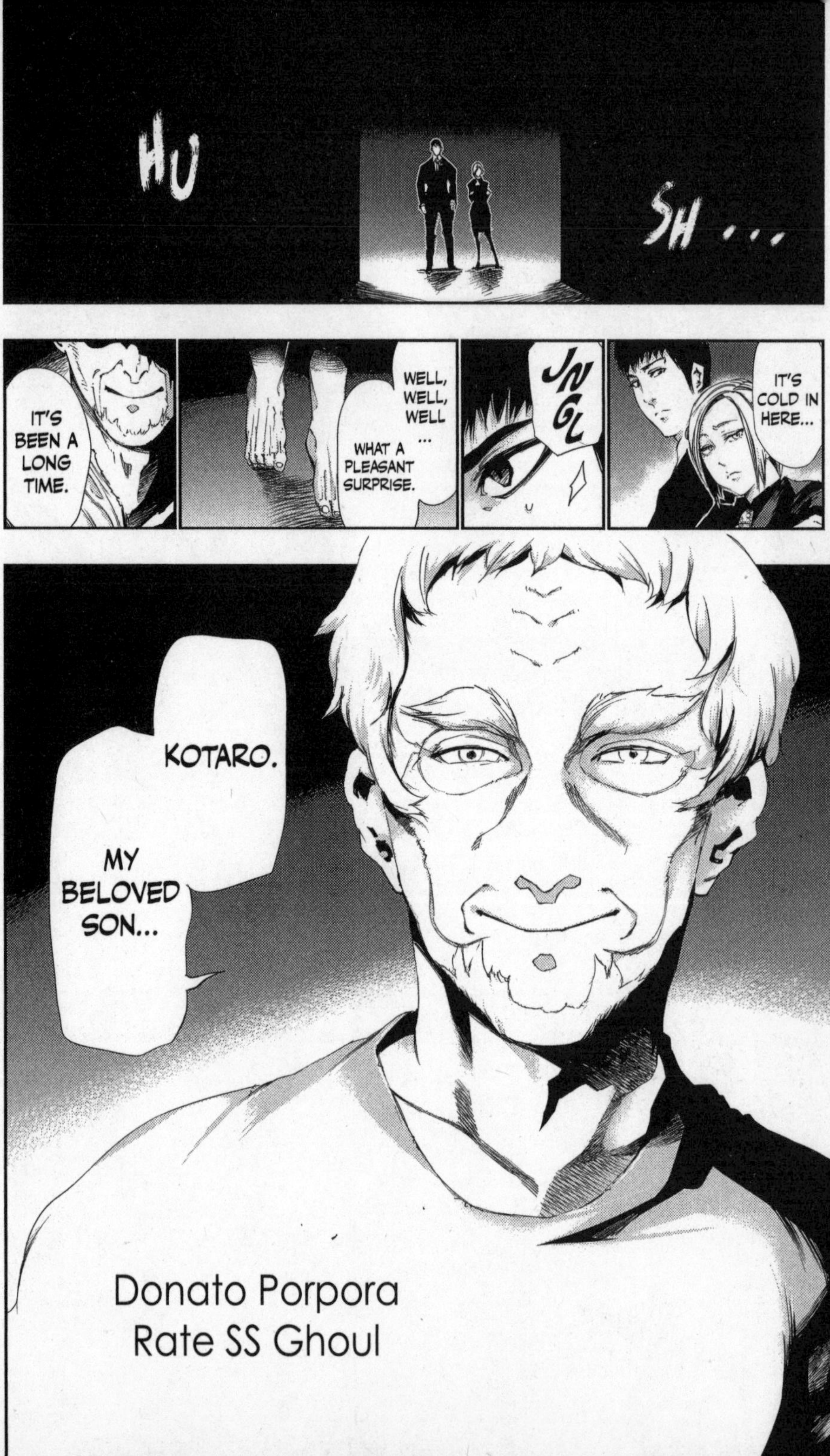
HU
SH . . .
IT'S COLD IN HERE...
JNGL
WELL, WELL, WELL ...
WHAT A PLEASANT SURPRISE.
IT'S BEEN A LONG TIME.
KOTARO.
MY BELOVED SON...
Donato Porpora
Rate SS Ghoul

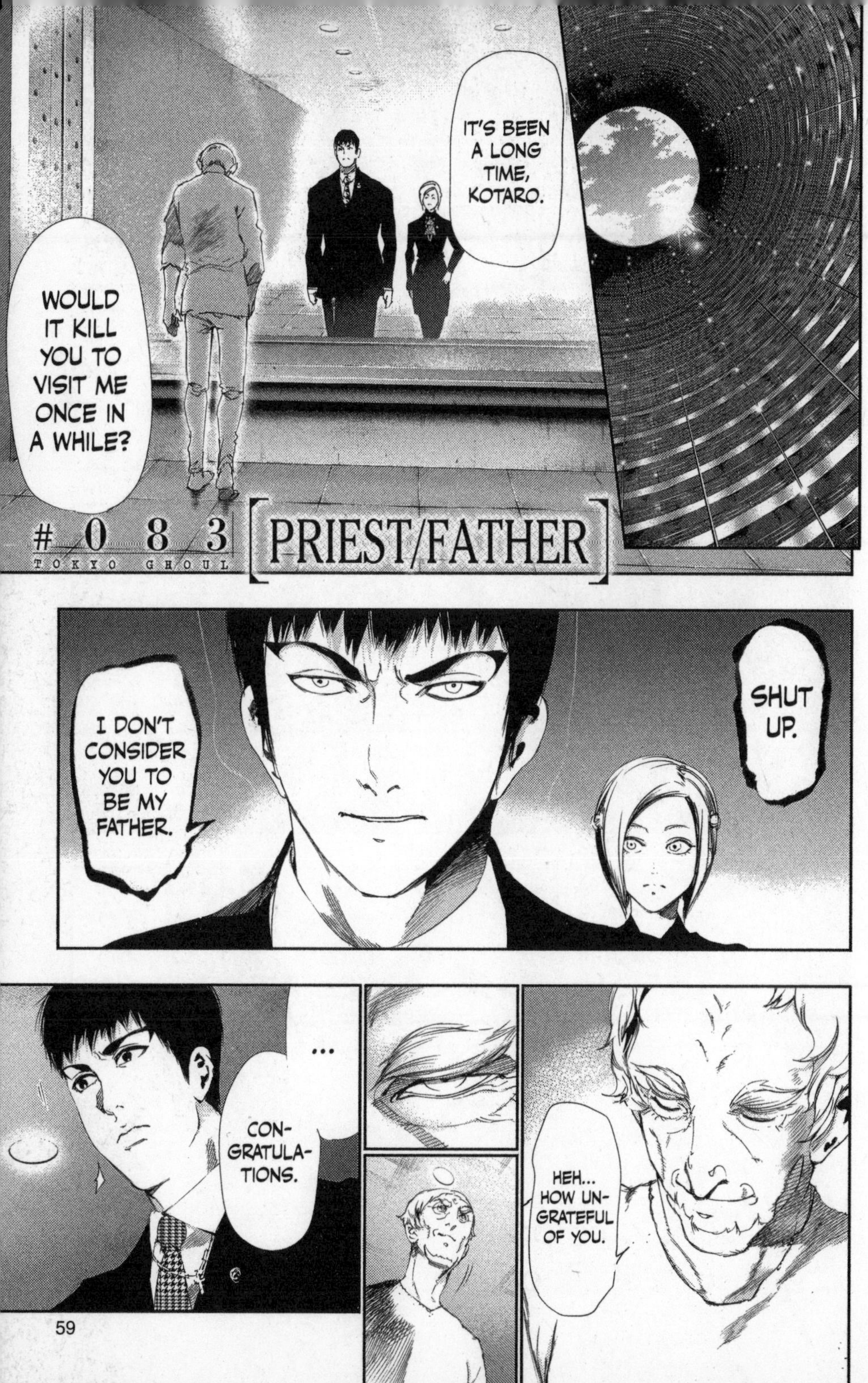
IT'S BEEN A LONG TIME, KOTARO.
WOULD IT KILL YOU TO VISIT ME ONCE IN A WHILE?
#083 TOKYO GHOUL
PRIEST/FATHER
SHUT UP.
I DON'T CONSIDER YOU TO BE MY FATHER.
HEH... HOW UNGRATEFUL OF YOU.
...
CONGRATULATIONS.

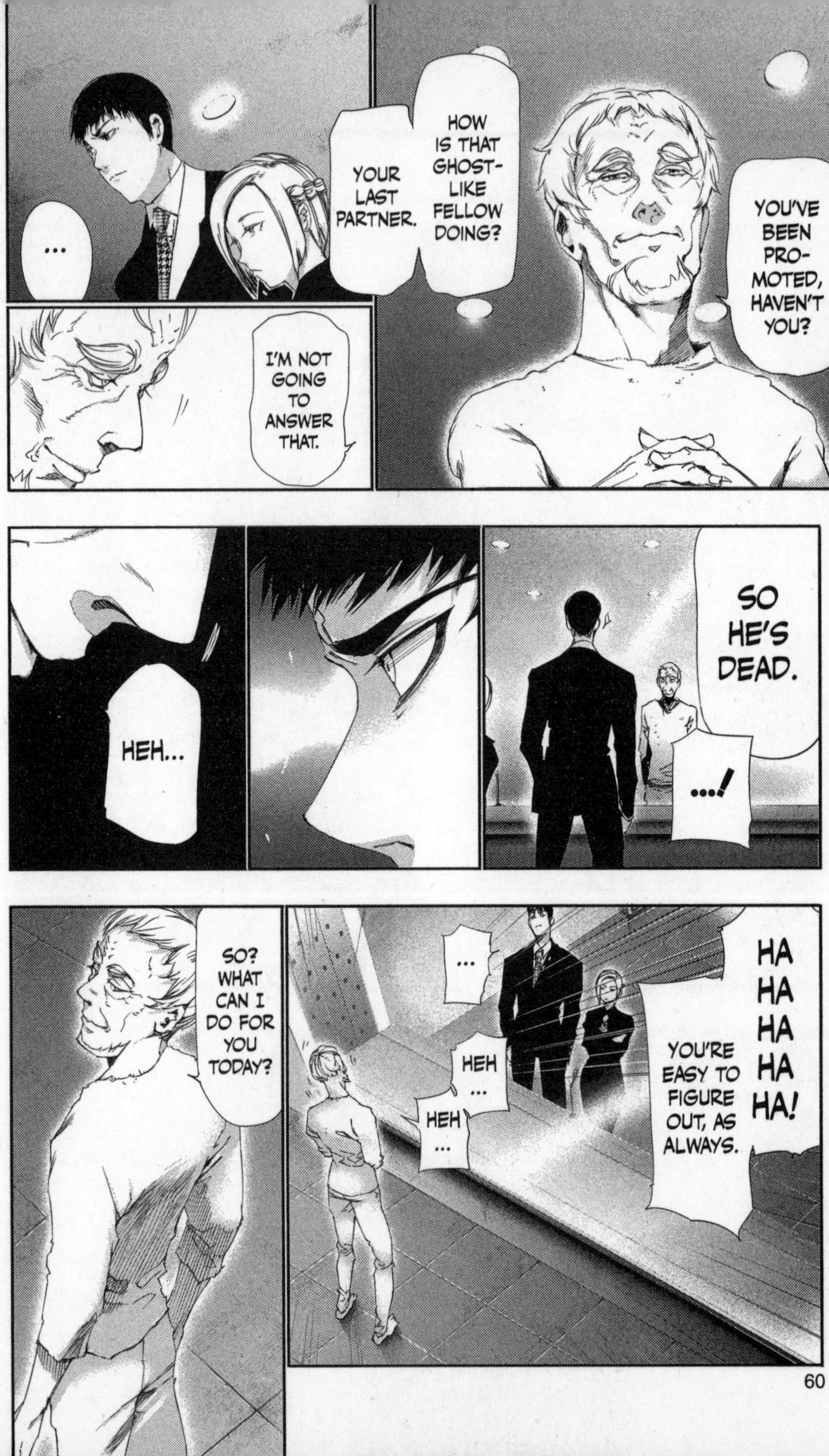
YOU'VE BEEN PRO-MOTED, HAVEN'T YOU?
HOW IS THAT GHOST-LIKE FELLOW DOING?
YOUR LAST PARTNER.
...
I'M NOT GOING TO ANSWER THAT.
SO HE'S DEAD.
...!
HEH...
HA HA HA HA HA!
YOU'RE EASY TO FIGURE OUT, AS ALWAYS.
...
HEH ...
HEH ...
SO? WHAT CAN I DO FOR YOU TODAY?

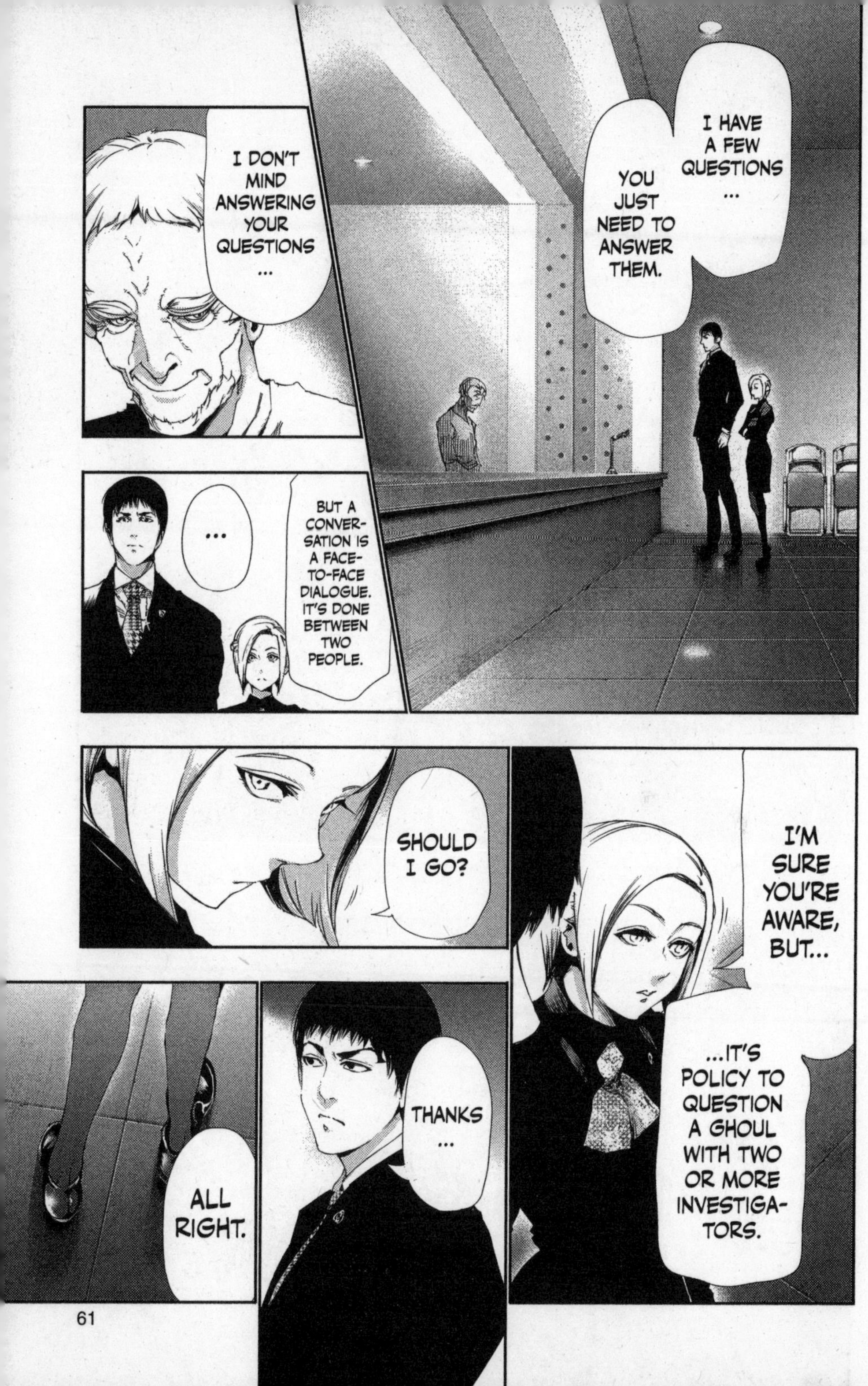
I HAVE A FEW QUESTIONS...
YOU JUST NEED TO ANSWER THEM.
I DON'T MIND ANSWERING YOUR QUESTIONS...
BUT A CONVERSATION IS A FACE-TO-FACE DIALOGUE. IT'S DONE BETWEEN TWO PEOPLE.
...
I'M SURE YOU'RE AWARE, BUT...
...IT'S POLICY TO QUESTION A GHOUL WITH TWO OR MORE INVESTIGATORS.
SHOULD I GO?
THANKS...
ALL RIGHT.

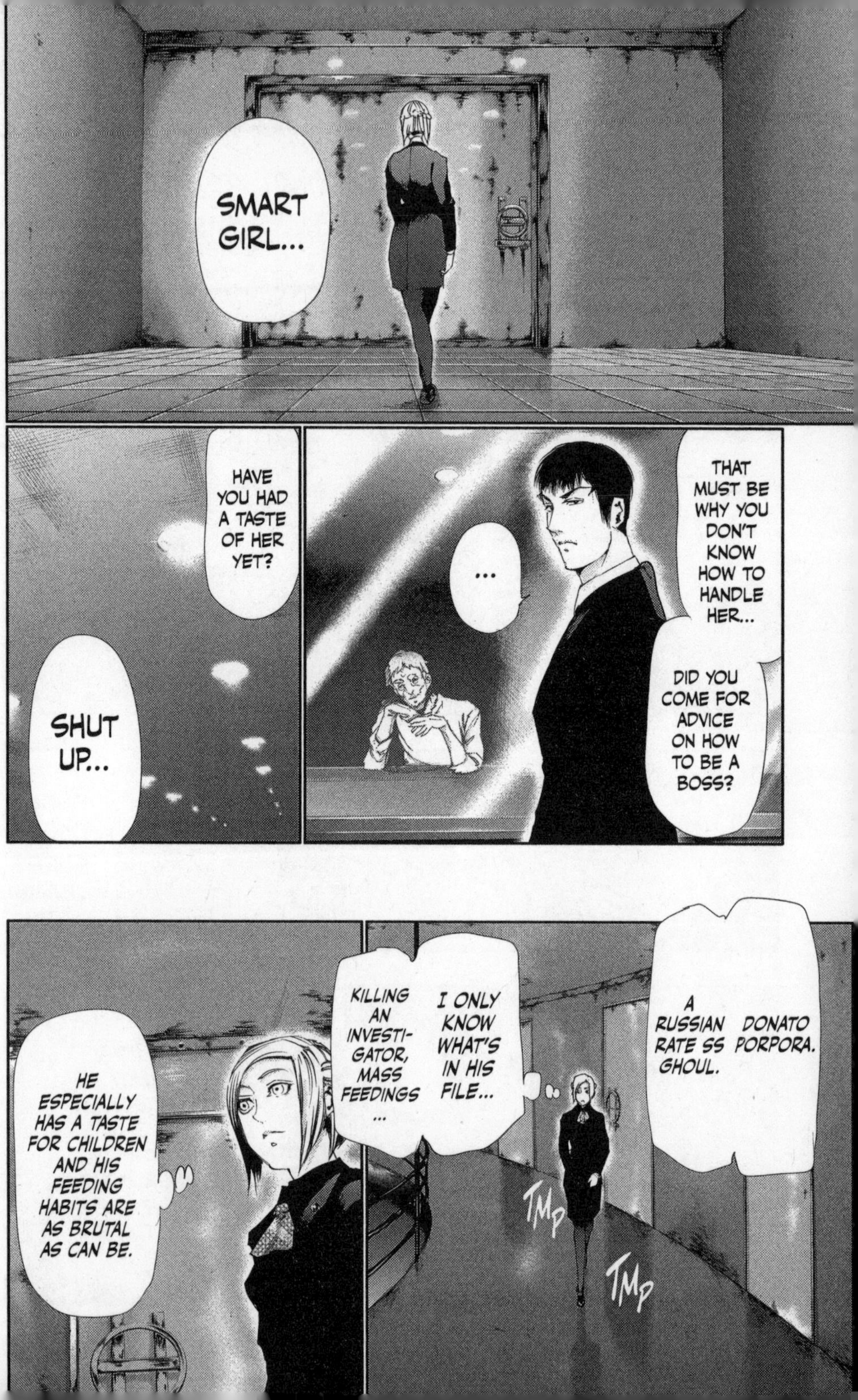
SMART GIRL...
THAT MUST BE WHY YOU DON'T KNOW HOW TO HANDLE HER...
DID YOU COME FOR ADVICE ON HOW TO BE A BOSS?
...
HAVE YOU HAD A TASTE OF HER YET?
SHUT UP...
DONATO PORPORA.
A RUSSIAN RATE SS GHOUL.
I ONLY KNOW WHAT'S IN HIS FILE...
KILLING AN INVESTIGATOR, MASS FEEDINGS...
TMP
TMP
HE ESPECIALLY HAS A TASTE FOR CHILDREN AND HIS FEEDING HABITS ARE AS BRUTAL AS CAN BE.

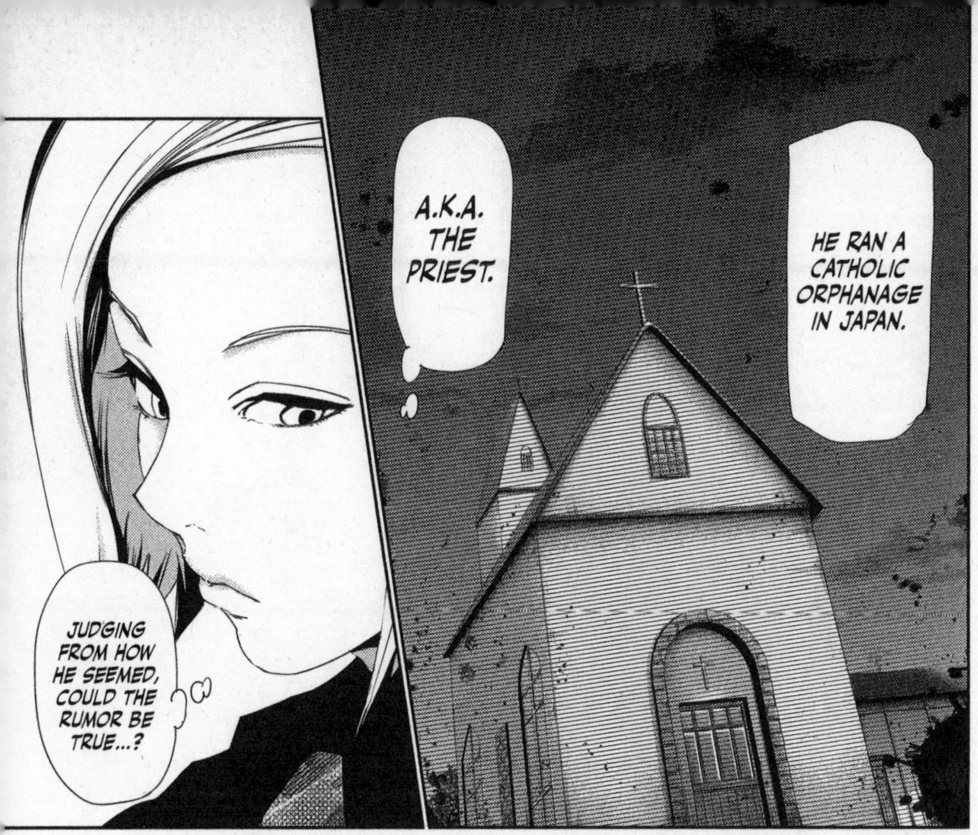
HE RAN A CATHOLIC ORPHANAGE IN JAPAN.
A.K.A. THE PRIEST.
JUDGING FROM HOW HE SEEMED, COULD THE RUMOR BE TRUE...?

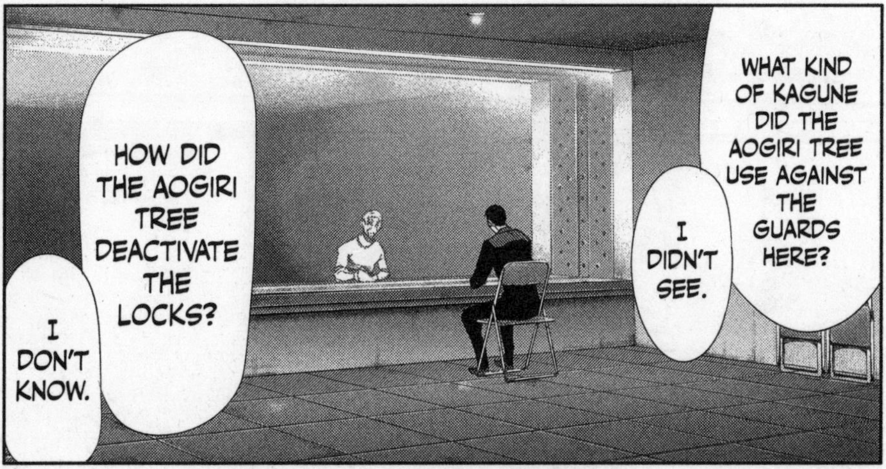
WHAT KIND OF KAGUNE DID THE AOGIRI TREE USE AGAINST THE GUARDS HERE?
I DIDN'T SEE.
HOW DID THE AOGIRI TREE DEACTIVATE THE LOCKS?
I DON'T KNOW.

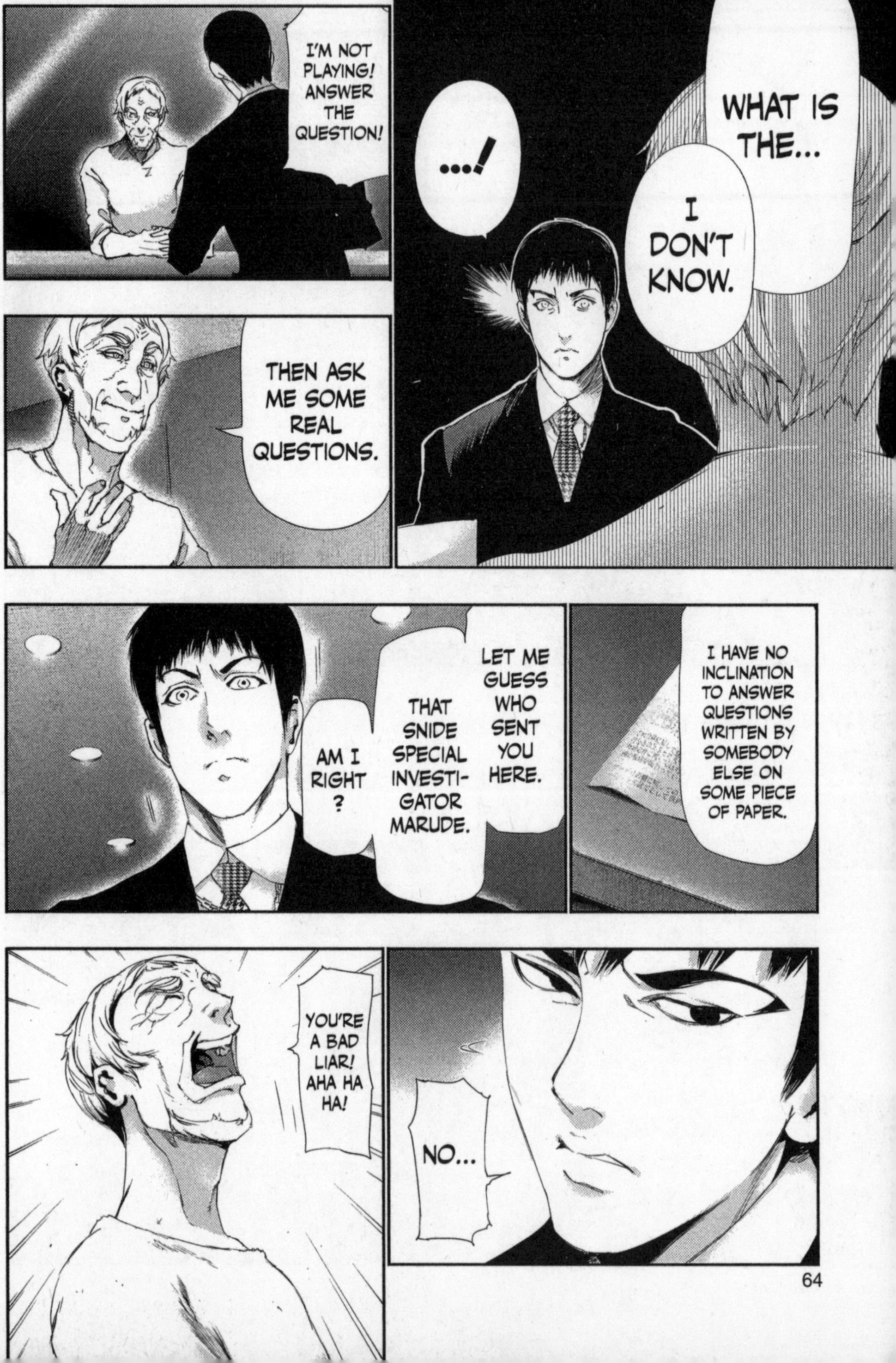
WHAT IS THE...
I DON'T KNOW.
...!
I'M NOT PLAYING! ANSWER THE QUESTION!
THEN ASK ME SOME REAL QUESTIONS.
I HAVE NO INCLINATION TO ANSWER QUESTIONS WRITTEN BY SOMEBODY ELSE ON SOME PIECE OF PAPER.
LET ME GUESS WHO SENT YOU HERE.
THAT SNIDE SPECIAL INVESTI-GATOR MARUDE.
AM I RIGHT?
NO...
YOU'RE A BAD LIAR! AHA HA HA!

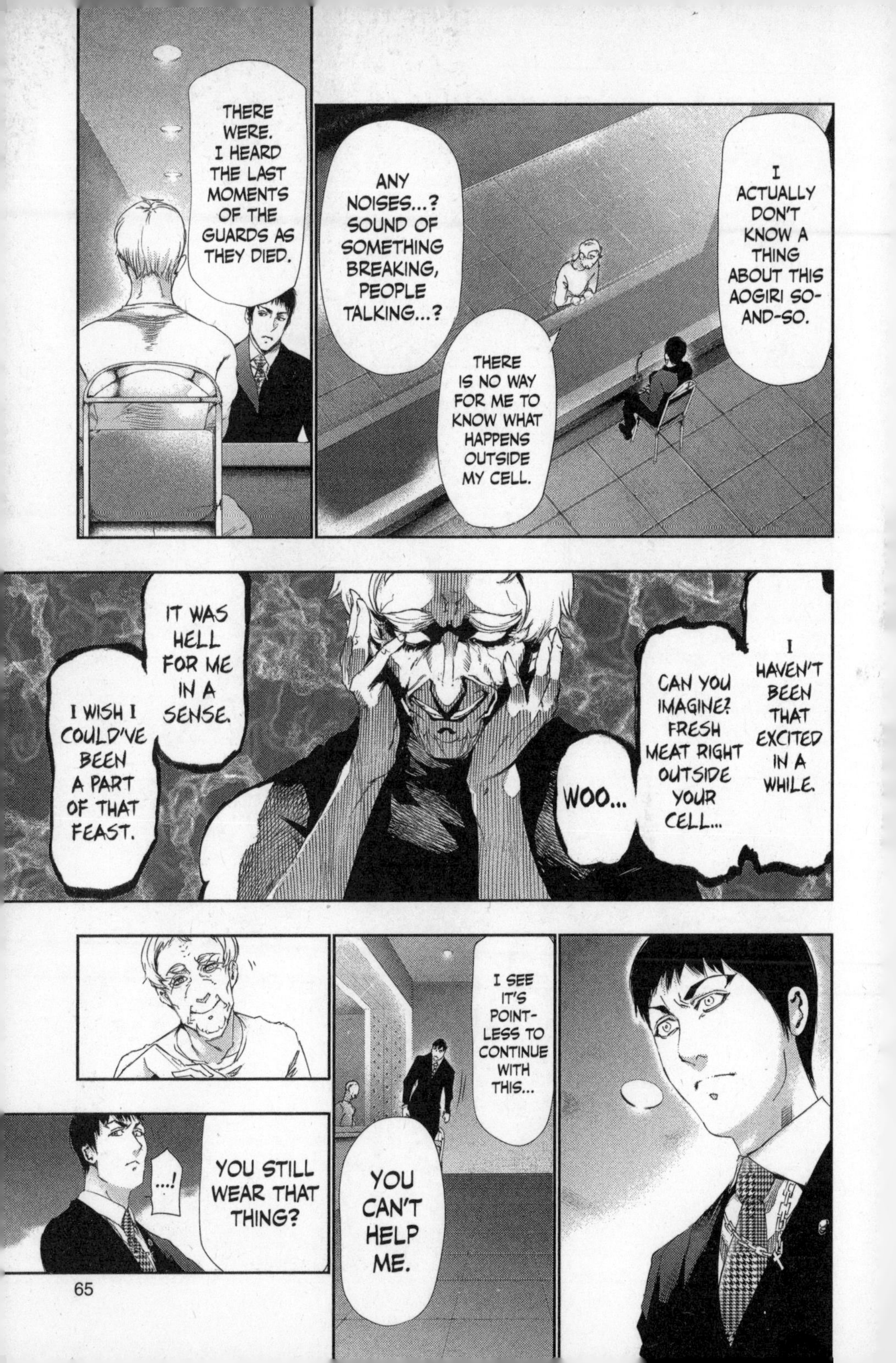
I ACTUALLY DON'T KNOW A THING ABOUT THIS AOGIRI SO-AND-SO.
THERE IS NO WAY FOR ME TO KNOW WHAT HAPPENS OUTSIDE MY CELL.
ANY NOISES...? SOUND OF SOMETHING BREAKING, PEOPLE TALKING...?
THERE WERE. I HEARD THE LAST MOMENTS OF THE GUARDS AS THEY DIED.
I HAVEN'T BEEN THAT EXCITED IN A WHILE.
CAN YOU IMAGINE? FRESH MEAT RIGHT OUTSIDE YOUR CELL...
WOO...
IT WAS HELL FOR ME IN A SENSE.
I WISH I COULD'VE BEEN A PART OF THAT FEAST.
I SEE IT'S POINTLESS TO CONTINUE WITH THIS...
YOU CAN'T HELP ME.
YOU STILL WEAR THAT THING?
...!

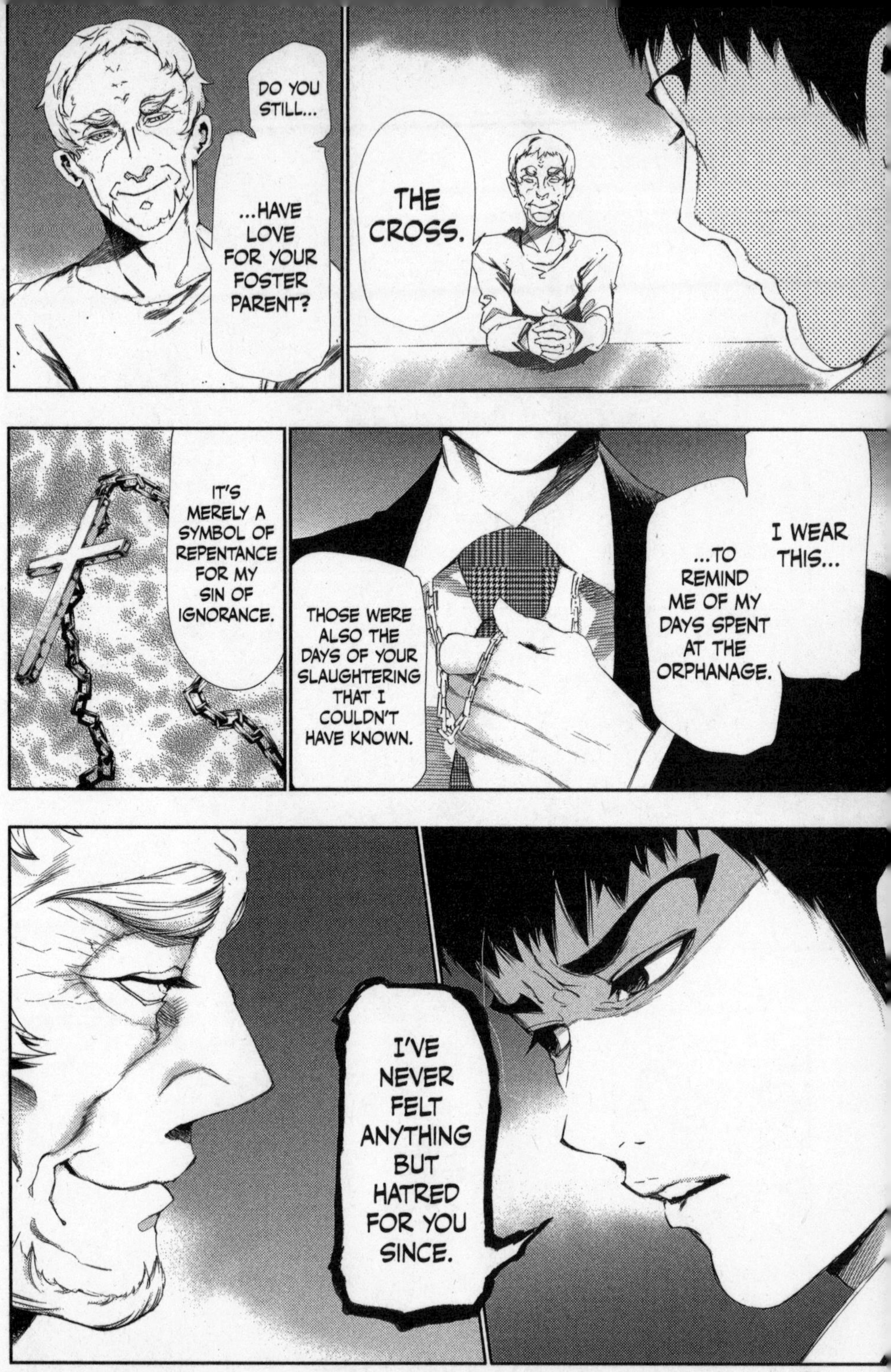
THE CROSS.
DO YOU STILL...
...HAVE LOVE FOR YOUR FOSTER PARENT?
I WEAR THIS...
...TO REMIND ME OF MY DAYS SPENT AT THE ORPHANAGE.
THOSE WERE ALSO THE DAYS OF YOUR SLAUGHTERING THAT I COULDN'T HAVE KNOWN.
IT'S MERELY A SYMBOL OF REPENTANCE FOR MY SIN OF IGNORANCE.
I'VE NEVER FELT ANYTHING BUT HATRED FOR YOU SINCE.

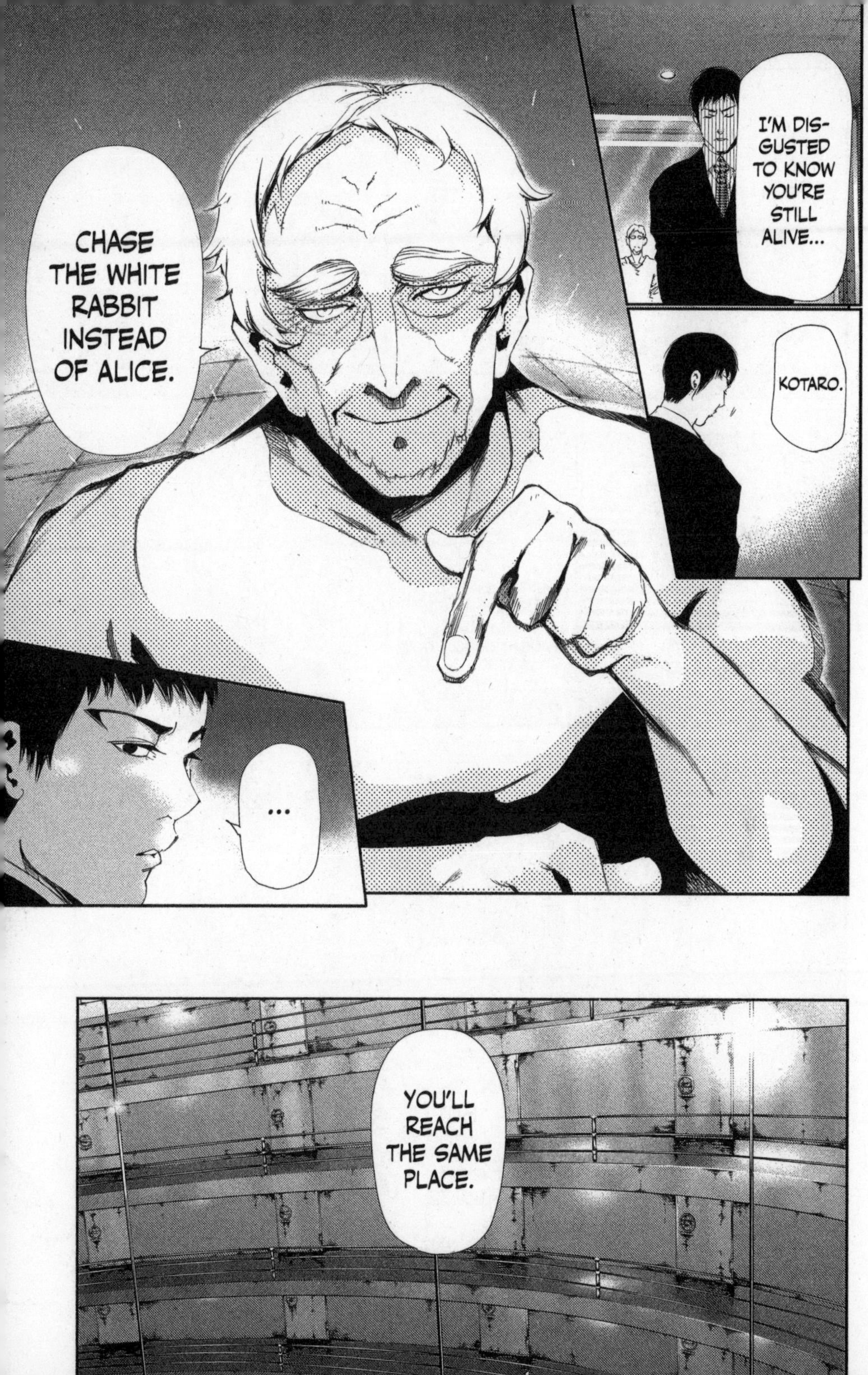
I'M DIS-GUSTED TO KNOW YOU'RE STILL ALIVE...
KOTARO.
CHASE THE WHITE RABBIT INSTEAD OF ALICE.
...
YOU'LL REACH THE SAME PLACE.

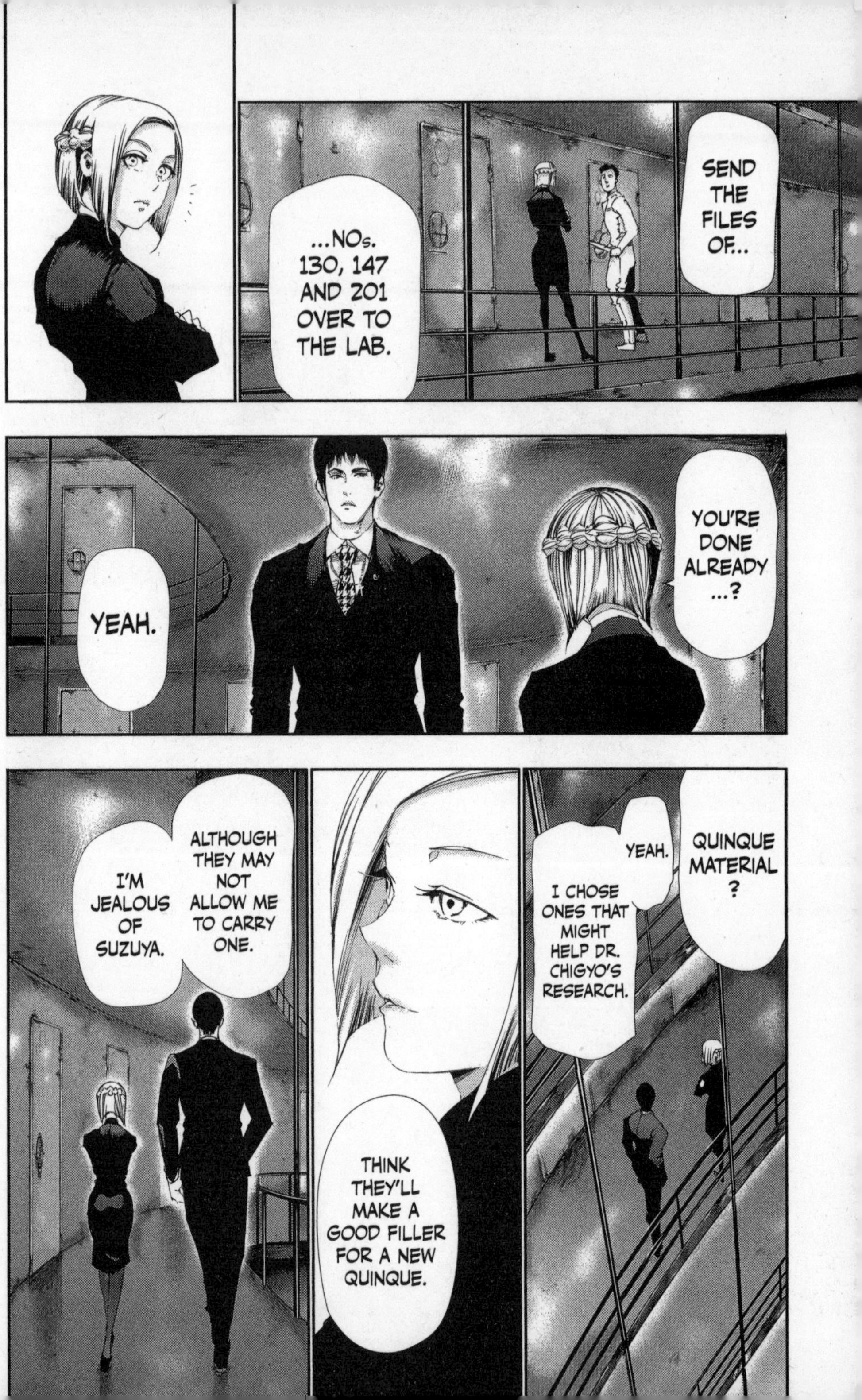
SEND THE FILES OF...
...NOs. 130, 147 AND 201 OVER TO THE LAB.
YOU'RE DONE ALREADY ...?
YEAH.
QUINQUE MATERIAL ?
YEAH.
I CHOSE ONES THAT MIGHT HELP DR. CHIGYO'S RESEARCH.
THINK THEY'LL MAKE A GOOD FILLER FOR A NEW QUINQUE.
ALTHOUGH THEY MAY NOT ALLOW ME TO CARRY ONE.
I'M JEALOUS OF SUZUYA.

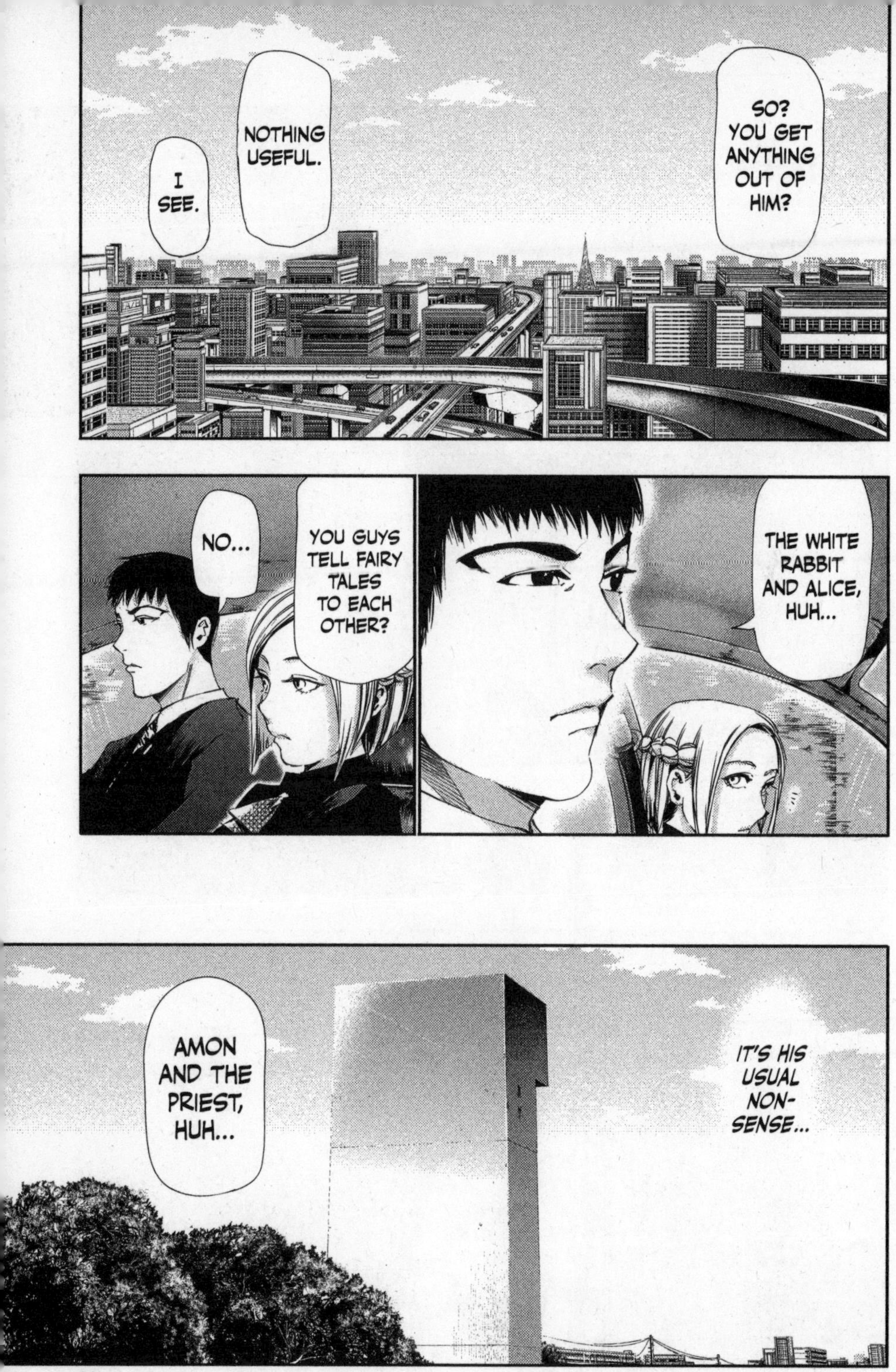
SO? YOU GET ANYTHING OUT OF HIM?
NOTHING USEFUL.
I SEE.
THE WHITE RABBIT AND ALICE, HUH...
YOU GUYS TELL FAIRY TALES TO EACH OTHER?
NO...
IT'S HIS USUAL NON-SENSE...
AMON AND THE PRIEST, HUH...

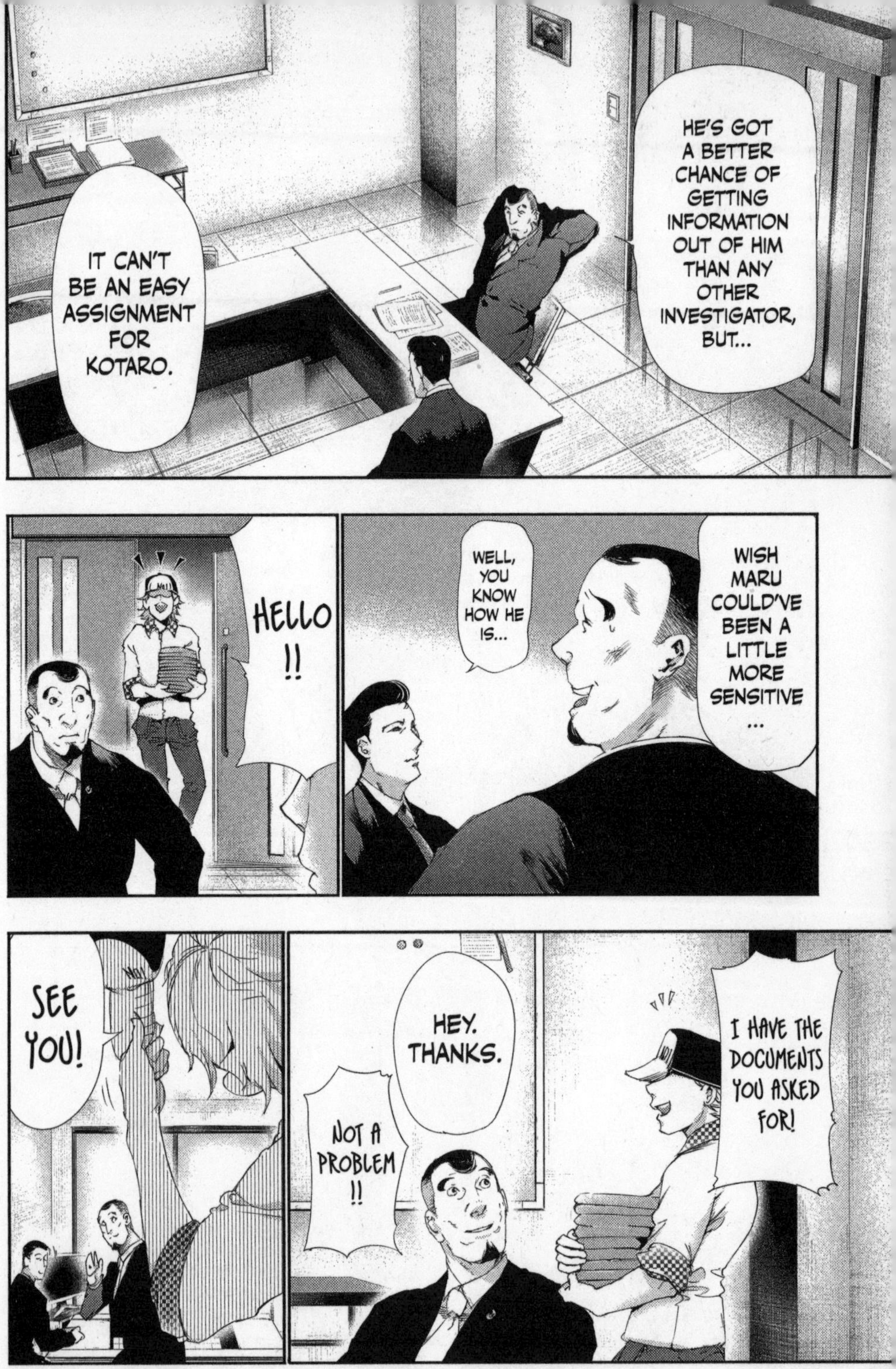
HE'S GOT A BETTER CHANCE OF GETTING INFORMATION OUT OF HIM THAN ANY OTHER INVESTIGATOR, BUT...
IT CAN'T BE AN EASY ASSIGNMENT FOR KOTARO.
WISH MARU COULD'VE BEEN A LITTLE MORE SENSITIVE...
WELL, YOU KNOW HOW HE IS...
HELLO !!
I HAVE THE DOCUMENTS YOU ASKED FOR!
HEY. THANKS.
NOT A PROBLEM !!
SEE YOU!

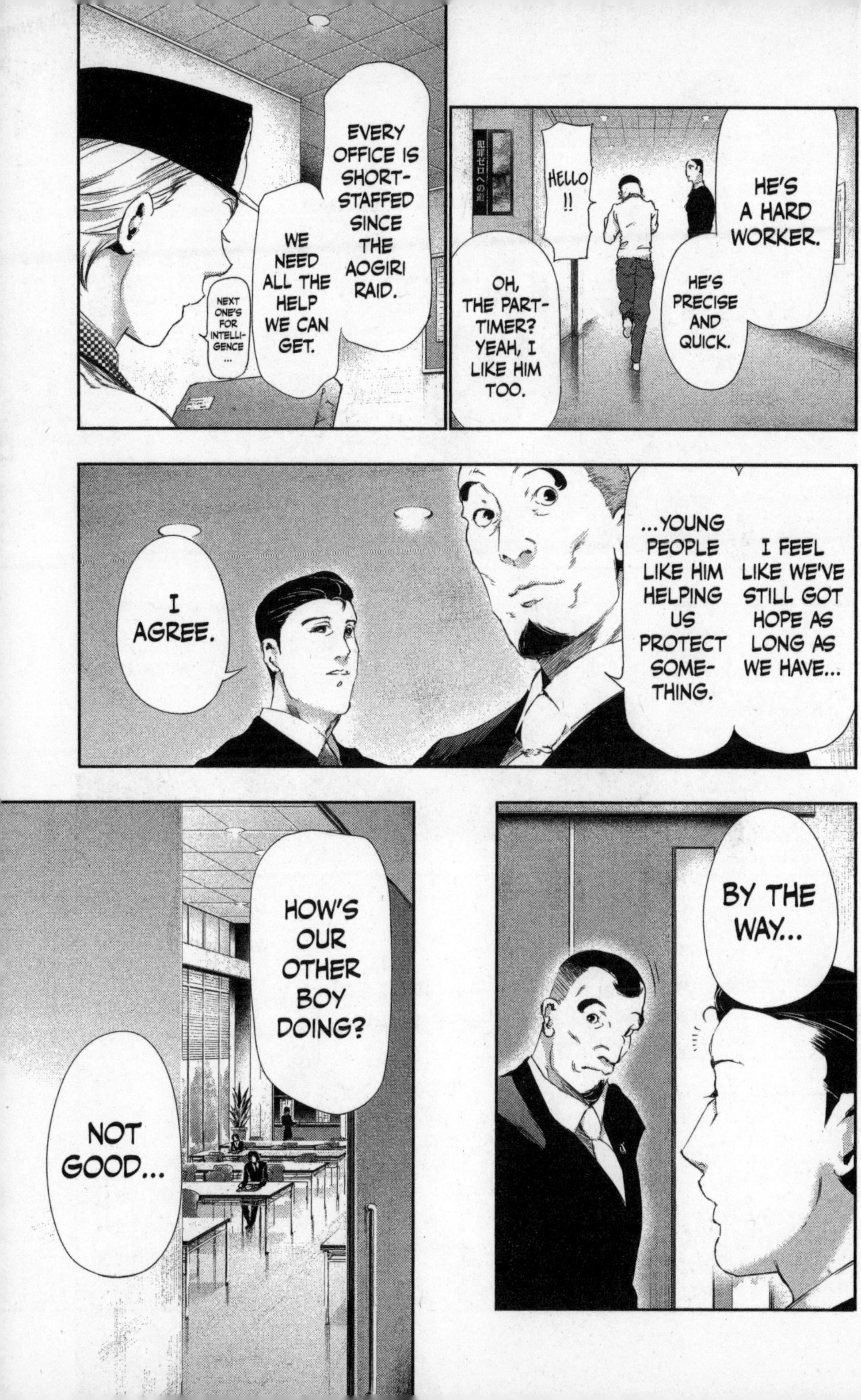
HE'S A HARD WORKER.
HE'S PRECISE AND QUICK.
犯罪ゼロへの道
HELLO !!
OH, THE PART-TIMER? YEAH, I LIKE HIM TOO.
EVERY OFFICE IS SHORT-STAFFED SINCE THE AOGIRI RAID.
WE NEED ALL THE HELP WE CAN GET.
NEXT ONE'S FOR INTELLIGENCE...
I FEEL LIKE WE'VE STILL GOT HOPE AS LONG AS WE HAVE...
...YOUNG PEOPLE LIKE HIM HELPING US PROTECT SOMETHING.
I AGREE.
BY THE WAY...
HOW'S OUR OTHER BOY DOING?
NOT GOOD...

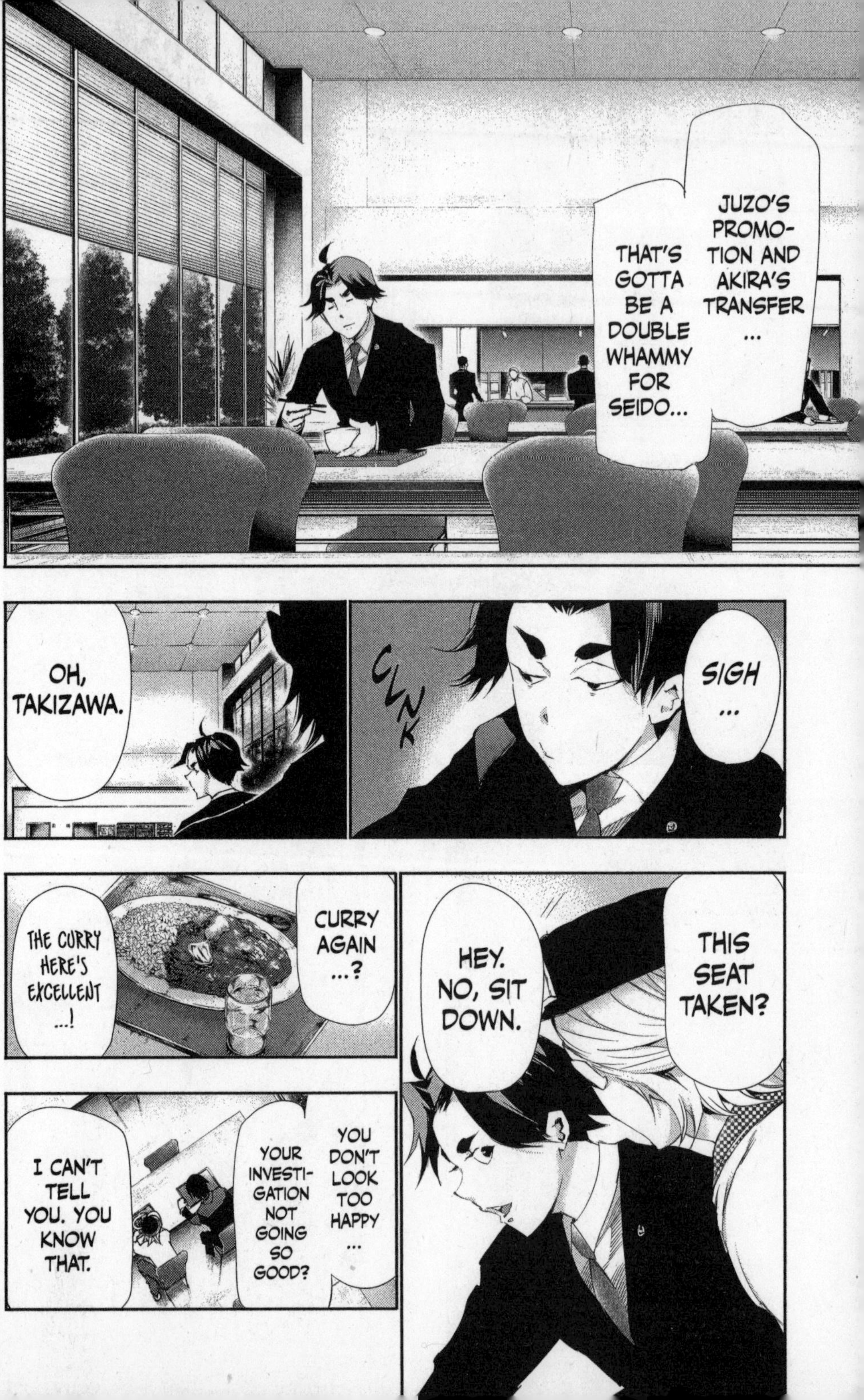
JUZO'S PROMOTION AND AKIRA'S TRANSFER ...
THAT'S GOTTA BE A DOUBLE WHAMMY FOR SEIDO...
SIGH ...
CLNK
OH, TAKIZAWA.
THIS SEAT TAKEN?
HEY. NO, SIT DOWN.
CURRY AGAIN ...?
THE CURRY HERE'S EXCELLENT ...!
YOU DON'T LOOK TOO HAPPY ...
YOUR INVESTIGATION NOT GOING SO GOOD?
I CAN'T TELL YOU. YOU KNOW THAT.

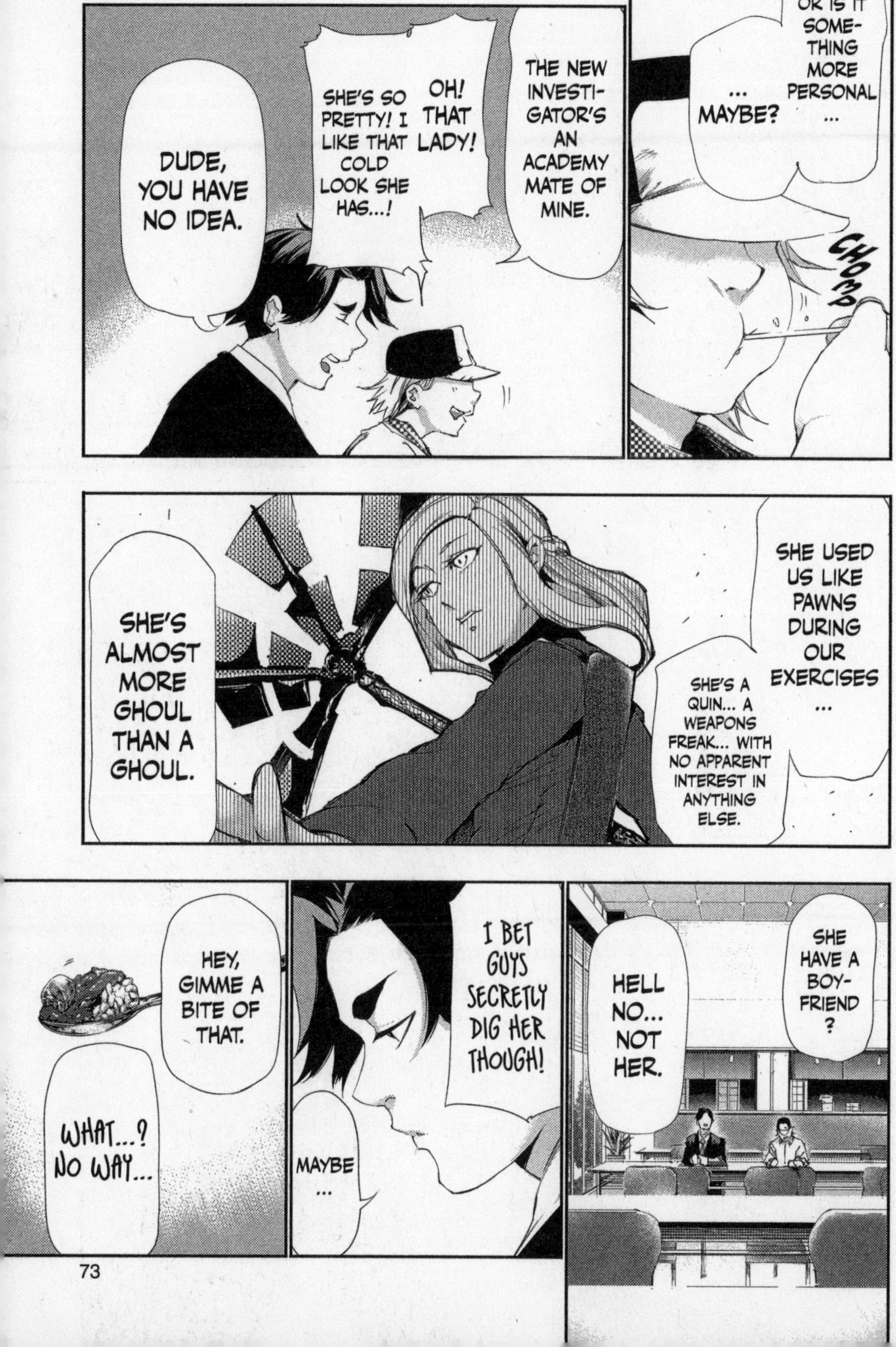
OR IS IT SOMETHING MORE PERSONAL ...
... MAYBE?
CHOMP
THE NEW INVESTIGATOR'S AN ACADEMY MATE OF MINE.
OH! THAT LADY!
SHE'S SO PRETTY! I LIKE THAT COLD LOOK SHE HAS...!
DUDE, YOU HAVE NO IDEA.
SHE USED US LIKE PAWNS DURING OUR EXERCISES ...
SHE'S A QUIN... A WEAPONS FREAK... WITH NO APPARENT INTEREST IN ANYTHING ELSE.
SHE'S ALMOST MORE GHOUL THAN A GHOUL.
SHE HAVE A BOYFRIEND?
HELL NO... NOT HER.
I BET GUYS SECRETLY DIG HER THOUGH!
MAYBE ...
HEY, GIMME A BITE OF THAT.
WHAT...? NO WAY...

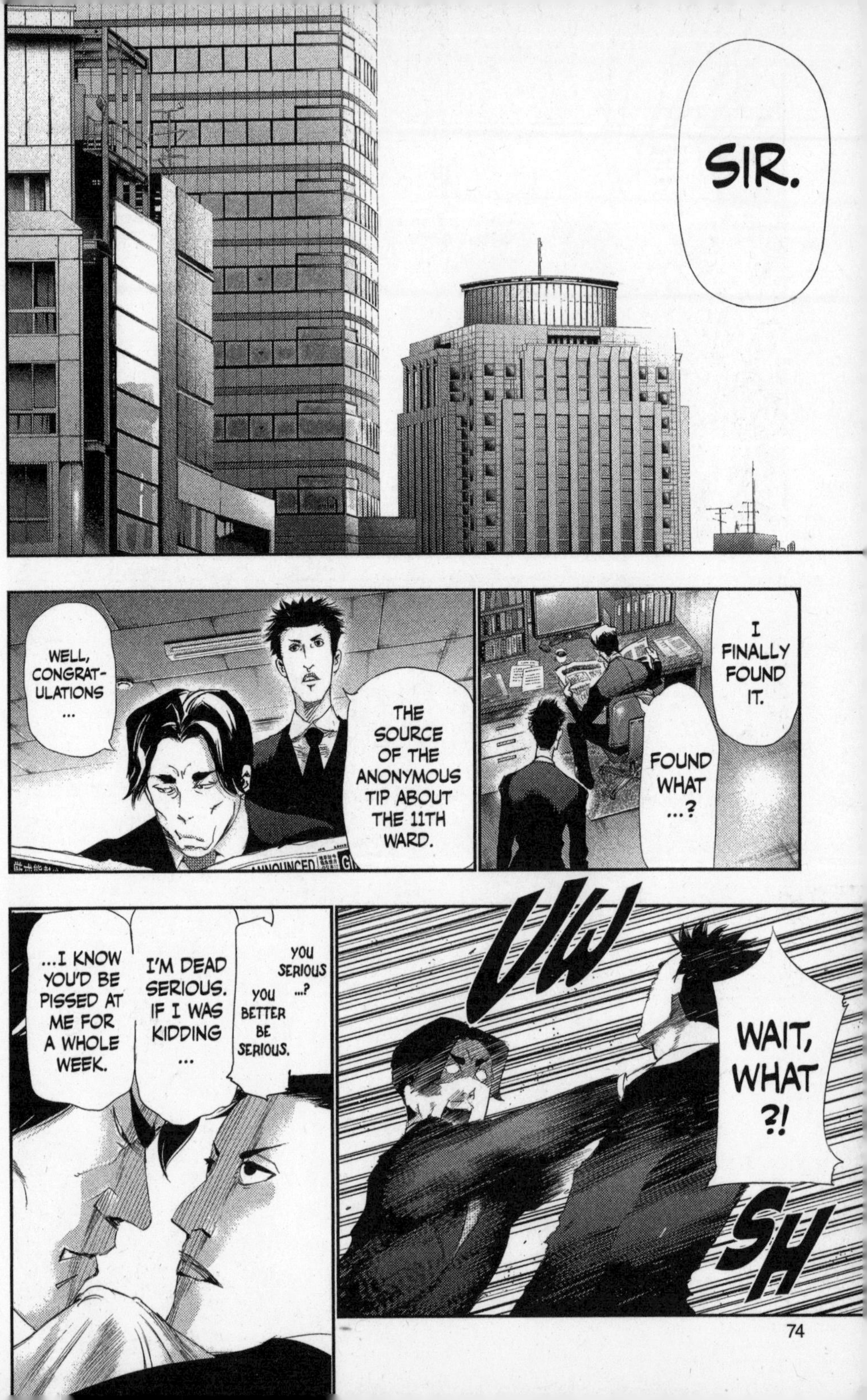
SIR.
I FINALLY FOUND IT.
FOUND WHAT ...?
THE SOURCE OF THE ANONYMOUS TIP ABOUT THE 11TH WARD.
WELL, CONGRAT-ULATIONS ...
ANNOUNCED
WAIT, WHAT ?!
YOU SERIOUS ...?
YOU BETTER BE SERIOUS.
I'M DEAD SERIOUS. IF I WAS KIDDING ...
...I KNOW YOU'D BE PISSED AT ME FOR A WHOLE WEEK.

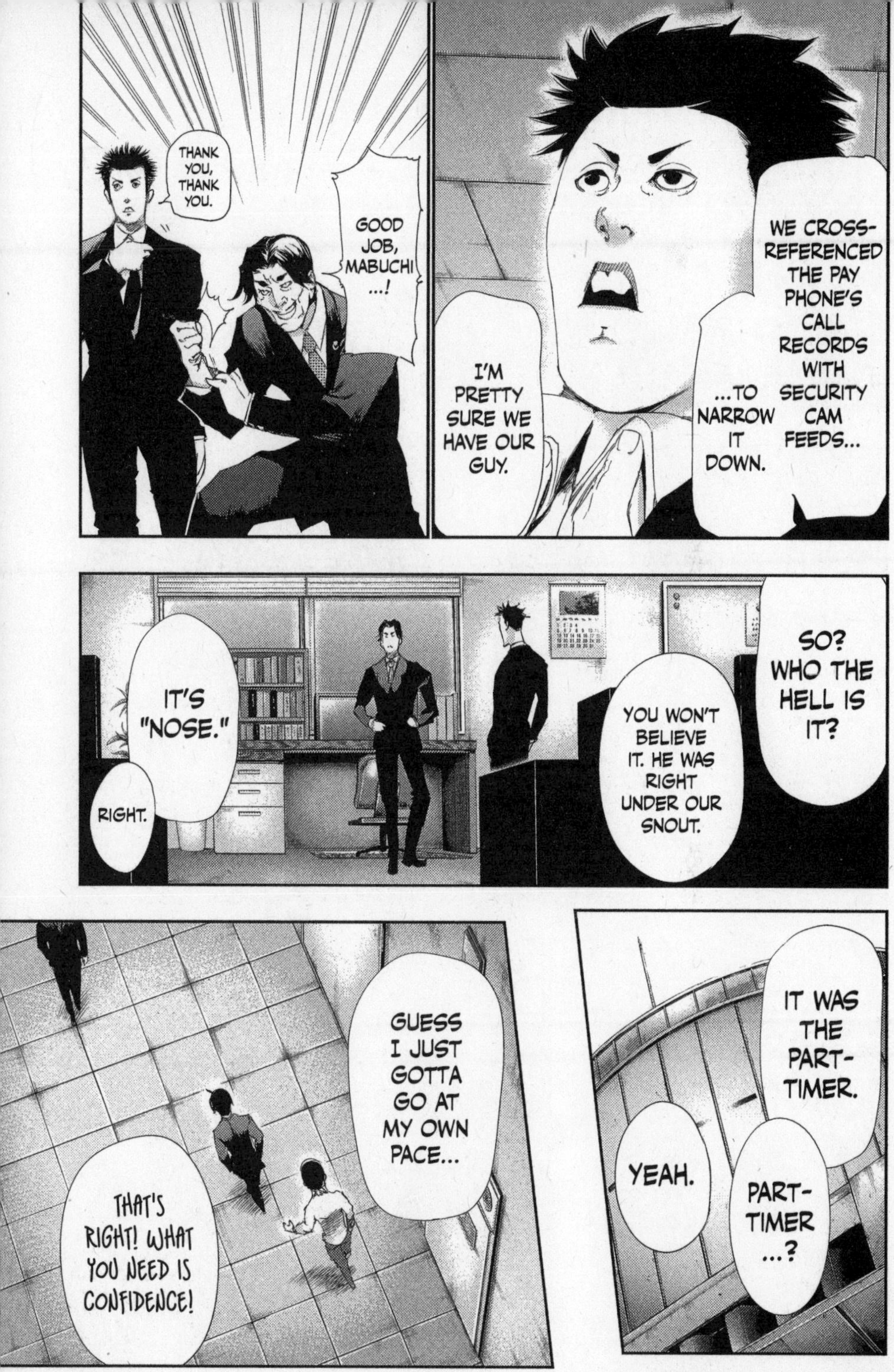
WE CROSS-REFERENCED THE PAY PHONE'S CALL RECORDS WITH SECURITY CAM FEEDS...
...TO NARROW IT DOWN.
I'M PRETTY SURE WE HAVE OUR GUY.
GOOD JOB, MABUCHI ...!
THANK YOU, THANK YOU.
SO? WHO THE HELL IS IT?
YOU WON'T BELIEVE IT. HE WAS RIGHT UNDER OUR SNOUT.
IT'S "NOSE."
RIGHT.
IT WAS THE PART-TIMER.
YEAH.
PART-TIMER ...?
GUESS I JUST GOTTA GO AT MY OWN PACE...
THAT'S RIGHT! WHAT YOU NEED IS CONFIDENCE!

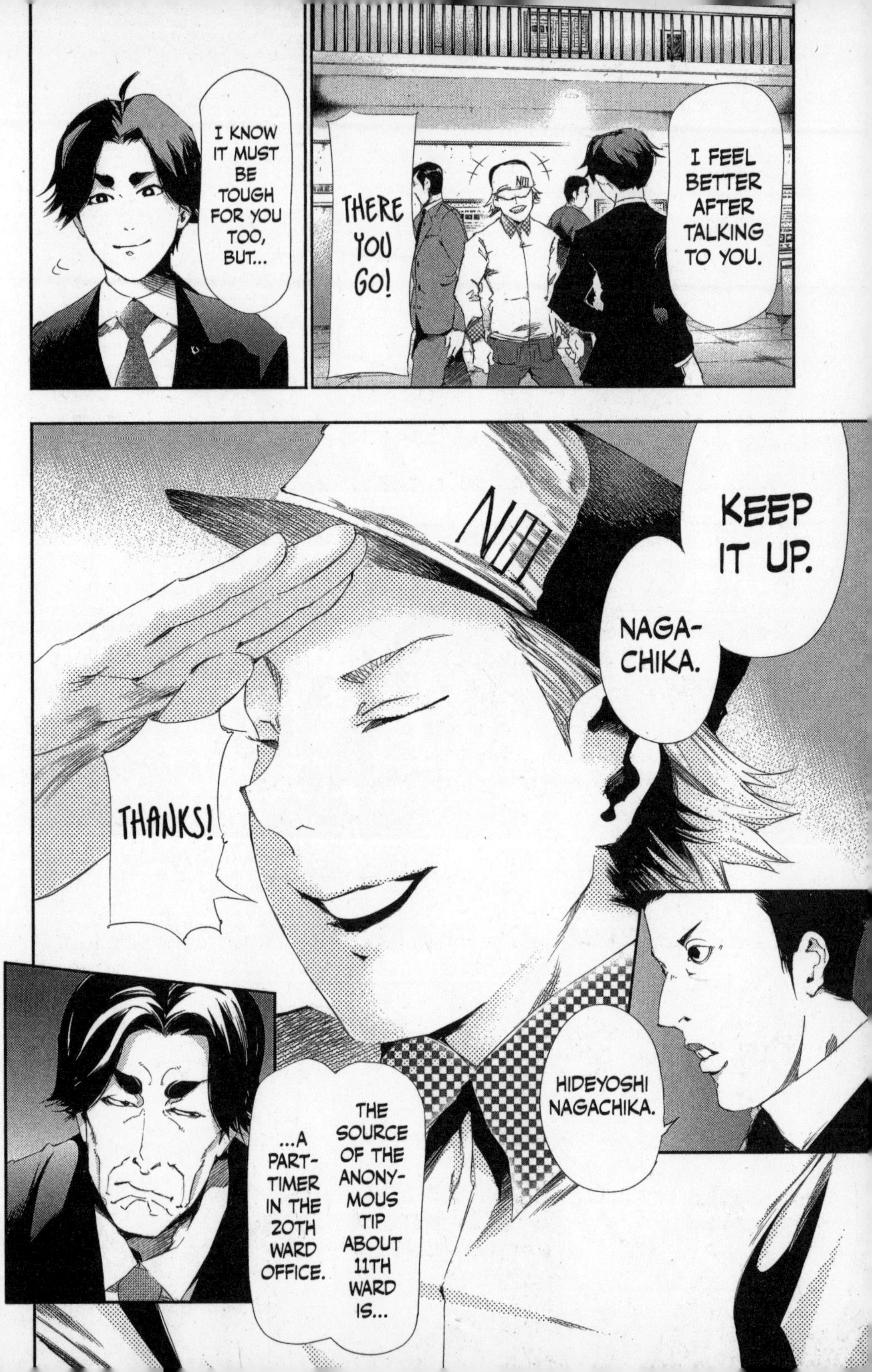
I FEEL BETTER AFTER TALKING TO YOU.
THERE YOU GO!
I KNOW IT MUST BE TOUGH FOR YOU TOO, BUT...
KEEP IT UP.
NAGA-CHIKA.
THANKS!
HIDEYOSHI NAGACHIKA.
THE SOURCE OF THE ANONYMOUS TIP ABOUT 11TH WARD IS...
...A PART-TIMER IN THE 20TH WARD OFFICE.

#084
TOKYO GHOUL

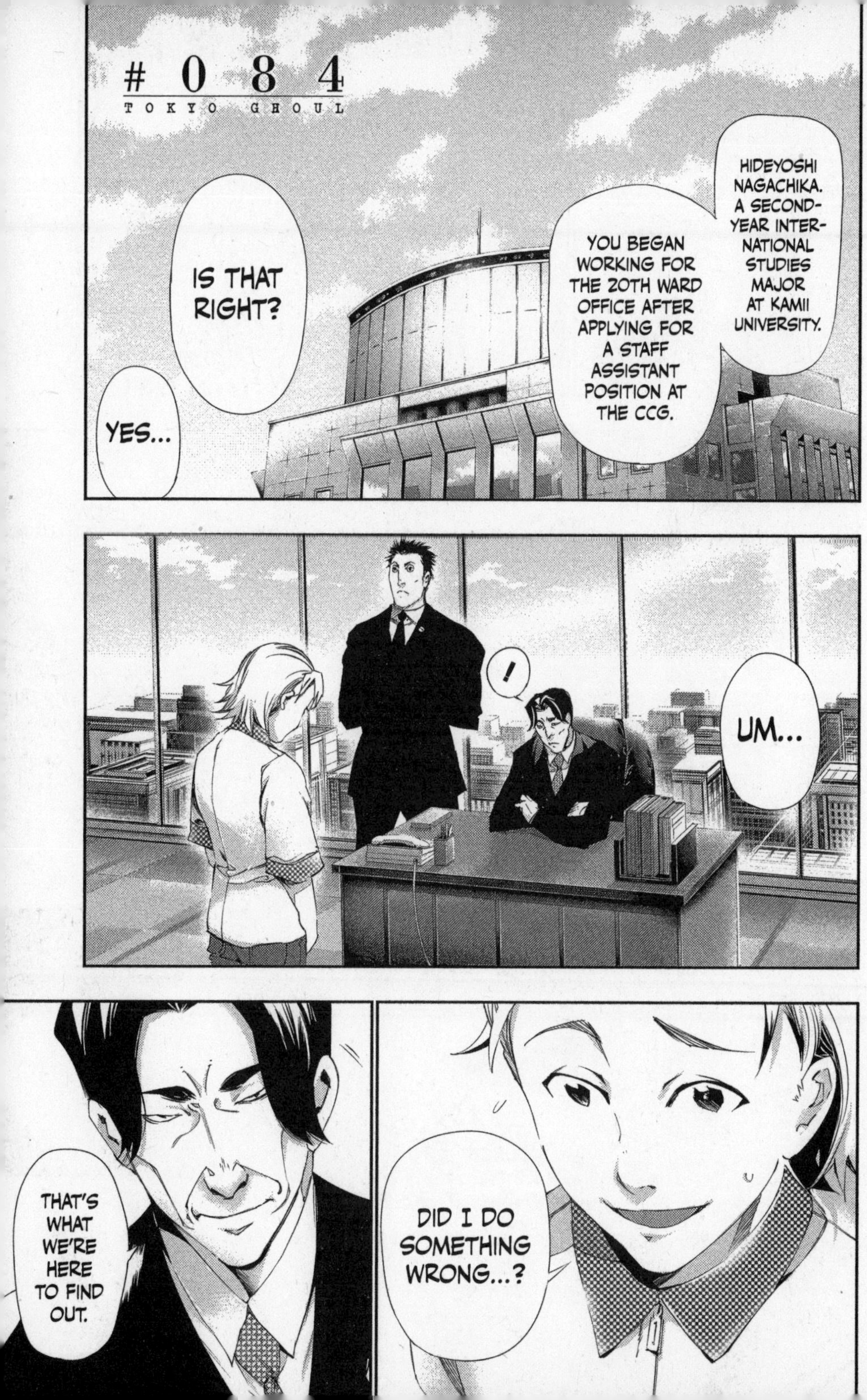
HIDEYOSHI NAGACHIKA. A SECOND-YEAR INTERNATIONAL STUDIES MAJOR AT KAMII UNIVERSITY.
YOU BEGAN WORKING FOR THE 20TH WARD OFFICE AFTER APPLYING FOR A STAFF ASSISTANT POSITION AT THE CCG.
IS THAT RIGHT?
YES...
UM...
!
DID I DO SOMETHING WRONG...?
THAT'S WHAT WE'RE HERE TO FIND OUT.

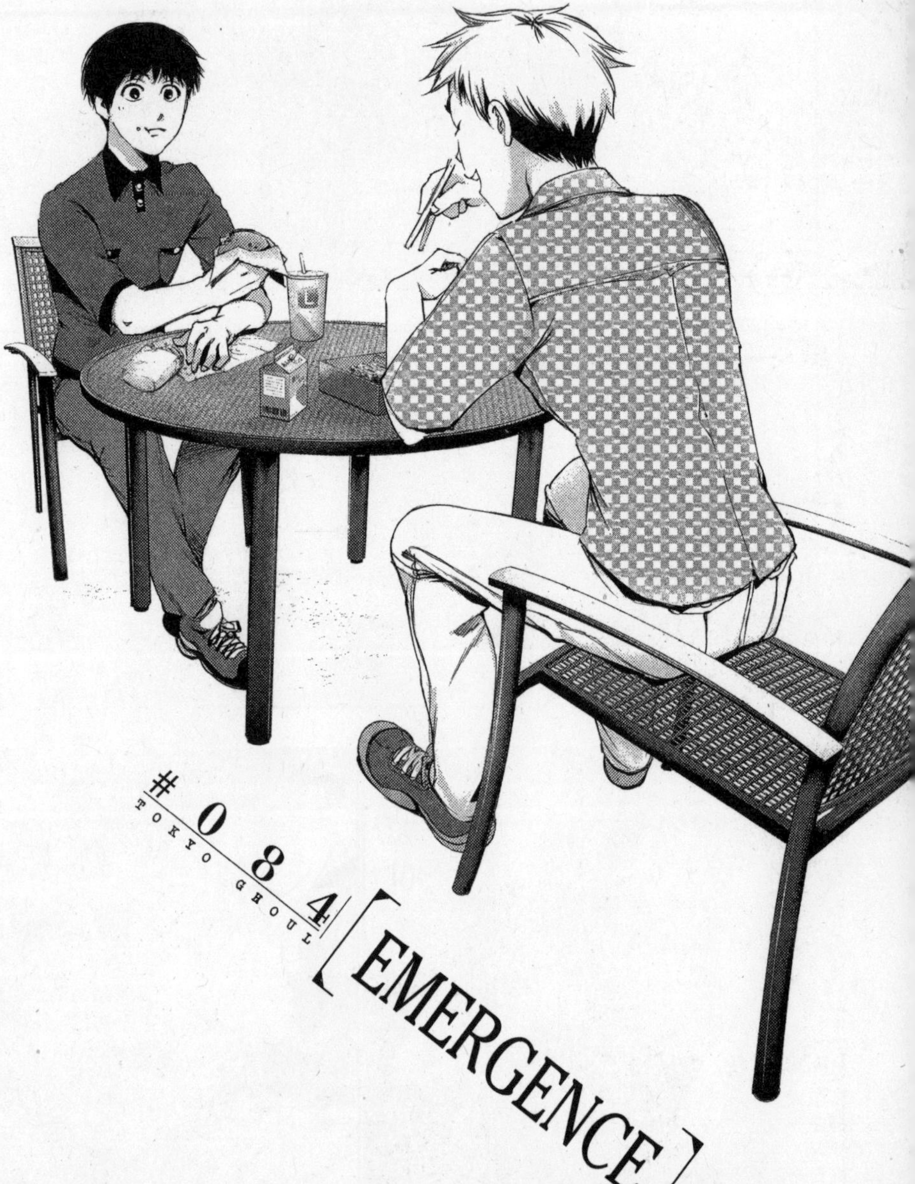
#084
TOKYO GHOUL
[EMERGENCE]

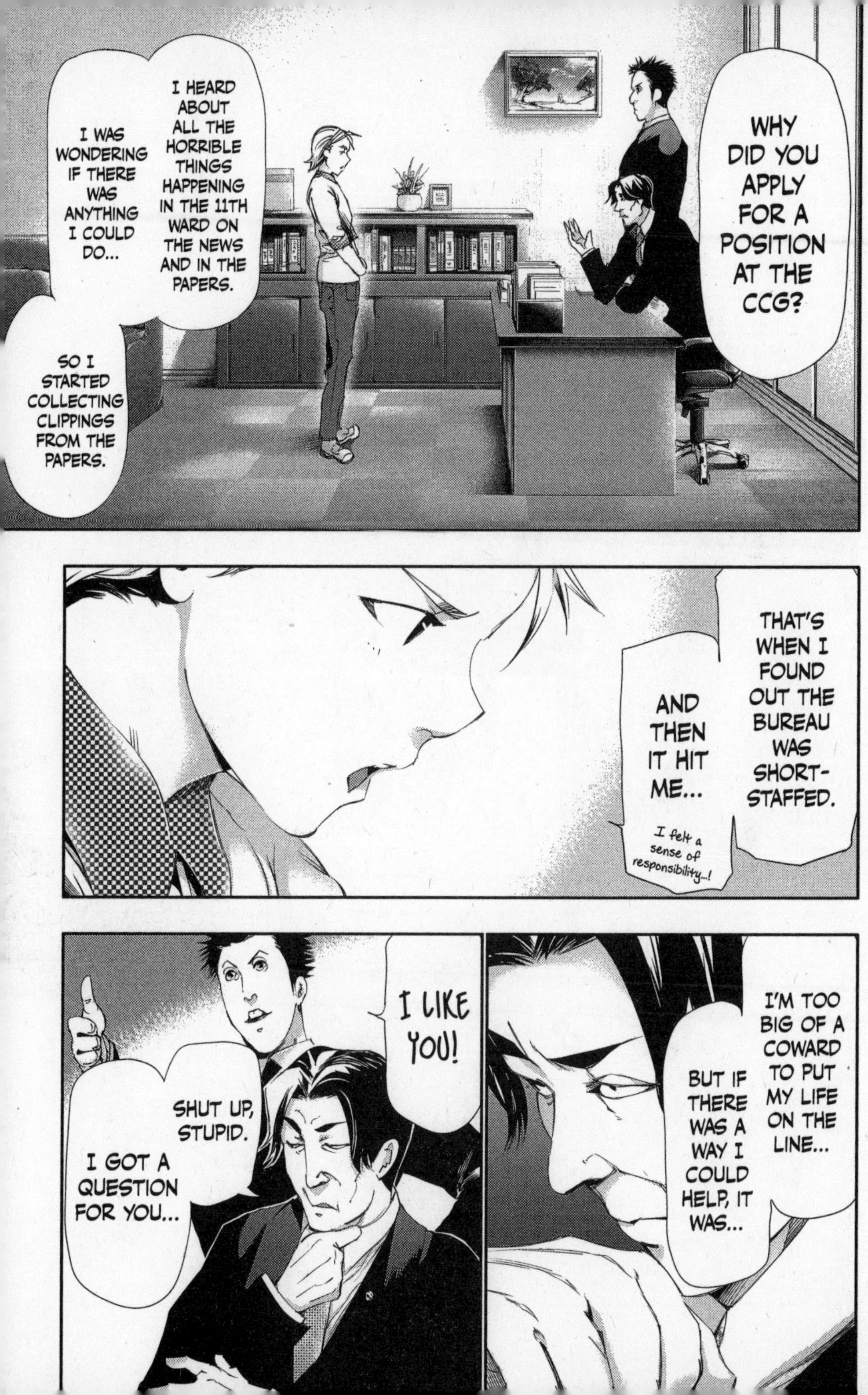
WHY DID YOU APPLY FOR A POSITION AT THE CCG?
I HEARD ABOUT ALL THE HORRIBLE THINGS HAPPENING IN THE 11TH WARD ON THE NEWS AND IN THE PAPERS.
I WAS WONDERING IF THERE WAS ANYTHING I COULD DO...
SO I STARTED COLLECTING CLIPPINGS FROM THE PAPERS.
THAT'S WHEN I FOUND OUT THE BUREAU WAS SHORT-STAFFED.
AND THEN IT HIT ME...
I felt a sense of responsibility...!
I'M TOO BIG OF A COWARD TO PUT MY LIFE ON THE LINE...
BUT IF THERE WAS A WAY I COULD HELP, IT WAS...
I LIKE YOU!
SHUT UP, STUPID.
I GOT A QUESTION FOR YOU...

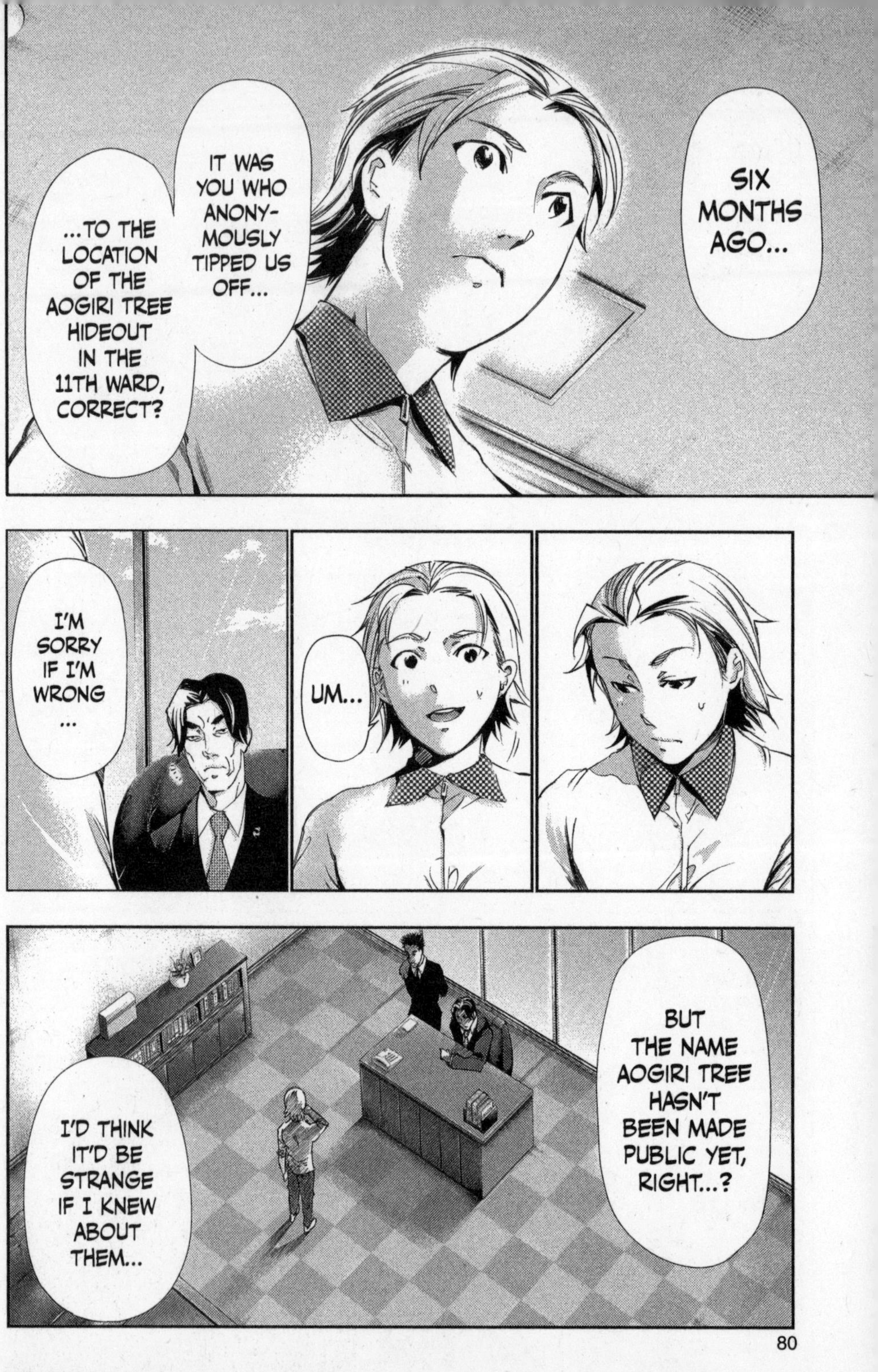
SIX MONTHS AGO...
IT WAS YOU WHO ANONYMOUSLY TIPPED US OFF...
...TO THE LOCATION OF THE AOGIRI TREE HIDEOUT IN THE 11TH WARD, CORRECT?
UM...
I'M SORRY IF I'M WRONG...
BUT THE NAME AOGIRI TREE HASN'T BEEN MADE PUBLIC YET, RIGHT...?
I'D THINK IT'D BE STRANGE IF I KNEW ABOUT THEM...

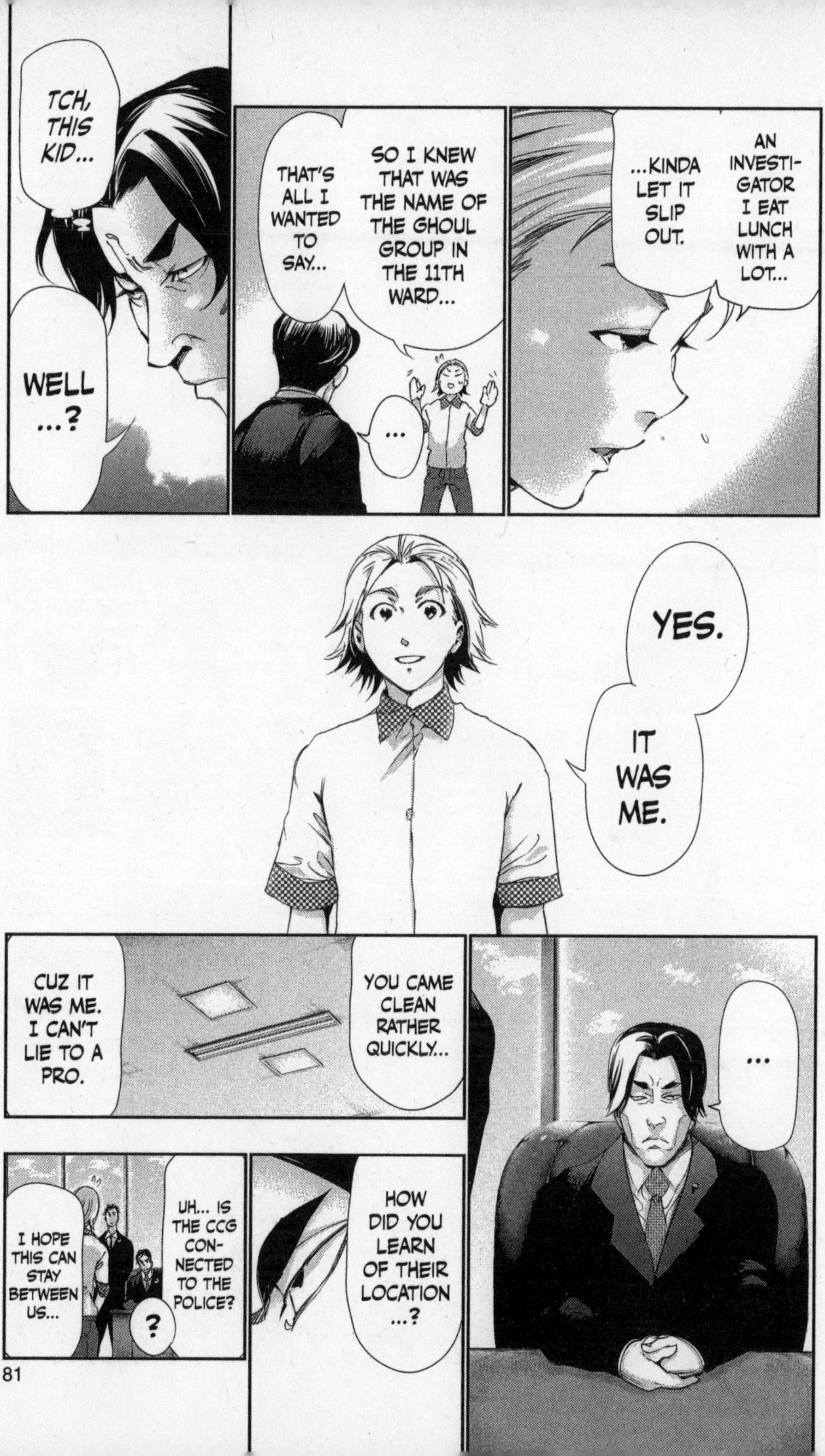
AN INVESTI-GATOR I EAT LUNCH WITH A LOT...
...KINDA LET IT SLIP OUT.
SO I KNEW THAT WAS THE NAME OF THE GHOUL GROUP IN THE 11TH WARD...
THAT'S ALL I WANTED TO SAY...
...
TCH, THIS KID...
WELL ...?
YES.
IT WAS ME.
...
YOU CAME CLEAN RATHER QUICKLY...
CUZ IT WAS ME. I CAN'T LIE TO A PRO.
HOW DID YOU LEARN OF THEIR LOCATION ...?
UH... IS THE CCG CON-NECTED TO THE POLICE?
?
I HOPE THIS CAN STAY BETWEEN US...

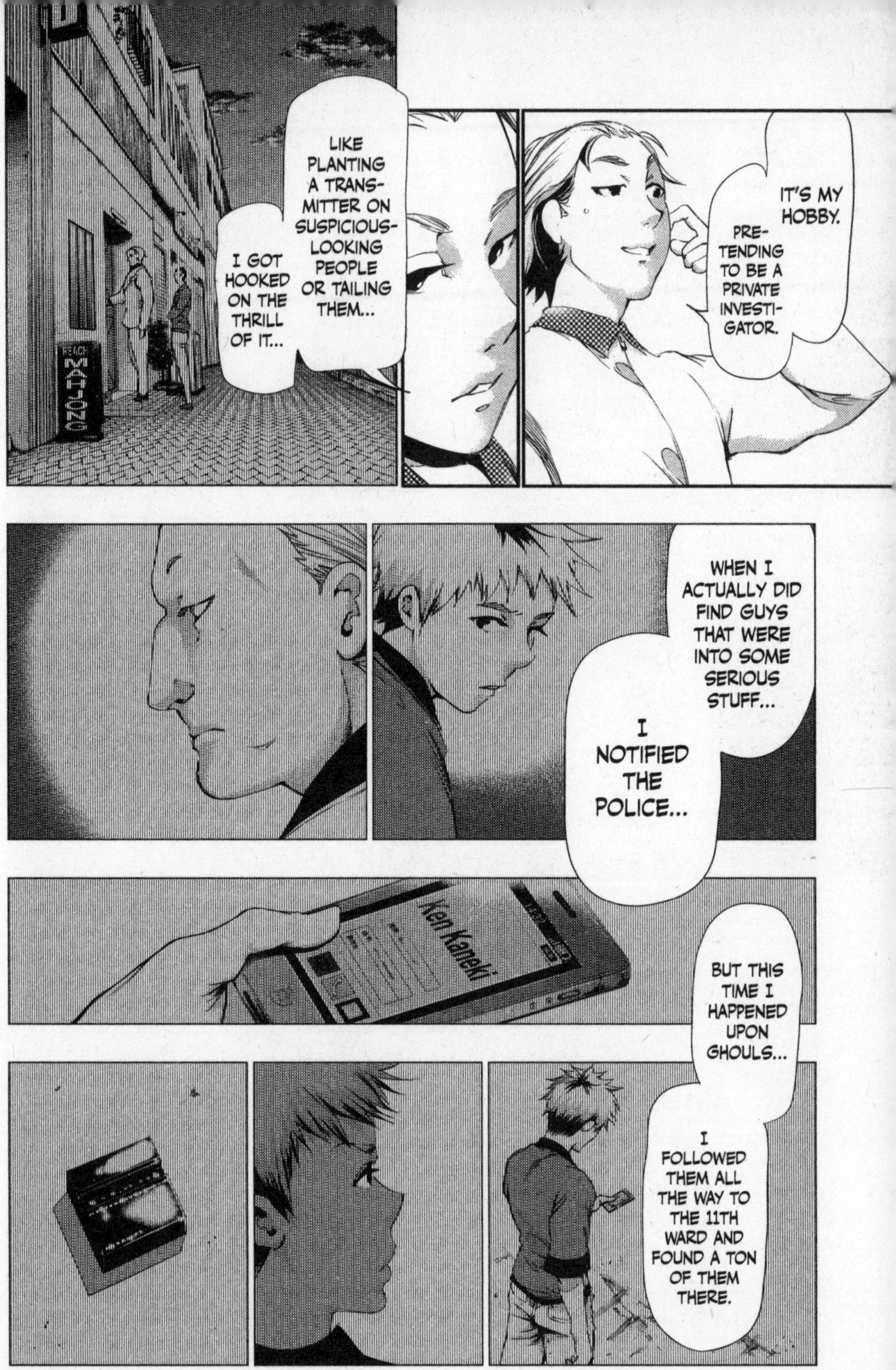
IT'S MY HOBBY.
PRETENDING TO BE A PRIVATE INVESTIGATOR.
LIKE PLANTING A TRANSMITTER ON SUSPICIOUS-LOOKING PEOPLE OR TAILING THEM...
I GOT HOOKED ON THE THRILL OF IT...
WHEN I ACTUALLY DID FIND GUYS THAT WERE INTO SOME SERIOUS STUFF...
I NOTIFIED THE POLICE...
Ken Kaneki
BUT THIS TIME I HAPPENED UPON GHOULS...
I FOLLOWED THEM ALL THE WAY TO THE 11TH WARD AND FOUND A TON OF THEM THERE.

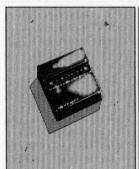

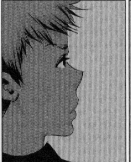

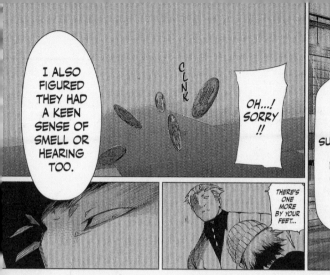

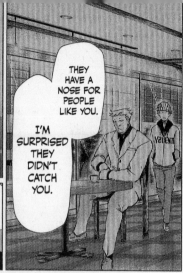

THEY HAVE A NOSE FOR PEOPLE LIKE YOU.
I'M SURPRISED THEY DIDN'T CATCH YOU.
CLINK
OH...! SORRY!!
I ALSO FIGURED THEY HAD A KEEN SENSE OF SMELL OR HEARING TOO.
THERE'S ONE MORE BY YOUR FEET...
SO I SNAGGED THE CLOTHES OFF A DEAD GHOUL...
WALKED IN MY SOCKS TO HIDE MY FOOTSTEPS...
...
...AND TIPTOED AWAY FROM HIM WITH MY LIFE.
BE CAREFUL, MAN!
I DISCOVERED SOMETHING SO TERRIBLE...
I COULDN'T KEEP IT TO MYSELF.
I CALLED IT IN ANONYMOUSLY BECAUSE...
... I DIDN'T WANT TO BE SUSPECTED MYSELF.
THAT'S WHY I KEPT QUIET ABOUT IT. I'M SORRY.
A COLLEGE STUDENT WHO LIKES TO TAIL PEOPLE...?
AND HIS MARK JUST HAPPENED TO BE A MEMBER OF AOGIRI...
SOUNDS TOO GOOD TO BE TRUE, BUT NOT ENTIRELY UNBELIEVABLE...
LET 'EM IN.
YES, SIR.

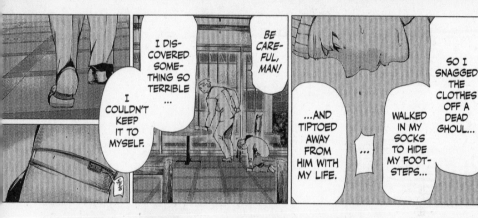

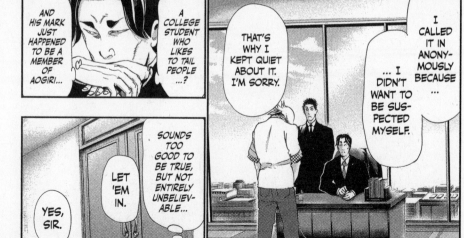

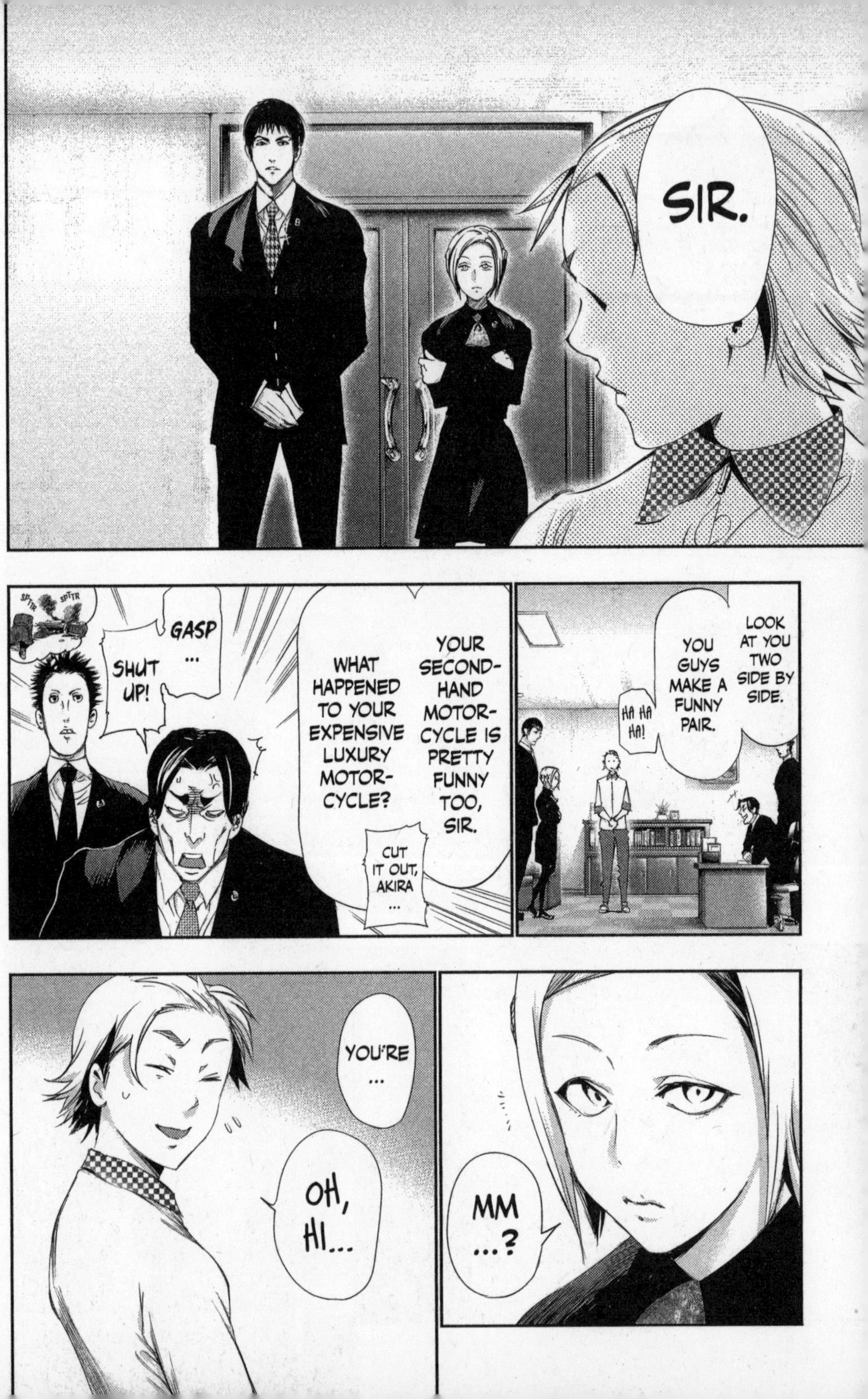
SIR.
LOOK AT YOU TWO SIDE BY SIDE.
YOU GUYS MAKE A FUNNY PAIR.
HA HA HA!
YOUR SECOND-HAND MOTORCYCLE IS PRETTY FUNNY TOO, SIR.
WHAT HAPPENED TO YOUR EXPENSIVE LUXURY MOTORCYCLE?
CUT IT OUT, AKIRA ...
GASP ...
SHUT UP!
SPTTR SPTTR
MM ...?
YOU'RE ...
OH, HI...

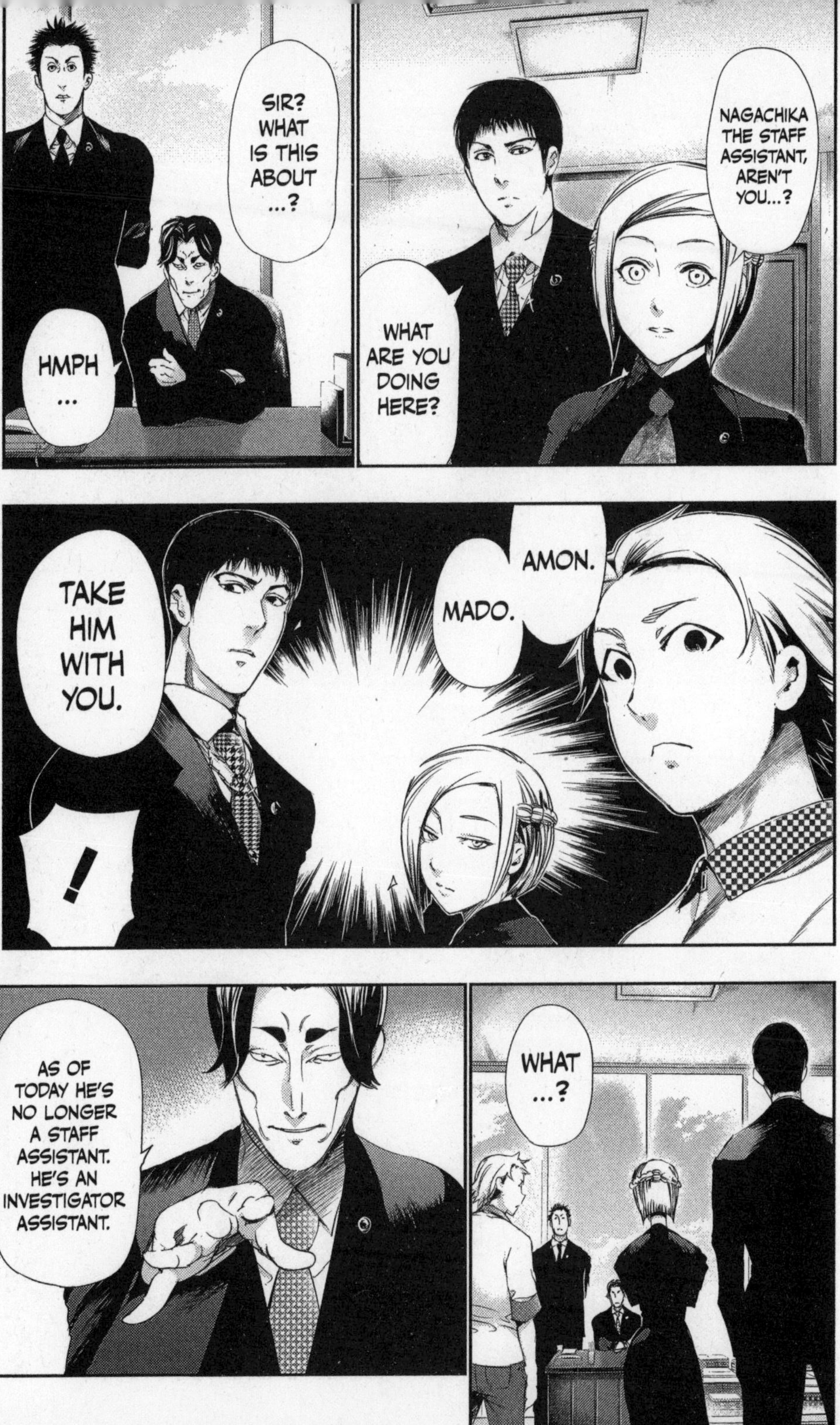
NAGACHIKA THE STAFF ASSISTANT, AREN'T YOU...?
WHAT ARE YOU DOING HERE?
SIR? WHAT IS THIS ABOUT ...?
HMPH ...
AMON.
MADO.
TAKE HIM WITH YOU.
!
WHAT ...?
AS OF TODAY HE'S NO LONGER A STAFF ASSISTANT. HE'S AN INVESTIGATOR ASSISTANT.

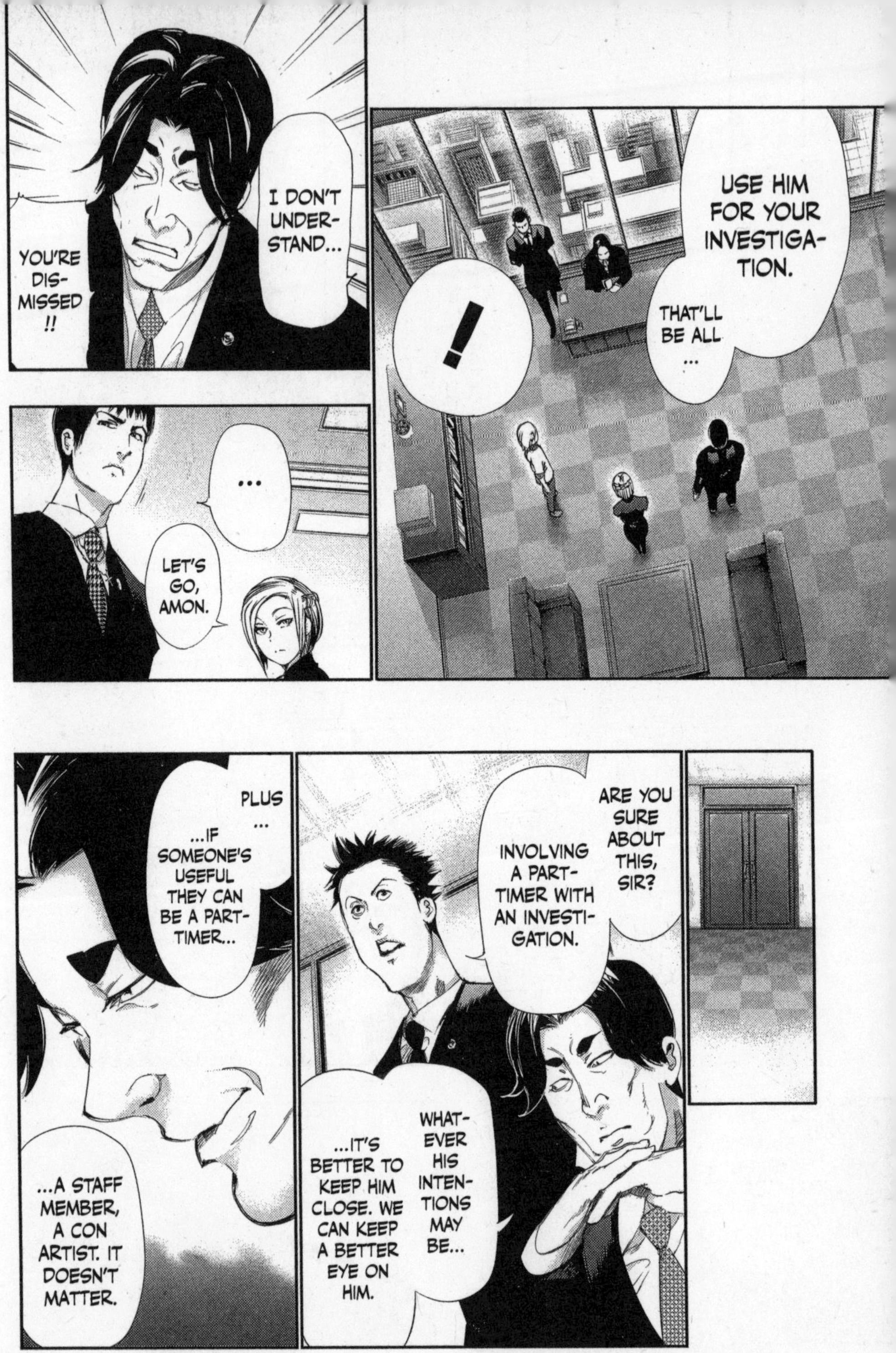
USE HIM FOR YOUR INVESTIGATION.
THAT'LL BE ALL...
!
I DON'T UNDERSTAND...
YOU'RE DISMISSED!!
...
LET'S GO, AMON.
ARE YOU SURE ABOUT THIS, SIR?
INVOLVING A PART-TIMER WITH AN INVESTIGATION.
WHATEVER HIS INTENTIONS MAY BE...
...IT'S BETTER TO KEEP HIM CLOSE. WE CAN KEEP A BETTER EYE ON HIM.
PLUS...
...IF SOMEONE'S USEFUL THEY CAN BE A PART-TIMER...
...A STAFF MEMBER, A CON ARTIST. IT DOESN'T MATTER.

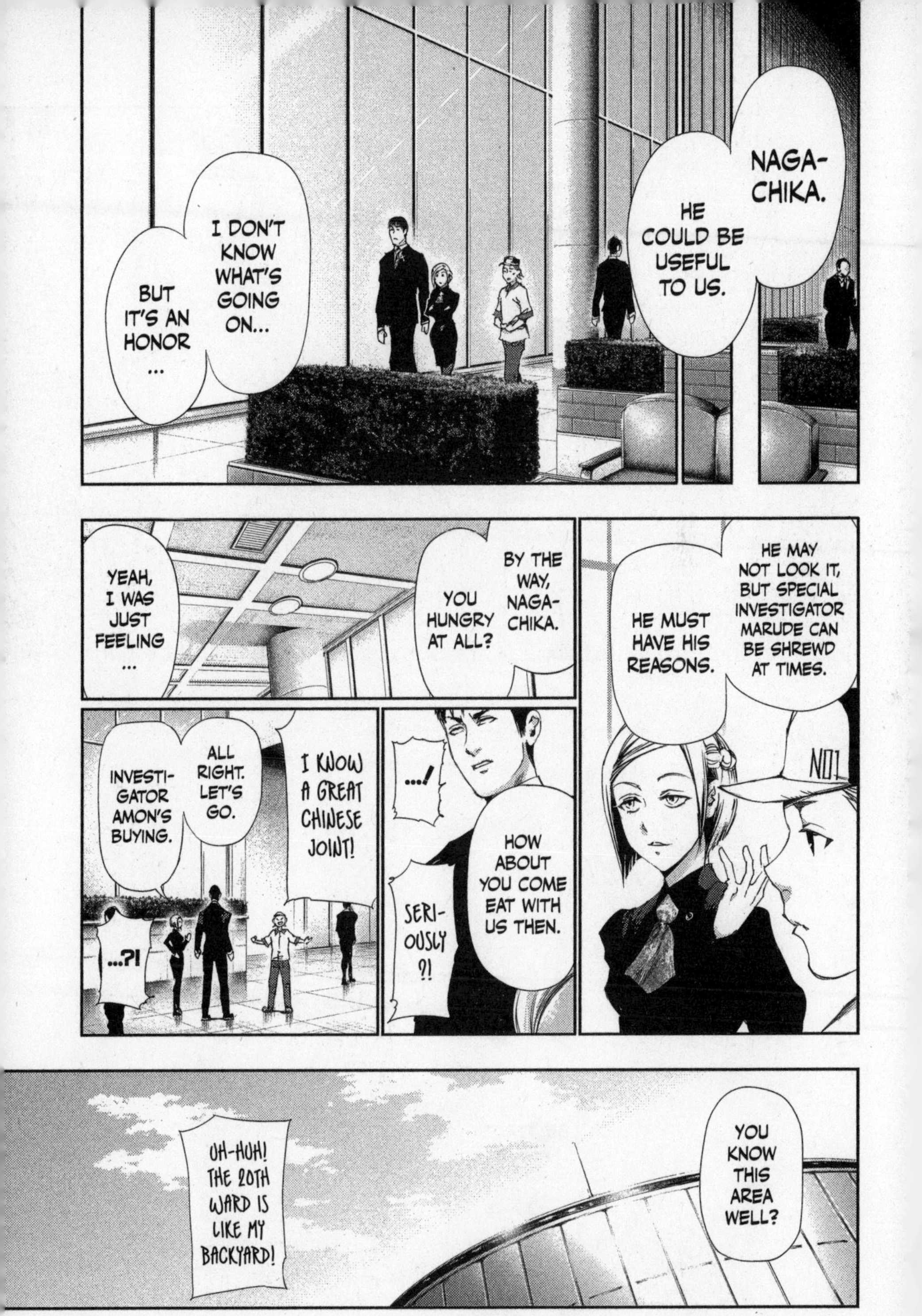
NAGA-CHIKA.
HE COULD BE USEFUL TO US.
I DON'T KNOW WHAT'S GOING ON...
BUT IT'S AN HONOR...
HE MAY NOT LOOK IT, BUT SPECIAL INVESTIGATOR MARUDE CAN BE SHREWD AT TIMES.
HE MUST HAVE HIS REASONS.
NO1
BY THE WAY, NAGA-CHIKA.
YOU HUNGRY AT ALL?
YEAH, I WAS JUST FEELING...
...!
HOW ABOUT YOU COME EAT WITH US THEN.
SERI-OUSLY?!
I KNOW A GREAT CHINESE JOINT!
ALL RIGHT. LET'S GO.
INVESTI-GATOR AMON'S BUYING.
...?!
YOU KNOW THIS AREA WELL?
UH-HUH! THE 20TH WARD IS LIKE MY BACKYARD!

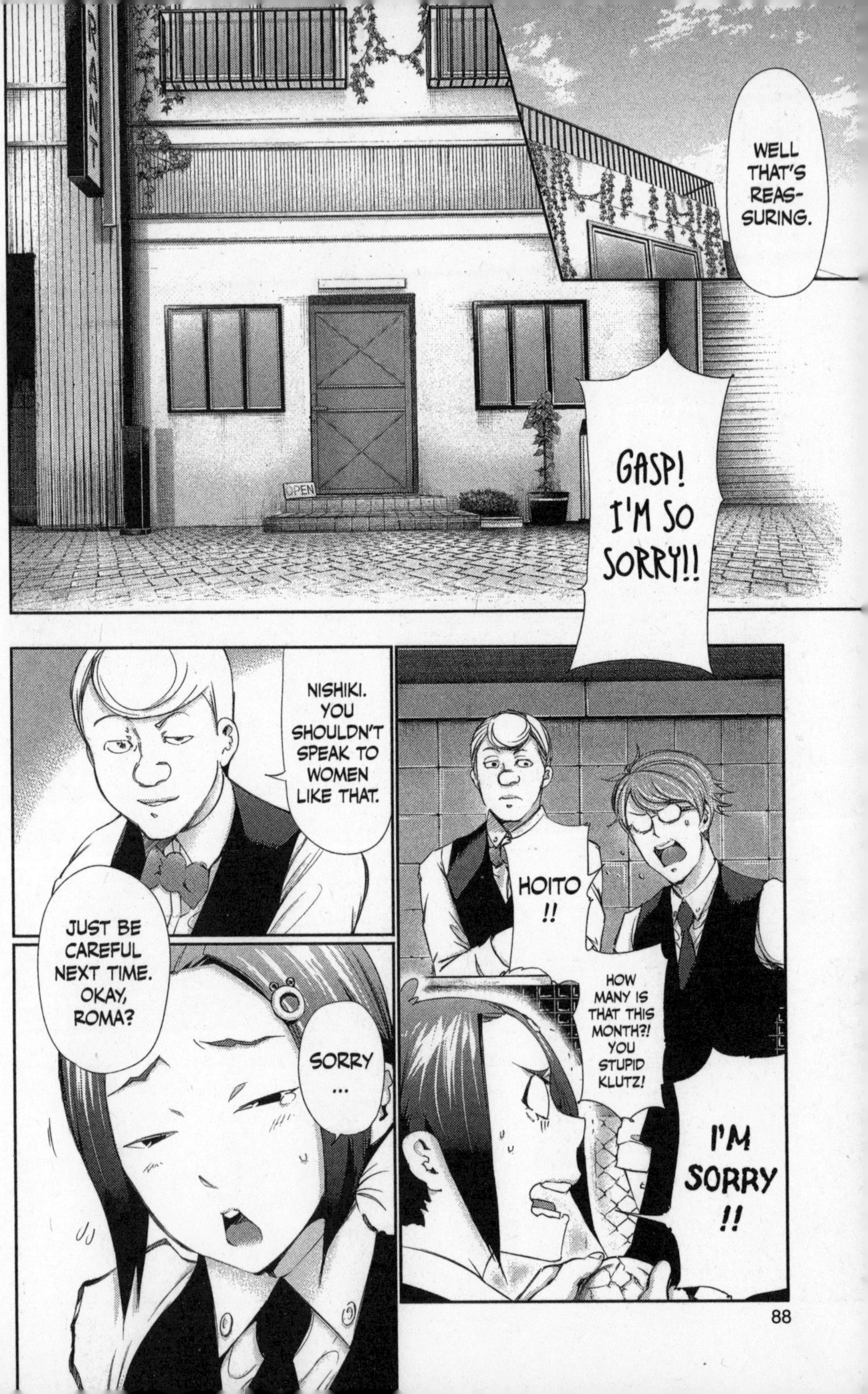
WELL THAT'S REAS-SURING.
GASP! I'M SO SORRY!!
HOITO !!
HOW MANY IS THAT THIS MONTH?! YOU STUPID KLUTZ!
I'M SORRY !!
NISHIKI. YOU SHOULDN'T SPEAK TO WOMEN LIKE THAT.
JUST BE CAREFUL NEXT TIME. OKAY, ROMA?
SORRY ...
OPEN

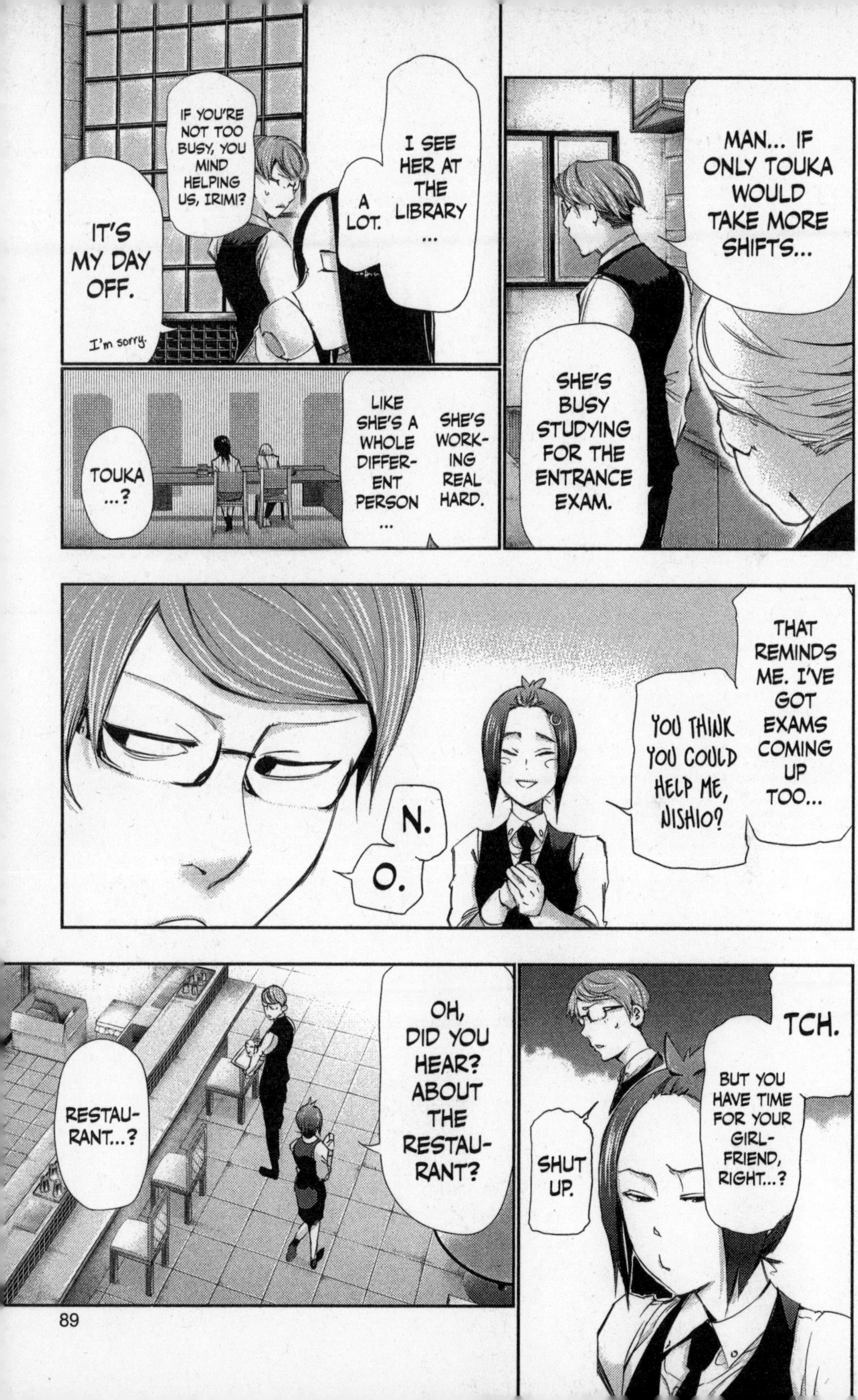
MAN... IF ONLY TOUKA WOULD TAKE MORE SHIFTS...
SHE'S BUSY STUDYING FOR THE ENTRANCE EXAM.
I SEE HER AT THE LIBRARY...
A LOT.
IF YOU'RE NOT TOO BUSY, YOU MIND HELPING US, IRIMI?
IT'S MY DAY OFF.
I'm sorry.
SHE'S WORKING REAL HARD.
LIKE SHE'S A WHOLE DIFFERENT PERSON...
TOUKA...?
THAT REMINDS ME. I'VE GOT EXAMS COMING UP TOO...
YOU THINK YOU COULD HELP ME, NISHIO?
N.
O.
TCH.
BUT YOU HAVE TIME FOR YOUR GIRLFRIEND, RIGHT...?
SHUT UP.
OH, DID YOU HEAR? ABOUT THE RESTAURANT?
RESTAURANT...?

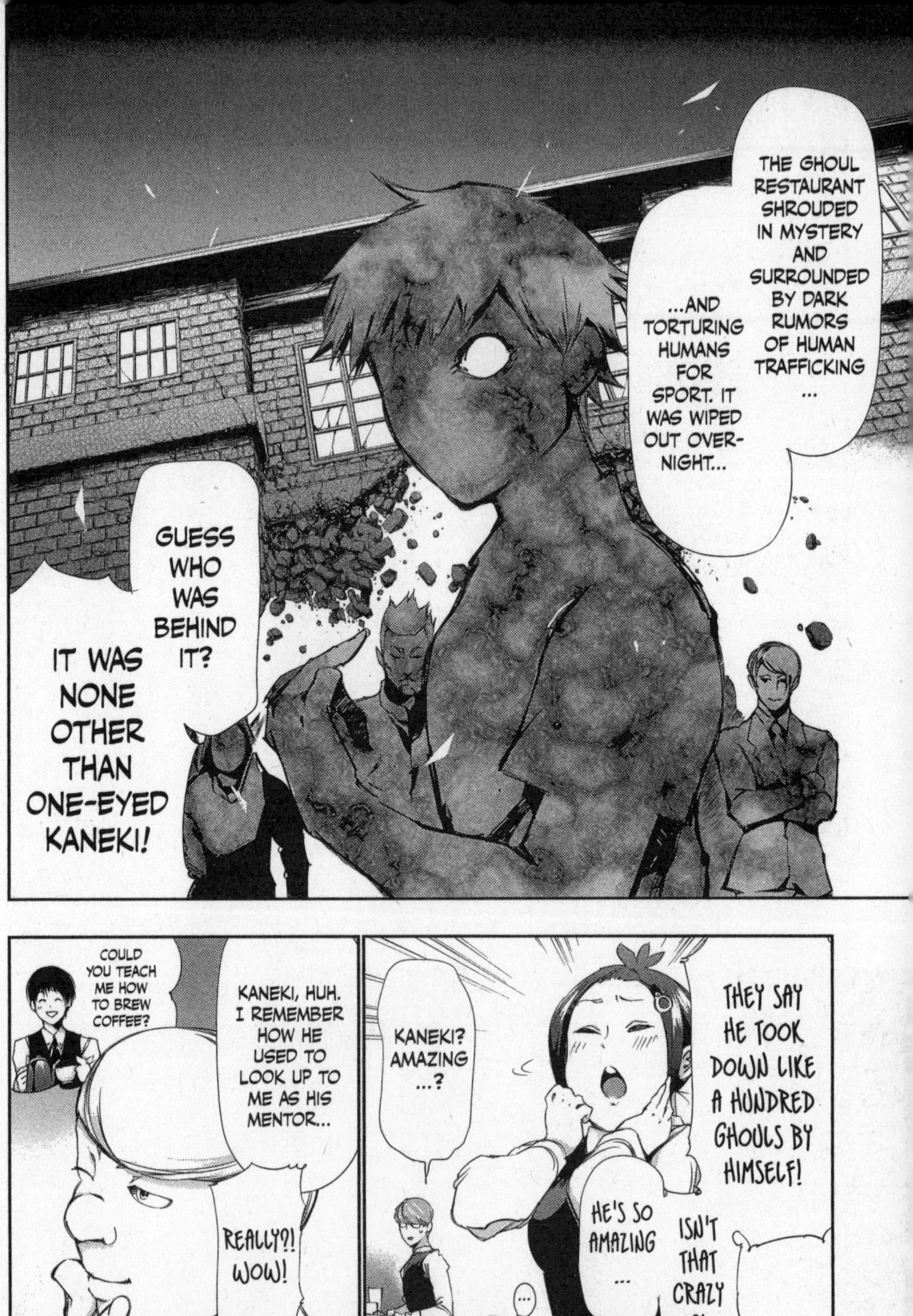
THE GHOUL RESTAURANT SHROUDED IN MYSTERY AND SURROUNDED BY DARK RUMORS OF HUMAN TRAFFICKING ...
...AND TORTURING HUMANS FOR SPORT. IT WAS WIPED OUT OVER-NIGHT...
GUESS WHO WAS BEHIND IT?
IT WAS NONE OTHER THAN ONE-EYED KANEKI!
THEY SAY HE TOOK DOWN LIKE A HUNDRED GHOULS BY HIMSELF!
KANEKI? AMAZING ...?
ISN'T THAT CRAZY ?!
HE'S SO AMAZING ...
...
KANEKI, HUH. I REMEMBER HOW HE USED TO LOOK UP TO ME AS HIS MENTOR...
COULD YOU TEACH ME HOW TO BREW COFFEE?
REALLY?! WOW!

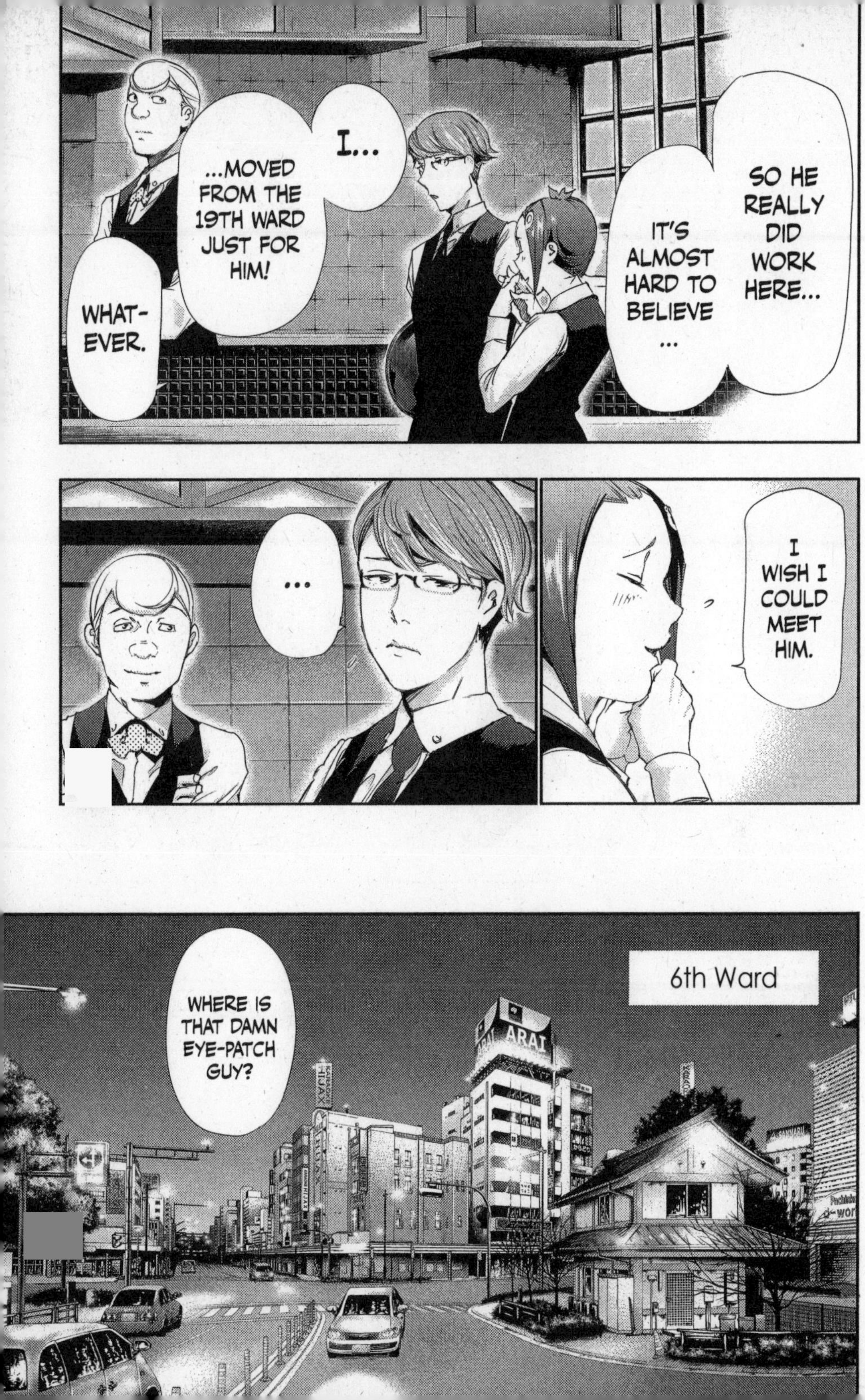
SO HE REALLY DID WORK HERE...
IT'S ALMOST HARD TO BELIEVE ...
I...
...MOVED FROM THE 19TH WARD JUST FOR HIM!
WHAT-EVER.
I WISH I COULD MEET HIM.
...
6th Ward
WHERE IS THAT DAMN EYE-PATCH GUY?

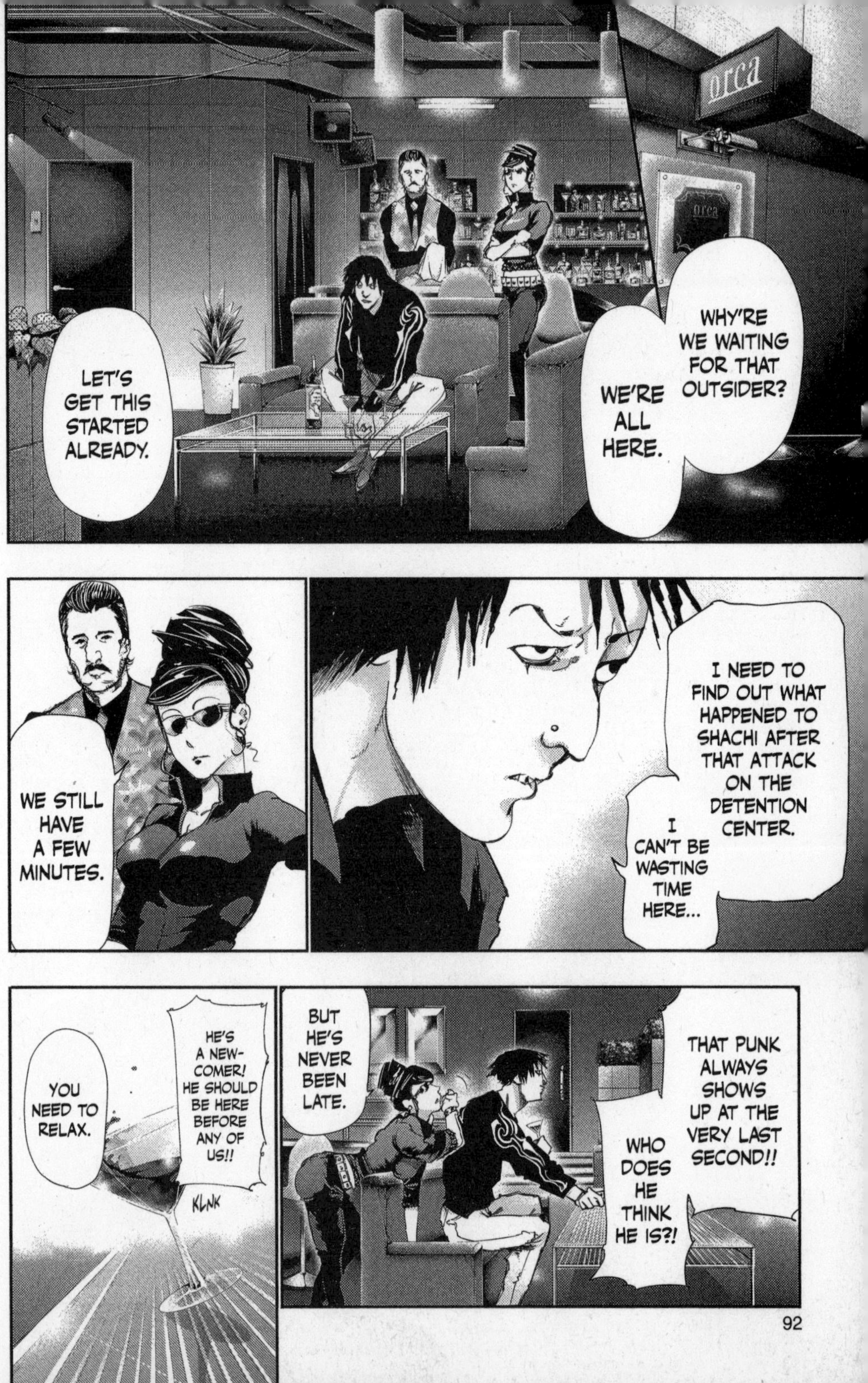
orca
WHY'RE WE WAITING FOR THAT OUTSIDER?
WE'RE ALL HERE.
LET'S GET THIS STARTED ALREADY.
I NEED TO FIND OUT WHAT HAPPENED TO SHACHI AFTER THAT ATTACK ON THE DETENTION CENTER.
I CAN'T BE WASTING TIME HERE...
WE STILL HAVE A FEW MINUTES.
THAT PUNK ALWAYS SHOWS UP AT THE VERY LAST SECOND!!
WHO DOES HE THINK HE IS?!
BUT HE'S NEVER BEEN LATE.
HE'S A NEW-COMER! HE SHOULD BE HERE BEFORE ANY OF US!!
YOU NEED TO RELAX.
KLNK

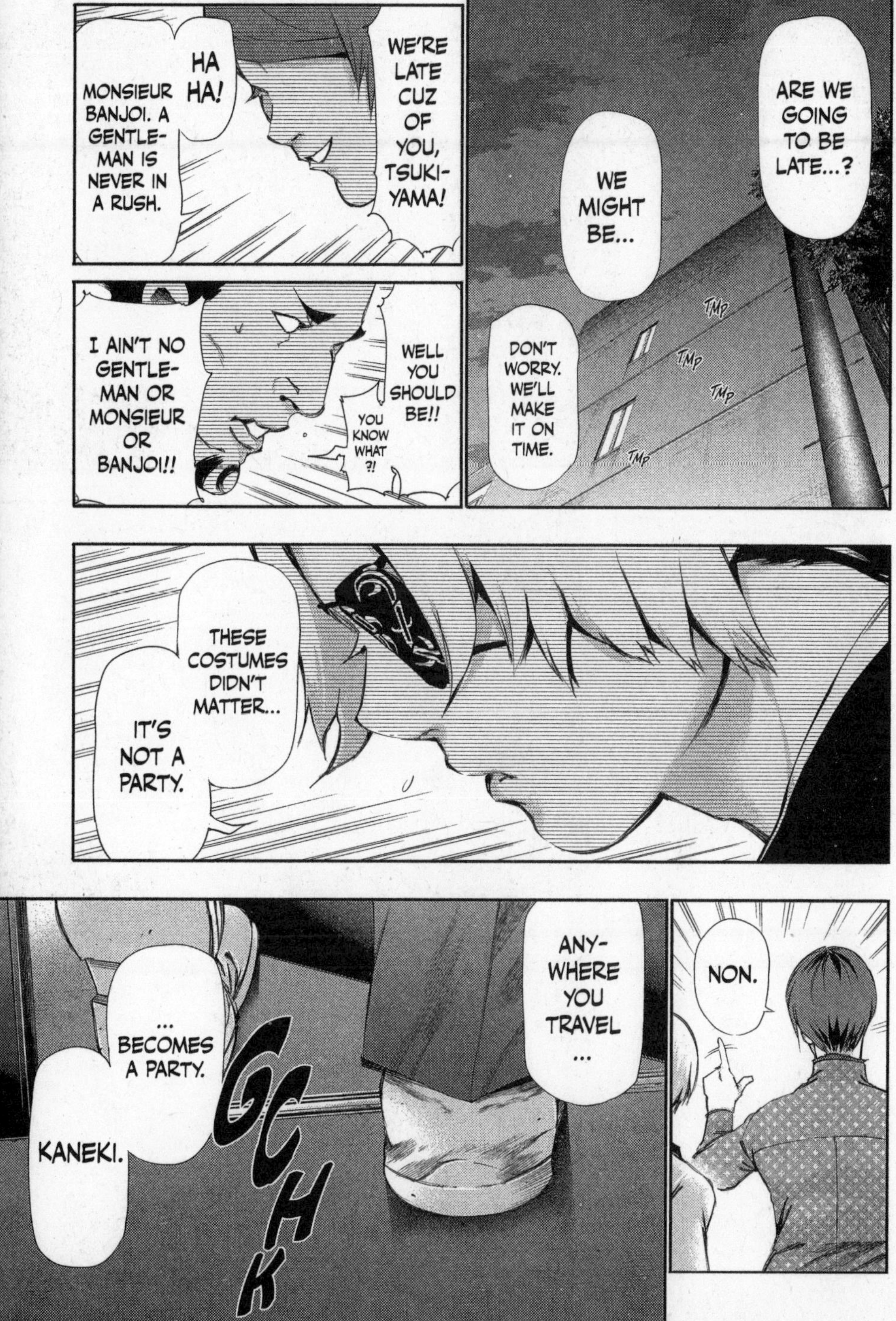
ARE WE GOING TO BE LATE...?
WE MIGHT BE...
TMP
TMP
TMP
TMP
DON'T WORRY. WE'LL MAKE IT ON TIME.
WE'RE LATE CUZ OF YOU, TSUKIYAMA!
HA HA!
MONSIEUR BANJOI. A GENTLEMAN IS NEVER IN A RUSH.
WELL YOU SHOULD BE!!
YOU KNOW WHAT?!
I AIN'T NO GENTLEMAN OR MONSIEUR OR BANJOI!!
THESE COSTUMES DIDN'T MATTER...
IT'S NOT A PARTY.
NON.
ANYWHERE YOU TRAVEL...
...BECOMES A PARTY.
GCHK
KANEKI.

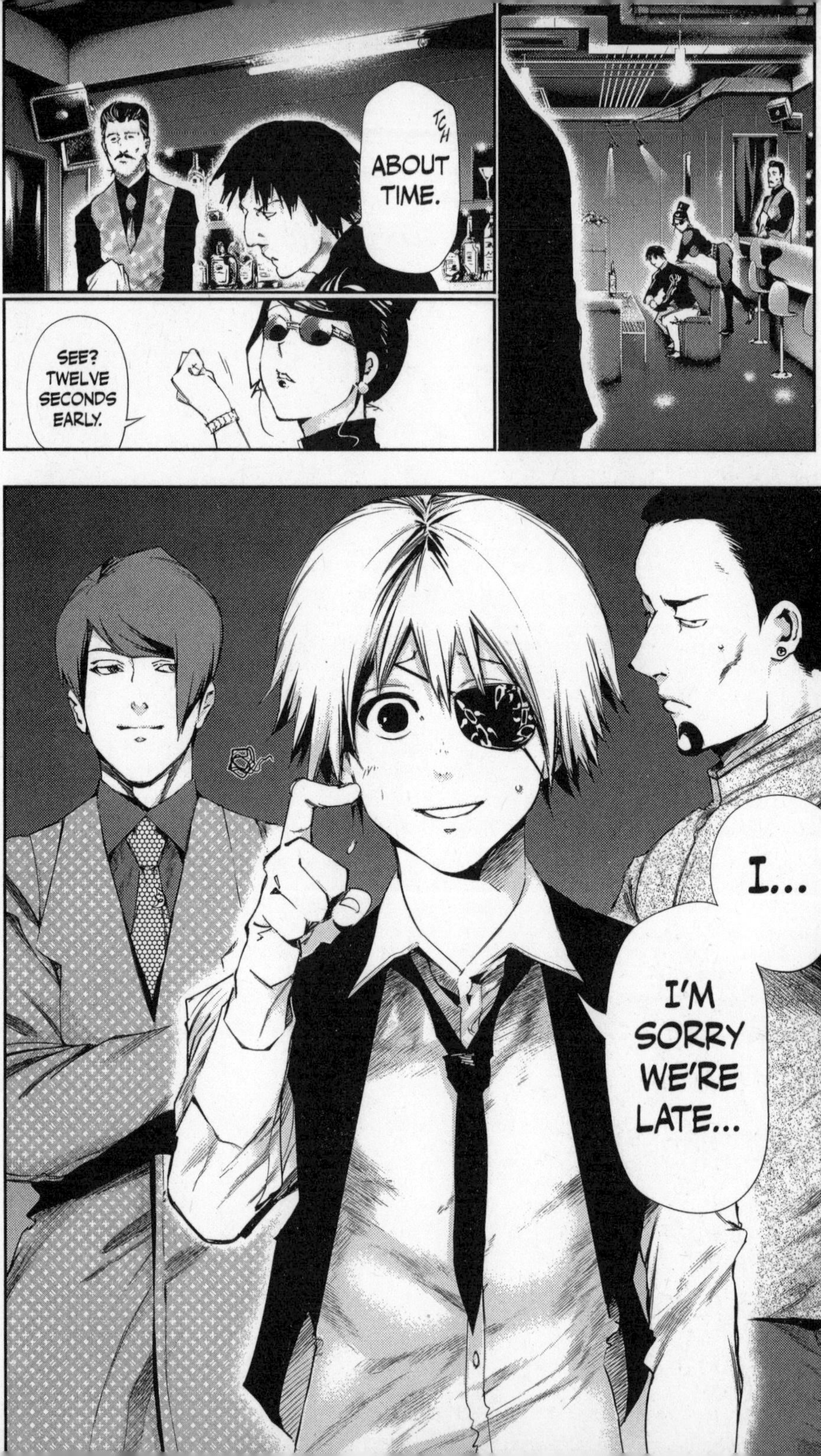
TCH
ABOUT TIME.
SEE? TWELVE SECONDS EARLY.
I...
I'M SORRY WE'RE LATE...

東京喰種
トーキョーグール
喰種
Tokyo
Ghoul

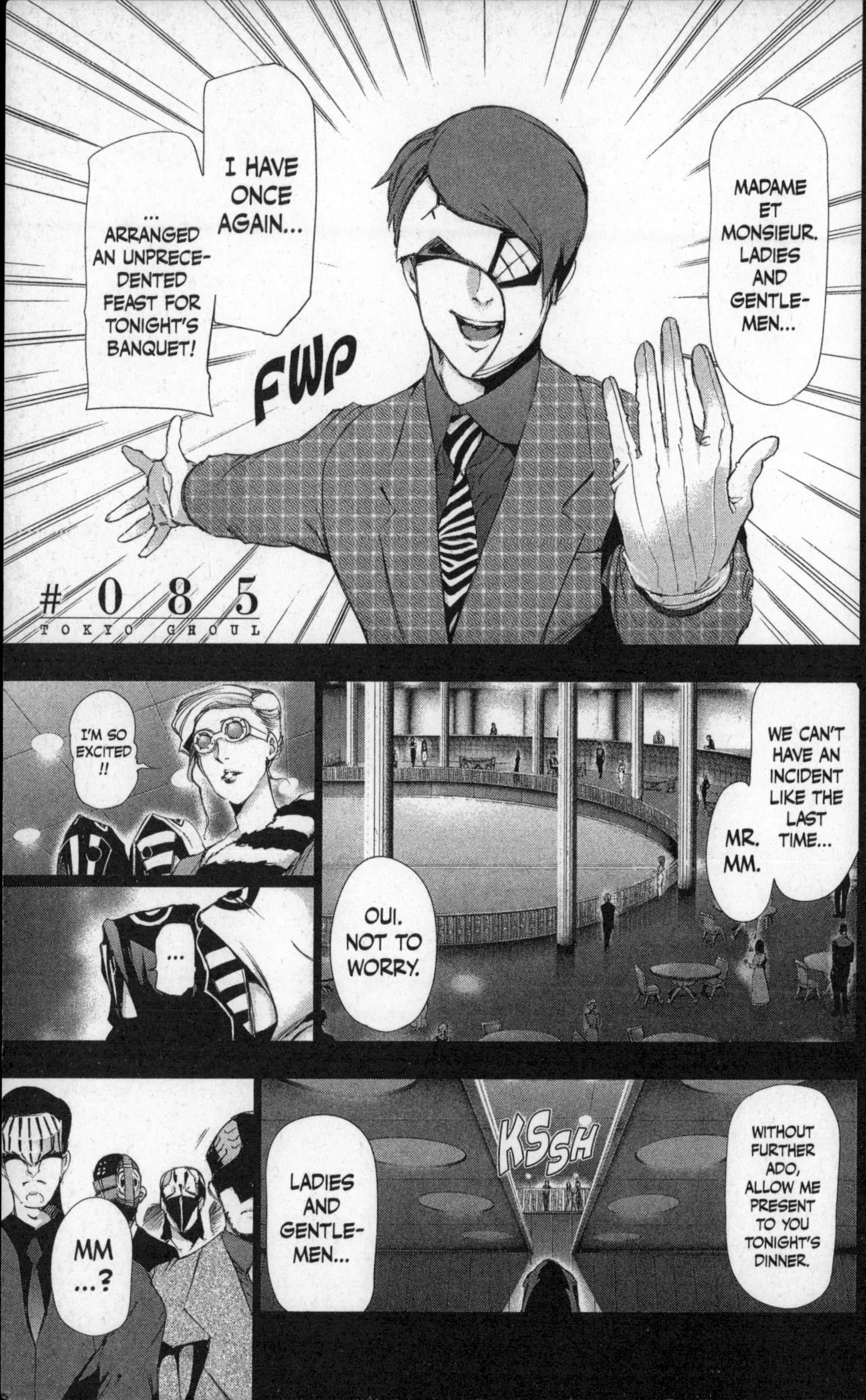
MADAME ET MONSIEUR. LADIES AND GENTLEMEN...
I HAVE ONCE AGAIN...
... ARRANGED AN UNPRECEDENTED FEAST FOR TONIGHT'S BANQUET!
FWP
#085
TOKYO GHOUL
WE CAN'T HAVE AN INCIDENT LIKE THE LAST TIME...
MR. MM.
OUI. NOT TO WORRY.
I'M SO EXCITED !!
...
WITHOUT FURTHER ADO, ALLOW ME PRESENT TO YOU TONIGHT'S DINNER.
KSSH
LADIES AND GENTLEMEN...
MM ...?

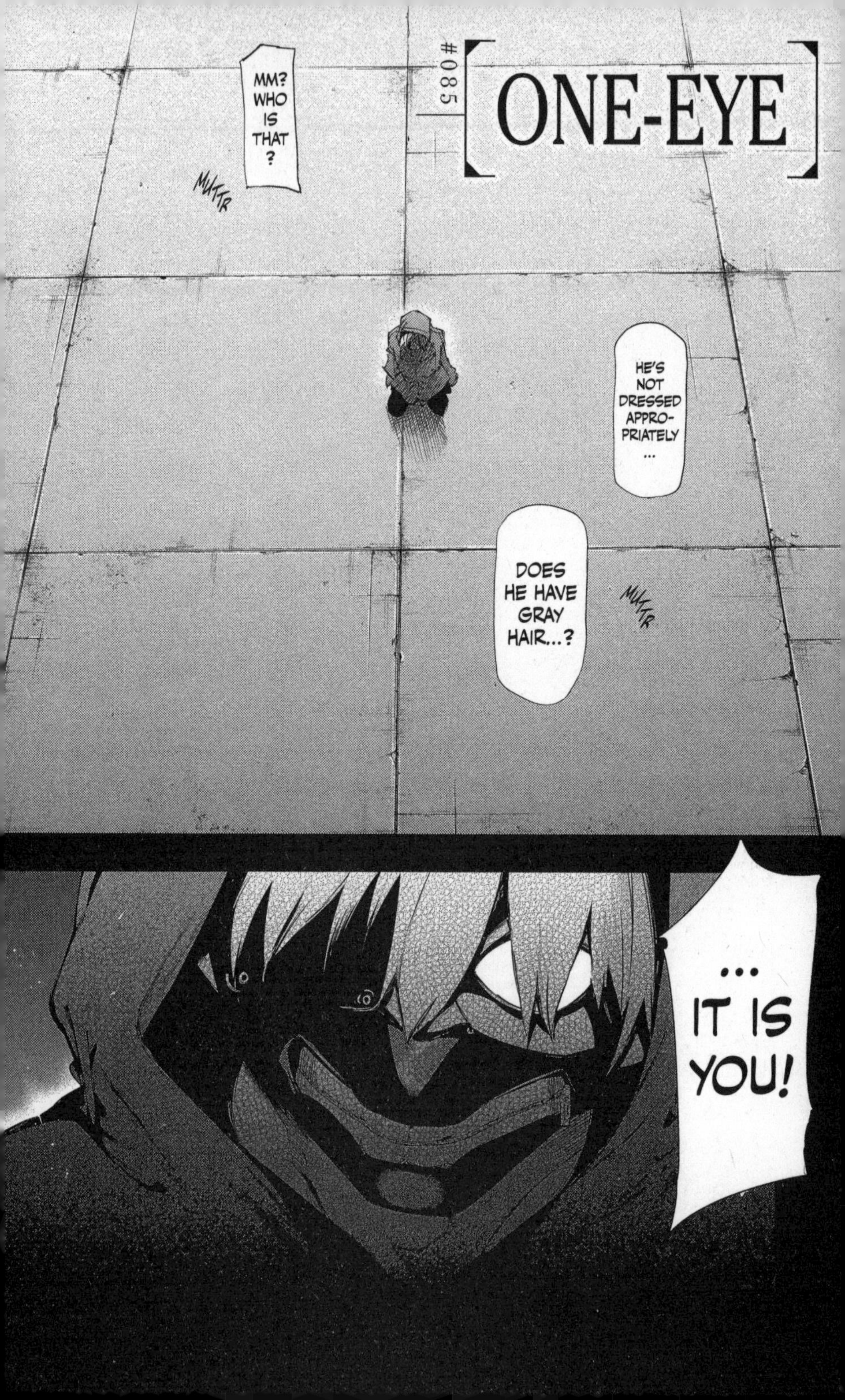
#085 [ONE-EYE]
MM? WHO IS THAT?
MUTTR
HE'S NOT DRESSED APPROPRIATELY...
DOES HE HAVE GRAY HAIR...?
MUTTR
...IT IS YOU!

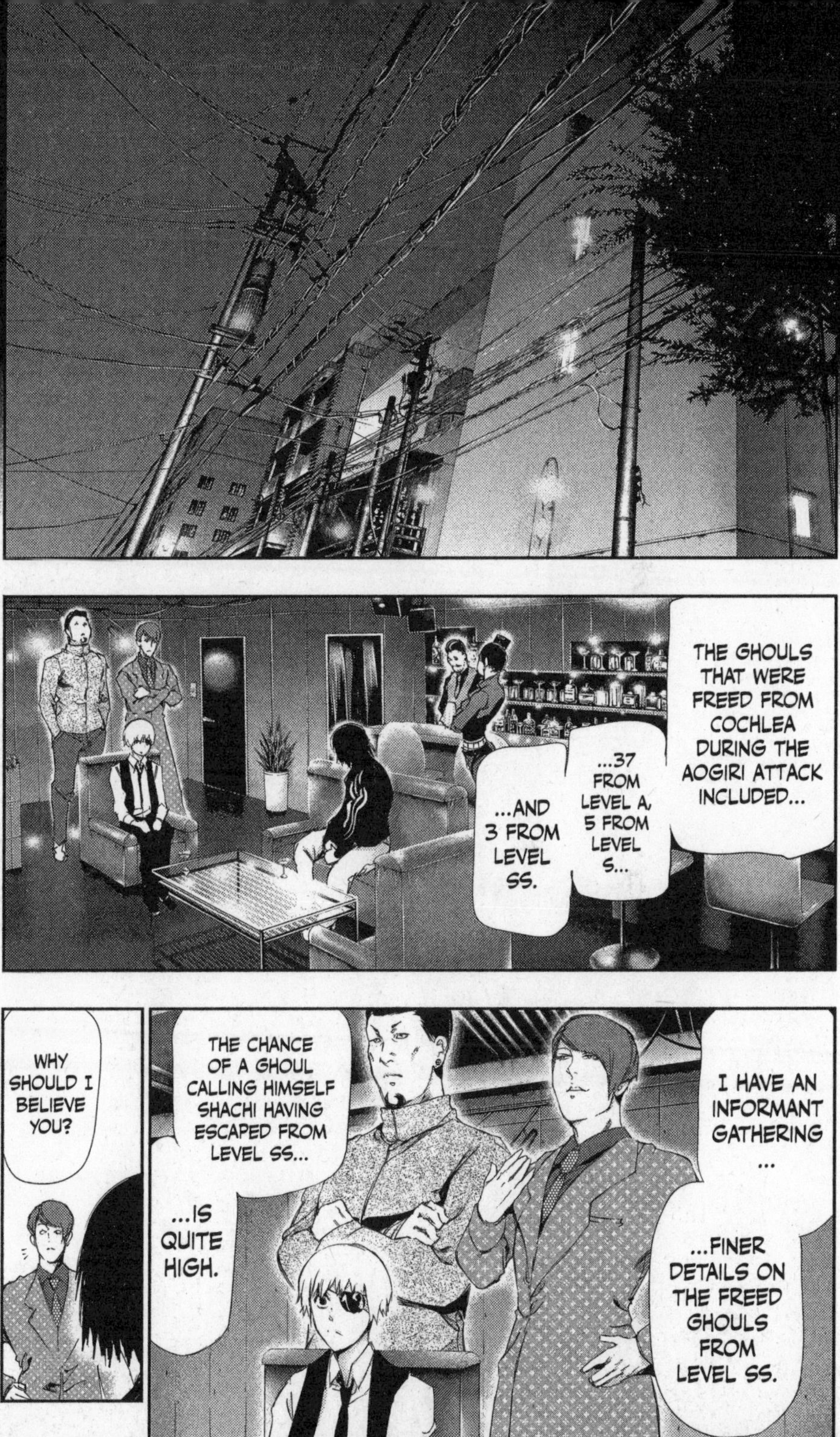
THE GHOULS THAT WERE FREED FROM COCHLEA DURING THE AOGIRI ATTACK INCLUDED...
...37 FROM LEVEL A, 5 FROM LEVEL S...
...AND 3 FROM LEVEL SS.
I HAVE AN INFORMANT GATHERING ...
...FINER DETAILS ON THE FREED GHOULS FROM LEVEL SS.
THE CHANCE OF A GHOUL CALLING HIMSELF SHACHI HAVING ESCAPED FROM LEVEL SS...
...IS QUITE HIGH.
WHY SHOULD I BELIEVE YOU?

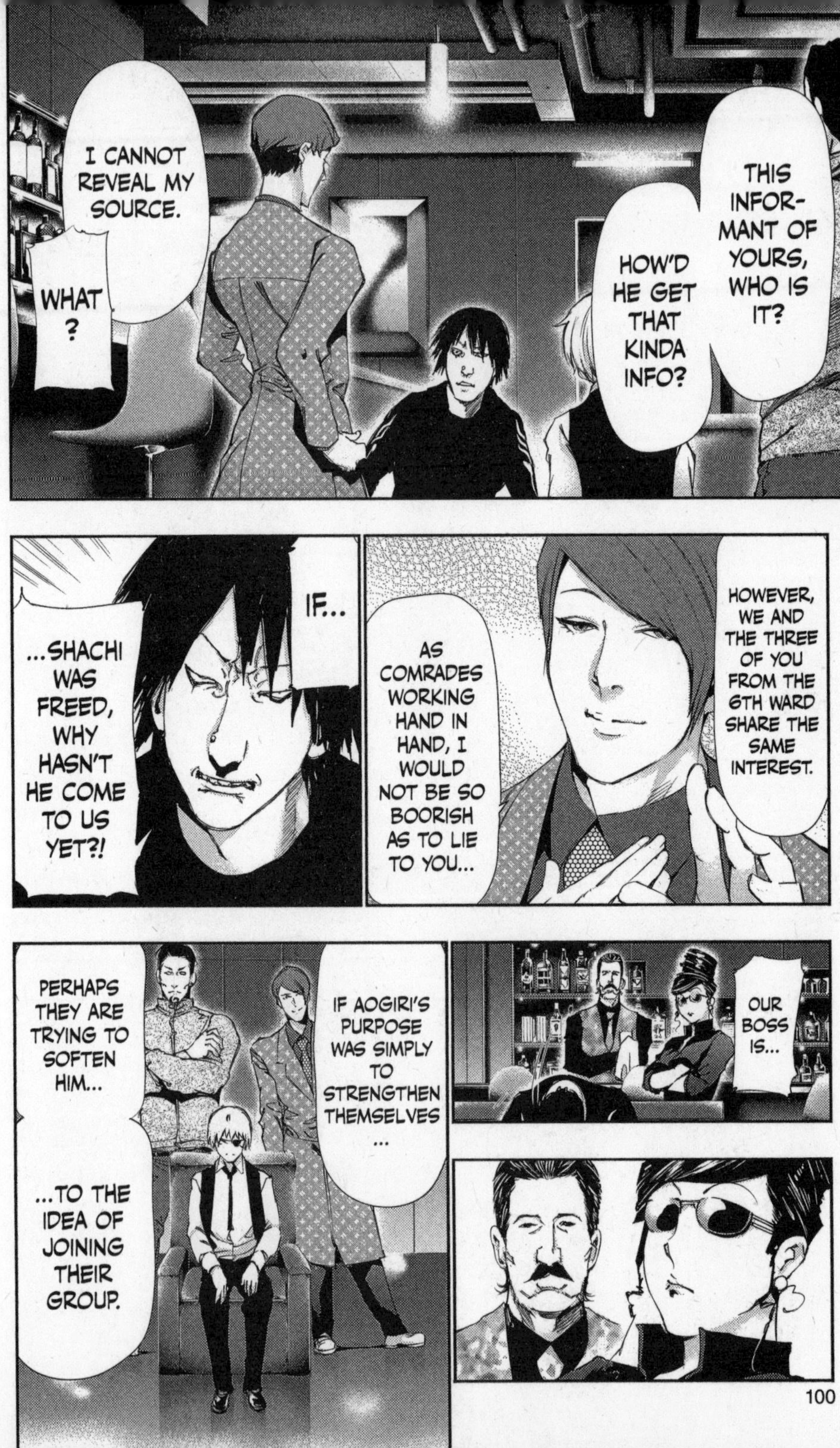
THIS INFORMANT OF YOURS, WHO IS IT?
HOW'D HE GET THAT KINDA INFO?
I CANNOT REVEAL MY SOURCE.
WHAT?
HOWEVER, WE AND THE THREE OF YOU FROM THE 6TH WARD SHARE THE SAME INTEREST.
AS COMRADES WORKING HAND IN HAND, I WOULD NOT BE SO BOORISH AS TO LIE TO YOU...
IF...
...SHACHI WAS FREED, WHY HASN'T HE COME TO US YET?!
OUR BOSS IS...
IF AOGIRI'S PURPOSE WAS SIMPLY TO STRENGTHEN THEMSELVES...
PERHAPS THEY ARE TRYING TO SOFTEN HIM...
...TO THE IDEA OF JOINING THEIR GROUP.

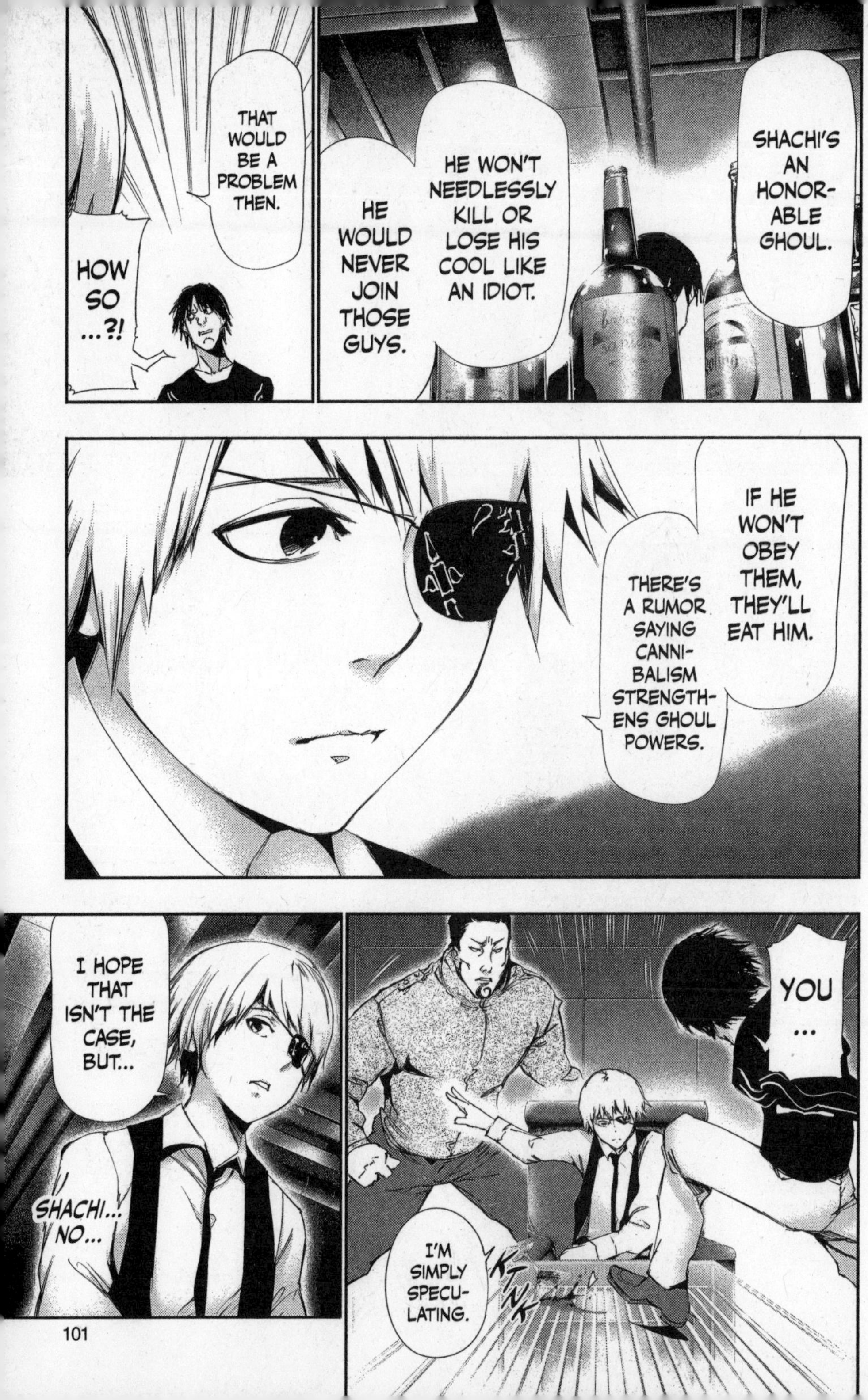
SHACHI'S AN HONORABLE GHOUL.
HE WON'T NEEDLESSLY KILL OR LOSE HIS COOL LIKE AN IDIOT.
HE WOULD NEVER JOIN THOSE GUYS.
THAT WOULD BE A PROBLEM THEN.
HOW SO ...?!
IF HE WON'T OBEY THEM, THEY'LL EAT HIM.
THERE'S A RUMOR SAYING CANNIBALISM STRENGTHENS GHOUL POWERS.
YOU ...
KTINK
I'M SIMPLY SPECULATING.
I HOPE THAT ISN'T THE CASE, BUT...
SHACHI... NO...

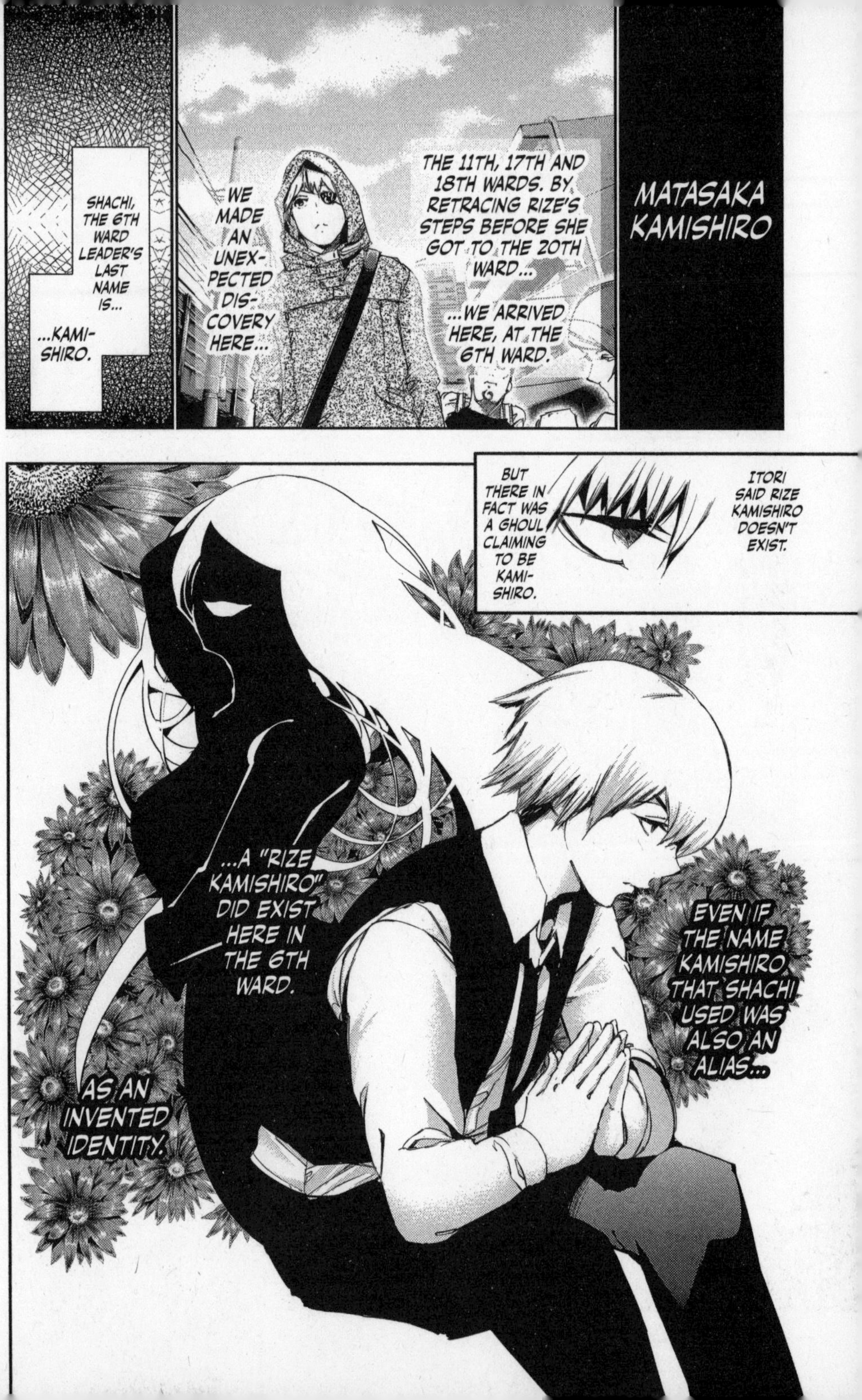
MATASAKA KAMISHIRO
THE 11TH, 17TH AND 18TH WARDS. BY RETRACING RIZE'S STEPS BEFORE SHE GOT TO THE 20TH WARD...
...WE ARRIVED HERE, AT THE 6TH WARD.
WE MADE AN UNEX-PECTED DIS-COVERY HERE...
SHACHI, THE 6TH WARD LEADER'S LAST NAME IS...
...KAMI-SHIRO.
ITORI SAID RIZE KAMISHIRO DOESN'T EXIST.
BUT THERE IN FACT WAS A GHOUL CLAIMING TO BE KAMI-SHIRO.
EVEN IF THE NAME KAMISHIRO THAT SHACHI USED WAS ALSO AN ALIAS...
...A "RIZE KAMISHIRO" DID EXIST HERE IN THE 6TH WARD.
AS AN INVENTED IDENTITY.

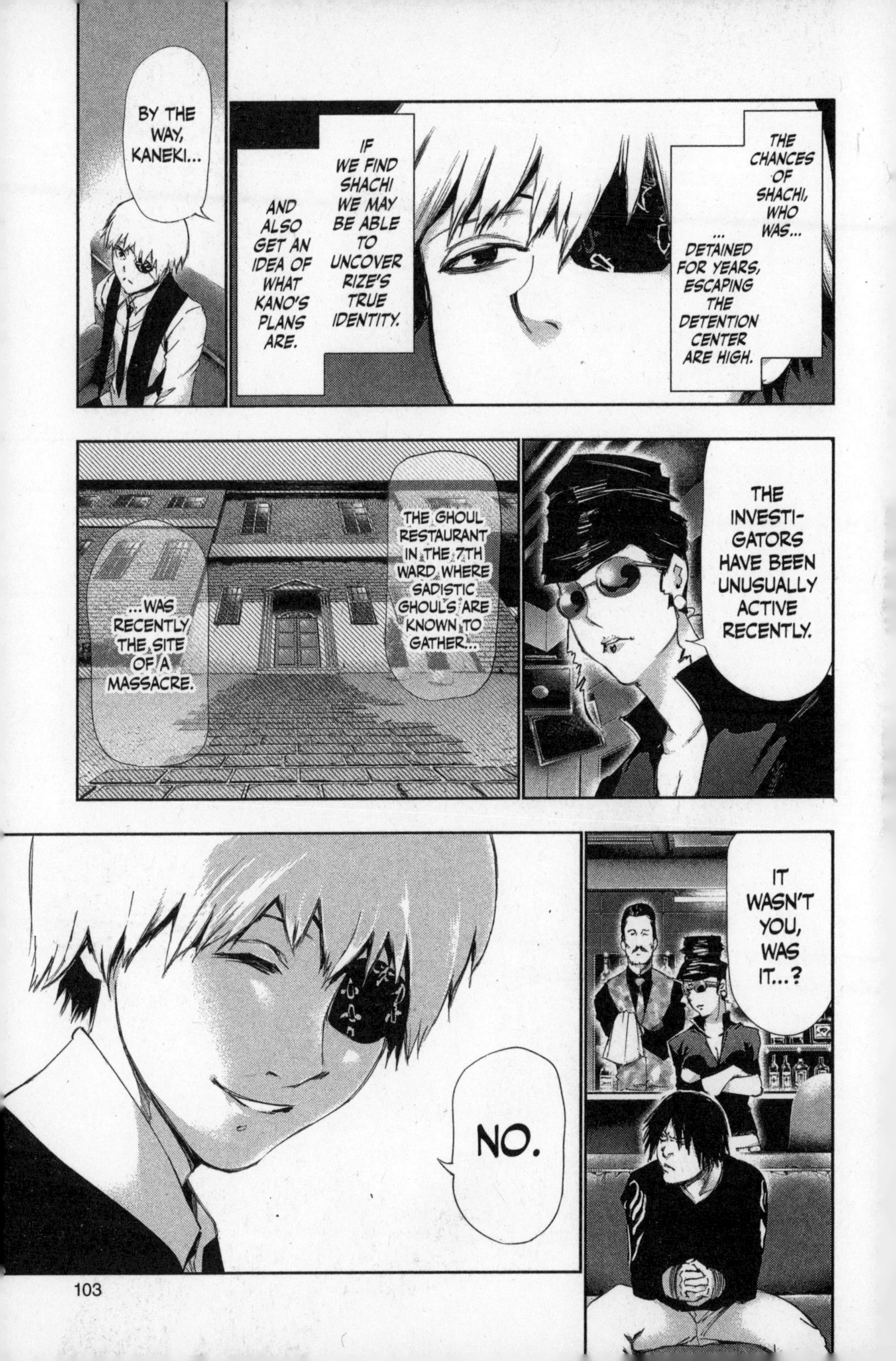
THE CHANCES OF SHACHI, WHO WAS...
...DETAINED FOR YEARS, ESCAPING THE DETENTION CENTER ARE HIGH.
IF WE FIND SHACHI WE MAY BE ABLE TO UNCOVER RIZE'S TRUE IDENTITY.
AND ALSO GET AN IDEA OF WHAT KANO'S PLANS ARE.
BY THE WAY, KANEKI...
THE INVESTIGATORS HAVE BEEN UNUSUALLY ACTIVE RECENTLY.
THE GHOUL RESTAURANT IN THE 7TH WARD WHERE SADISTIC GHOULS ARE KNOWN TO GATHER...
...WAS RECENTLY THE SITE OF A MASSACRE.
IT WASN'T YOU, WAS IT...?
NO.

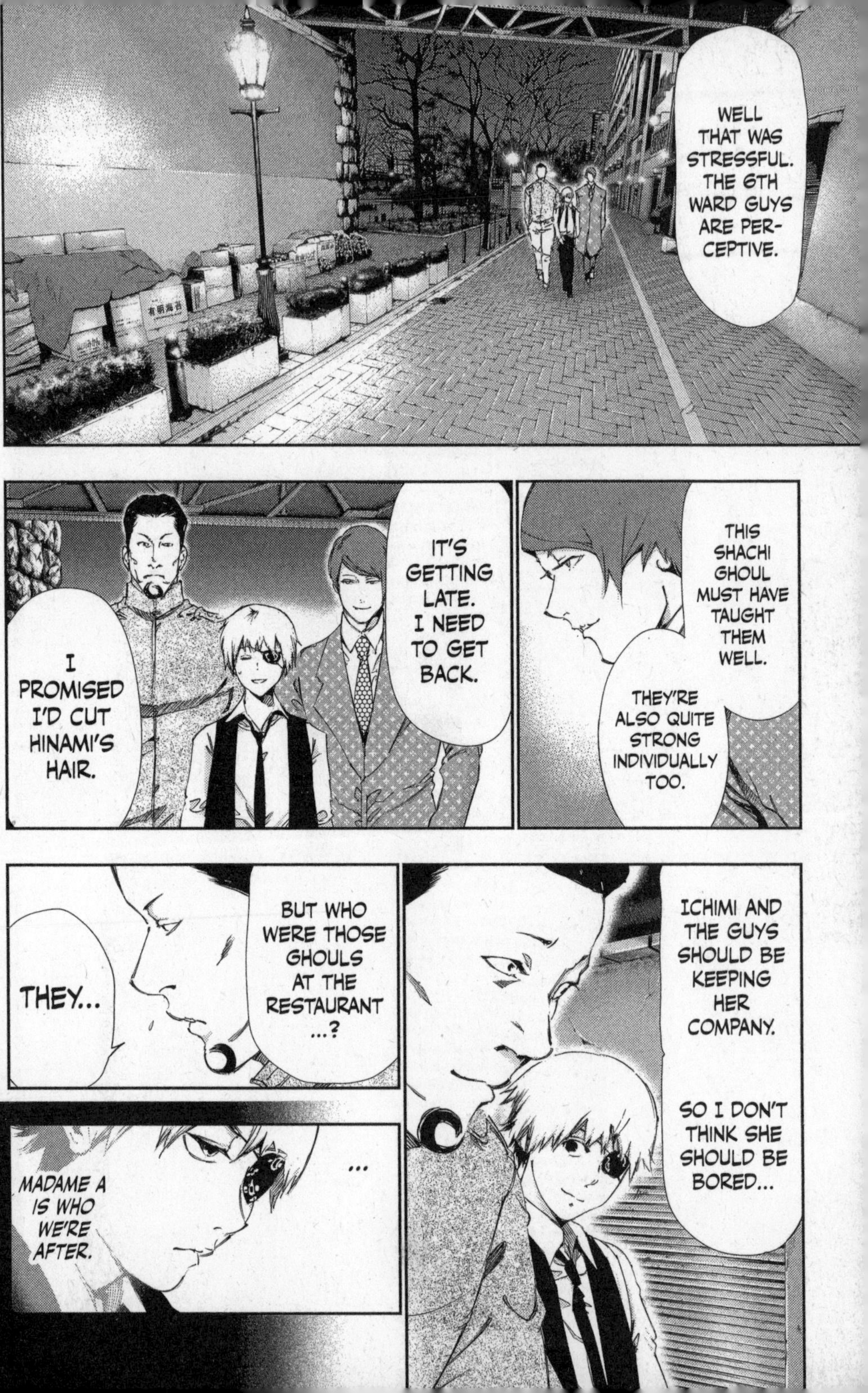
WELL THAT WAS STRESSFUL. THE 6TH WARD GUYS ARE PERCEPTIVE.
THIS SHACHI GHOUL MUST HAVE TAUGHT THEM WELL.
THEY'RE ALSO QUITE STRONG INDIVIDUALLY TOO.
IT'S GETTING LATE. I NEED TO GET BACK.
I PROMISED I'D CUT HINAMI'S HAIR.
ICHIMI AND THE GUYS SHOULD BE KEEPING HER COMPANY.
SO I DON'T THINK SHE SHOULD BE BORED...
BUT WHO WERE THOSE GHOULS AT THE RESTAURANT ...?
THEY...
...
MADAME A IS WHO WE'RE AFTER.

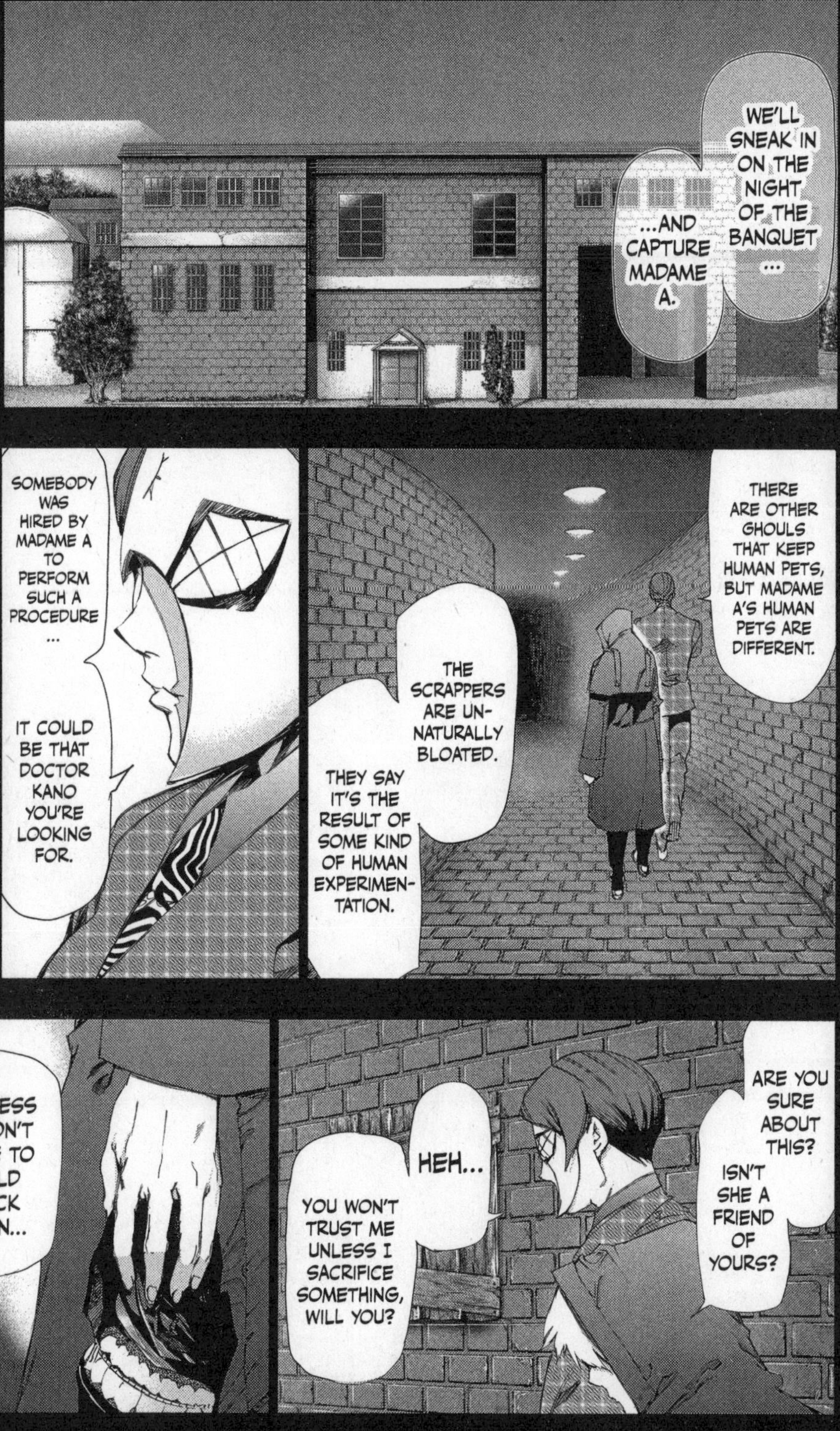
WE'LL SNEAK IN ON THE NIGHT OF THE BANQUET...
...AND CAPTURE MADAME A.
THERE ARE OTHER GHOULS THAT KEEP HUMAN PETS, BUT MADAME A'S HUMAN PETS ARE DIFFERENT.
THE SCRAPPERS ARE UNNATURALLY BLOATED.
THEY SAY IT'S THE RESULT OF SOME KIND OF HUMAN EXPERIMENTATION.
SOMEBODY WAS HIRED BY MADAME A TO PERFORM SUCH A PROCEDURE...
IT COULD BE THAT DOCTOR KANO YOU'RE LOOKING FOR.
ARE YOU SURE ABOUT THIS?
ISN'T SHE A FRIEND OF YOURS?
HEH...
YOU WON'T TRUST ME UNLESS I SACRIFICE SOMETHING, WILL YOU?
I GUESS I WON'T HAVE TO HOLD BACK THEN...

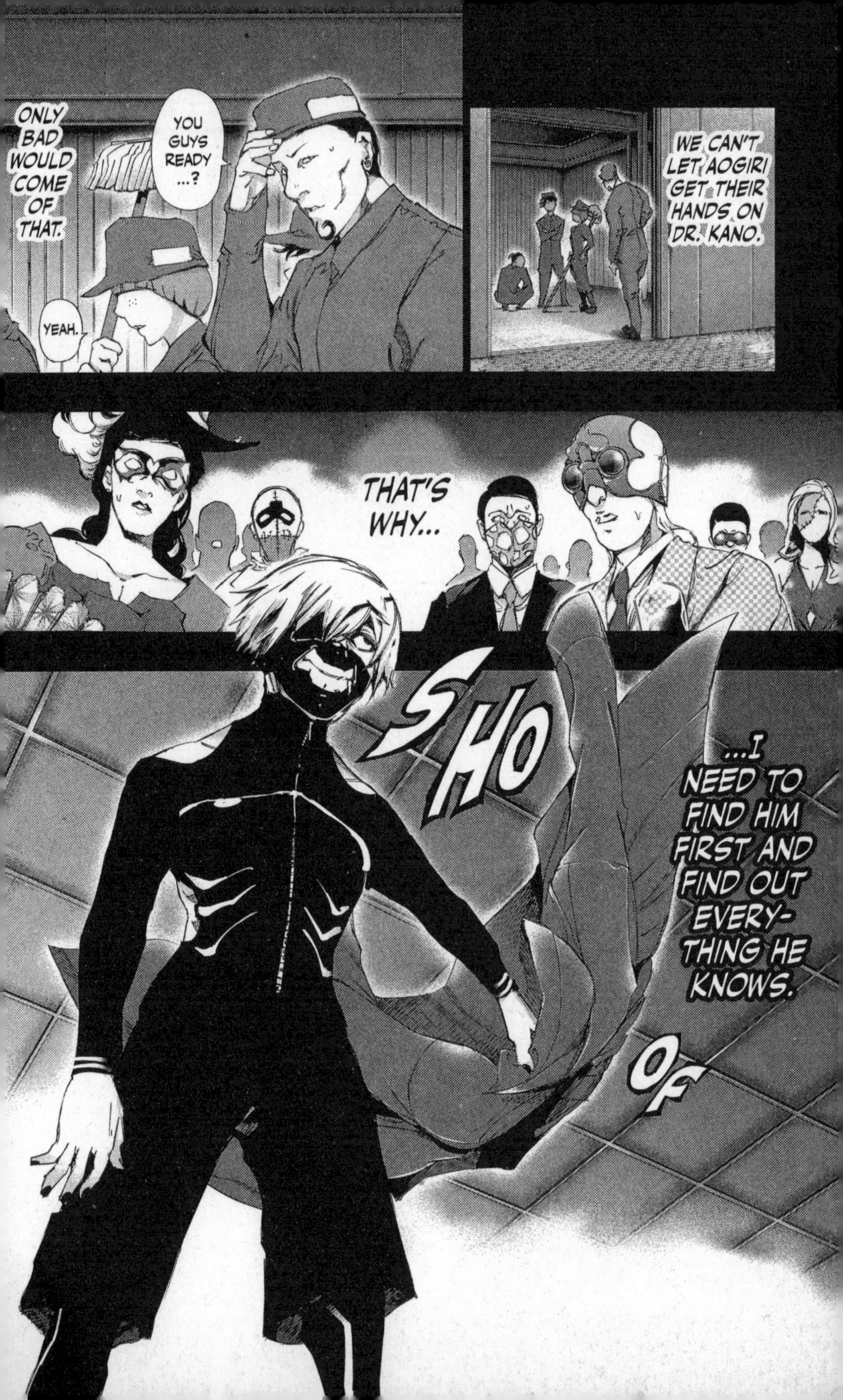
WE CAN'T LET AOGIRI GET THEIR HANDS ON DR. KANO.
ONLY BAD WOULD COME OF THAT.
YOU GUYS READY ...?
YEAH.
THAT'S WHY...
...I NEED TO FIND HIM FIRST AND FIND OUT EVERY-THING HE KNOWS.
SHO
OF

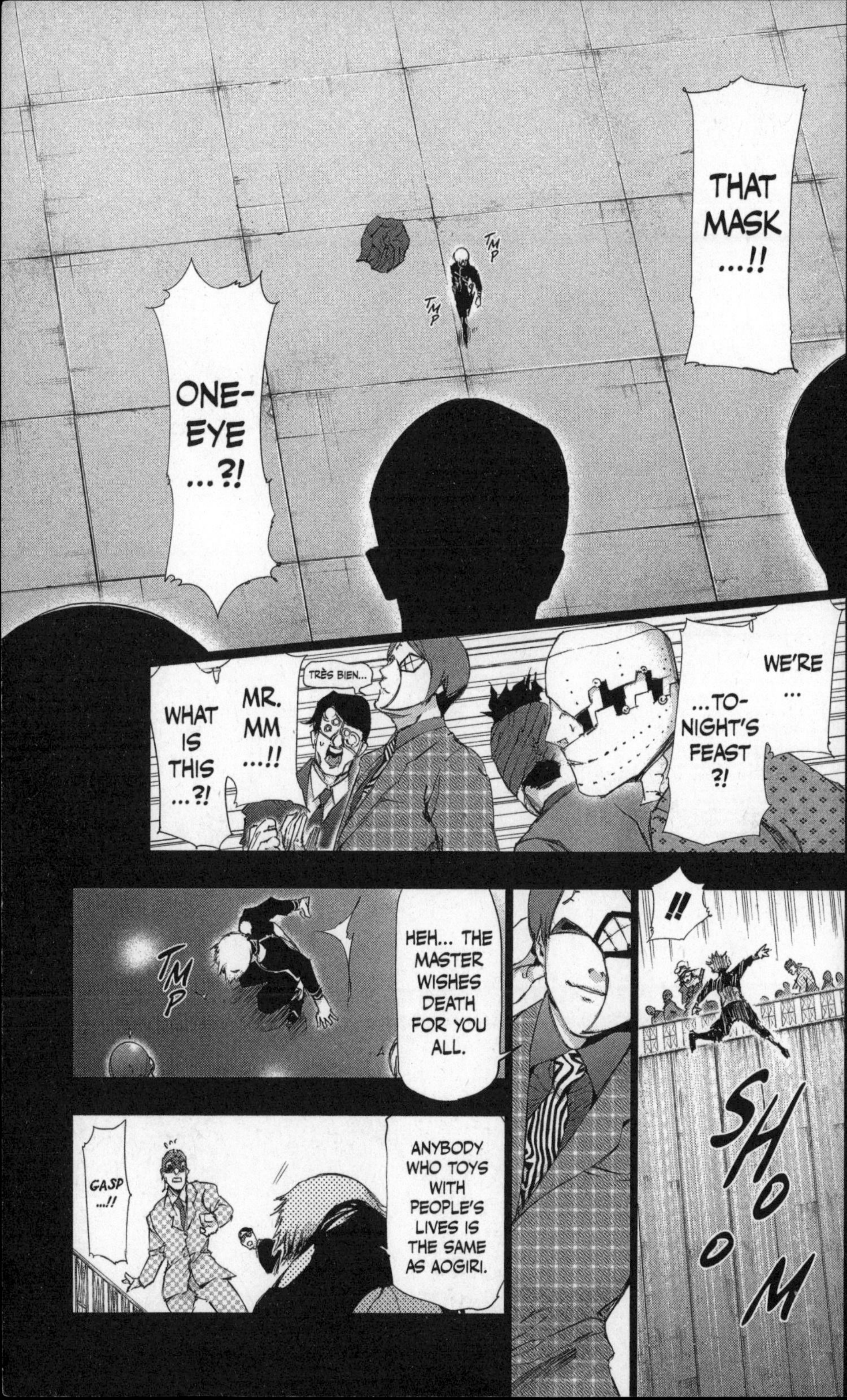
THAT MASK ...!!
TMP
TMP
ONE-EYE ...?!
WE'RE ...
...TO-NIGHT'S FEAST ?!
TRÈS BIEN...
MR. MM ...!!
WHAT IS THIS ...?!
!!
SHOOOM
TMP
HEH... THE MASTER WISHES DEATH FOR YOU ALL.
ANYBODY WHO TOYS WITH PEOPLE'S LIVES IS THE SAME AS AOGIRI.
GASP ...!!

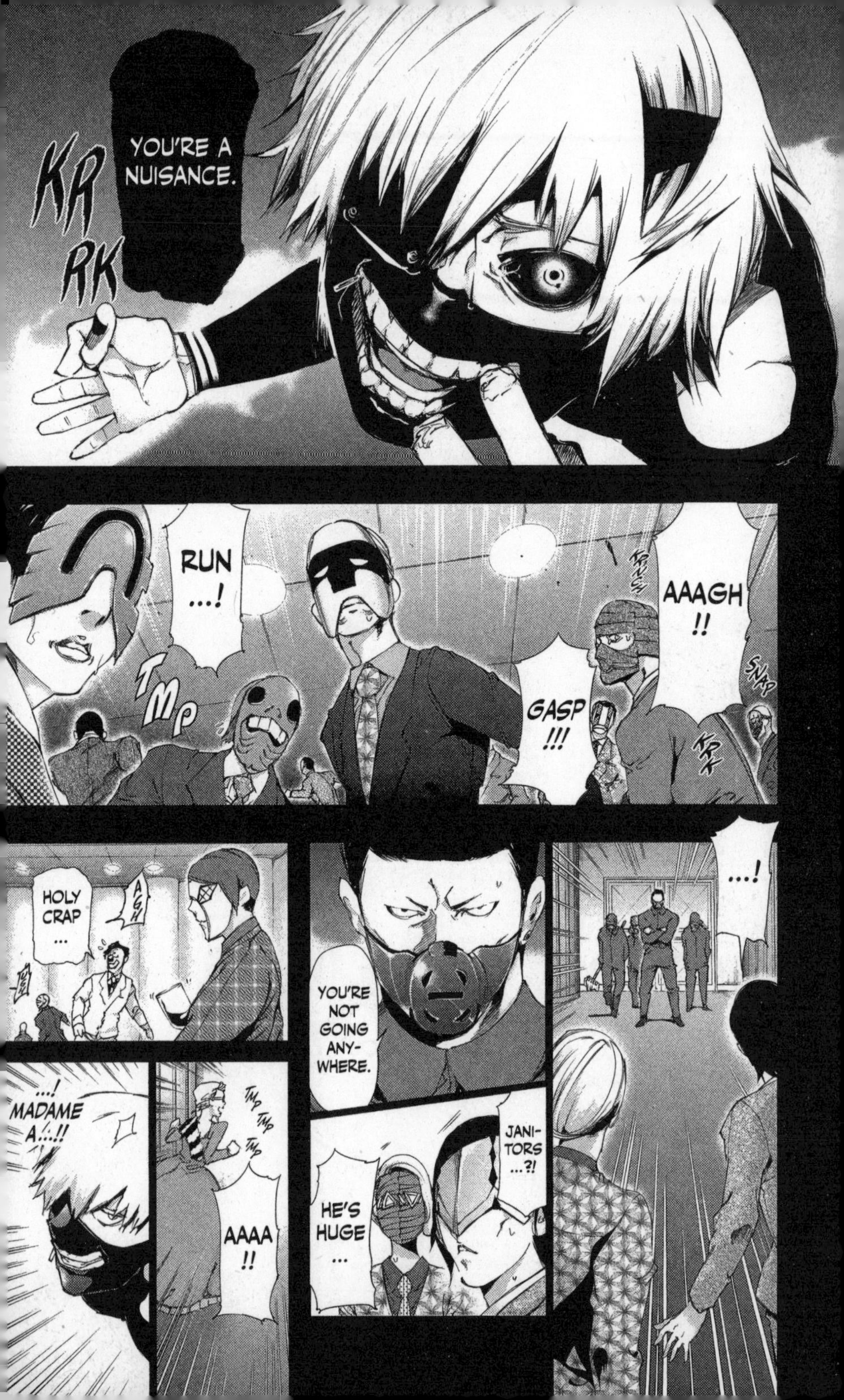
YOU'RE A NUISANCE.
KR RK
AAAGH !!
SNAP
KRK
GASP !!!
RUN ...!
TMP
...!
YOU'RE NOT GOING ANY-WHERE.
HOLY CRAP ...
AGH
JANI-TORS ...?!
HE'S HUGE ...
TMP TMP TMP
AAAA !!
...! MADAME A...!!

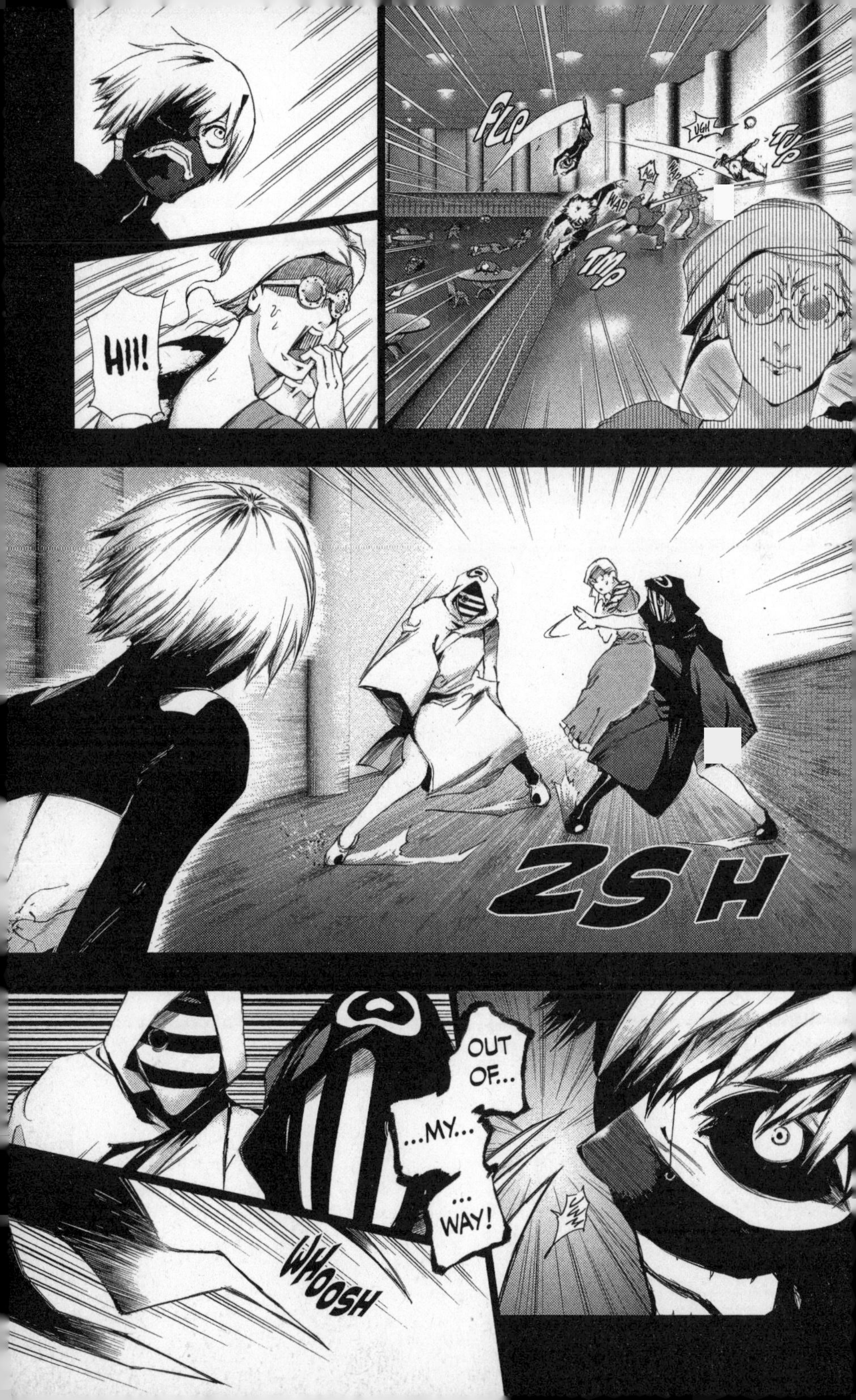
FUP
UGH
AGH
WAP
WAP
FLP
TMP
HIII!
ZSH
UMM
OUT OF...
...MY...
...WAY!
WHOOSH

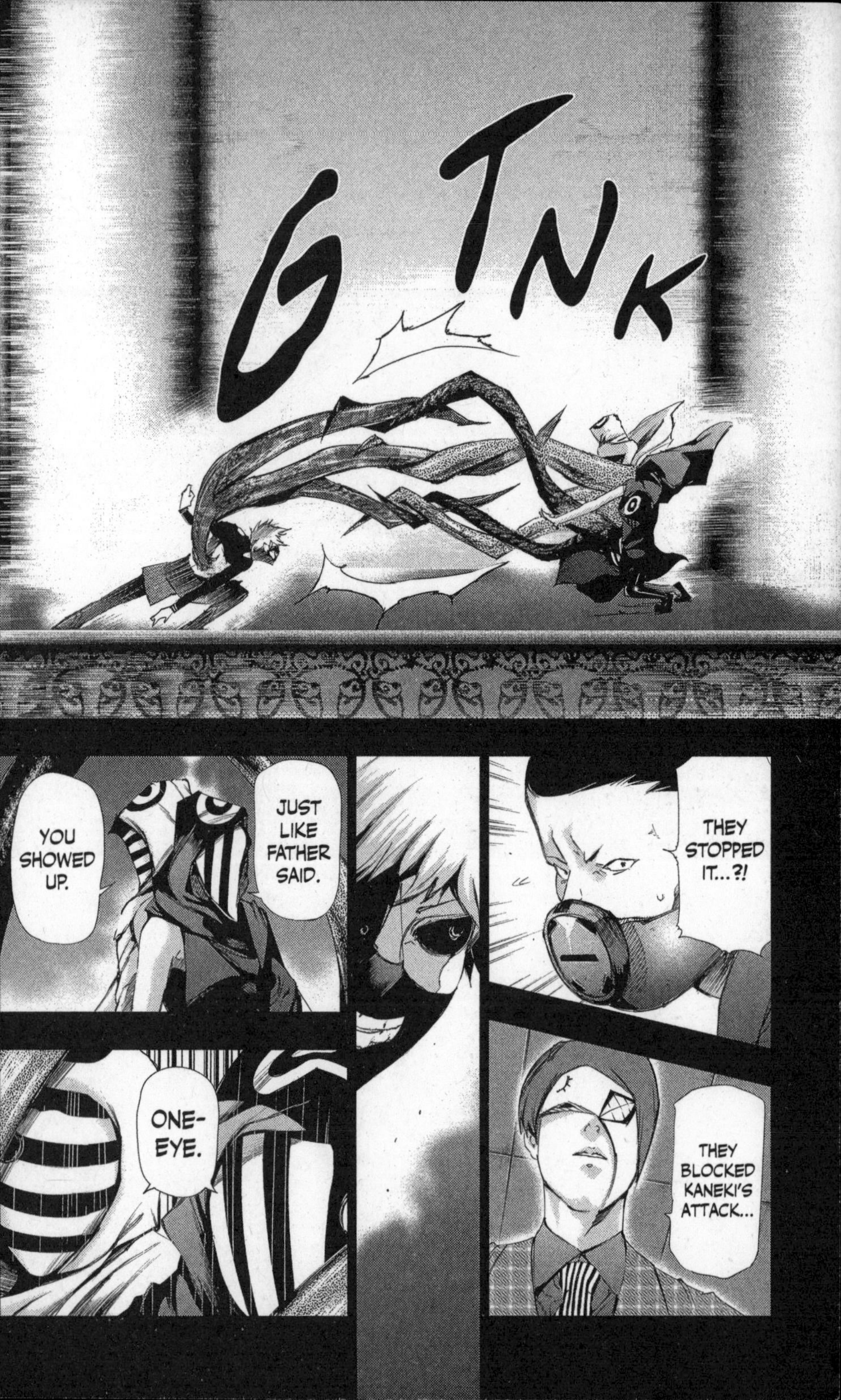
GTNK
THEY STOPPED IT...?!
THEY BLOCKED KANEKI'S ATTACK...
JUST LIKE FATHER SAID.
YOU SHOWED UP.
ONE-EYE.

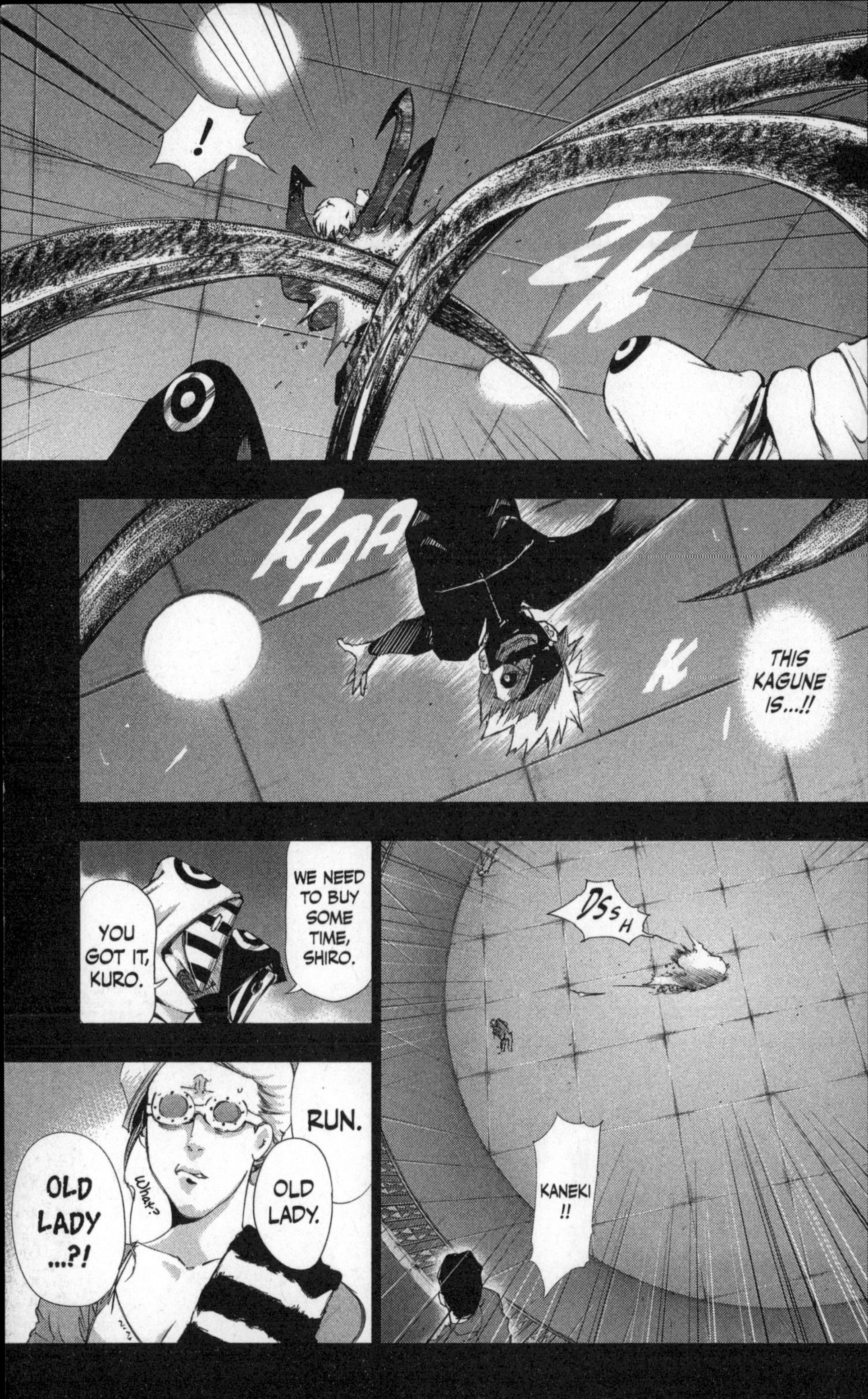
!
ZNK
THIS KAGUNE IS...!!
RAAK
DSSH
KANEKI !!
WE NEED TO BUY SOME TIME, SHIRO.
YOU GOT IT, KURO.
RUN.
OLD LADY.
What?
OLD LADY ...?!

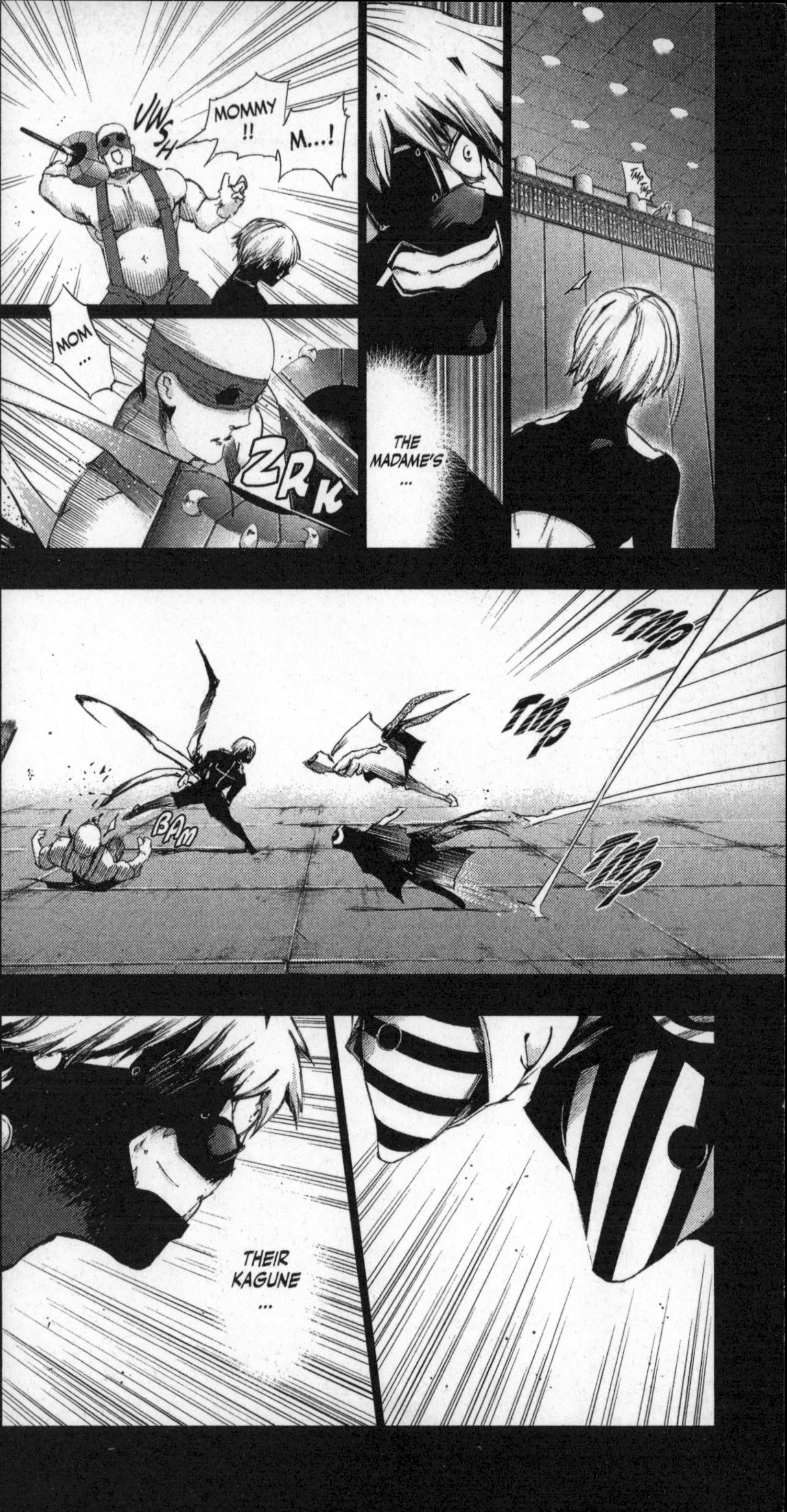
TMP TMP
THE MADAME'S ...
MOMMY !!
M...!
UWSH
MOM ...
ZRK
TMP
TMP
TMP
BAM
THEIR KAGUNE ...

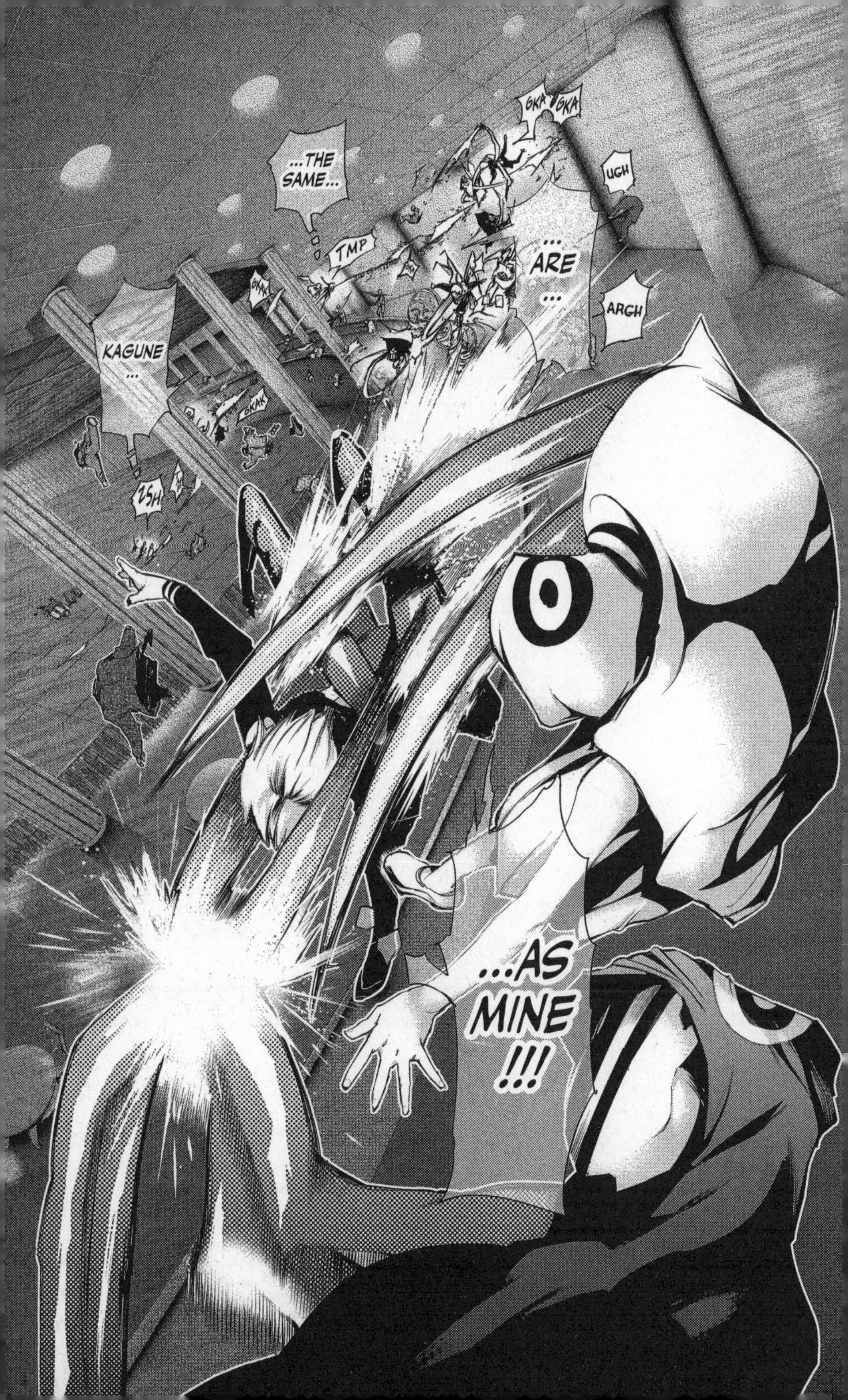
GKA GKA
UGH
ARGH
KAGUNE...
...ARE...
...THE SAME...
TMP
GKAK
ZSH
...AS MINE!!!

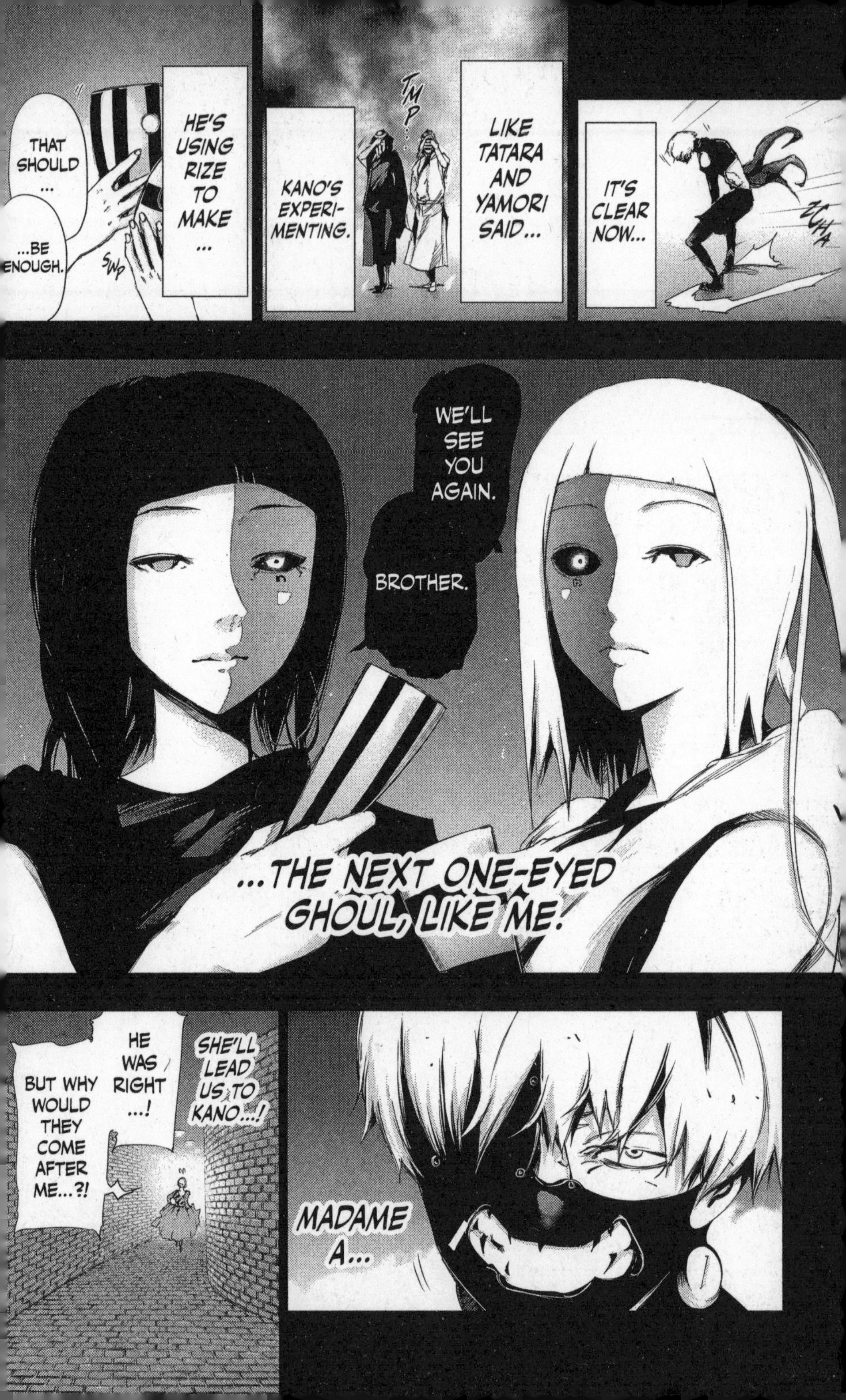
IT'S CLEAR NOW...
ZCHA
LIKE TATARA AND YAMORI SAID...
TMP...
KANO'S EXPERI-MENTING.
HE'S USING RIZE TO MAKE...
THAT SHOULD...
...BE ENOUGH.
SWP
WE'LL SEE YOU AGAIN.
BROTHER.
...THE NEXT ONE-EYED GHOUL, LIKE ME.
MADAME A...
SHE'LL LEAD US TO KANO...!
HE WAS RIGHT...!
BUT WHY WOULD THEY COME AFTER ME...?!

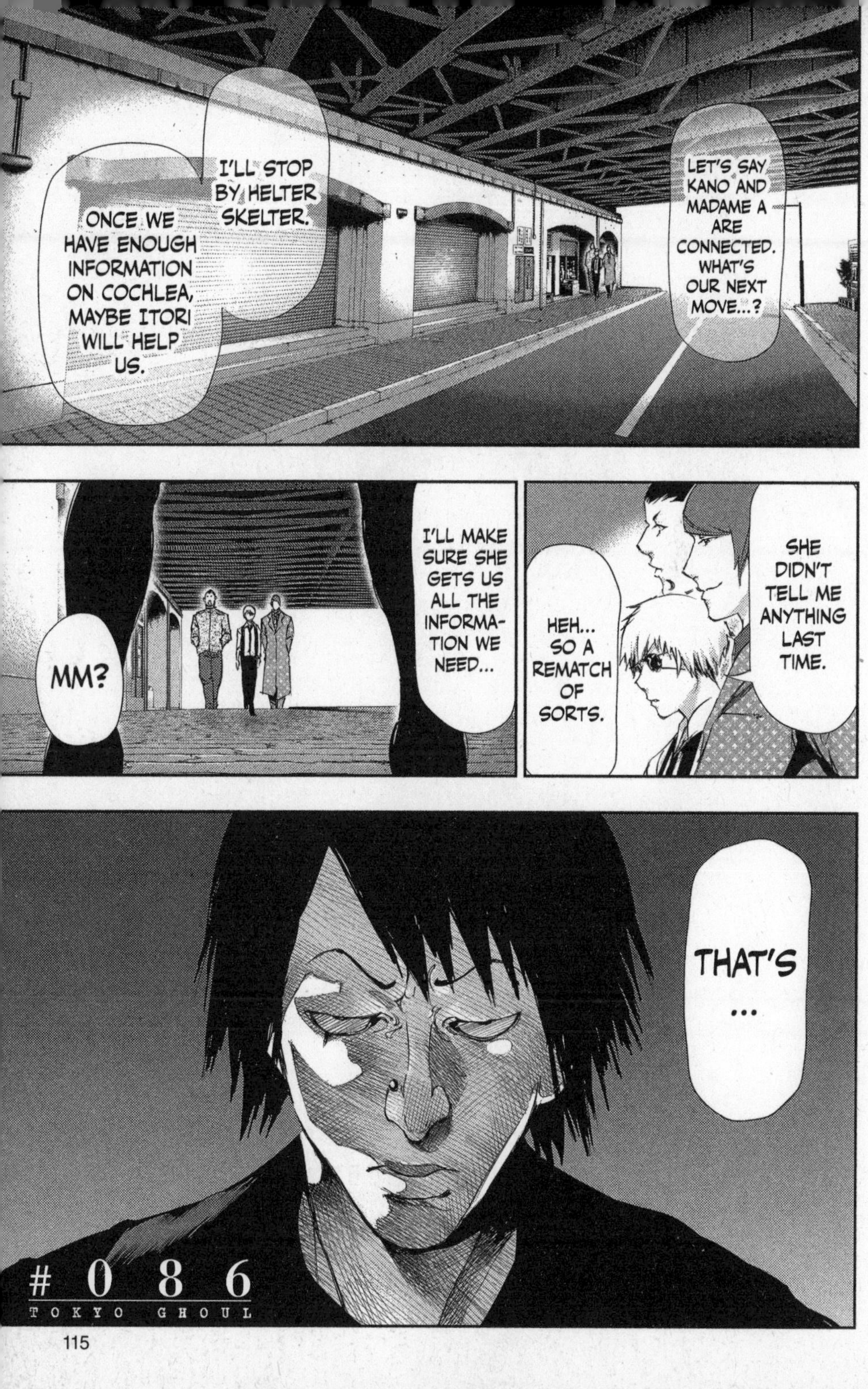
LET'S SAY KANO AND MADAME A ARE CONNECTED. WHAT'S OUR NEXT MOVE...?
I'LL STOP BY HELTER SKELTER.
ONCE WE HAVE ENOUGH INFORMATION ON COCHLEA, MAYBE ITORI WILL HELP US.
SHE DIDN'T TELL ME ANYTHING LAST TIME.
HEH... SO A REMATCH OF SORTS.
I'LL MAKE SURE SHE GETS US ALL THE INFORMATION WE NEED...
MM?
THAT'S ...
#086
TOKYO GHOUL

#086 [VISITOR]

TOKYO GHOUL

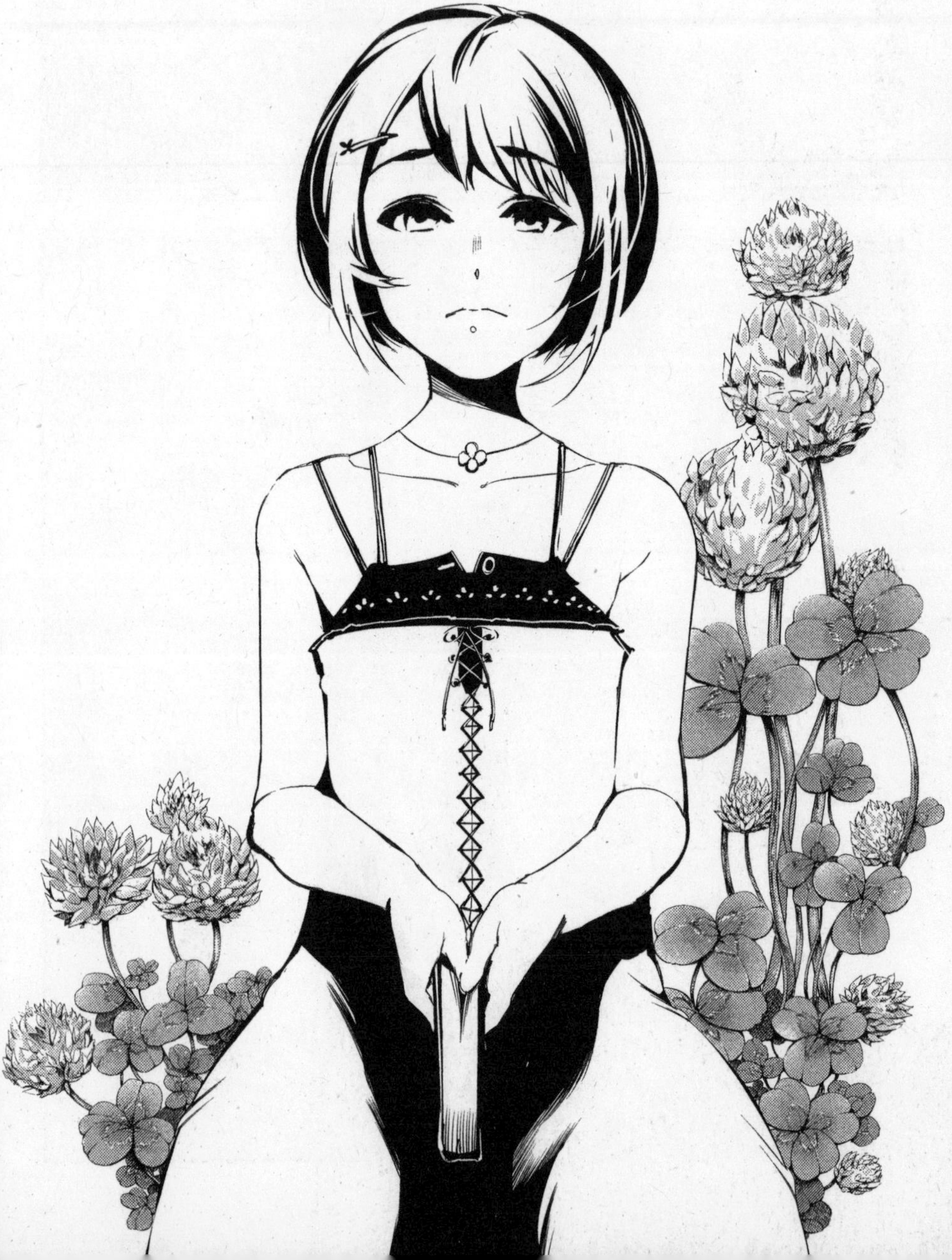

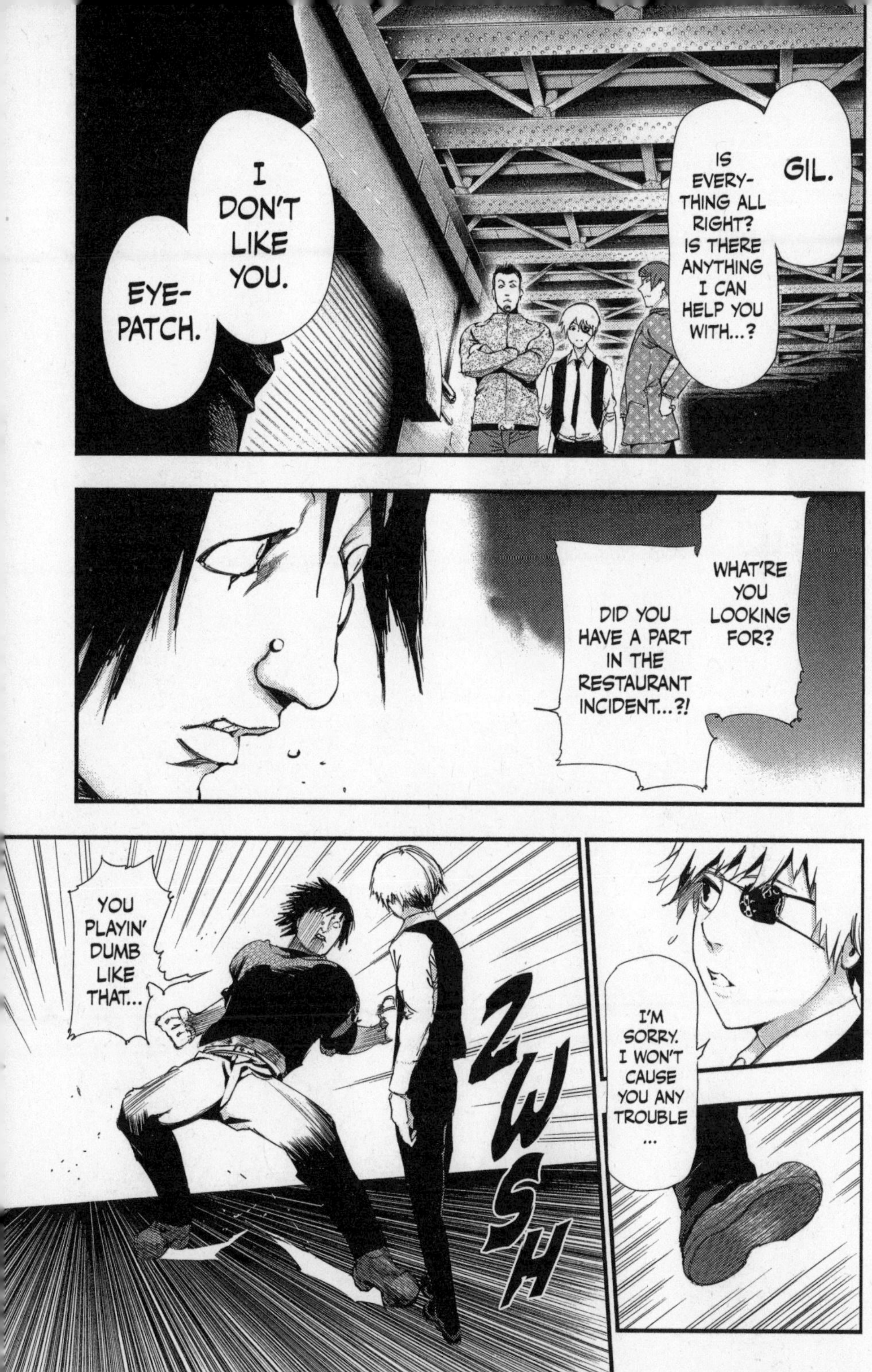
GIL.
IS EVERYTHING ALL RIGHT? IS THERE ANYTHING I CAN HELP YOU WITH...?
I DON'T LIKE YOU.
EYE-PATCH.
WHAT'RE YOU LOOKING FOR?
DID YOU HAVE A PART IN THE RESTAURANT INCIDENT...?!
I'M SORRY. I WON'T CAUSE YOU ANY TROUBLE ...
YOU PLAYIN' DUMB LIKE THAT...
ZWSH

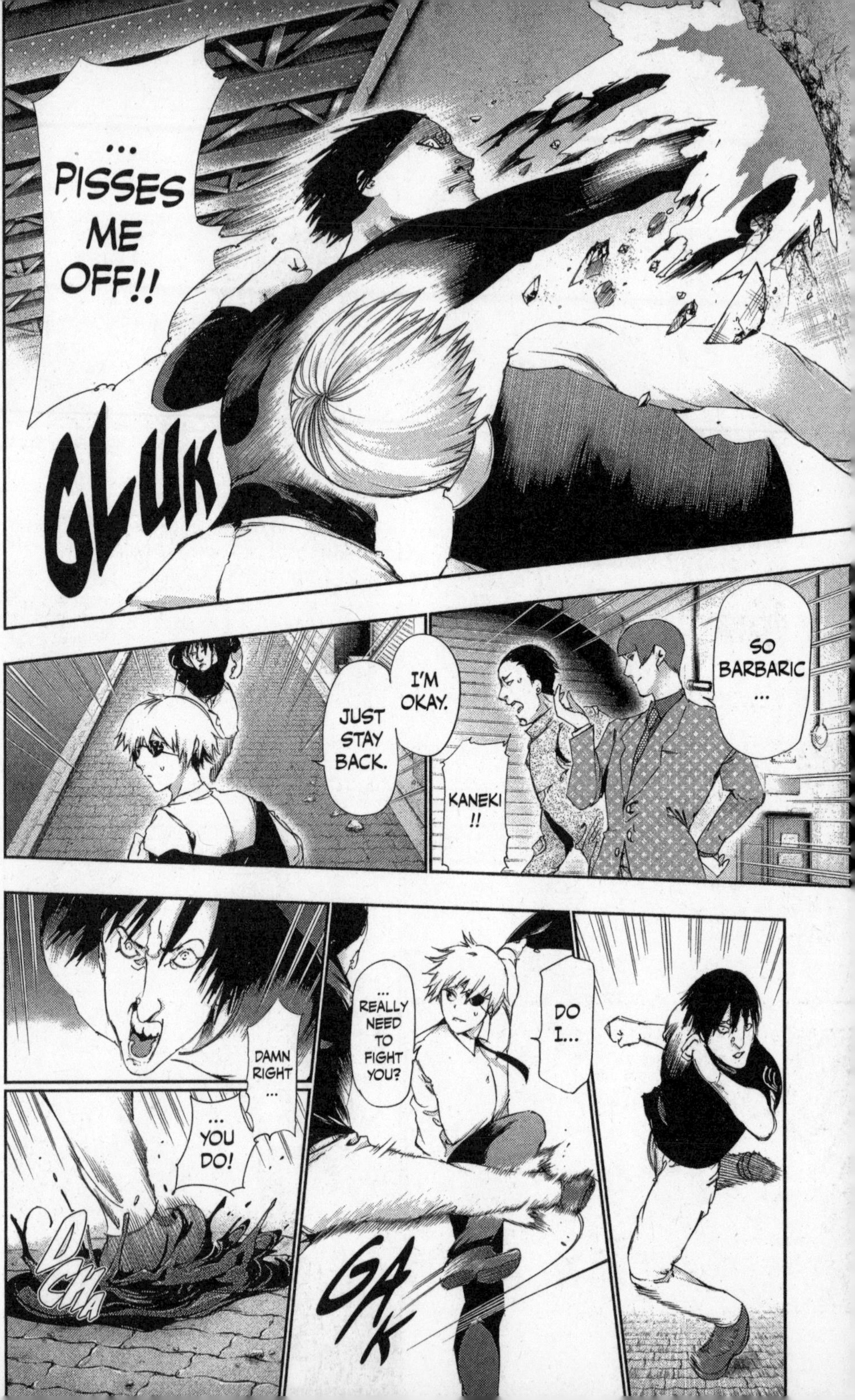

... PISSES ME OFF!!
GLUK
SO BARBARIC ...
KANEKI !!
I'M OKAY.
JUST STAY BACK.
DO I...
... REALLY NEED TO FIGHT YOU?
GAK
DAMN RIGHT ...
... YOU DO!
DOCHA

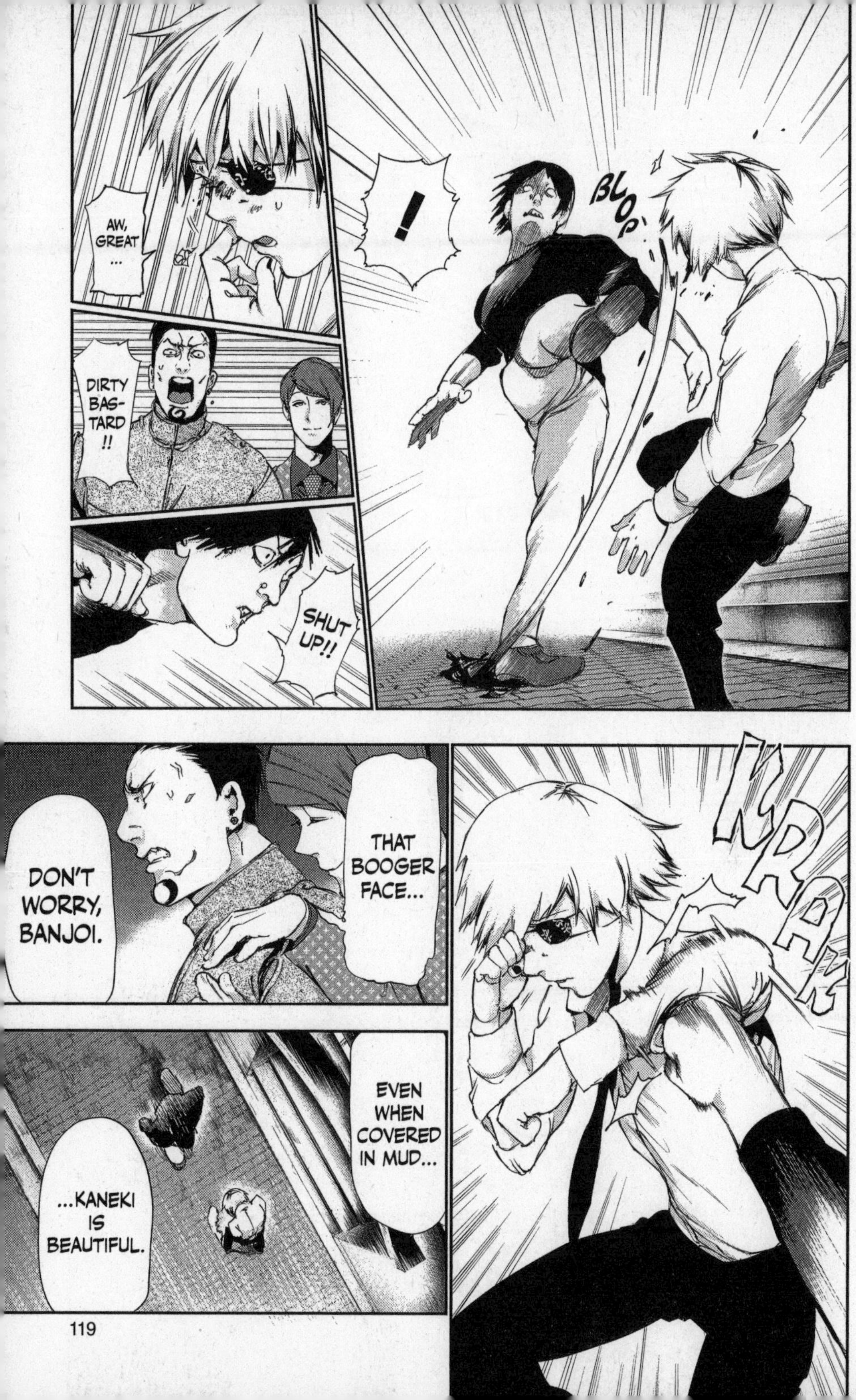
BLOP
!
AW, GREAT ...
DIRTY BASTARD !!
SHUT UP!!
KRAK
THAT BOOGER FACE...
DON'T WORRY, BANJOI.
EVEN WHEN COVERED IN MUD...
...KANEKI IS BEAUTIFUL.

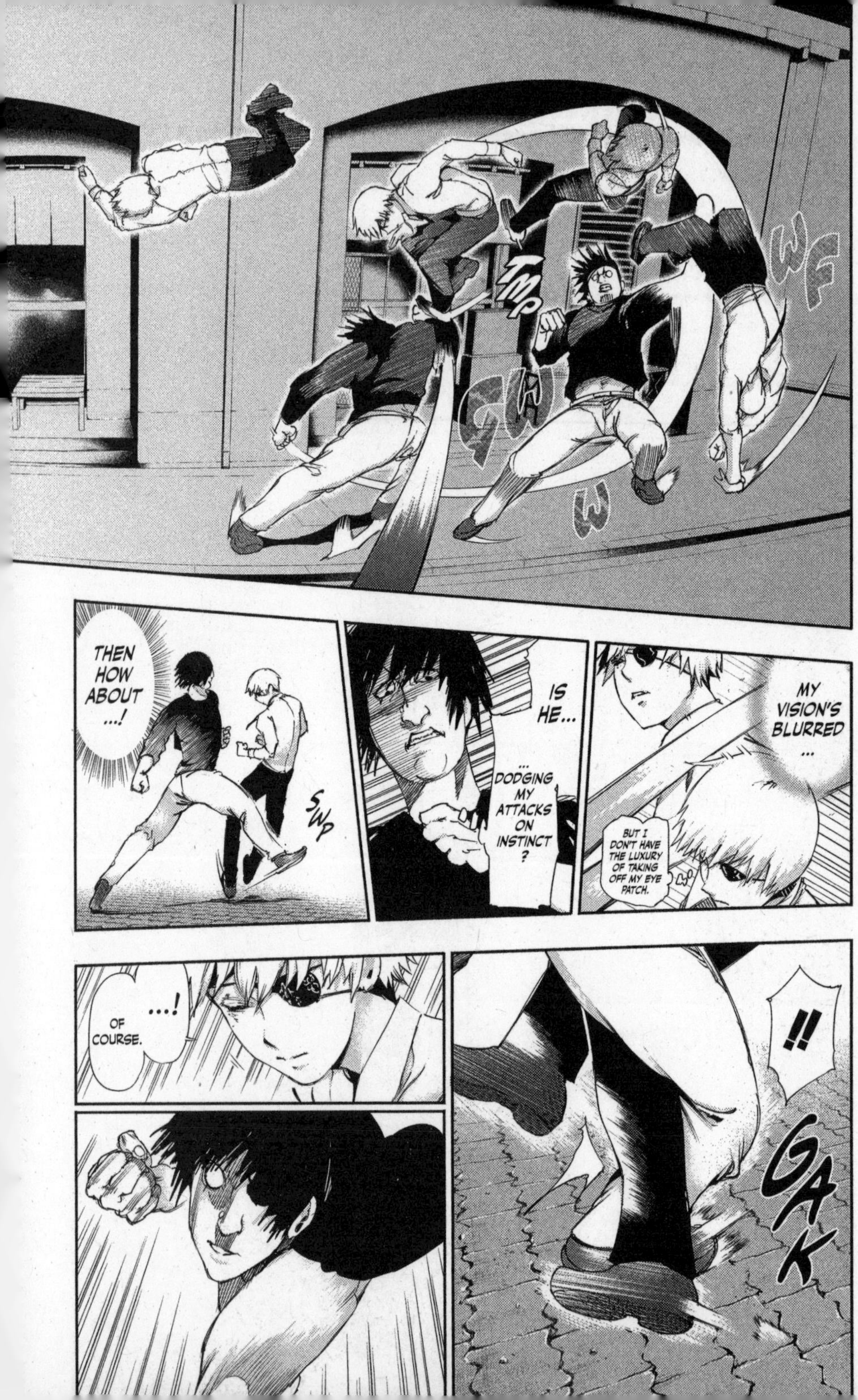
WF
TMP
GWA
W
MY VISION'S BLURRED ...
BUT I DON'T HAVE THE LUXURY OF TAKING OFF MY EYE PATCH.
IS HE...
... DODGING MY ATTACKS ON INSTINCT ?
THEN HOW ABOUT ...!
SWP
!!
GAK
...!
OF COURSE.

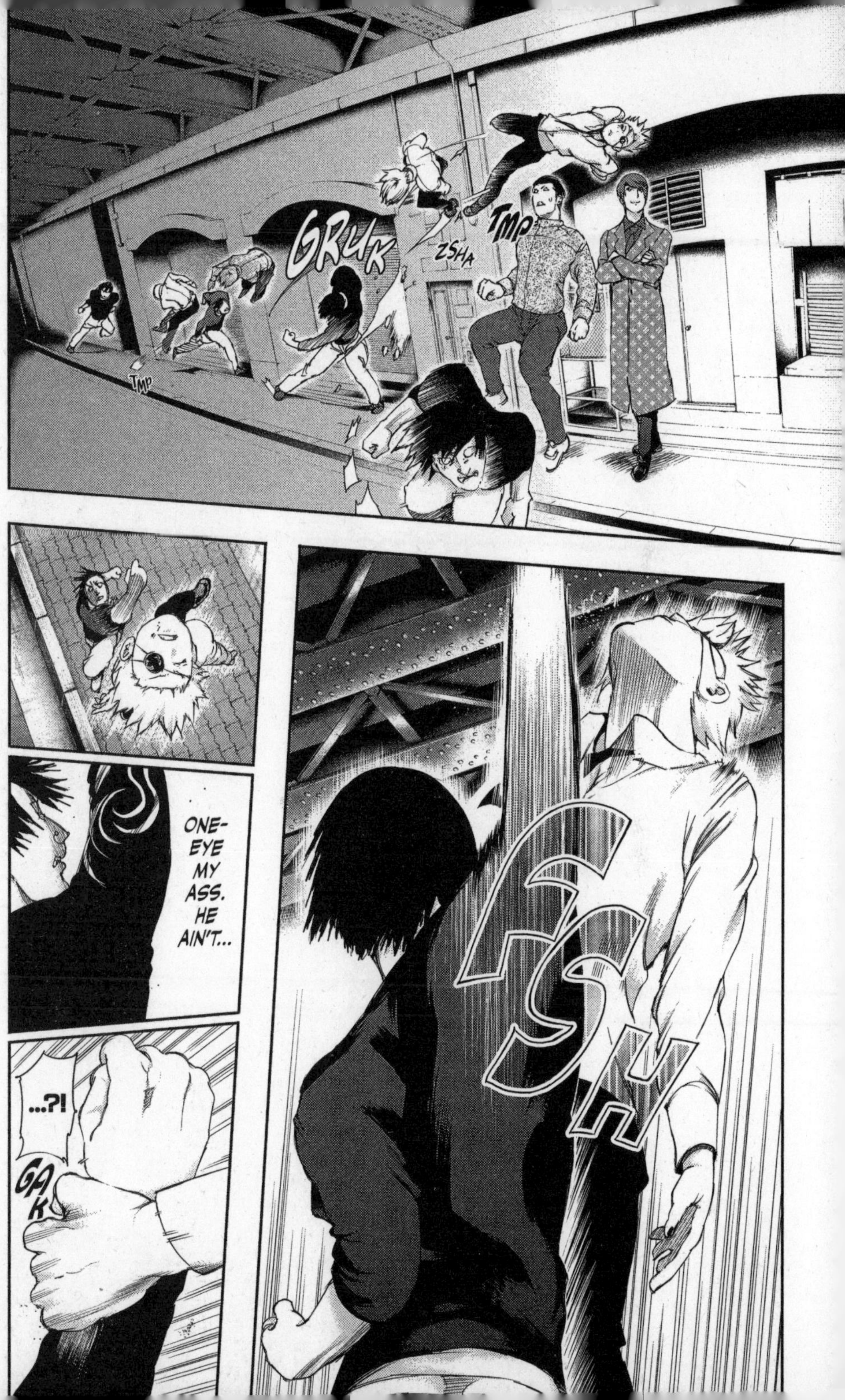
TMP
ZSHA
GRUK
TMP
FSSH
ONE-EYE MY ASS. HE AIN'T...
...?!
GAK

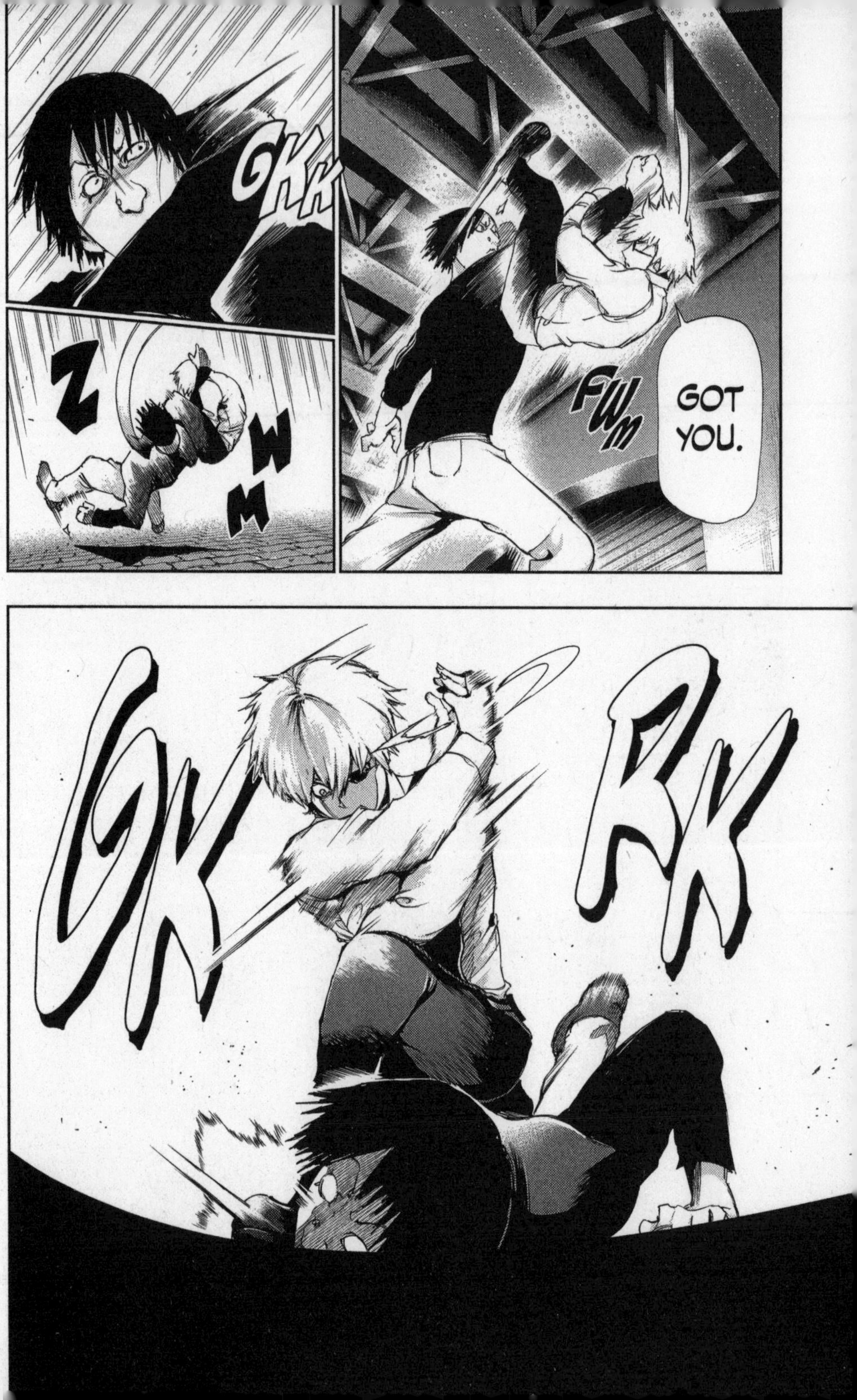
FWM
GOT YOU.
GKK
ZWM
GK
RK

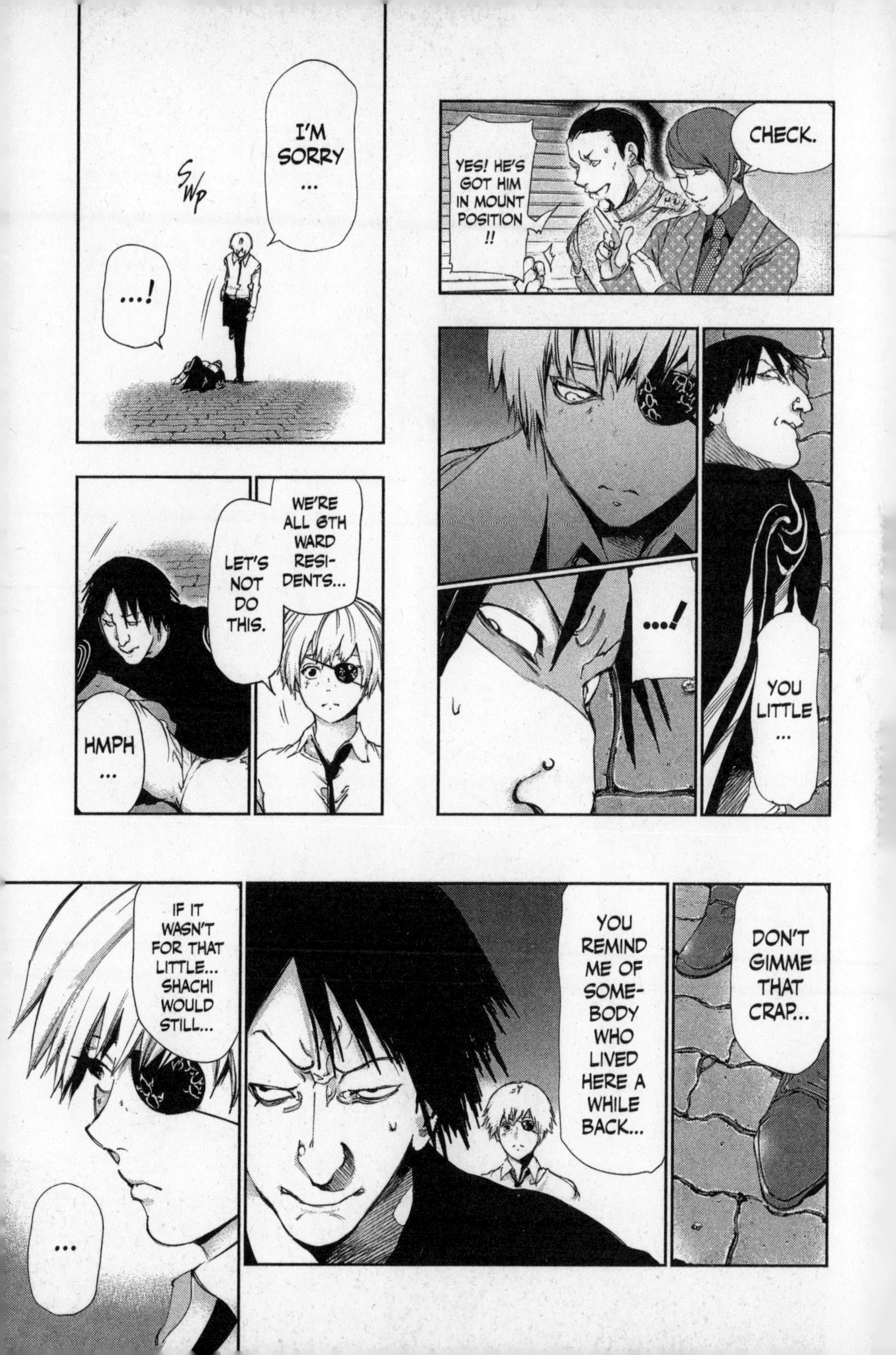
CHECK.
YES! HE'S GOT HIM IN MOUNT POSITION !!
I'M SORRY ...
SWP
...!
YOU LITTLE ...
...!
WE'RE ALL 6TH WARD RESI- DENTS...
LET'S NOT DO THIS.
HMPH ...
DON'T GIMME THAT CRAP...
YOU REMIND ME OF SOME- BODY WHO LIVED HERE A WHILE BACK...
IF IT WASN'T FOR THAT LITTLE... SHACHI WOULD STILL...
...

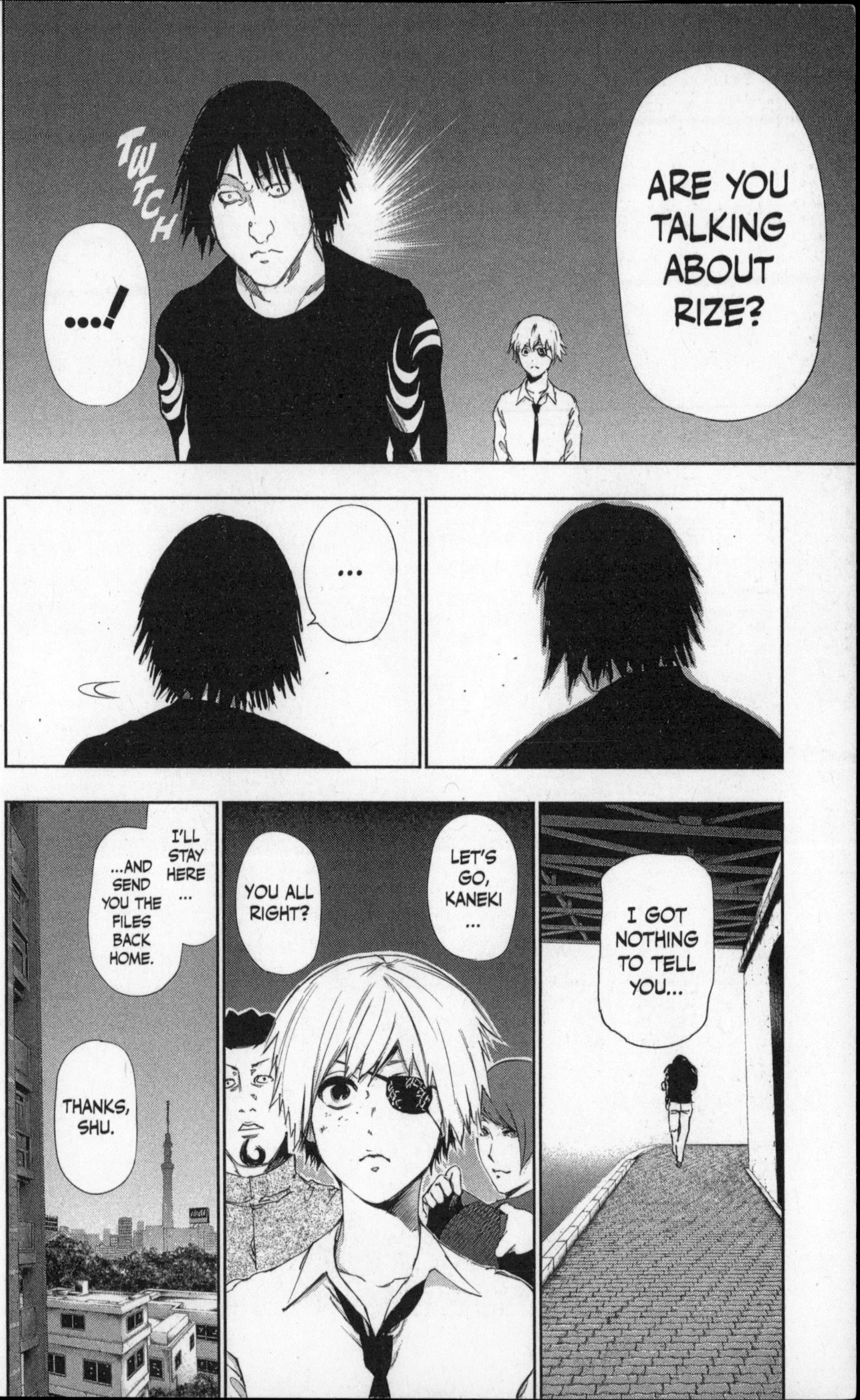
ARE YOU TALKING ABOUT RIZE?
TWITCH
...!
...
I GOT NOTHING TO TELL YOU...
LET'S GO, KANEKI ...
YOU ALL RIGHT?
I'LL STAY HERE ...
...AND SEND YOU THE FILES BACK HOME.
THANKS, SHU.

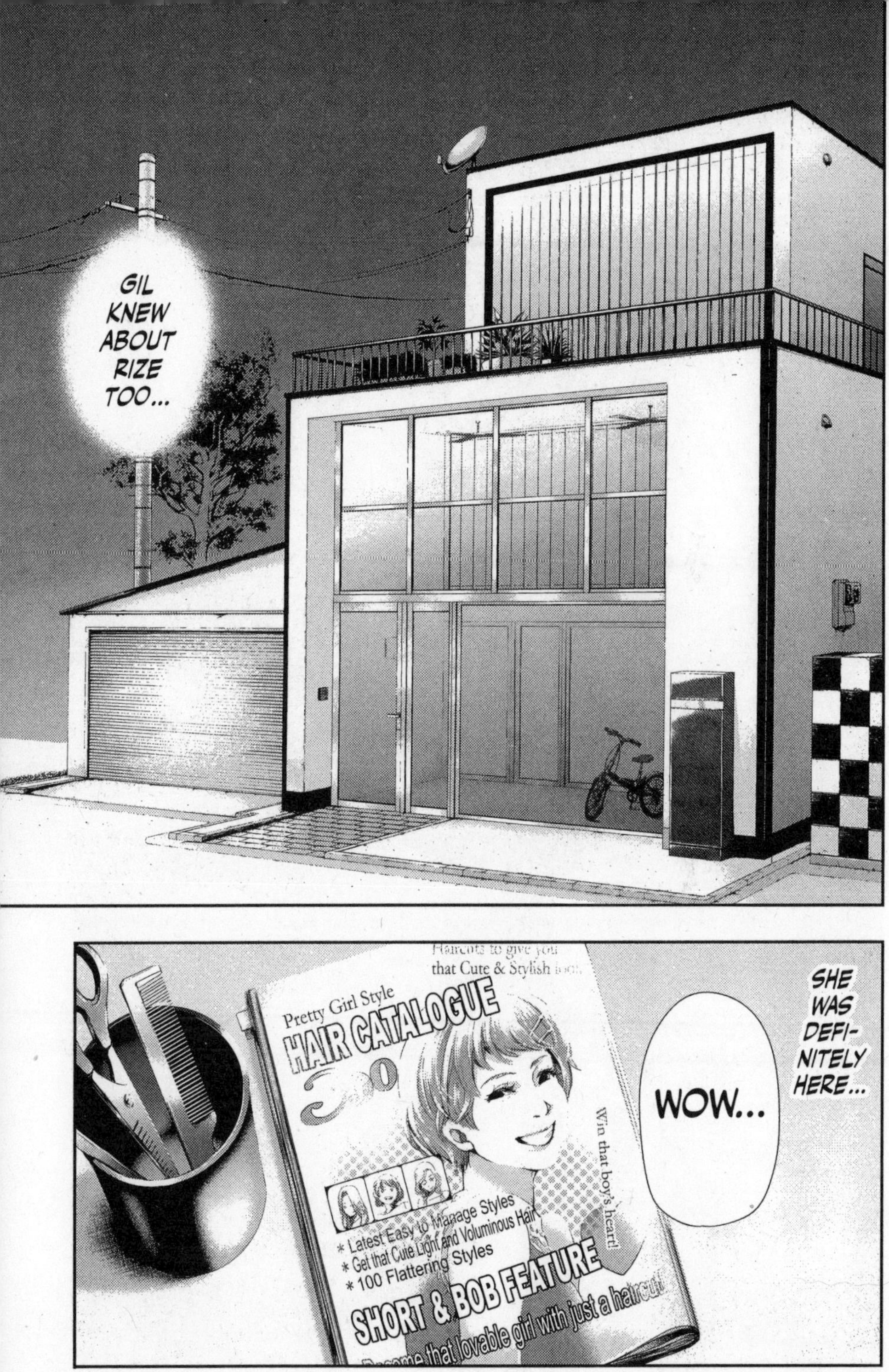
GIL KNEW ABOUT RIZE TOO...
SHE WAS DEFI-NITELY HERE...
WOW...
that Cute & Stylish
Pretty Girl Style
HAIR CATALOGUE
Win that boy's heart!
* Latest Easy to Manage Styles
* Get that Cute Light and Voluminous Hair
* 100 Flattering Styles
SHORT & BOB FEATURE

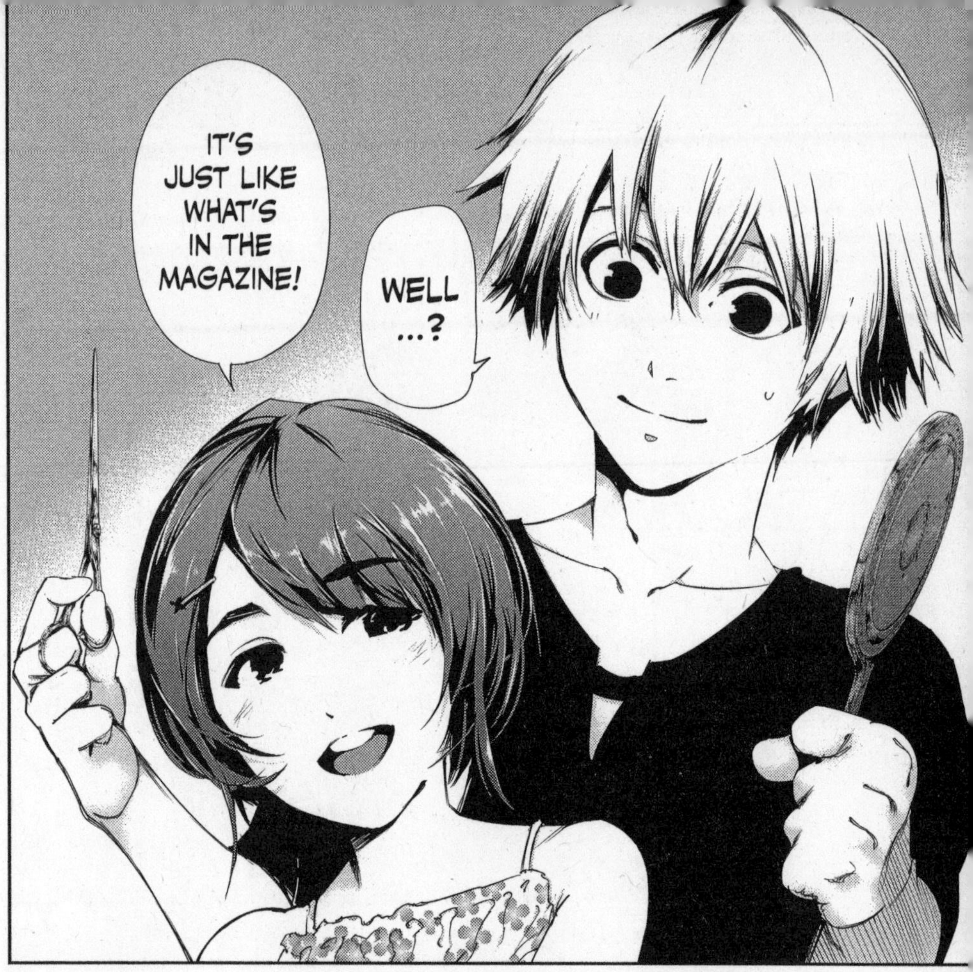
WELL ...?
IT'S JUST LIKE WHAT'S IN THE MAGAZINE!

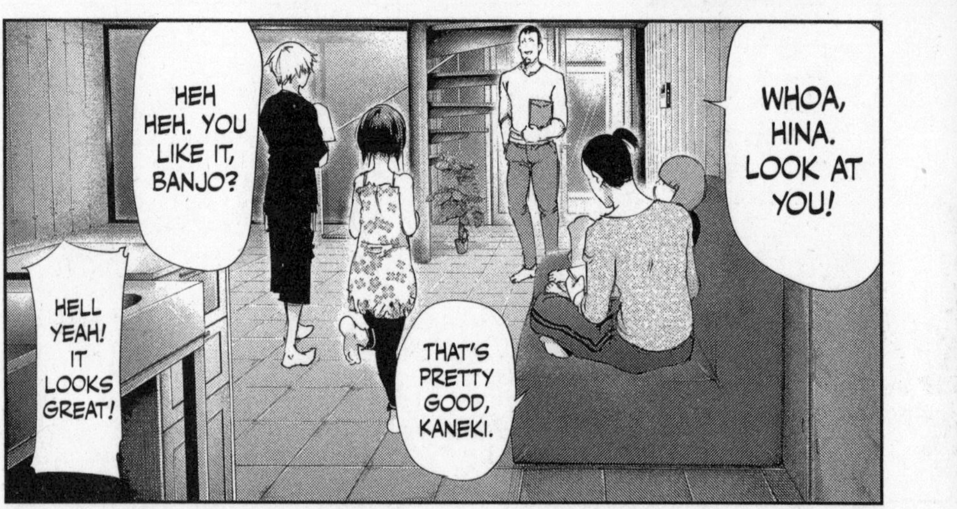
WHOA, HINA. LOOK AT YOU!
HEH HEH. YOU LIKE IT, BANJO?
THAT'S PRETTY GOOD, KANEKI.
HELL YEAH! IT LOOKS GREAT!

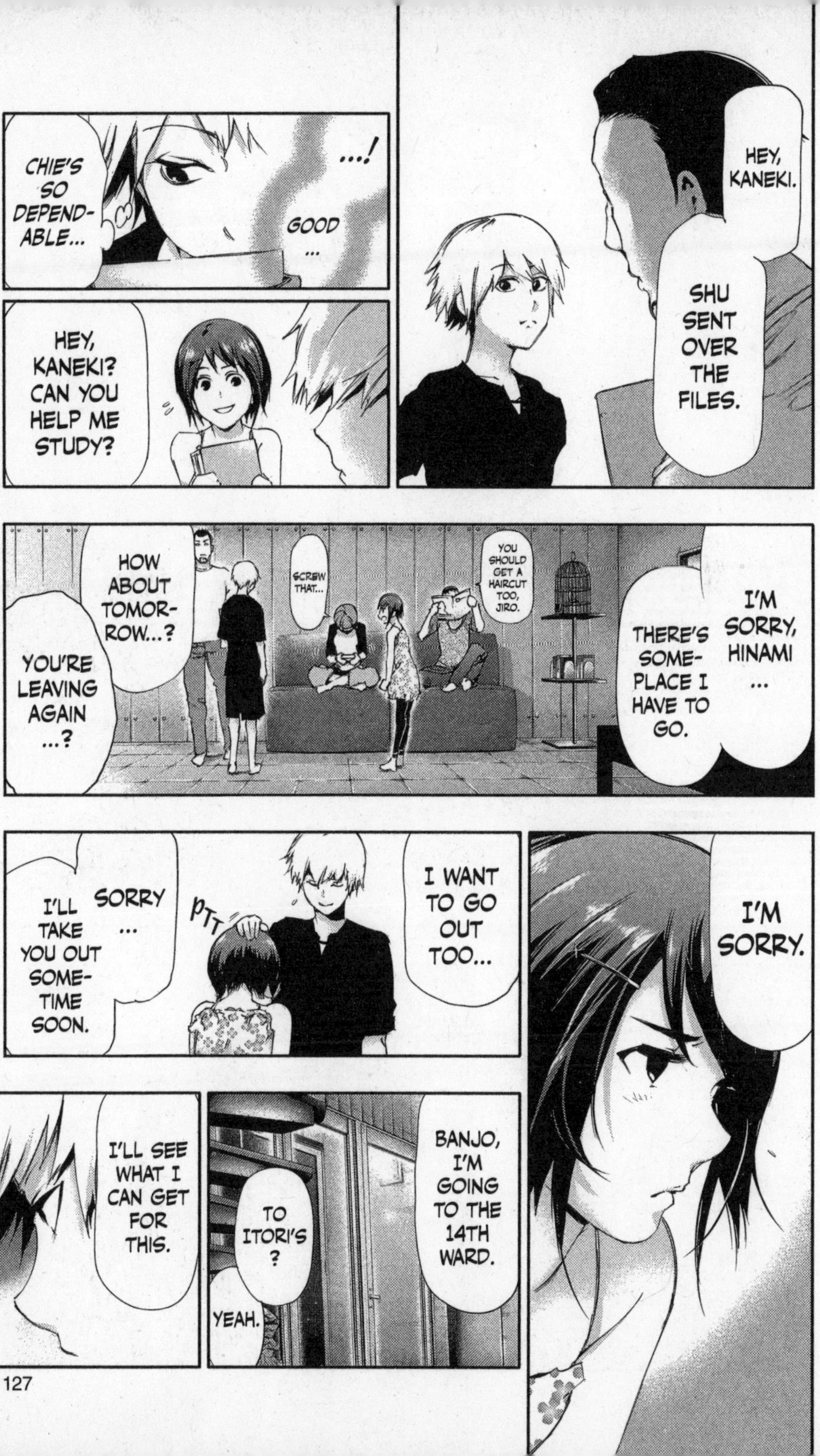
HEY, KANEKI.
SHU SENT OVER THE FILES.
...!
GOOD ...
CHIE'S SO DEPENDABLE...
HEY, KANEKI? CAN YOU HELP ME STUDY?
I'M SORRY, HINAMI ...
THERE'S SOMEPLACE I HAVE TO GO.
YOU SHOULD GET A HAIRCUT TOO, JIRO.
SCREW THAT...
HOW ABOUT TOMORROW...?
YOU'RE LEAVING AGAIN ...?
I'M SORRY.
I WANT TO GO OUT TOO...
PTT
SORRY ...
I'LL TAKE YOU OUT SOMETIME SOON.
BANJO, I'M GOING TO THE 14TH WARD.
TO ITORI'S ?
YEAH.
I'LL SEE WHAT I CAN GET FOR THIS.

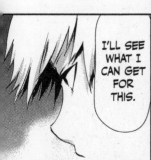

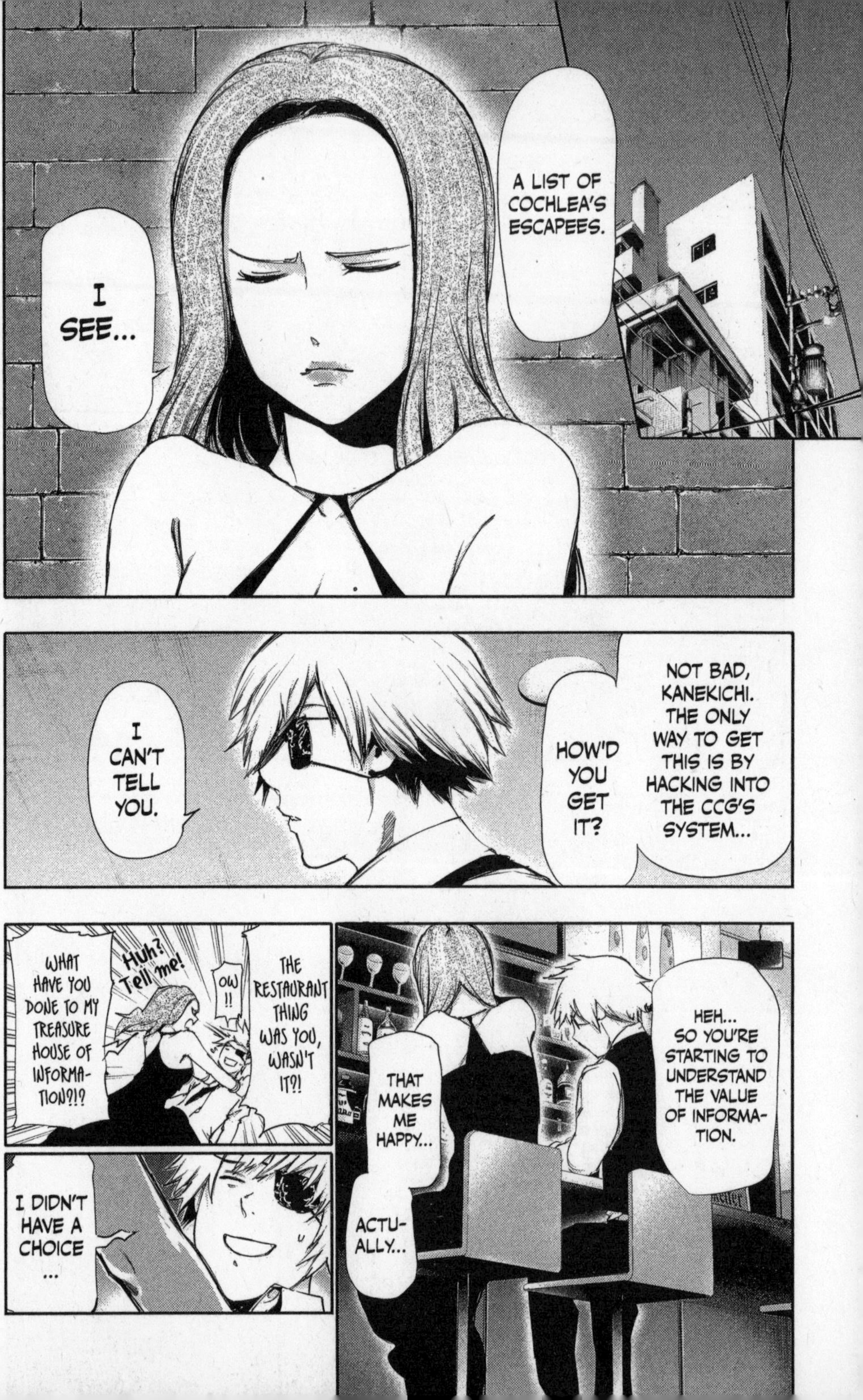
A LIST OF COCHLEA'S ESCAPEES.
I SEE...
NOT BAD, KANEKICHI. THE ONLY WAY TO GET THIS IS BY HACKING INTO THE CCG'S SYSTEM...
HOW'D YOU GET IT?
I CAN'T TELL YOU.
HEH... SO YOU'RE STARTING TO UNDERSTAND THE VALUE OF INFORMATION.
THAT MAKES ME HAPPY...
ACTU-ALLY...
THE RESTAURANT THING WAS YOU, WASN'T IT?!
OW !!
Huh? Tell me!
WHAT HAVE YOU DONE TO MY TREASURE HOUSE OF INFORMA-TION?!?
I DIDN'T HAVE A CHOICE ...

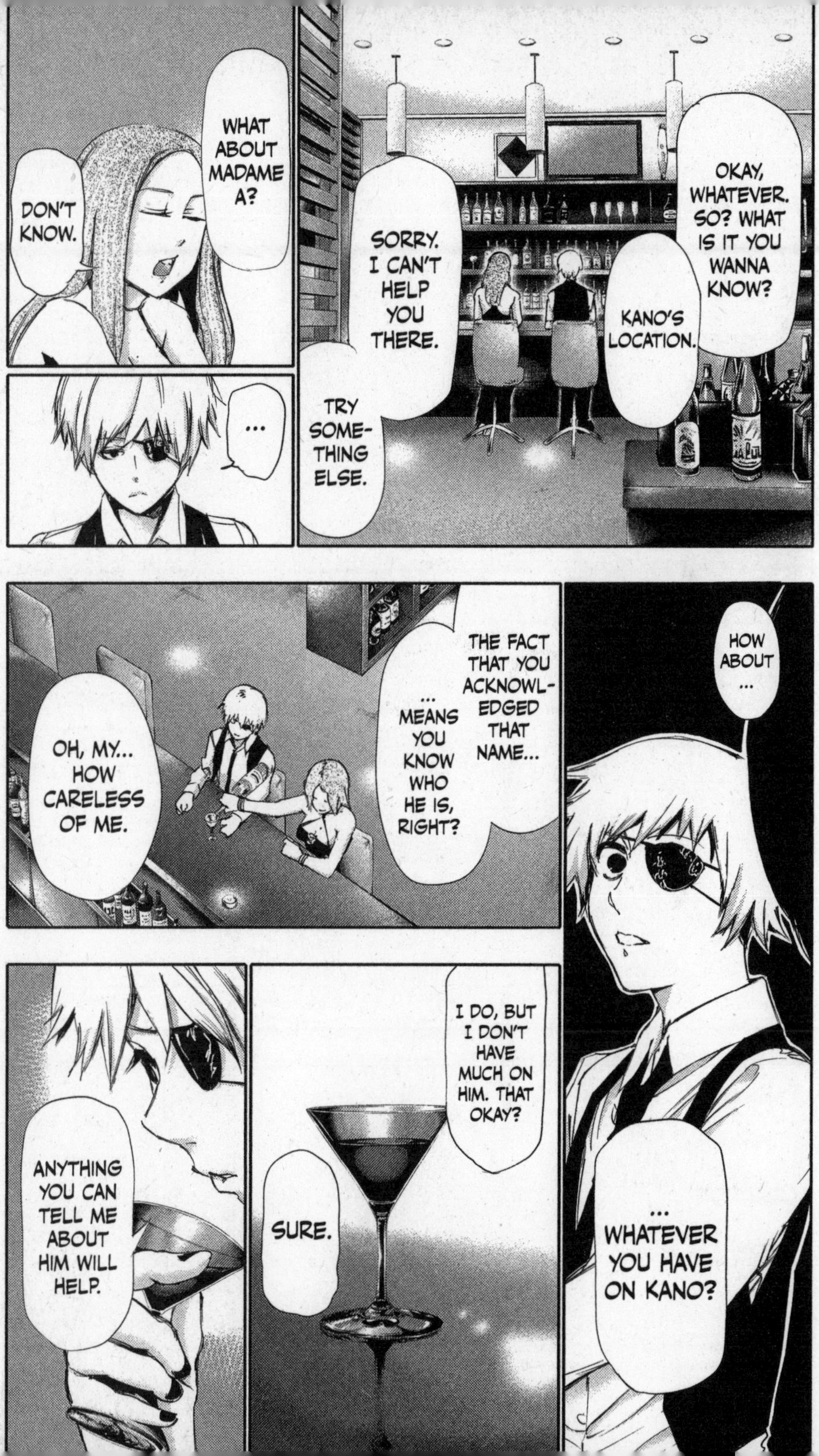
OKAY, WHATEVER. SO? WHAT IS IT YOU WANNA KNOW?
KANO'S LOCATION.
SORRY. I CAN'T HELP YOU THERE.
TRY SOME-THING ELSE.
WHAT ABOUT MADAME A?
DON'T KNOW.
...
HOW ABOUT ...
... WHATEVER YOU HAVE ON KANO?
THE FACT THAT YOU ACKNOWL-EDGED THAT NAME...
... MEANS YOU KNOW WHO HE IS, RIGHT?
OH, MY... HOW CARELESS OF ME.
I DO, BUT I DON'T HAVE MUCH ON HIM. THAT OKAY?
SURE.
ANYTHING YOU CAN TELL ME ABOUT HIM WILL HELP.

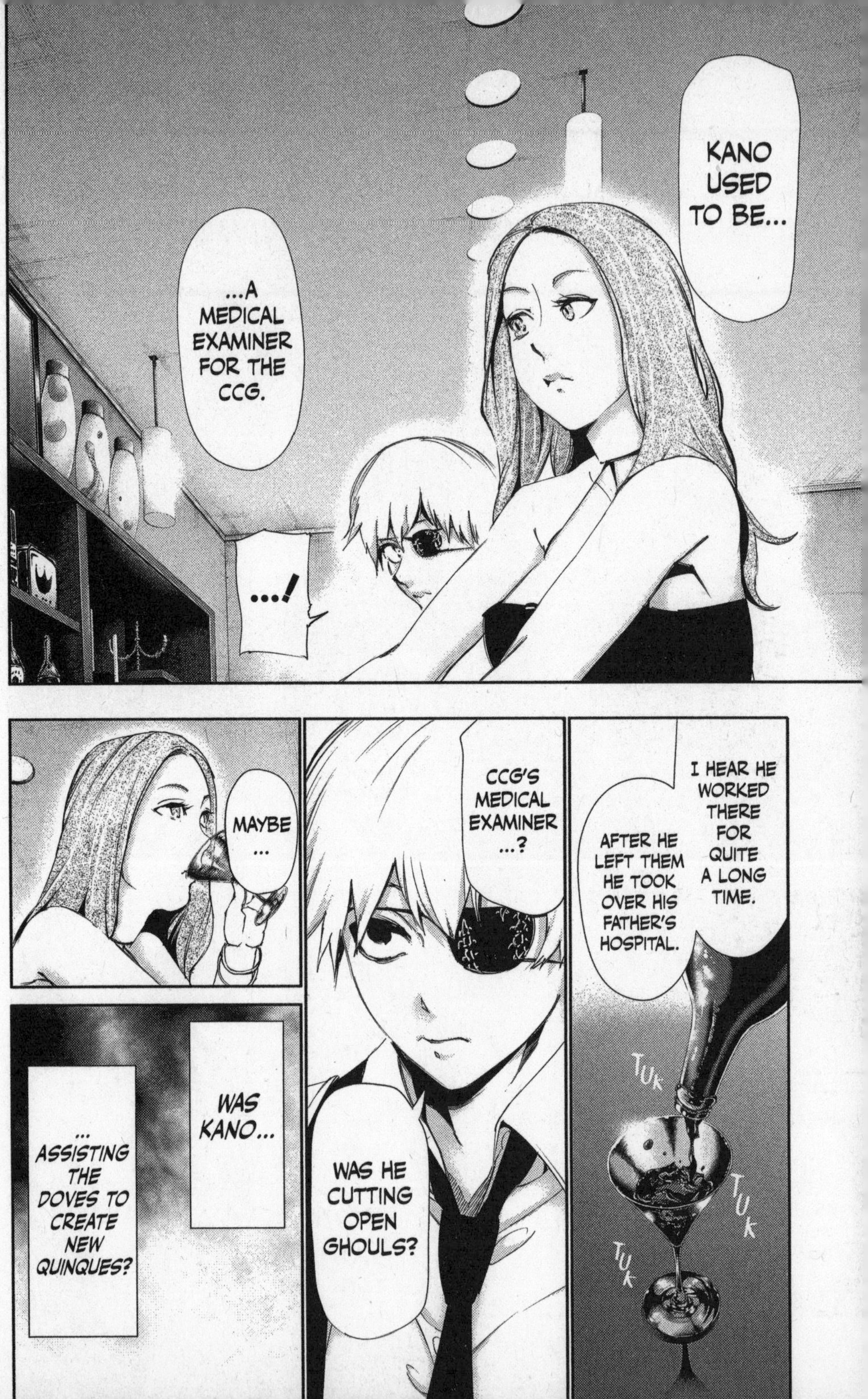
KANO USED TO BE...
...A MEDICAL EXAMINER FOR THE CCG.
...!
I HEAR HE WORKED THERE FOR QUITE A LONG TIME.
AFTER HE LEFT THEM HE TOOK OVER HIS FATHER'S HOSPITAL.
TUK
TUK
TUK
CCG'S MEDICAL EXAMINER ...?
WAS HE CUTTING OPEN GHOULS?
MAYBE ...
WAS KANO...
... ASSISTING THE DOVES TO CREATE NEW QUINQUES?

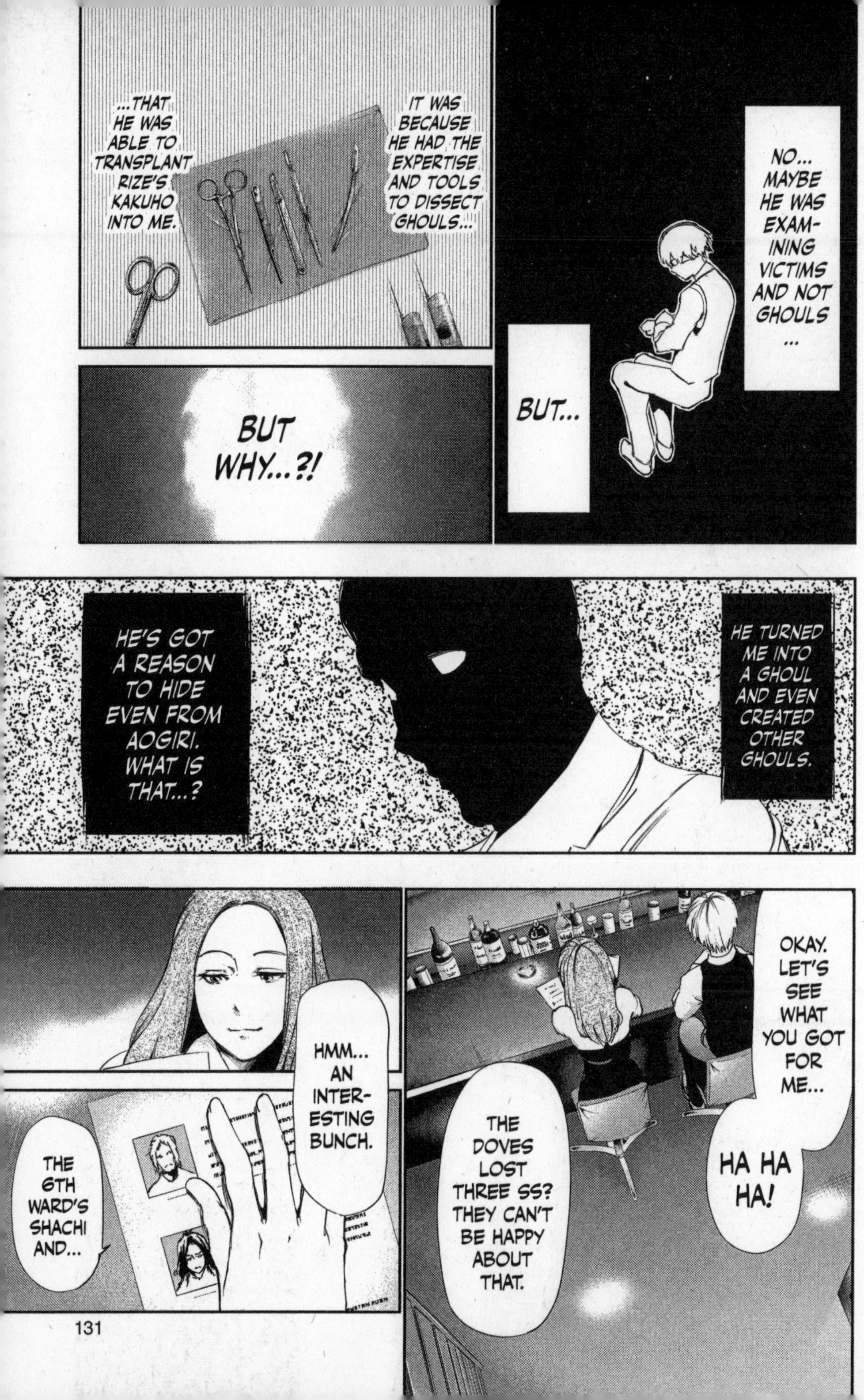
NO... MAYBE HE WAS EXAMINING VICTIMS AND NOT GHOULS...
BUT...
IT WAS BECAUSE HE HAD THE EXPERTISE AND TOOLS TO DISSECT GHOULS...
...THAT HE WAS ABLE TO TRANSPLANT RIZE'S KAKUHO INTO ME.
BUT WHY...?!
HE TURNED ME INTO A GHOUL AND EVEN CREATED OTHER GHOULS.
HE'S GOT A REASON TO HIDE EVEN FROM AOGIRI. WHAT IS THAT...?
OKAY. LET'S SEE WHAT YOU GOT FOR ME...
HA HA HA!
THE DOVES LOST THREE SS? THEY CAN'T BE HAPPY ABOUT THAT.
HMM... AN INTERESTING BUNCH.
THE 6TH WARD'S SHACHI AND...

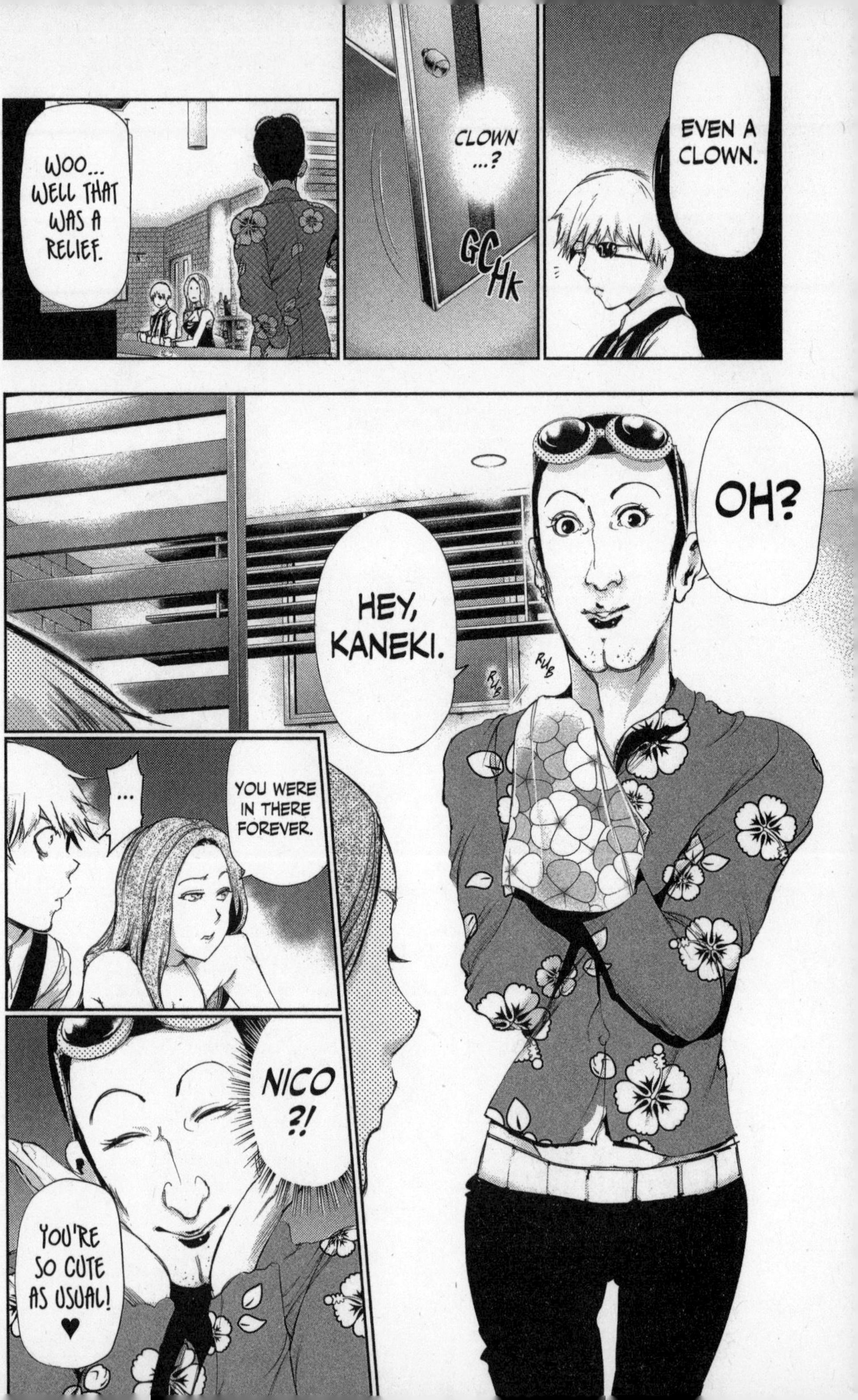
EVEN A CLOWN.
CLOWN ...?
GCHK
WOO... WELL THAT WAS A RELIEF.
OH?
HEY, KANEKI.
RUB
RUB
YOU WERE IN THERE FOREVER.
...
NICO?!
YOU'RE SO CUTE AS USUAL! ♥

東京喰種
トーキョーグール
喰種
Tokyo
Ghoul

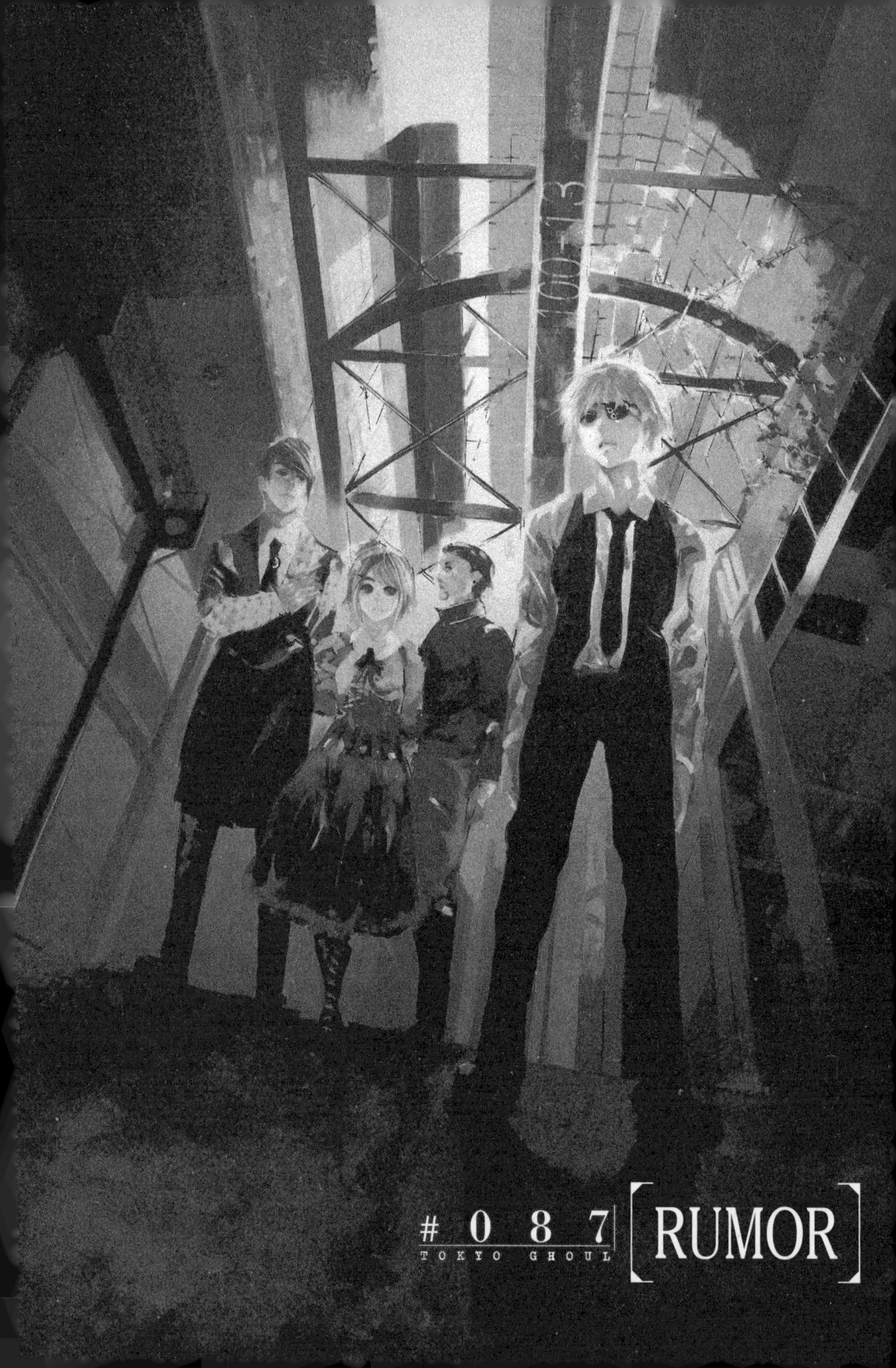
#087
TOKYO GHOUL
RUMOR

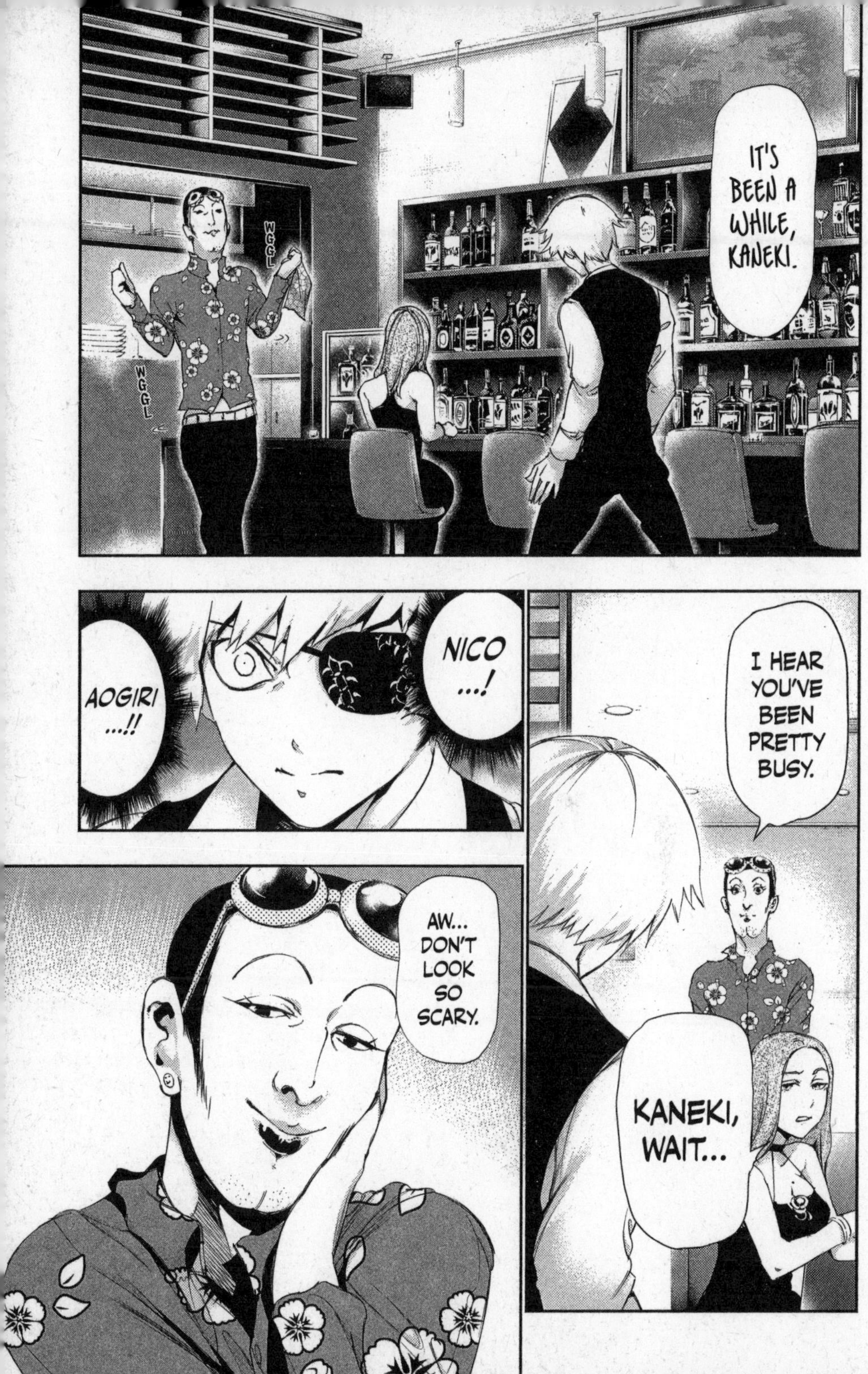
IT'S BEEN A WHILE, KANEKI.
WGGL
WGGL
I HEAR YOU'VE BEEN PRETTY BUSY.
KANEKI, WAIT...
NICO ...!
AOGIRI ...!!
AW... DON'T LOOK SO SCARY.

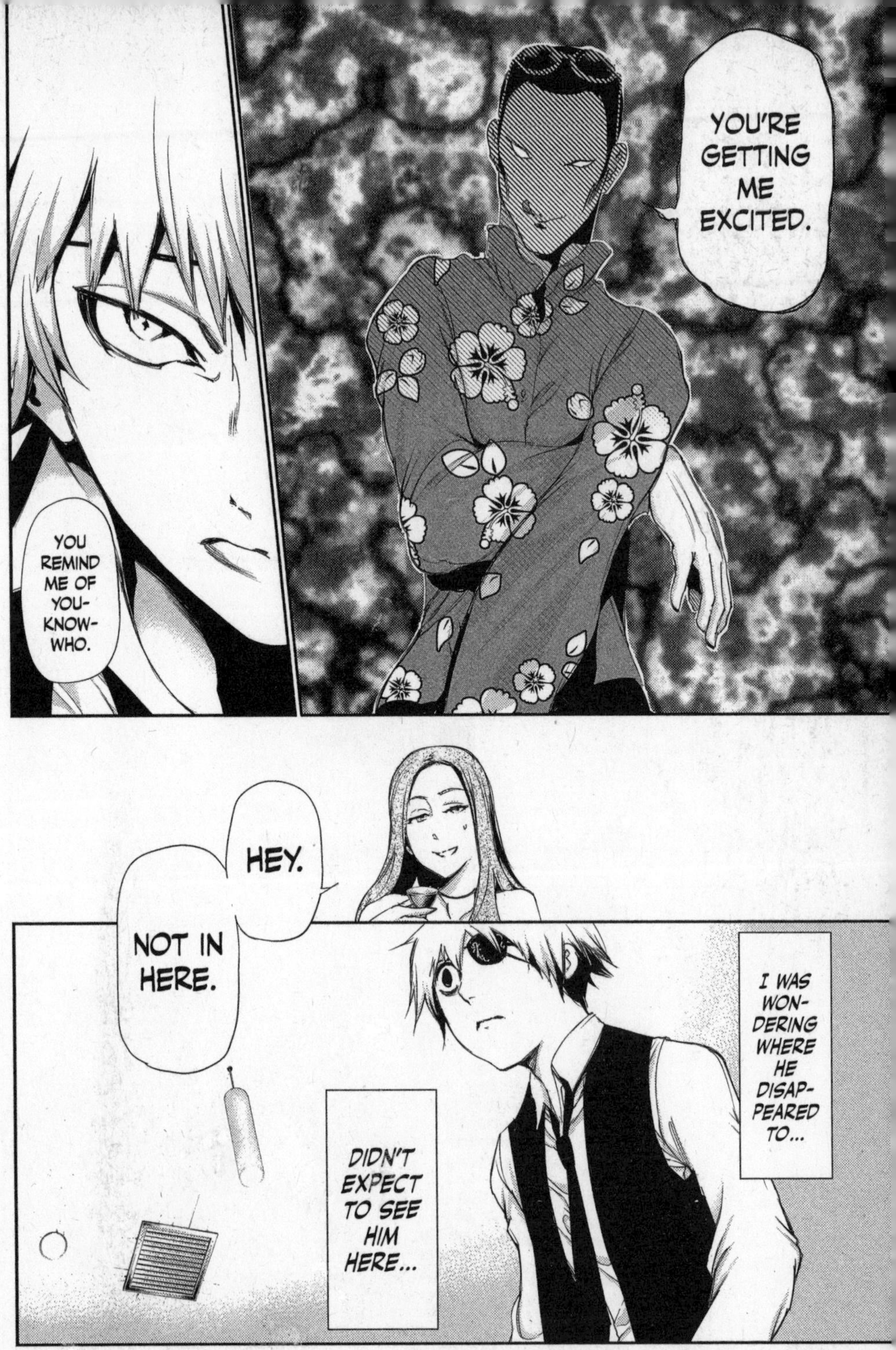

YOU'RE GETTING ME EXCITED.
YOU REMIND ME OF YOU-KNOW-WHO.
HEY.
NOT IN HERE.
I WAS WONDERING WHERE HE DISAPPEARED TO...
DIDN'T EXPECT TO SEE HIM HERE...

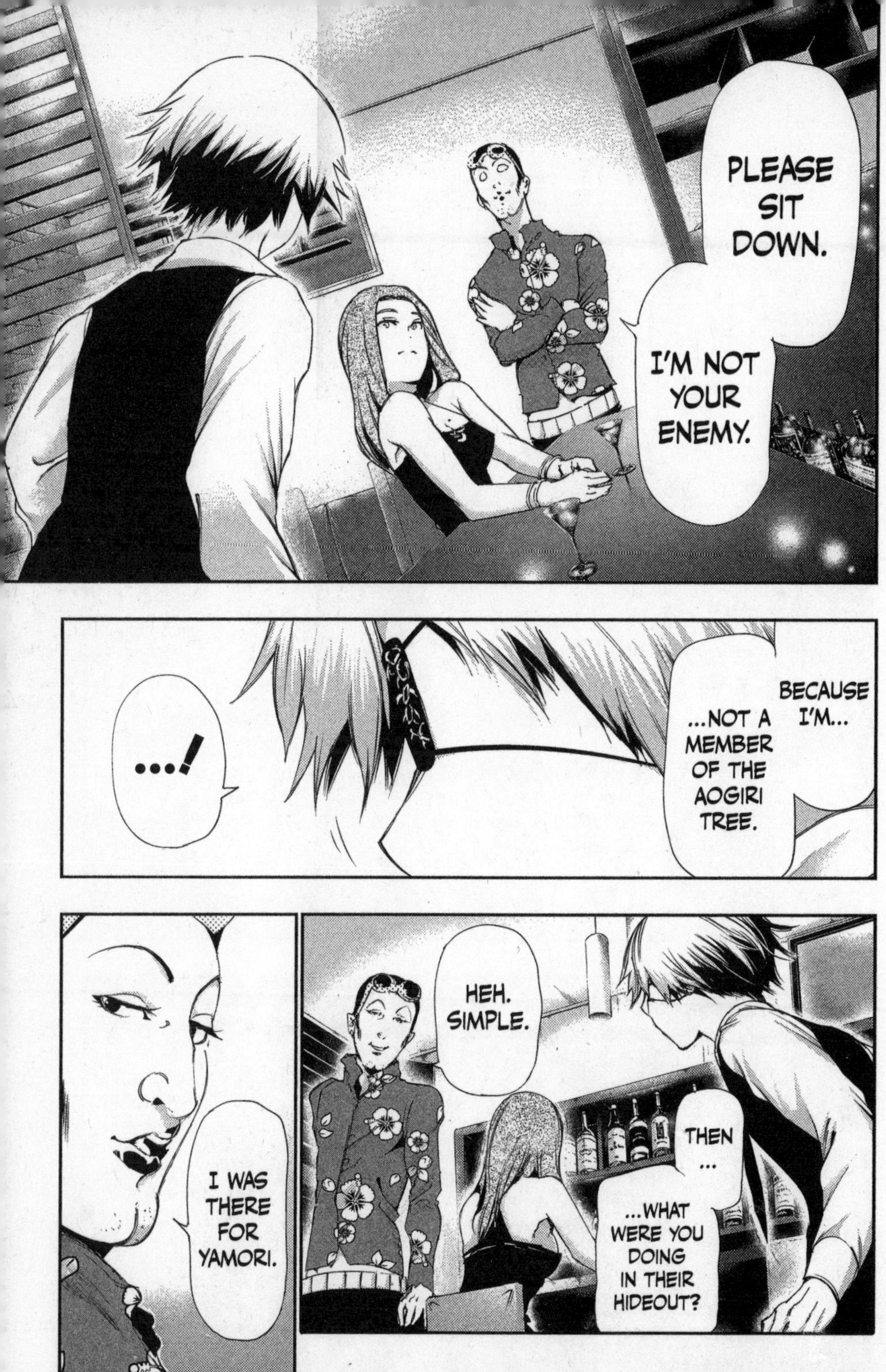
PLEASE SIT DOWN.
I'M NOT YOUR ENEMY.
BECAUSE I'M...
...NOT A MEMBER OF THE AOGIRI TREE.
...!
THEN...
...WHAT WERE YOU DOING IN THEIR HIDEOUT?
HEH. SIMPLE.
I WAS THERE FOR YAMORI.

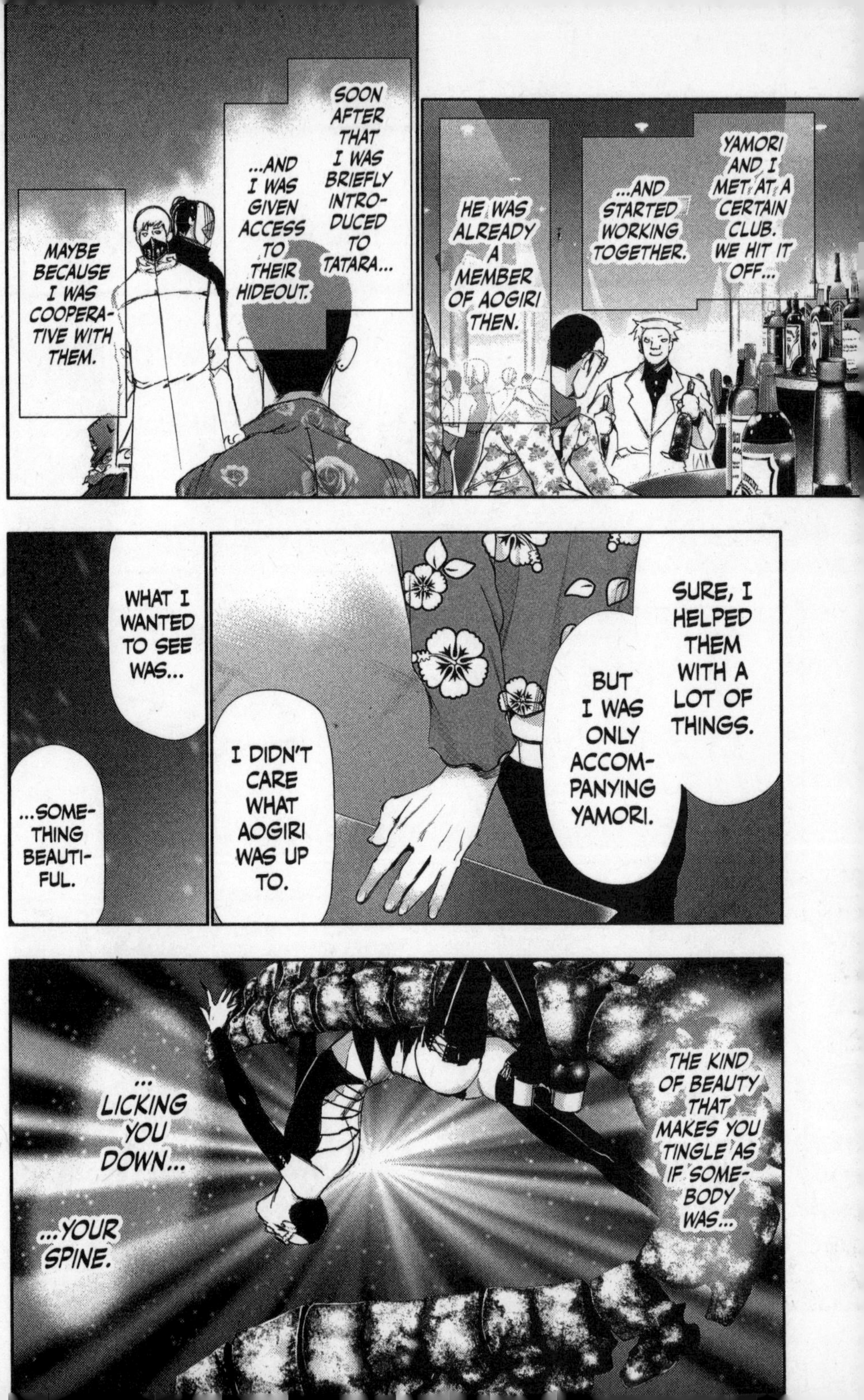
YAMORI AND I MET AT A CERTAIN CLUB. WE HIT IT OFF...
...AND STARTED WORKING TOGETHER.
HE WAS ALREADY A MEMBER OF AOGIRI THEN.
SOON AFTER THAT I WAS BRIEFLY INTRODUCED TO TATARA...
...AND I WAS GIVEN ACCESS TO THEIR HIDEOUT.
MAYBE BECAUSE I WAS COOPERATIVE WITH THEM.
SURE, I HELPED THEM WITH A LOT OF THINGS.
BUT I WAS ONLY ACCOMPANYING YAMORI.
I DIDN'T CARE WHAT AOGIRI WAS UP TO.
WHAT I WANTED TO SEE WAS...
...SOMETHING BEAUTIFUL.
THE KIND OF BEAUTY THAT MAKES YOU TINGLE AS IF SOMEBODY WAS...
...LICKING YOU DOWN...
...YOUR SPINE.

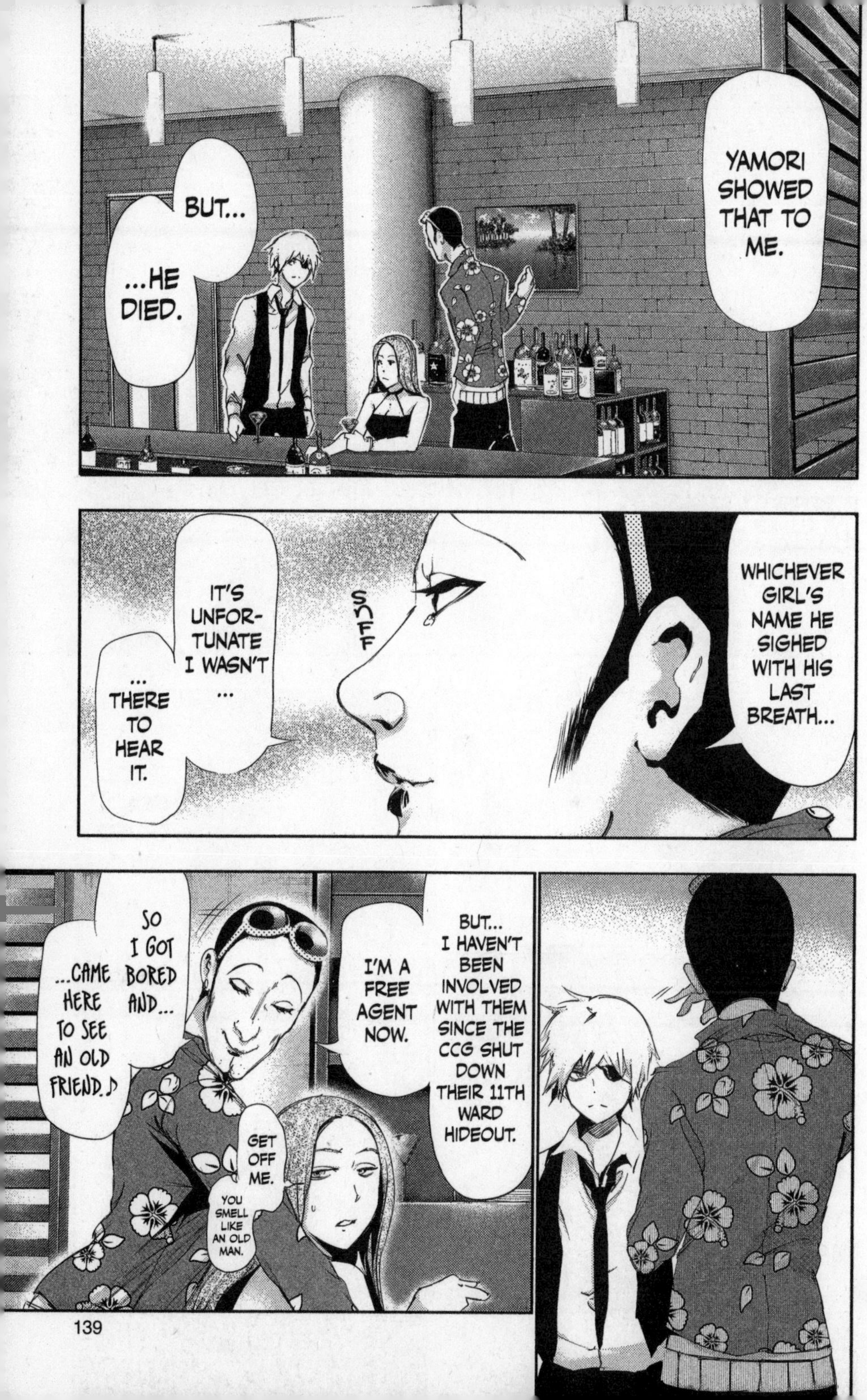
YAMORI SHOWED THAT TO ME.
BUT...
...HE DIED.
WHICHEVER GIRL'S NAME HE SIGHED WITH HIS LAST BREATH...
SNIFF
IT'S UNFOR-TUNATE I WASN'T ...
... THERE TO HEAR IT.
BUT... I HAVEN'T BEEN INVOLVED WITH THEM SINCE THE CCG SHUT DOWN THEIR 11TH WARD HIDEOUT.
I'M A FREE AGENT NOW.
SO I GOT BORED AND...
...CAME HERE TO SEE AN OLD FRIEND.♪
GET OFF ME.
YOU SMELL LIKE AN OLD MAN.

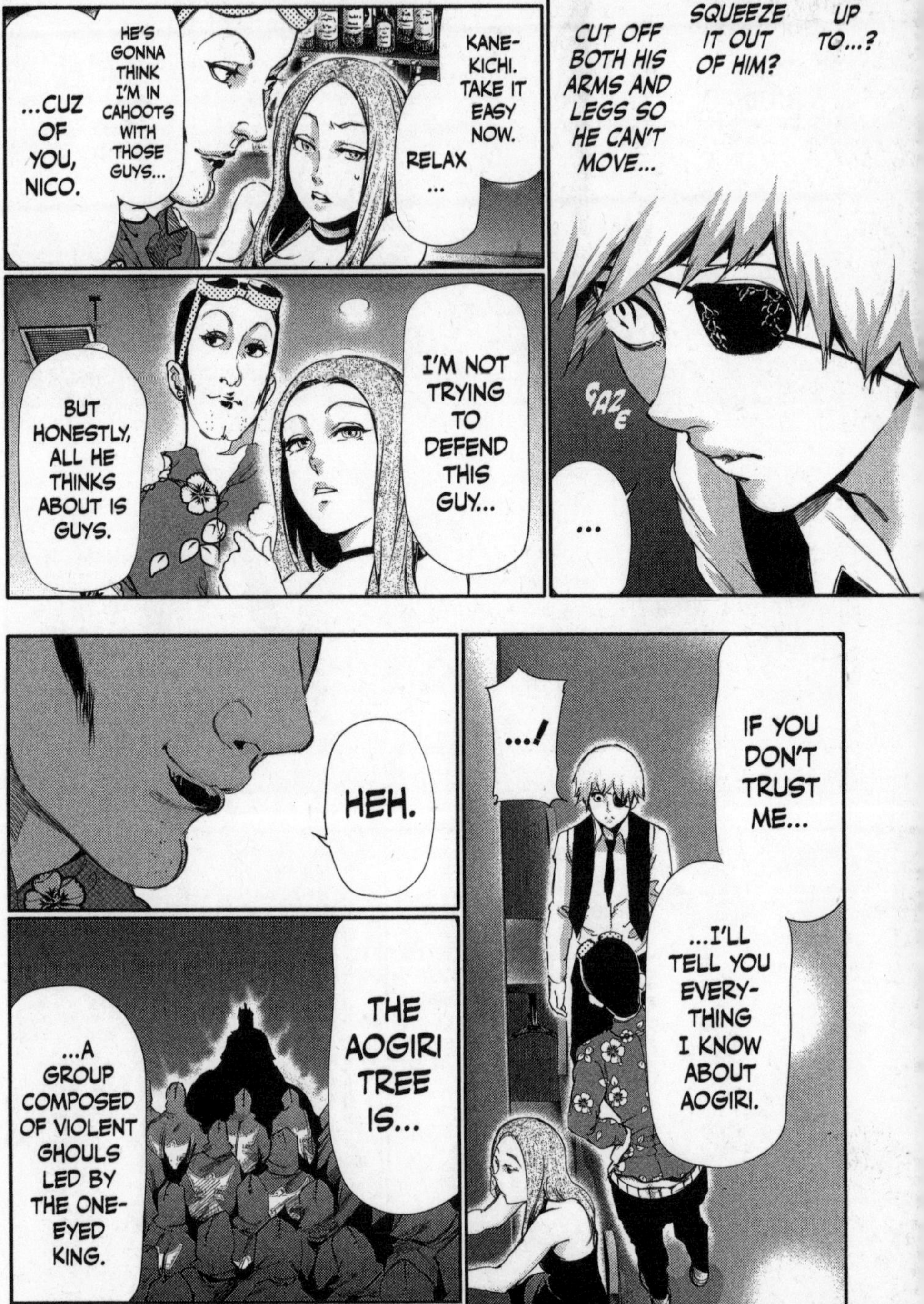
WHAT IS HE UP TO...?
SHOULD I SQUEEZE IT OUT OF HIM?
CUT OFF BOTH HIS ARMS AND LEGS SO HE CAN'T MOVE...
GAZE
...
KANE-KICHI. TAKE IT EASY NOW.
RELAX...
HE'S GONNA THINK I'M IN CAHOOTS WITH THOSE GUYS...
...CUZ OF YOU, NICO.
I'M NOT TRYING TO DEFEND THIS GUY...
BUT HONESTLY, ALL HE THINKS ABOUT IS GUYS.
...!
IF YOU DON'T TRUST ME...
...I'LL TELL YOU EVERY-THING I KNOW ABOUT AOGIRI.
HEH.
THE AOGIRI TREE IS...
...A GROUP COMPOSED OF VIOLENT GHOULS LED BY THE ONE-EYED KING.

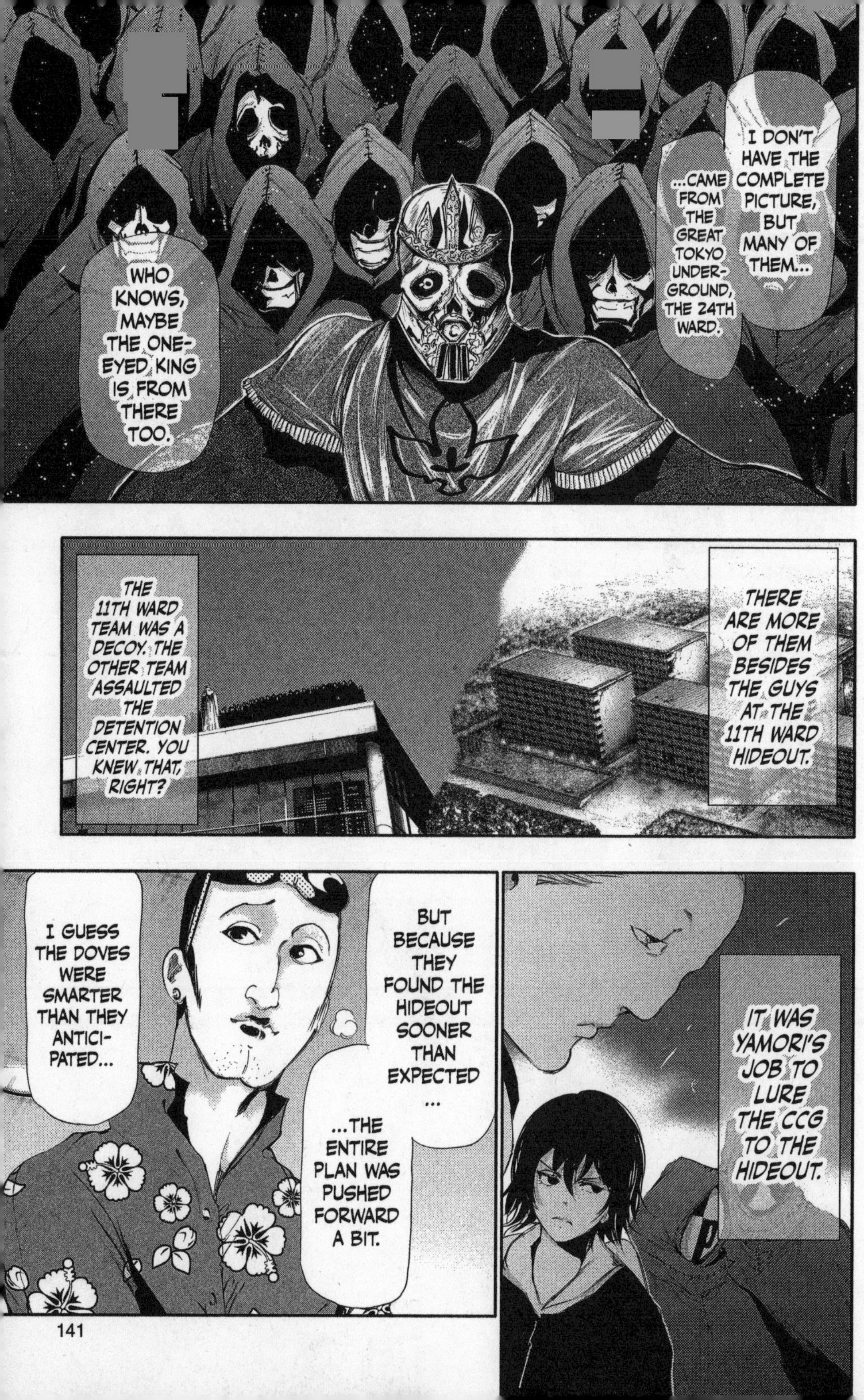
I DON'T HAVE THE COMPLETE PICTURE, BUT MANY OF THEM...
...CAME FROM THE GREAT TOKYO UNDER-GROUND, THE 24TH WARD.
WHO KNOWS, MAYBE THE ONE-EYED KING IS FROM THERE TOO.
THERE ARE MORE OF THEM BESIDES THE GUYS AT THE 11TH WARD HIDEOUT.
THE 11TH WARD TEAM WAS A DECOY. THE OTHER TEAM ASSAULTED THE DETENTION CENTER. YOU KNEW THAT, RIGHT?
IT WAS YAMORI'S JOB TO LURE THE CCG TO THE HIDEOUT.
I GUESS THE DOVES WERE SMARTER THAN THEY ANTICI-PATED...
BUT BECAUSE THEY FOUND THE HIDEOUT SOONER THAN EXPECTED ...
...THE ENTIRE PLAN WAS PUSHED FORWARD A BIT.

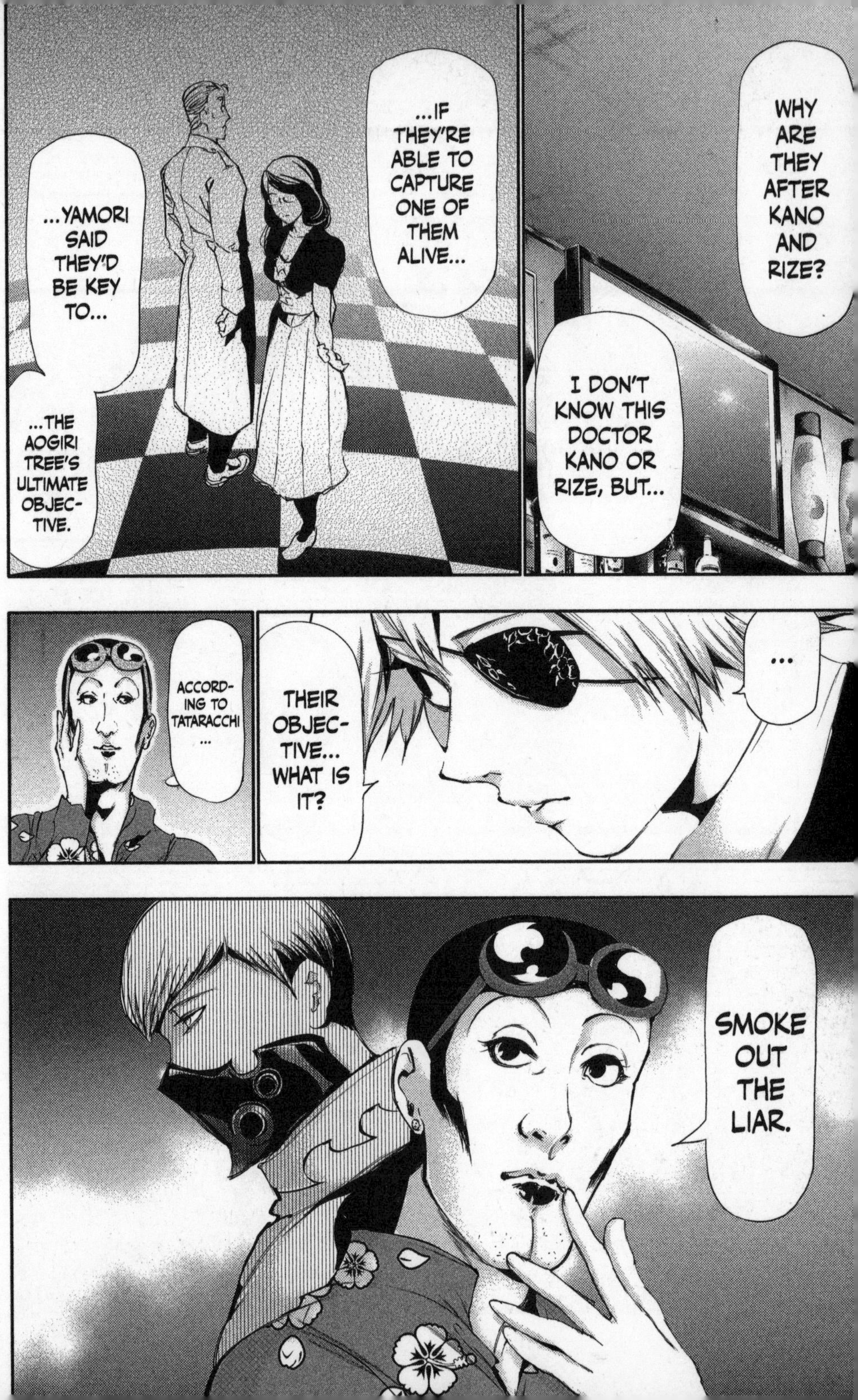
WHY ARE THEY AFTER KANO AND RIZE?
I DON'T KNOW THIS DOCTOR KANO OR RIZE, BUT...
...IF THEY'RE ABLE TO CAPTURE ONE OF THEM ALIVE...
...YAMORI SAID THEY'D BE KEY TO...
...THE AOGIRI TREE'S ULTIMATE OBJECTIVE.
...
THEIR OBJECTIVE... WHAT IS IT?
ACCORDING TO TATARACCHI...
SMOKE OUT THE LIAR.

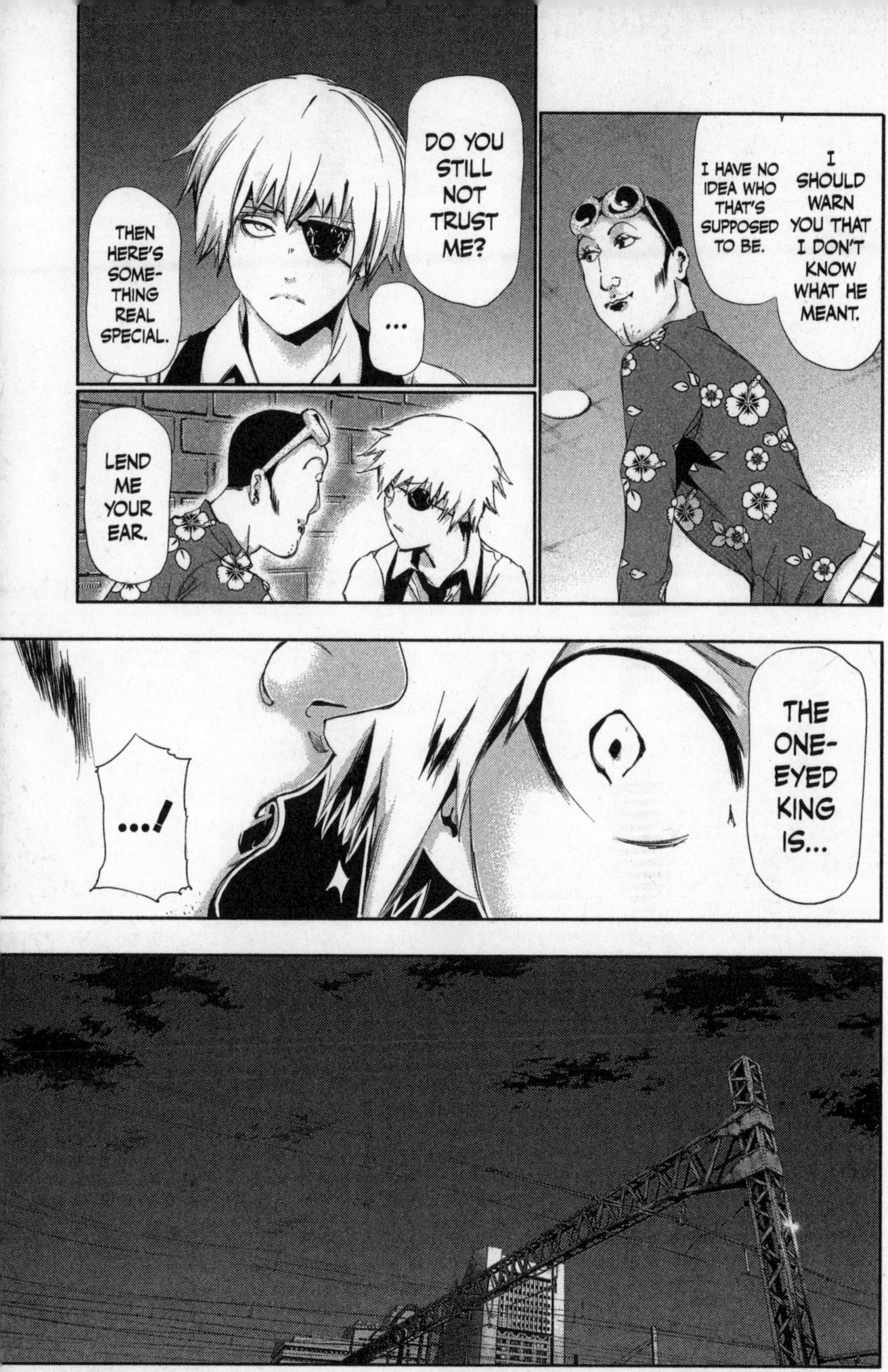
I SHOULD WARN YOU THAT I DON'T KNOW WHAT HE MEANT.
I HAVE NO IDEA WHO THAT'S SUPPOSED TO BE.
DO YOU STILL NOT TRUST ME?
...
THEN HERE'S SOME-THING REAL SPECIAL.
LEND ME YOUR EAR.
THE ONE-EYED KING IS...
...!

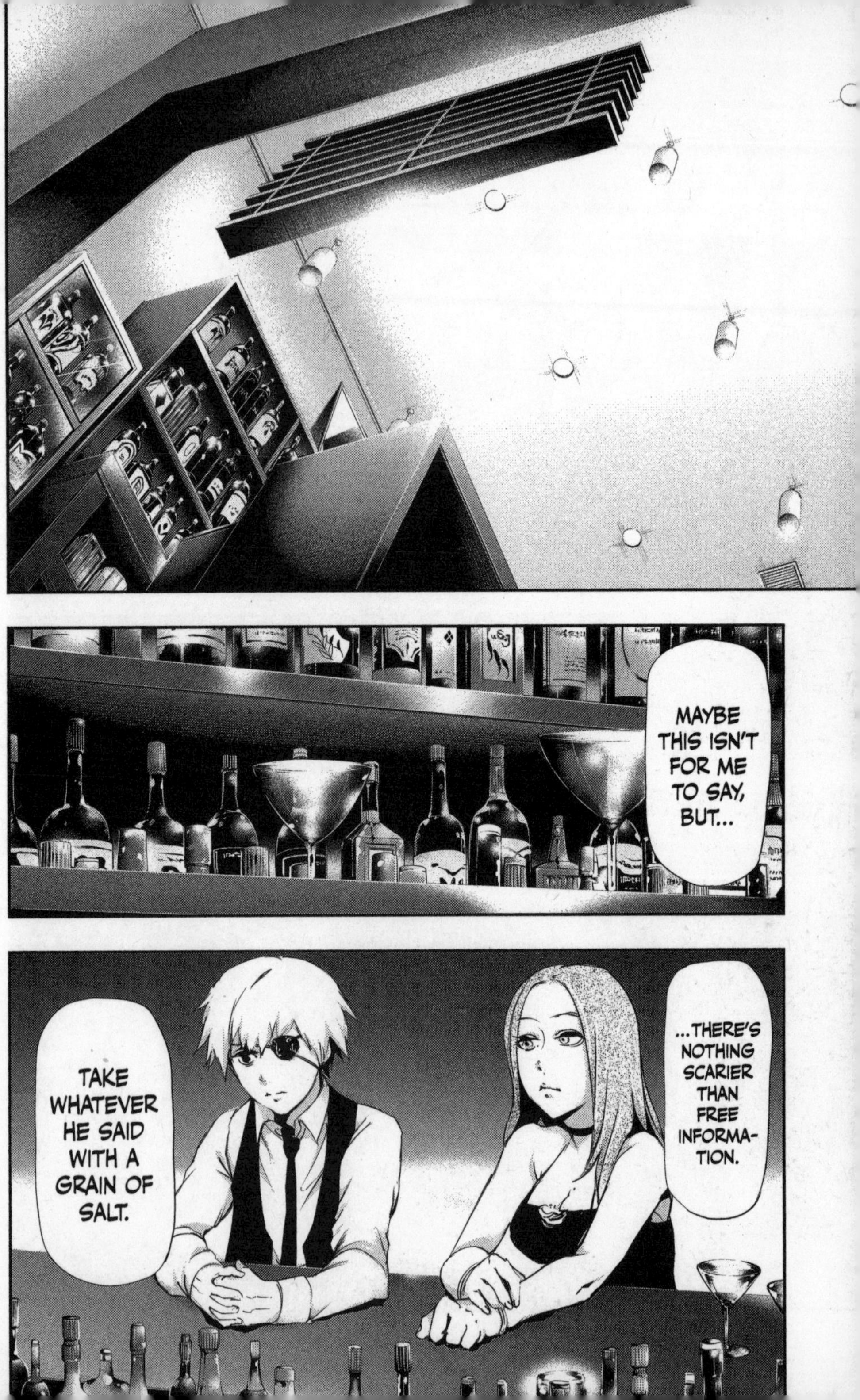
MAYBE THIS ISN'T FOR ME TO SAY, BUT...
...THERE'S NOTHING SCARIER THAN FREE INFORMA-TION.
TAKE WHATEVER HE SAID WITH A GRAIN OF SALT.

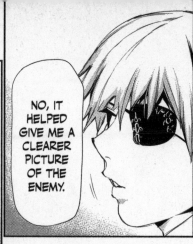

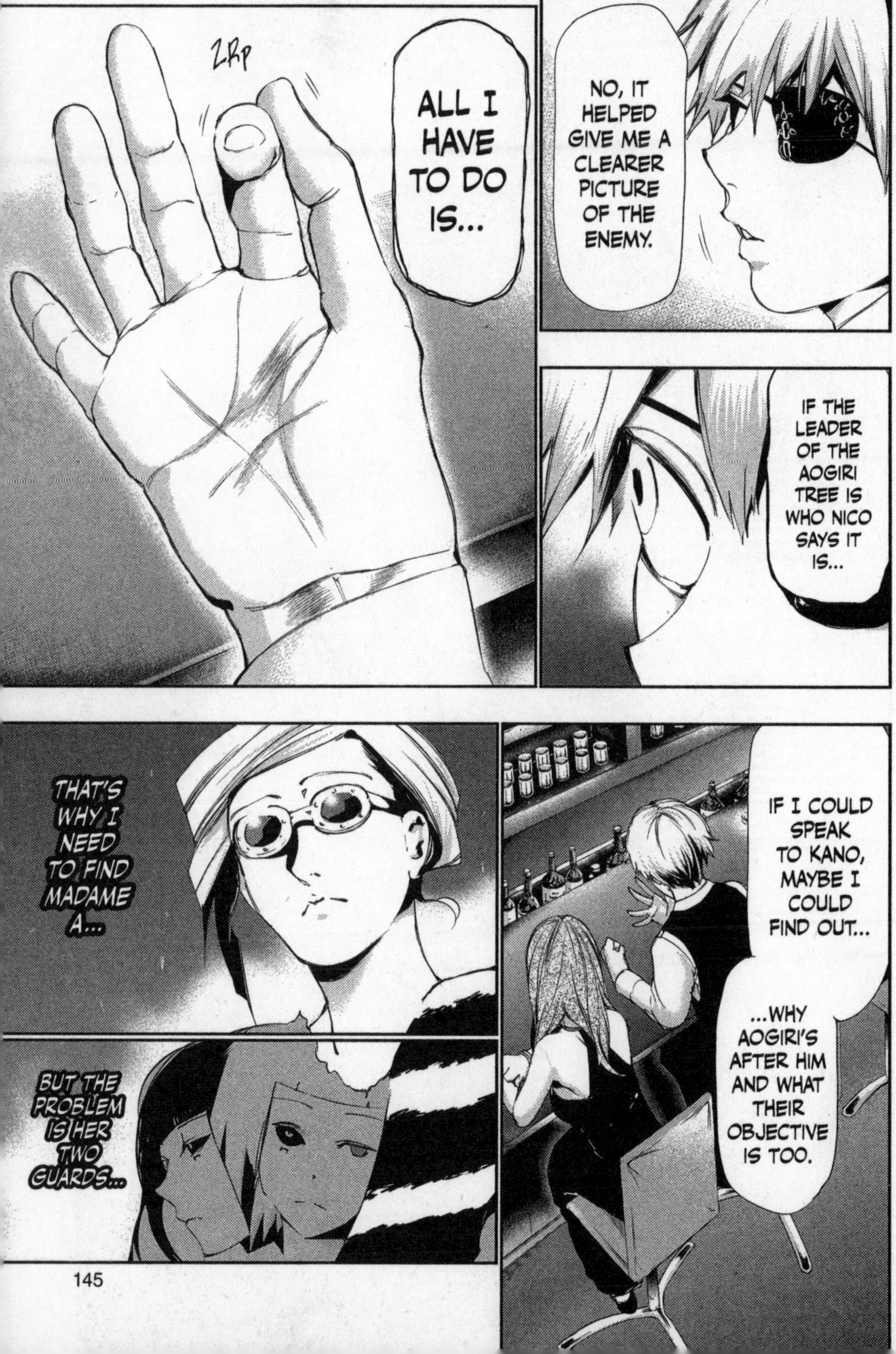
NO, IT HELPED GIVE ME A CLEARER PICTURE OF THE ENEMY.
IF THE LEADER OF THE AOGIRI TREE IS WHO NICO SAYS IT IS...
ZRP
ALL I HAVE TO DO IS...
IF I COULD SPEAK TO KANO, MAYBE I COULD FIND OUT...
...WHY AOGIRI'S AFTER HIM AND WHAT THEIR OBJECTIVE IS TOO.
THAT'S WHY I NEED TO FIND MADAME A...
BUT THE PROBLEM IS HER TWO GUARDS...

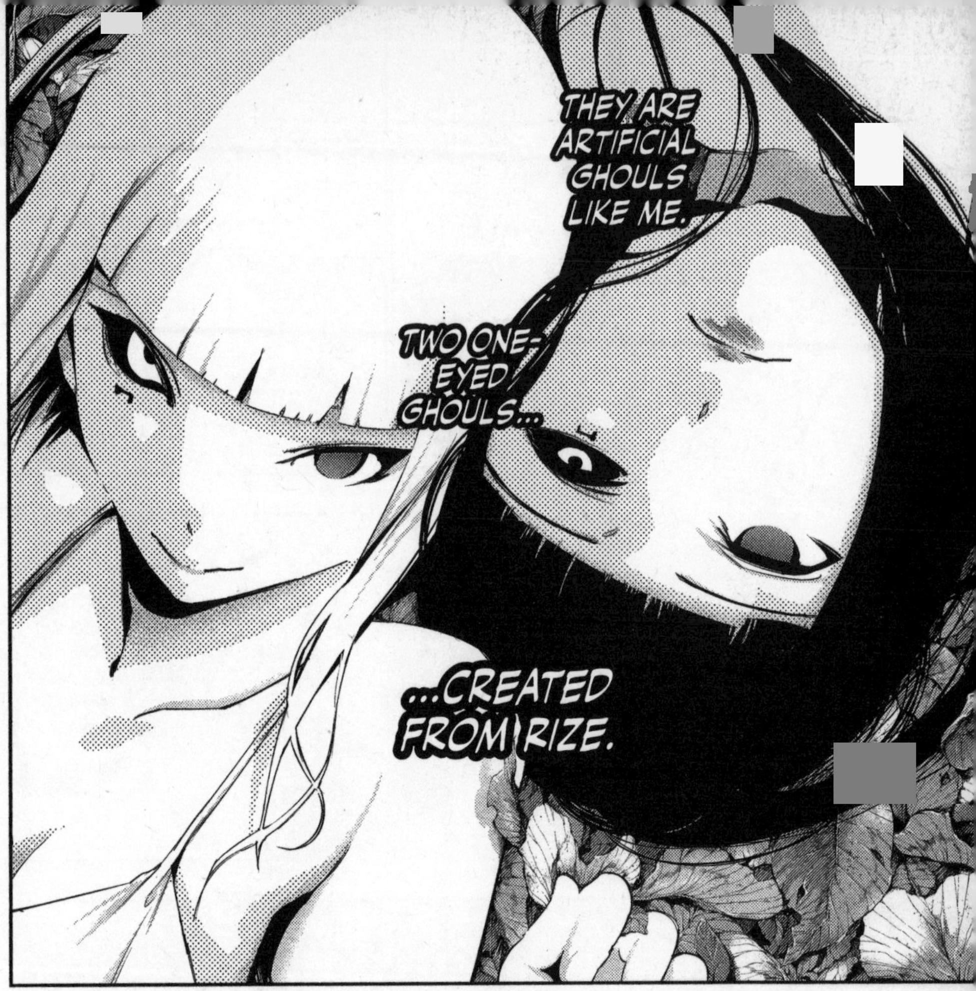
THEY ARE ARTIFICIAL GHOULS LIKE ME.
TWO ONE-EYED GHOULS...
...CREATED FROM RIZE.
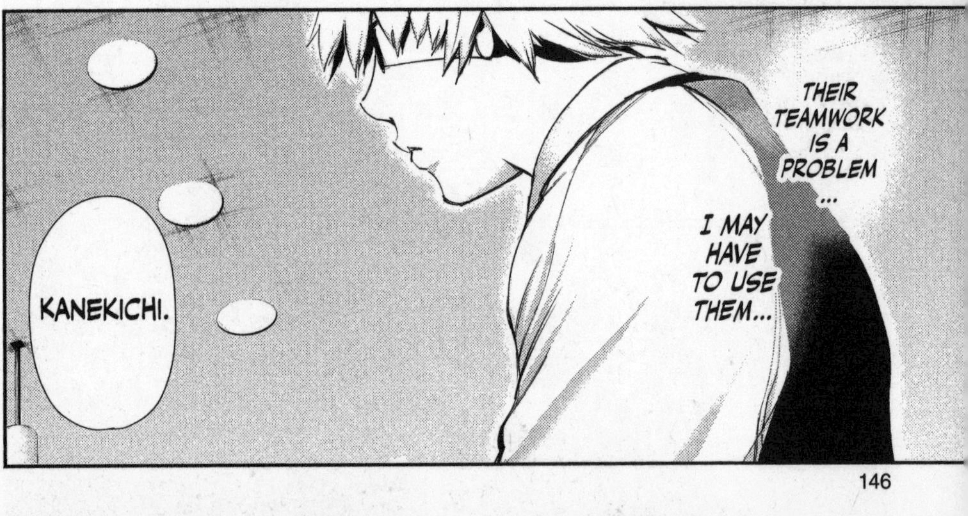
THEIR TEAMWORK IS A PROBLEM...
I MAY HAVE TO USE THEM...
KANEKICHI.

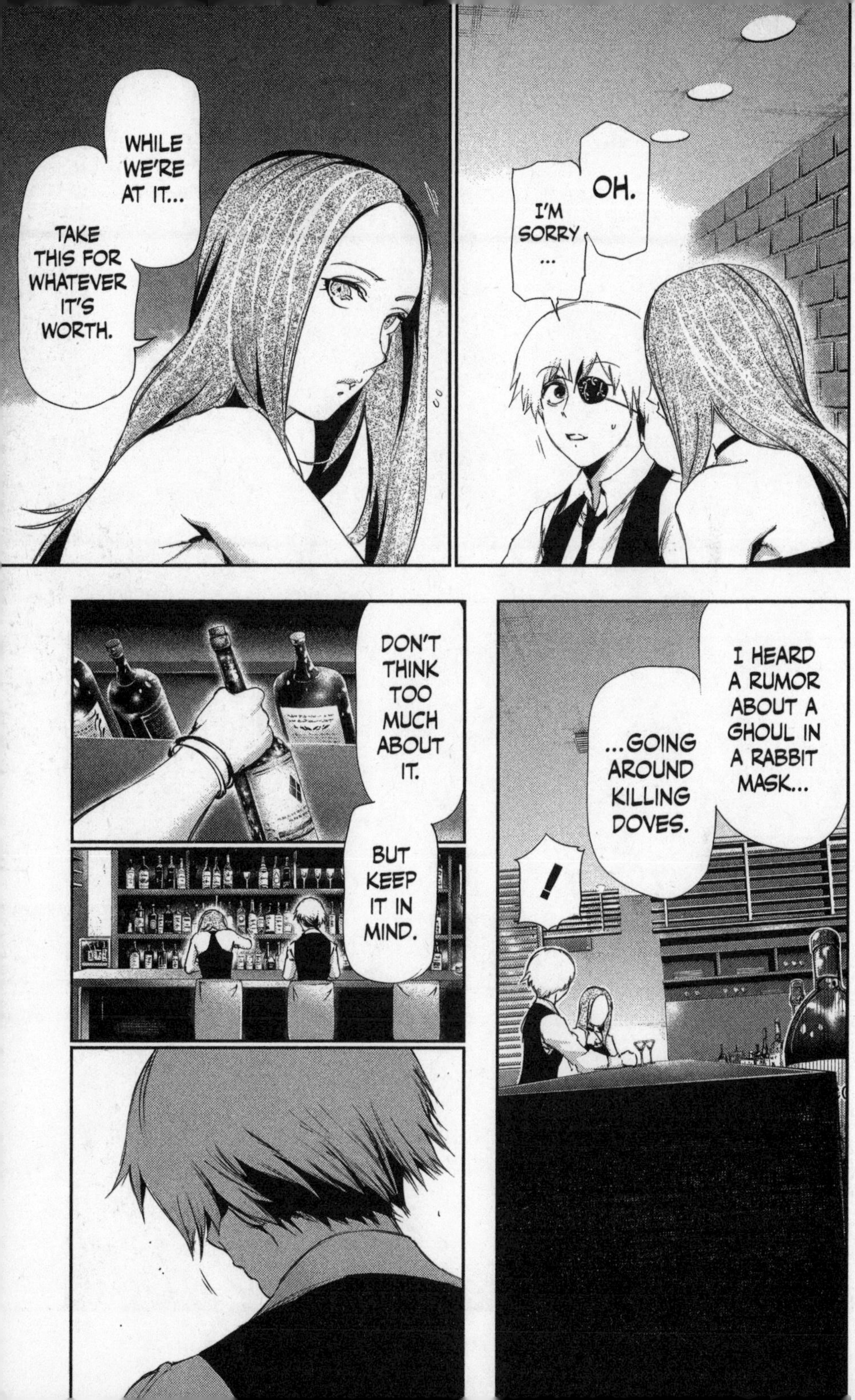
OH.
I'M SORRY ...
WHILE WE'RE AT IT...
TAKE THIS FOR WHATEVER IT'S WORTH.
I HEARD A RUMOR ABOUT A GHOUL IN A RABBIT MASK...
...GOING AROUND KILLING DOVES.
!
DON'T THINK TOO MUCH ABOUT IT.
BUT KEEP IT IN MIND.

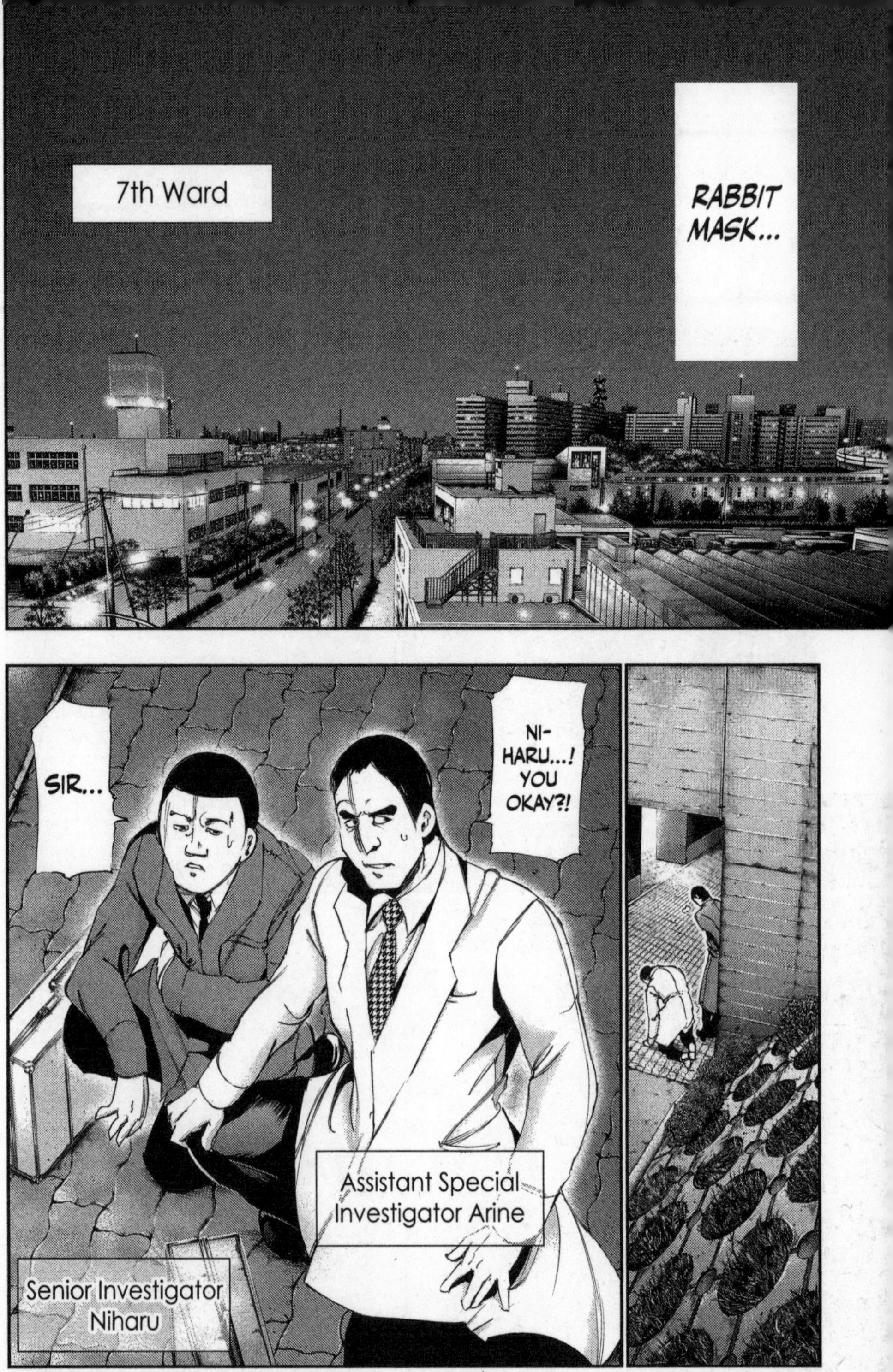
RABBIT MASK...
7th Ward
NI-HARU...! YOU OKAY?!
SIR...
Assistant Special Investigator Arine
Senior Investigator Niharu

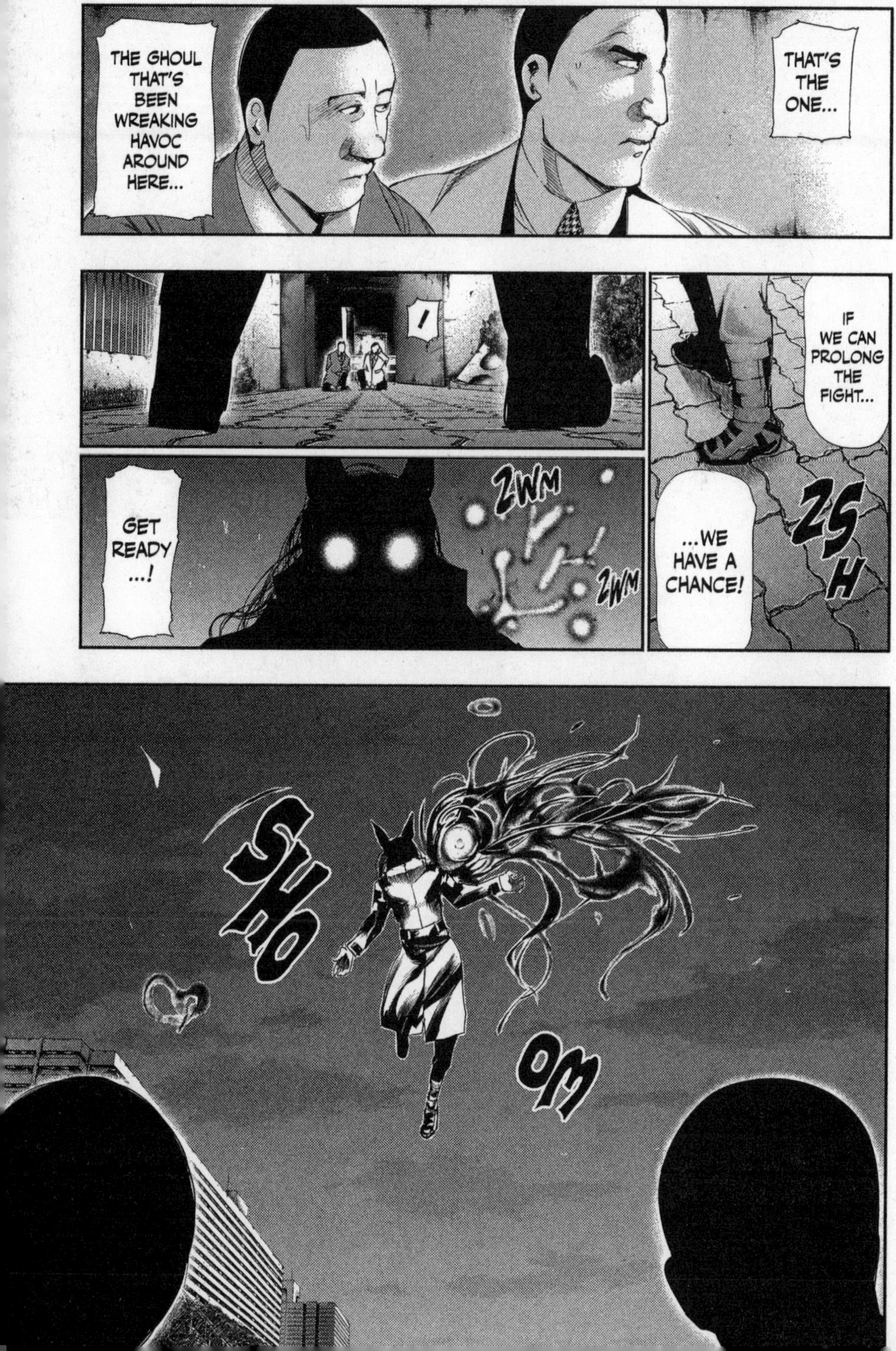
THAT'S THE ONE...
THE GHOUL THAT'S BEEN WREAKING HAVOC AROUND HERE...
IF WE CAN PROLONG THE FIGHT...
...WE HAVE A CHANCE!
ZSH
!
ZWM
ZWM
GET READY ...!
SHOOM

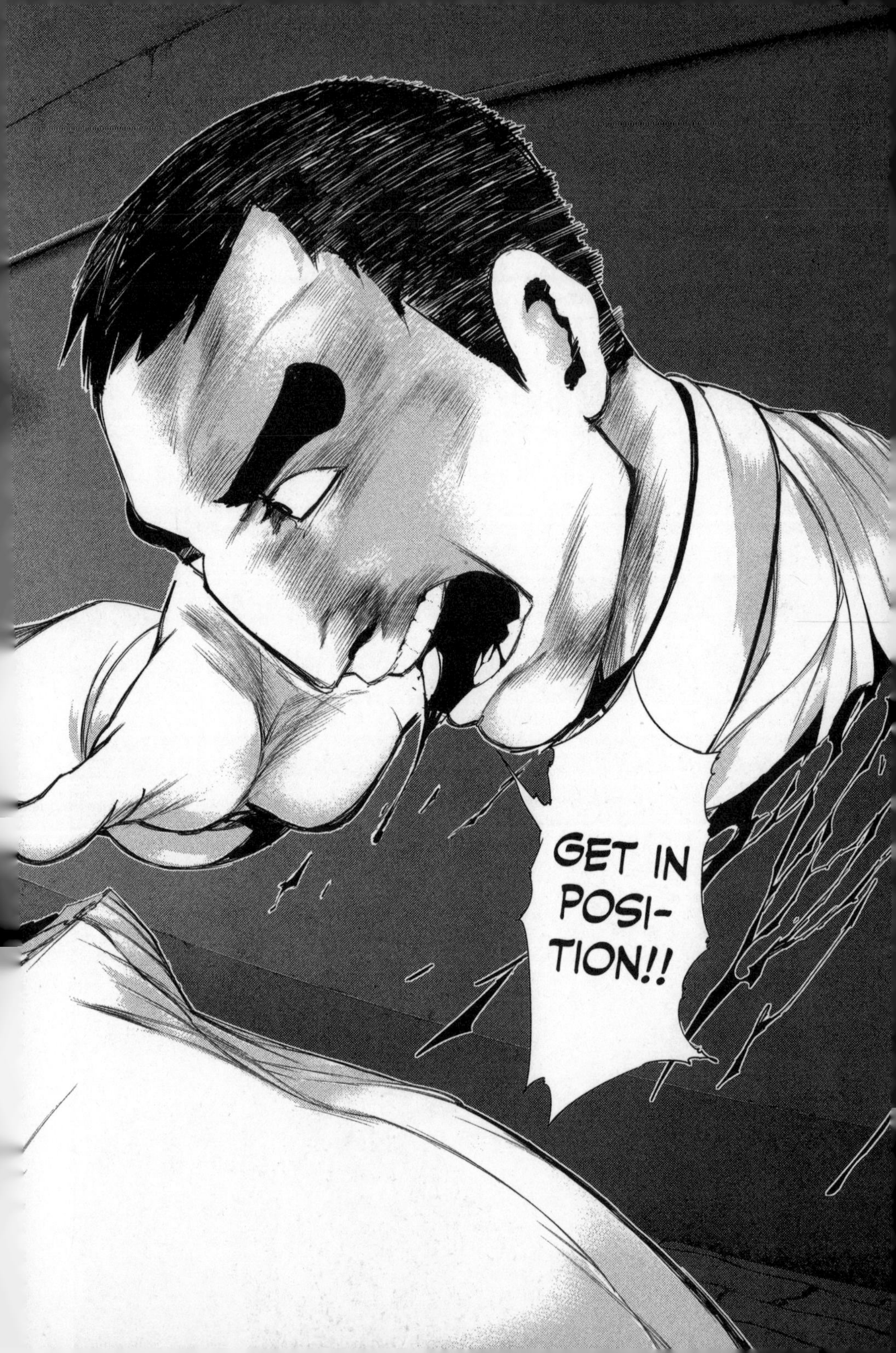
GET IN POSI-TION!!

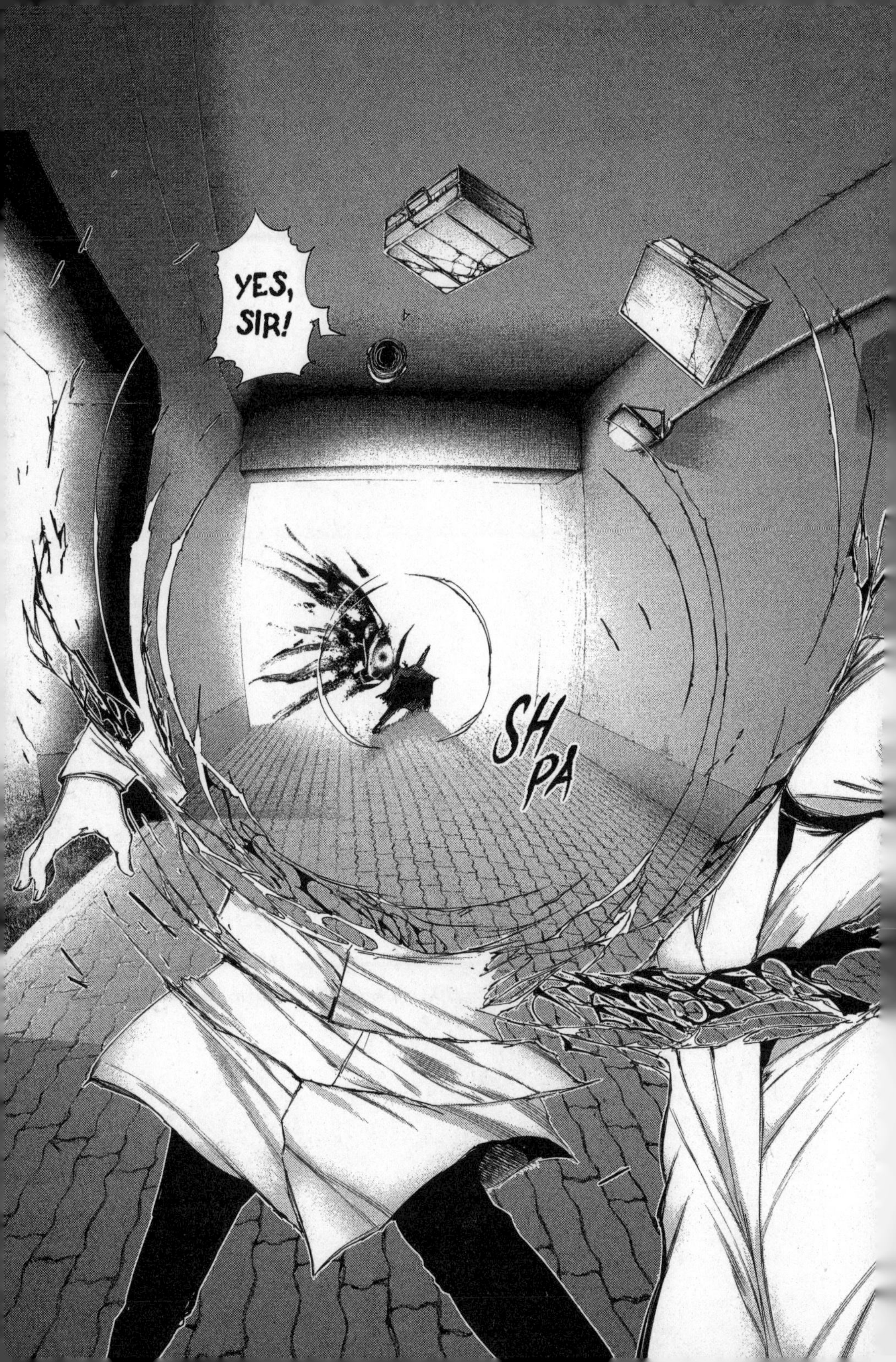
YES, SIR!
SHPA

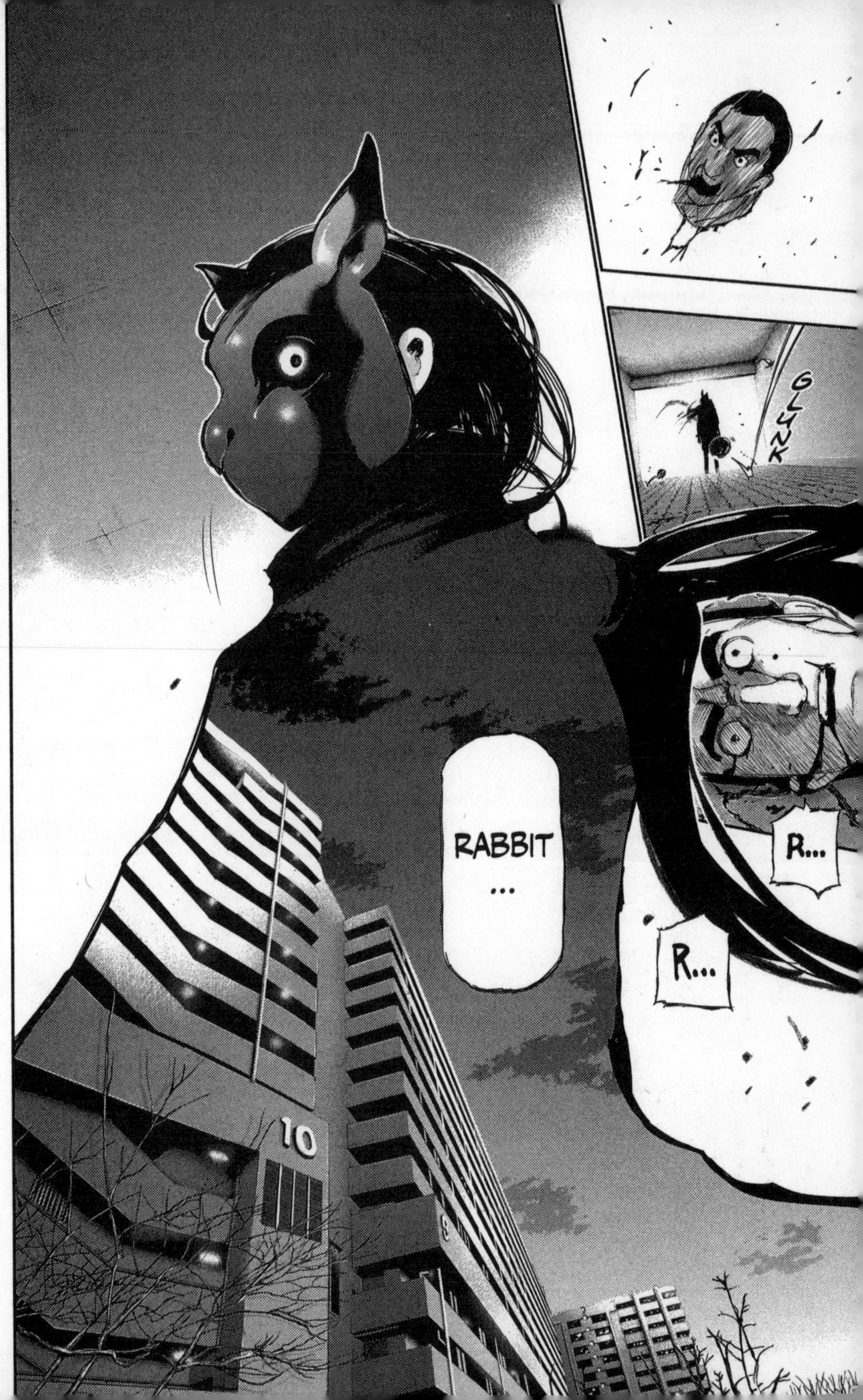
GLUNK
R...
R...
RABBIT ...

東京喰種
トーキョーグール
Tokyo
Ghoul

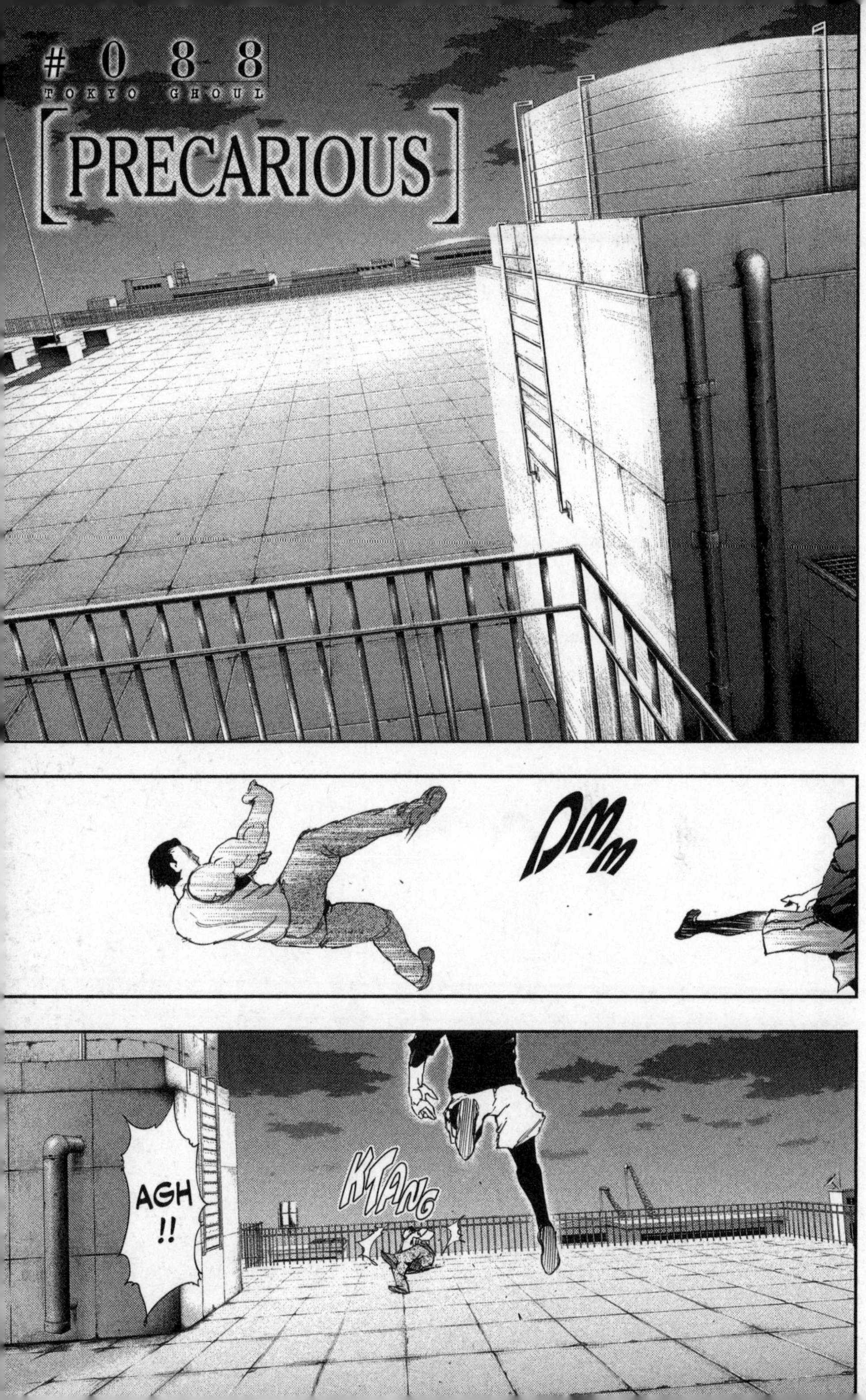

#088
TOKYO GHOUL
[PRECARIOUS]
DMM
KTANG
AGH!!

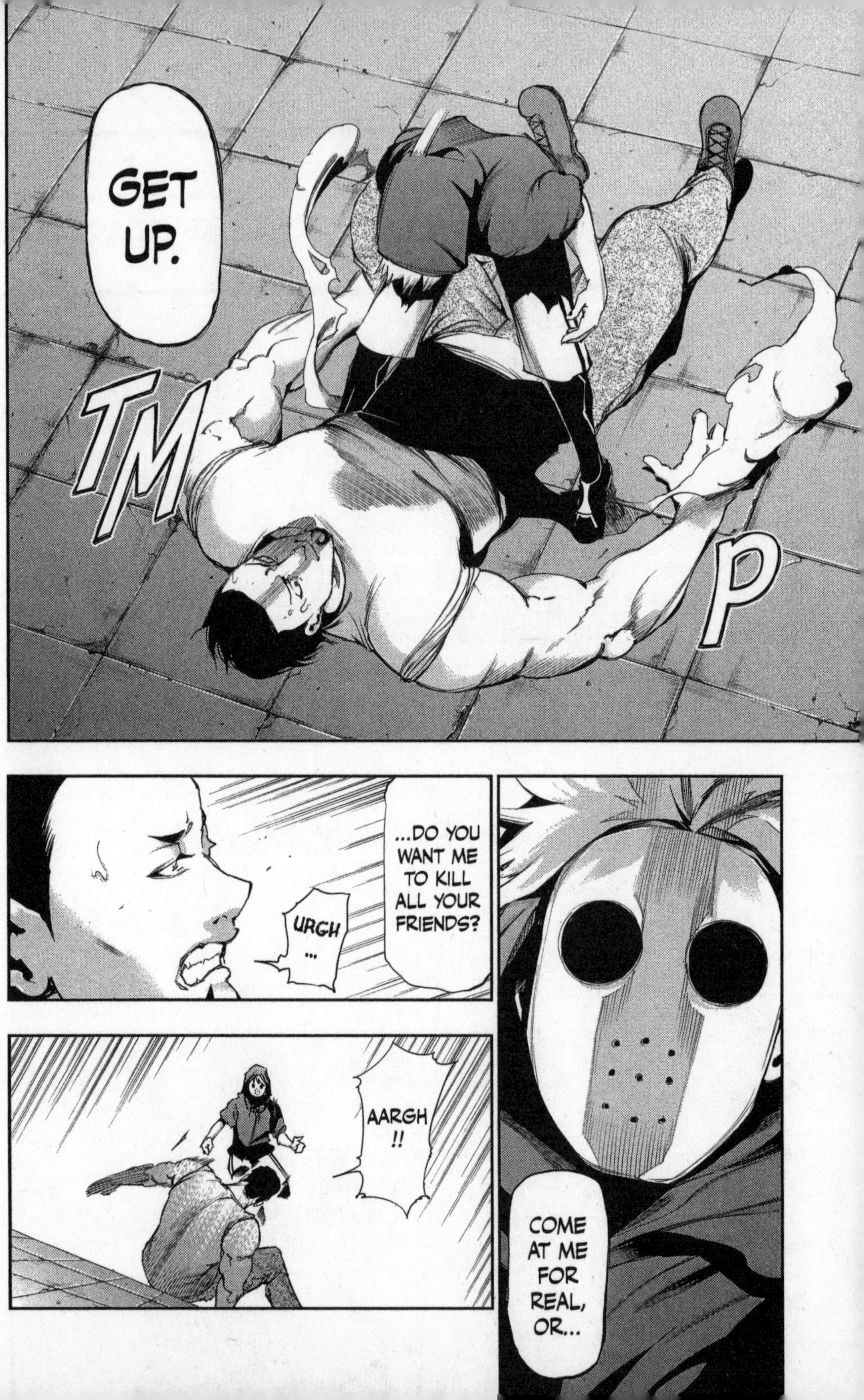
GET UP.
TMP
COME AT ME FOR REAL, OR...
...DO YOU WANT ME TO KILL ALL YOUR FRIENDS?
URGH...
AARGH!!

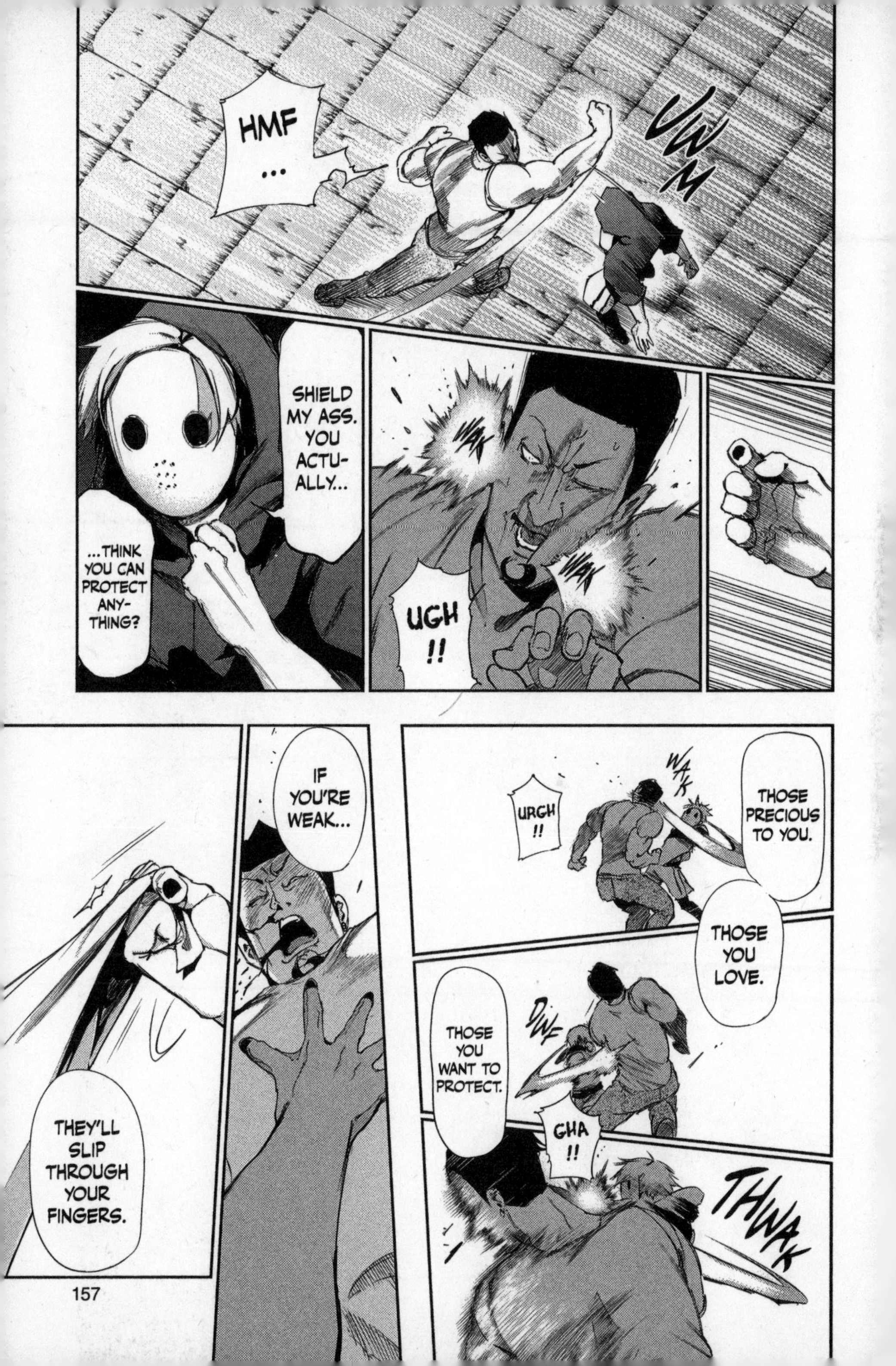
UWM
HMF ...
WAK
WAK
UGH!!
SHIELD MY ASS. YOU ACTU-ALLY...
...THINK YOU CAN PROTECT ANY-THING?
THOSE PRECIOUS TO YOU.
WAK
URGH!!
THOSE YOU LOVE.
DUF
THOSE YOU WANT TO PROTECT.
GHA!!
THWAK
IF YOU'RE WEAK...
THEY'LL SLIP THROUGH YOUR FINGERS.

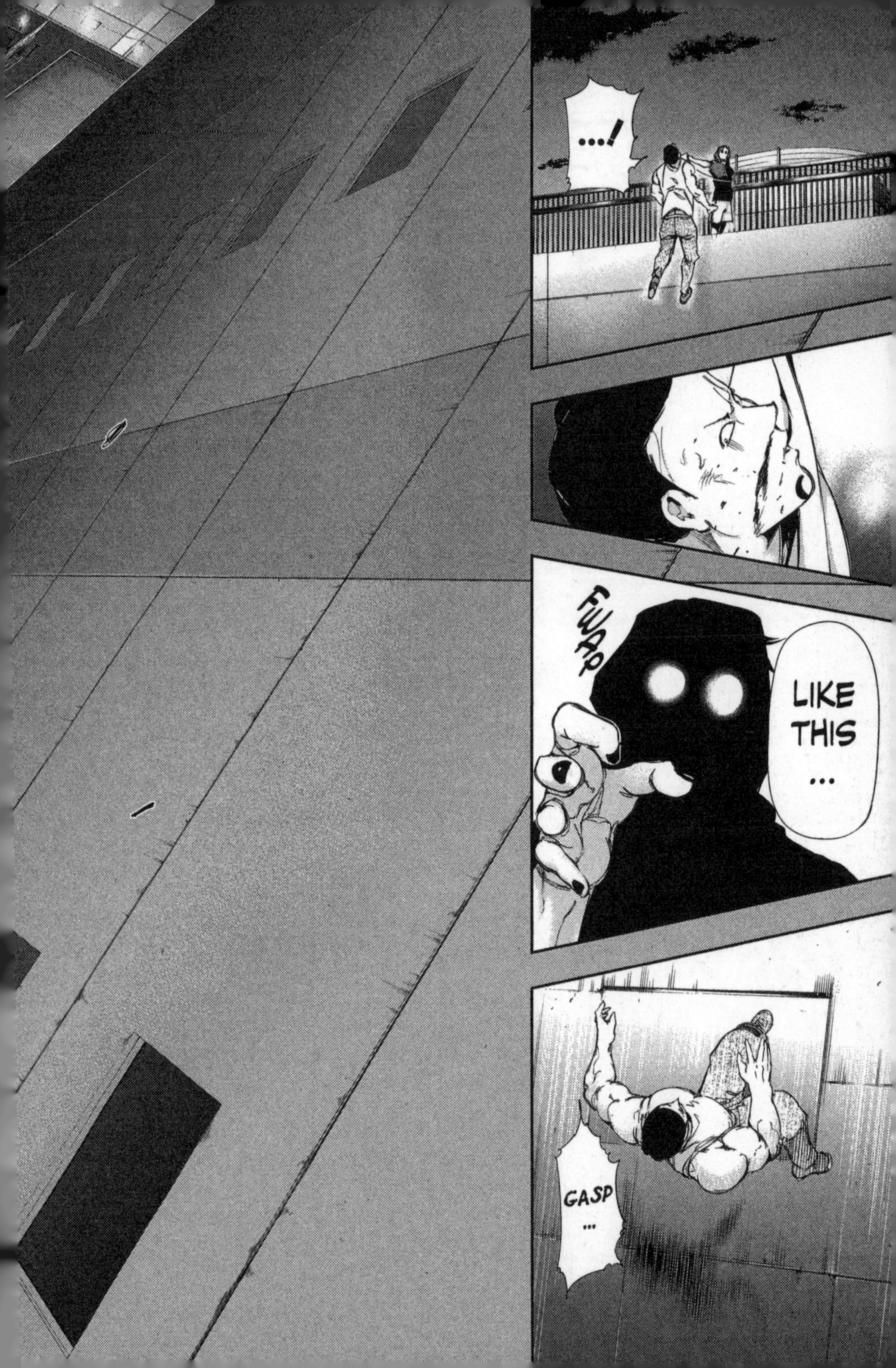
...!
FWAP
LIKE THIS ...
GASP ...

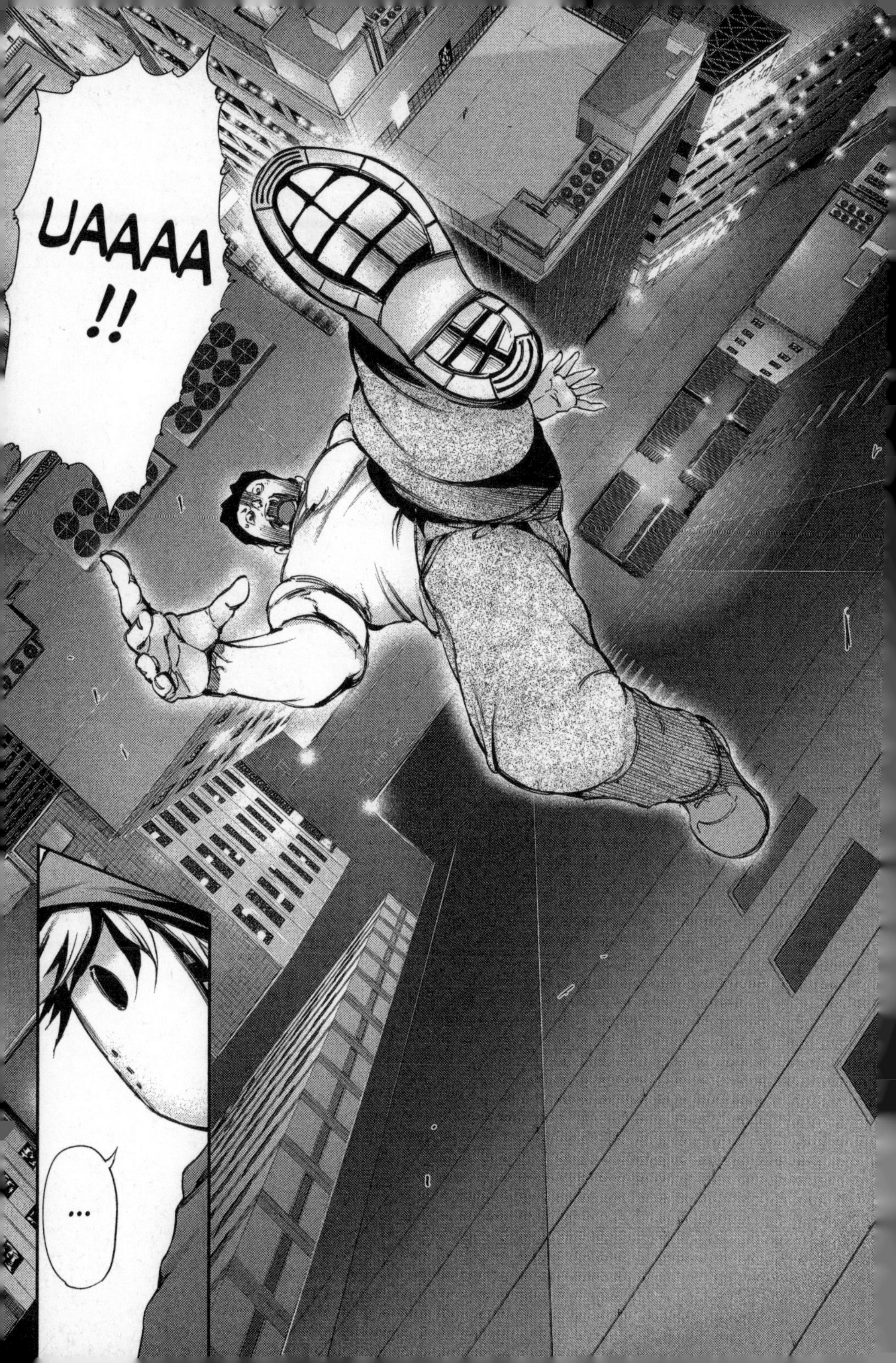
UAAAA !!
...

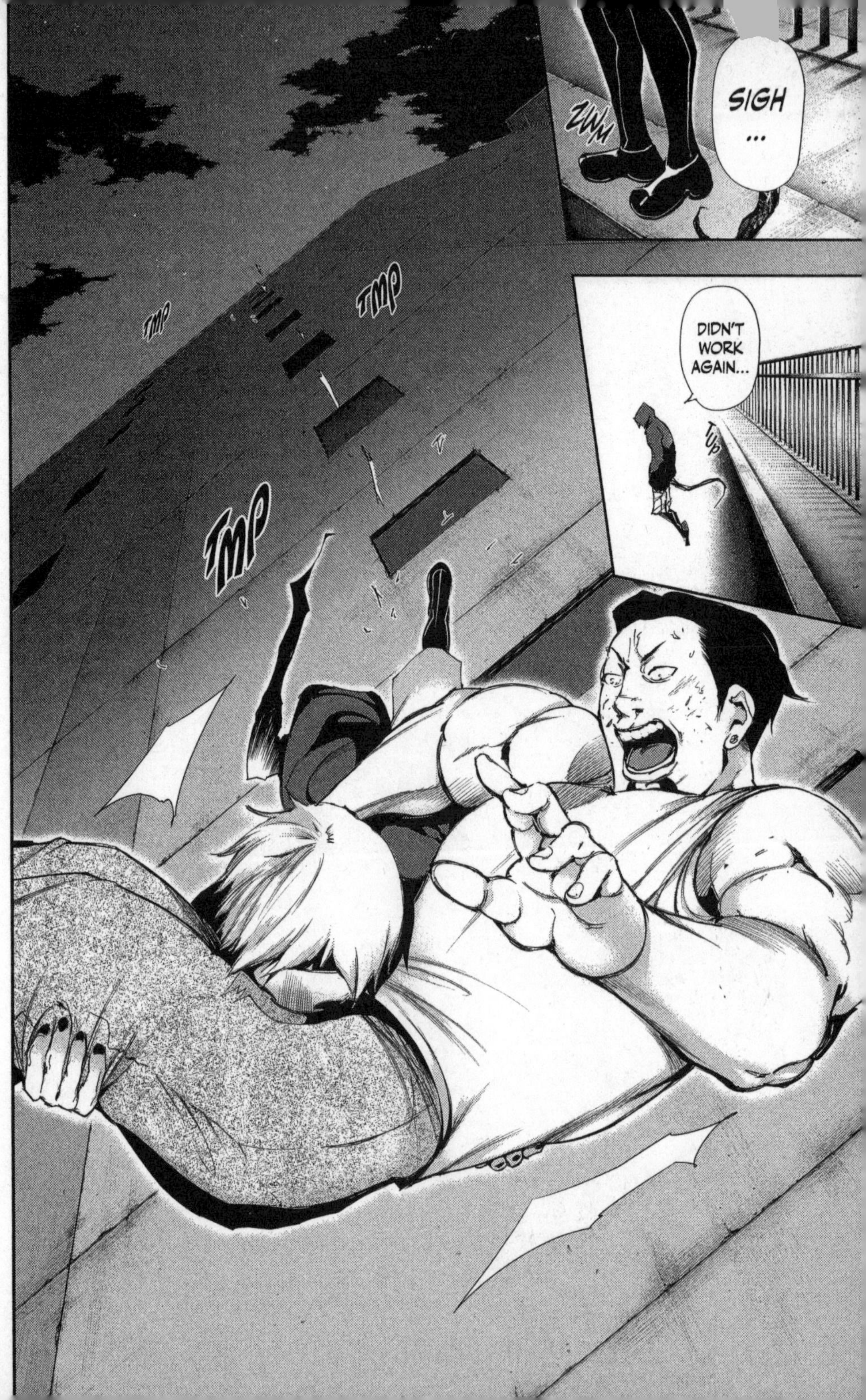
ZWM
SIGH ...
DIDN'T WORK AGAIN...
TUP
TMP
TMP
TMP

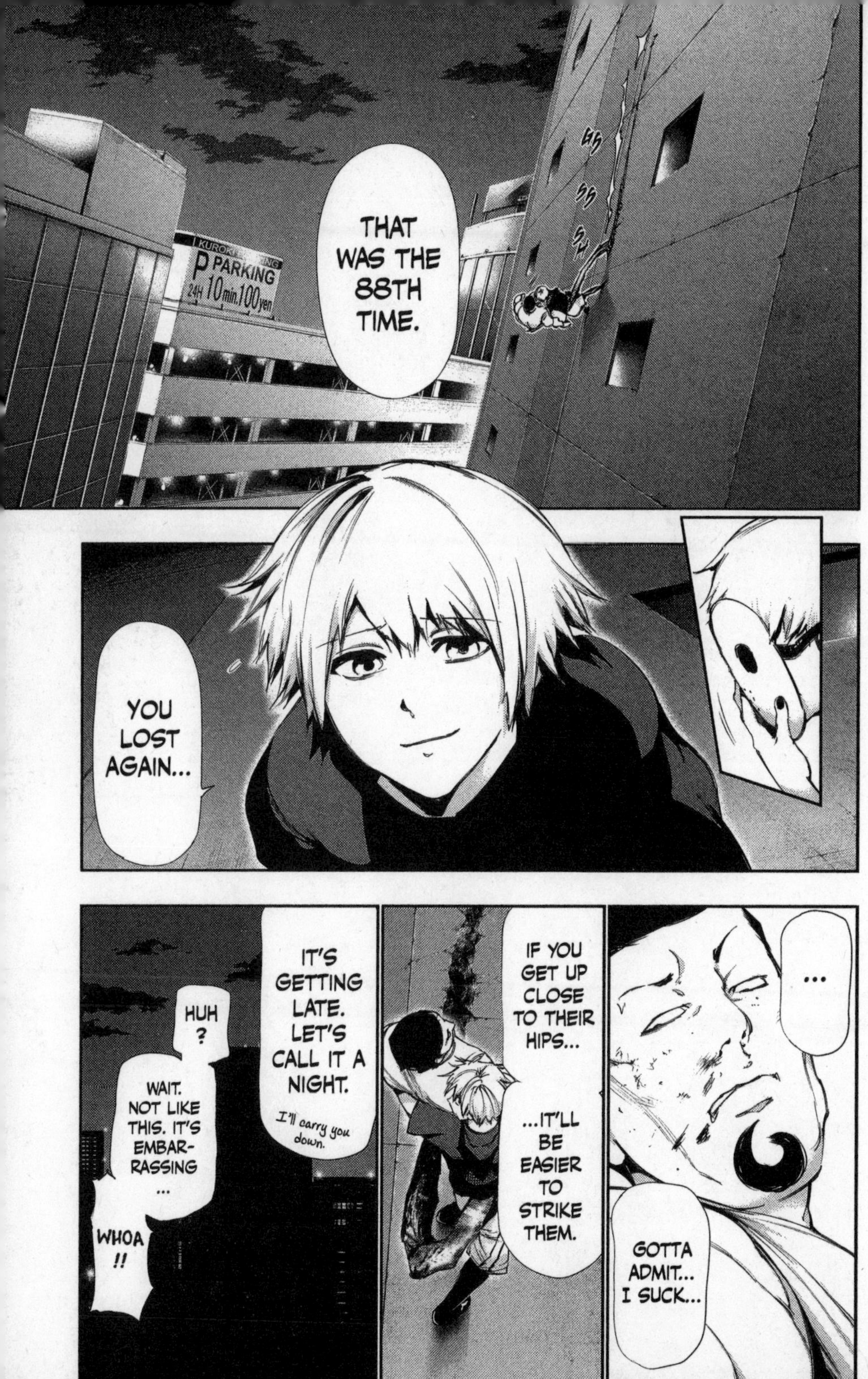

P PARKING
24H 10min.100yen
THAT WAS THE 88TH TIME.
YOU LOST AGAIN...
...
GOTTA ADMIT... I SUCK...
IF YOU GET UP CLOSE TO THEIR HIPS...
...IT'LL BE EASIER TO STRIKE THEM.
IT'S GETTING LATE. LET'S CALL IT A NIGHT.
I'll carry you down.
HUH?
WAIT. NOT LIKE THIS. IT'S EMBARRASSING...
WHOA!!

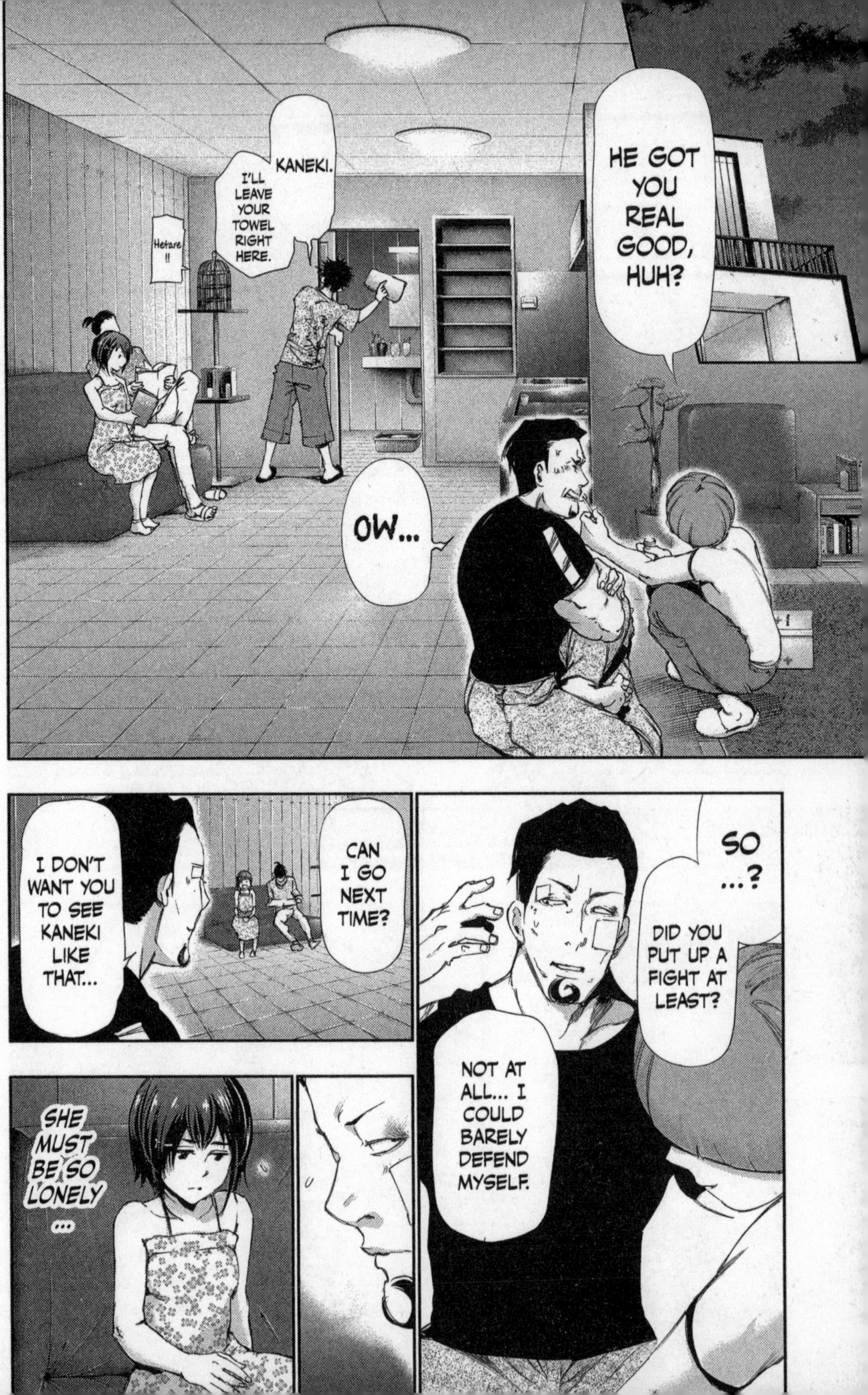

HE GOT YOU REAL GOOD, HUH?
KANEKI.
I'LL LEAVE YOUR TOWEL RIGHT HERE.
Hetare!!
OW...
SO ...?
DID YOU PUT UP A FIGHT AT LEAST?
NOT AT ALL... I COULD BARELY DEFEND MYSELF.
CAN I GO NEXT TIME?
I DON'T WANT YOU TO SEE KANEKI LIKE THAT...
SHE MUST BE SO LONELY ...

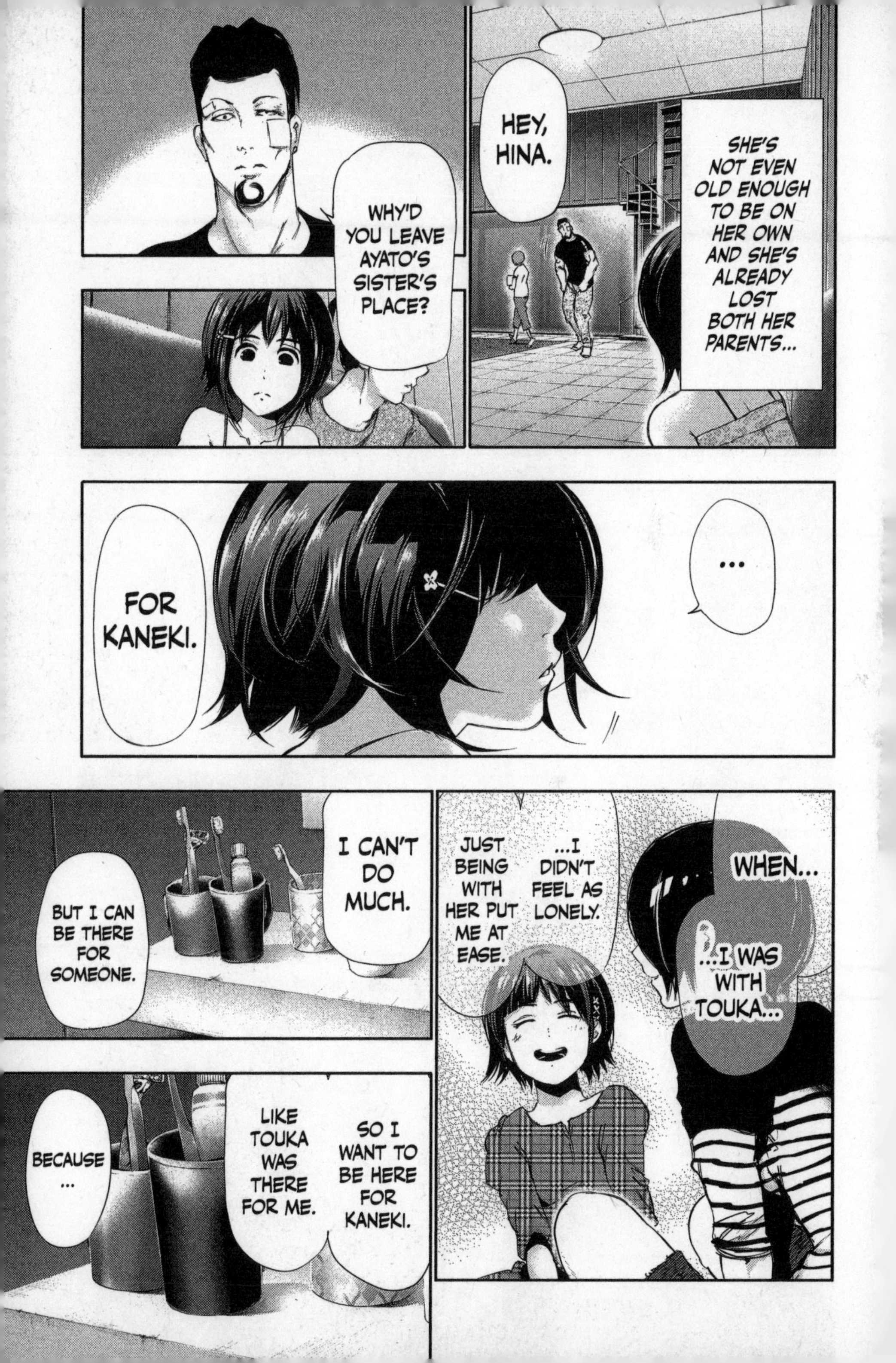
SHE'S NOT EVEN OLD ENOUGH TO BE ON HER OWN AND SHE'S ALREADY LOST BOTH HER PARENTS...
HEY, HINA.
WHY'D YOU LEAVE AYATO'S SISTER'S PLACE?
...
FOR KANEKI.
WHEN...
...I WAS WITH TOUKA...
...I DIDN'T FEEL AS LONELY.
JUST BEING WITH HER PUT ME AT EASE.
I CAN'T DO MUCH.
BUT I CAN BE THERE FOR SOMEONE.
SO I WANT TO BE HERE FOR KANEKI.
LIKE TOUKA WAS THERE FOR ME.
BECAUSE ...

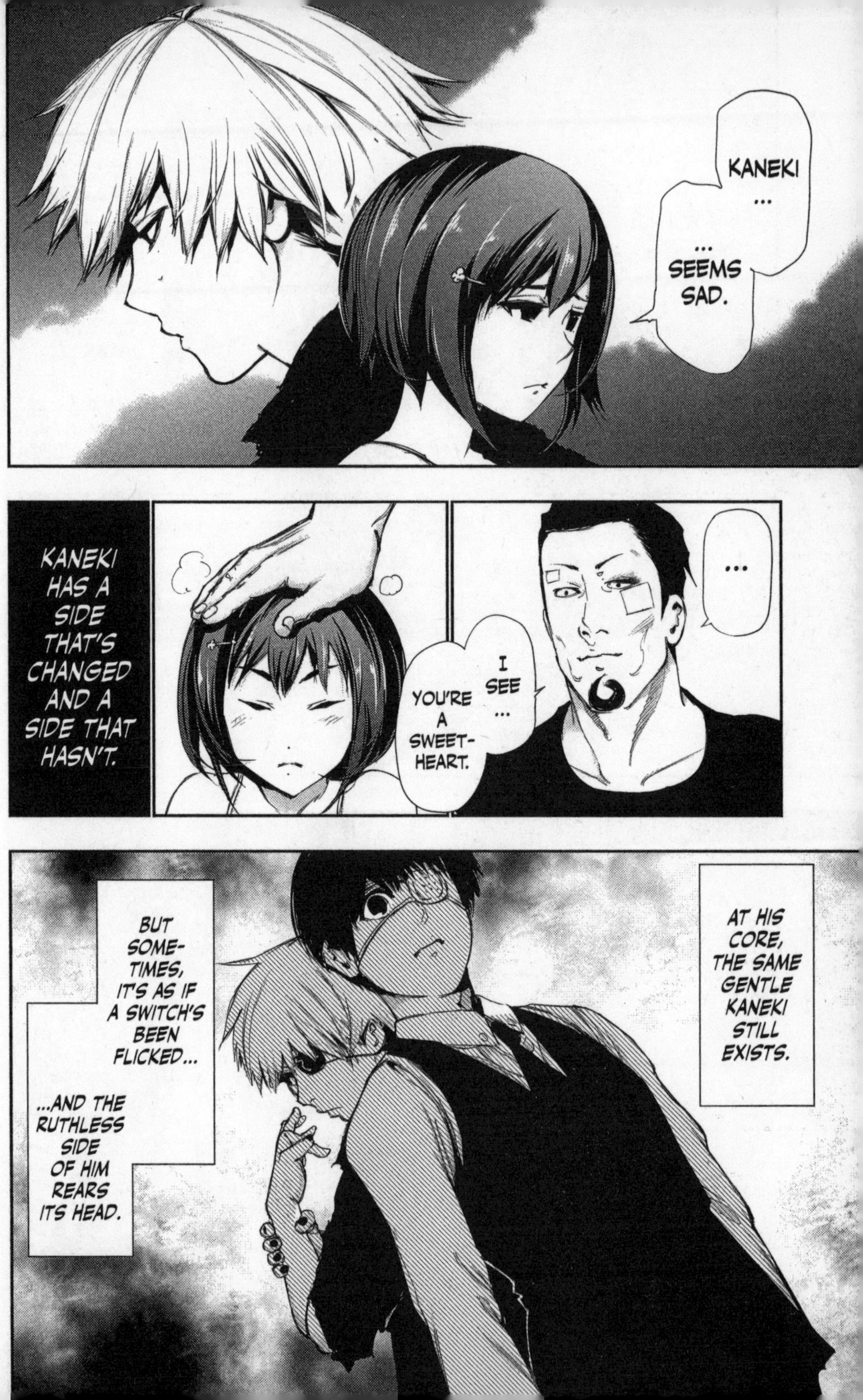
KANEKI ...
... SEEMS SAD.
...
I SEE ...
YOU'RE A SWEET-HEART.
KANEKI HAS A SIDE THAT'S CHANGED AND A SIDE THAT HASN'T.
AT HIS CORE, THE SAME GENTLE KANEKI STILL EXISTS.
BUT SOME-TIMES, IT'S AS IF A SWITCH'S BEEN FLICKED...
...AND THE RUTHLESS SIDE OF HIM REARS ITS HEAD.

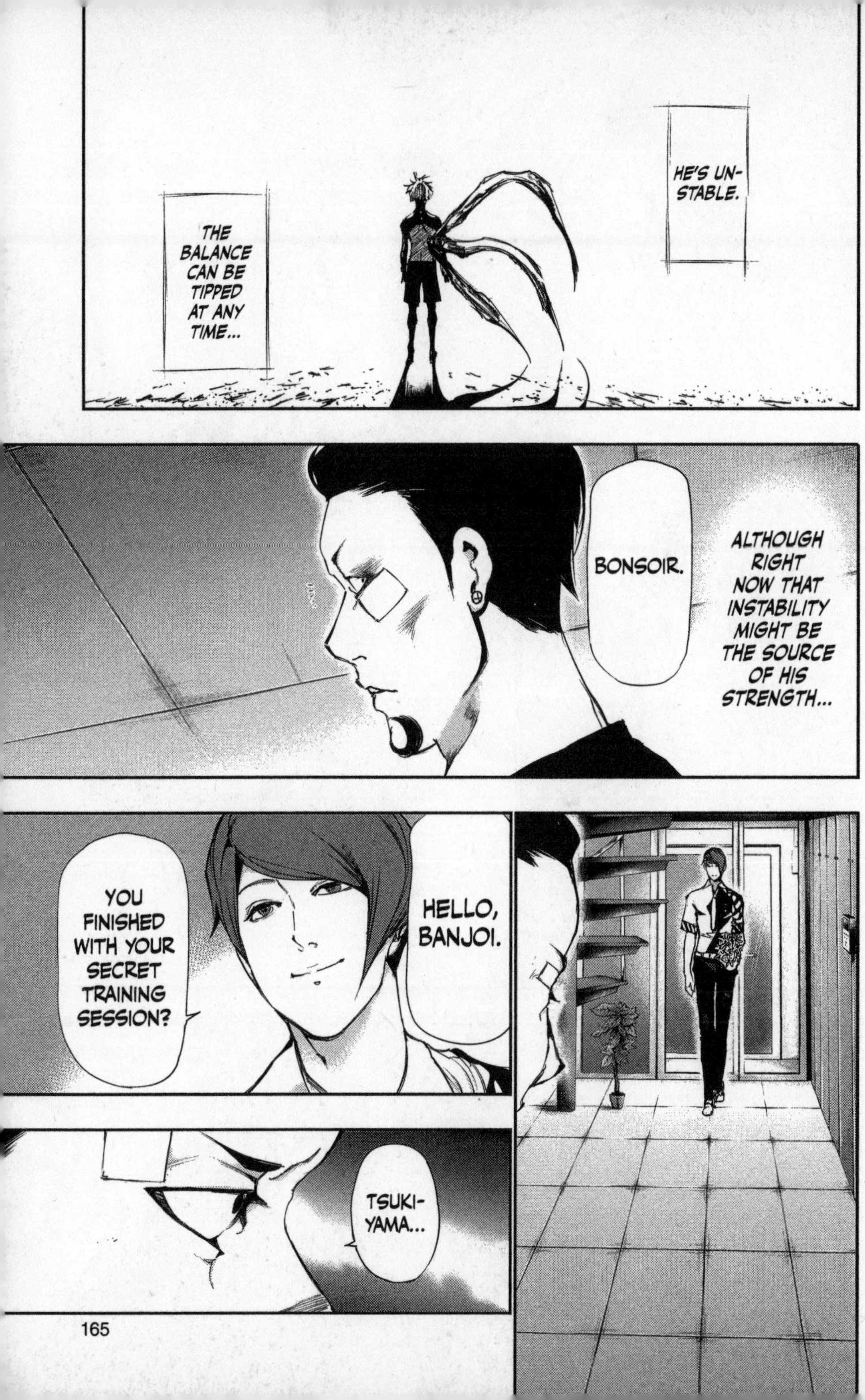
HE'S UN-STABLE.
THE BALANCE CAN BE TIPPED AT ANY TIME...
ALTHOUGH RIGHT NOW THAT INSTABILITY MIGHT BE THE SOURCE OF HIS STRENGTH...
BONSOIR.
HELLO, BANJOI.
YOU FINISHED WITH YOUR SECRET TRAINING SESSION?
TSUKI-YAMA...

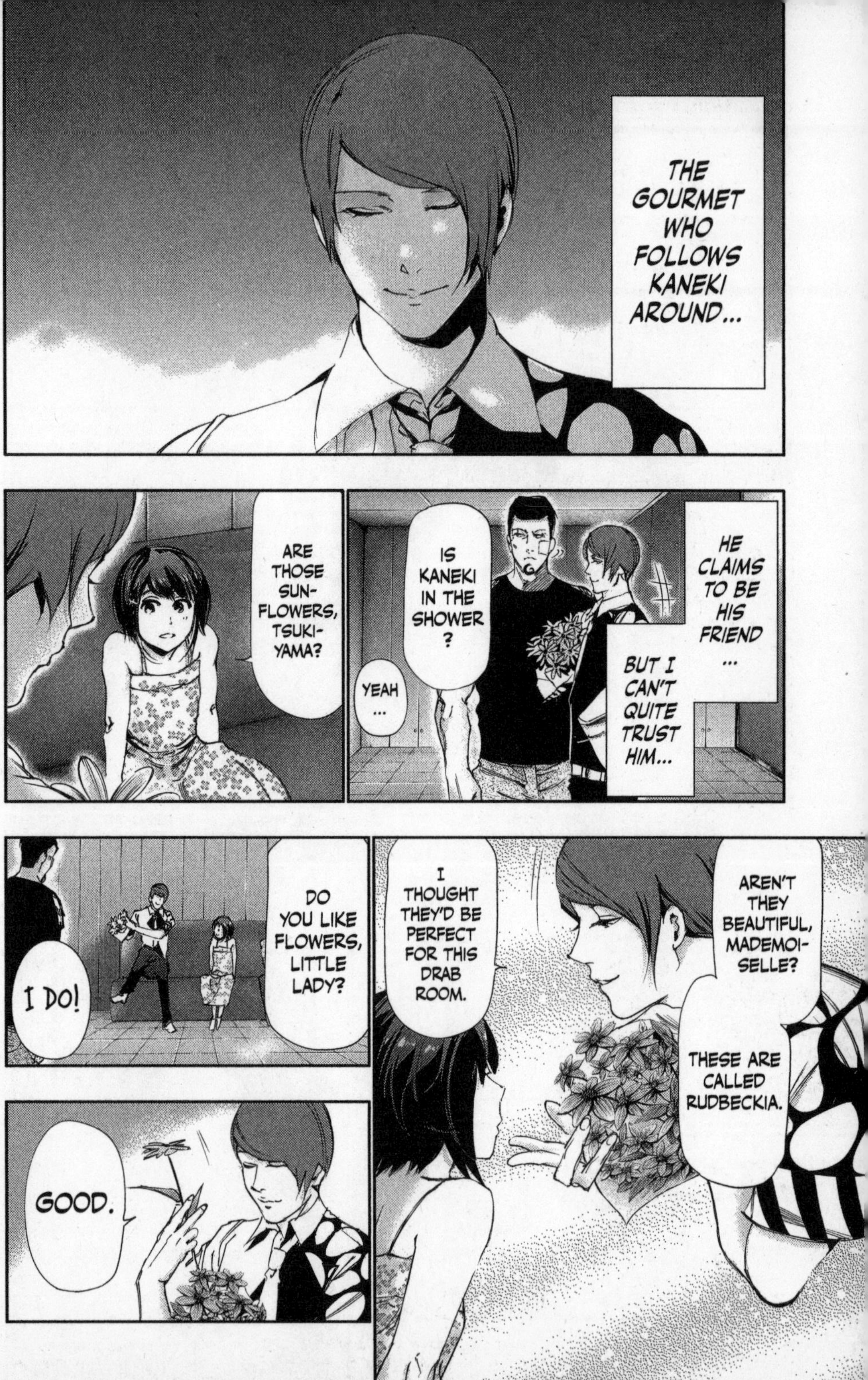
THE GOURMET WHO FOLLOWS KANEKI AROUND...
HE CLAIMS TO BE HIS FRIEND...
BUT I CAN'T QUITE TRUST HIM...
IS KANEKI IN THE SHOWER?
YEAH...
ARE THOSE SUN-FLOWERS, TSUKI-YAMA?
AREN'T THEY BEAUTIFUL, MADEMOI-SELLE?
THESE ARE CALLED RUDBECKIA.
I THOUGHT THEY'D BE PERFECT FOR THIS DRAB ROOM.
DO YOU LIKE FLOWERS, LITTLE LADY?
I DO!
GOOD.

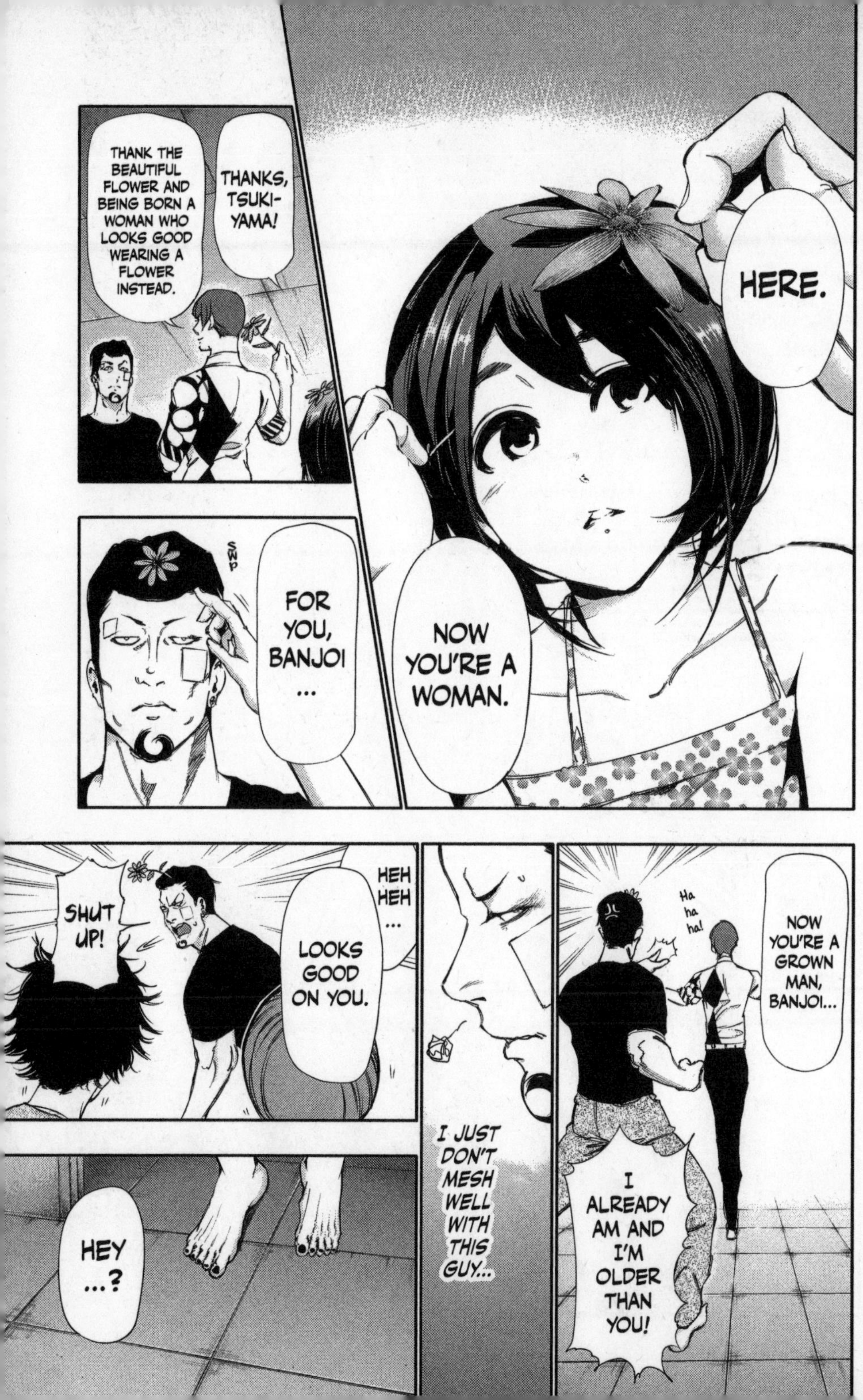
HERE.
NOW YOU'RE A WOMAN.
THANKS, TSUKI-YAMA!
THANK THE BEAUTIFUL FLOWER AND BEING BORN A WOMAN WHO LOOKS GOOD WEARING A FLOWER INSTEAD.
SWP
FOR YOU, BANJOI ...
Ha ha ha!
NOW YOU'RE A GROWN MAN, BANJOI...
I ALREADY AM AND I'M OLDER THAN YOU!
I JUST DON'T MESH WELL WITH THIS GUY...
HEH HEH ...
LOOKS GOOD ON YOU.
SHUT UP!
HEY ...?

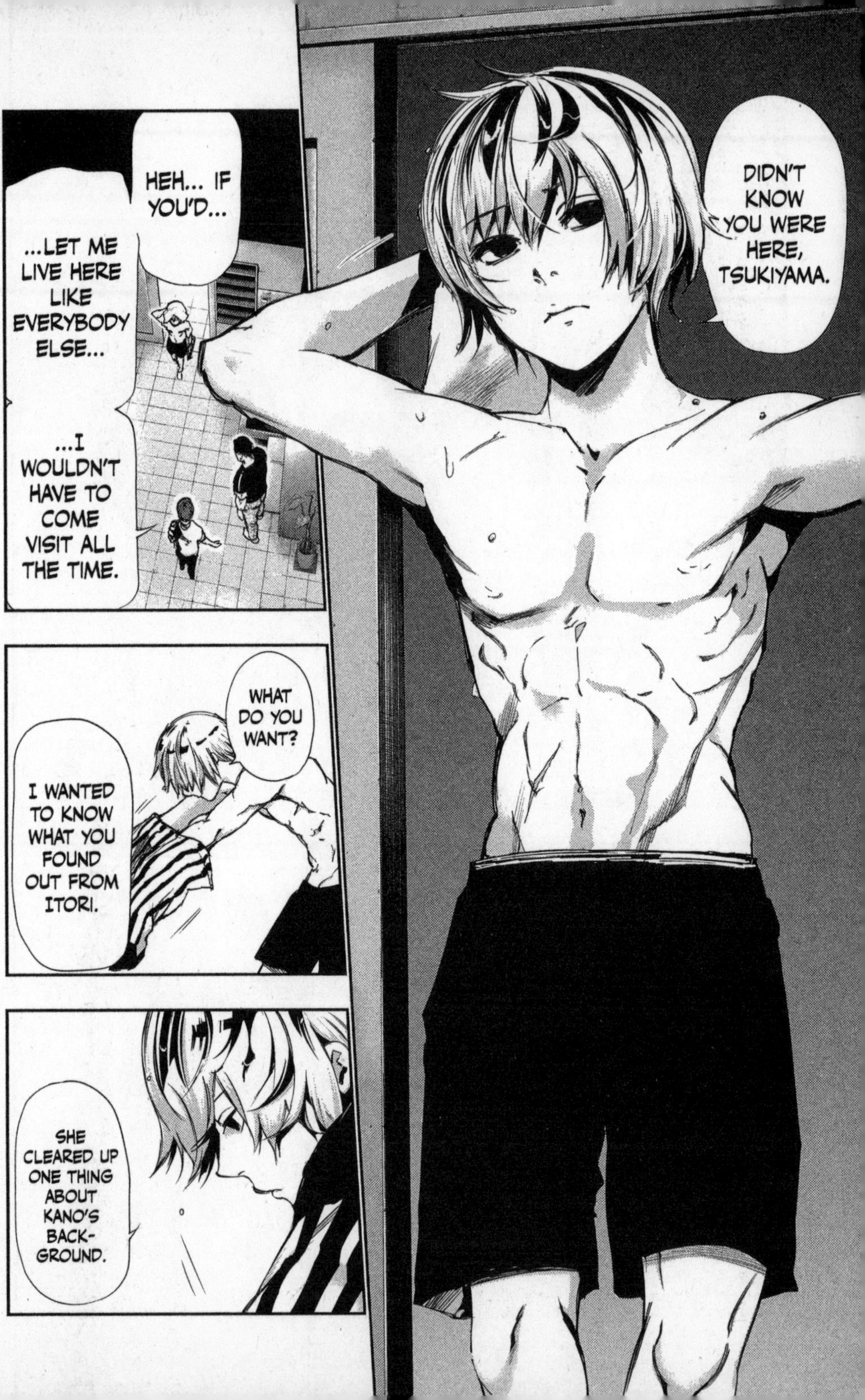
DIDN'T KNOW YOU WERE HERE, TSUKIYAMA.
HEH... IF YOU'D...
...LET ME LIVE HERE LIKE EVERYBODY ELSE...
...I WOULDN'T HAVE TO COME VISIT ALL THE TIME.
WHAT DO YOU WANT?
I WANTED TO KNOW WHAT YOU FOUND OUT FROM ITORI.
SHE CLEARED UP ONE THING ABOUT KANO'S BACK-GROUND.

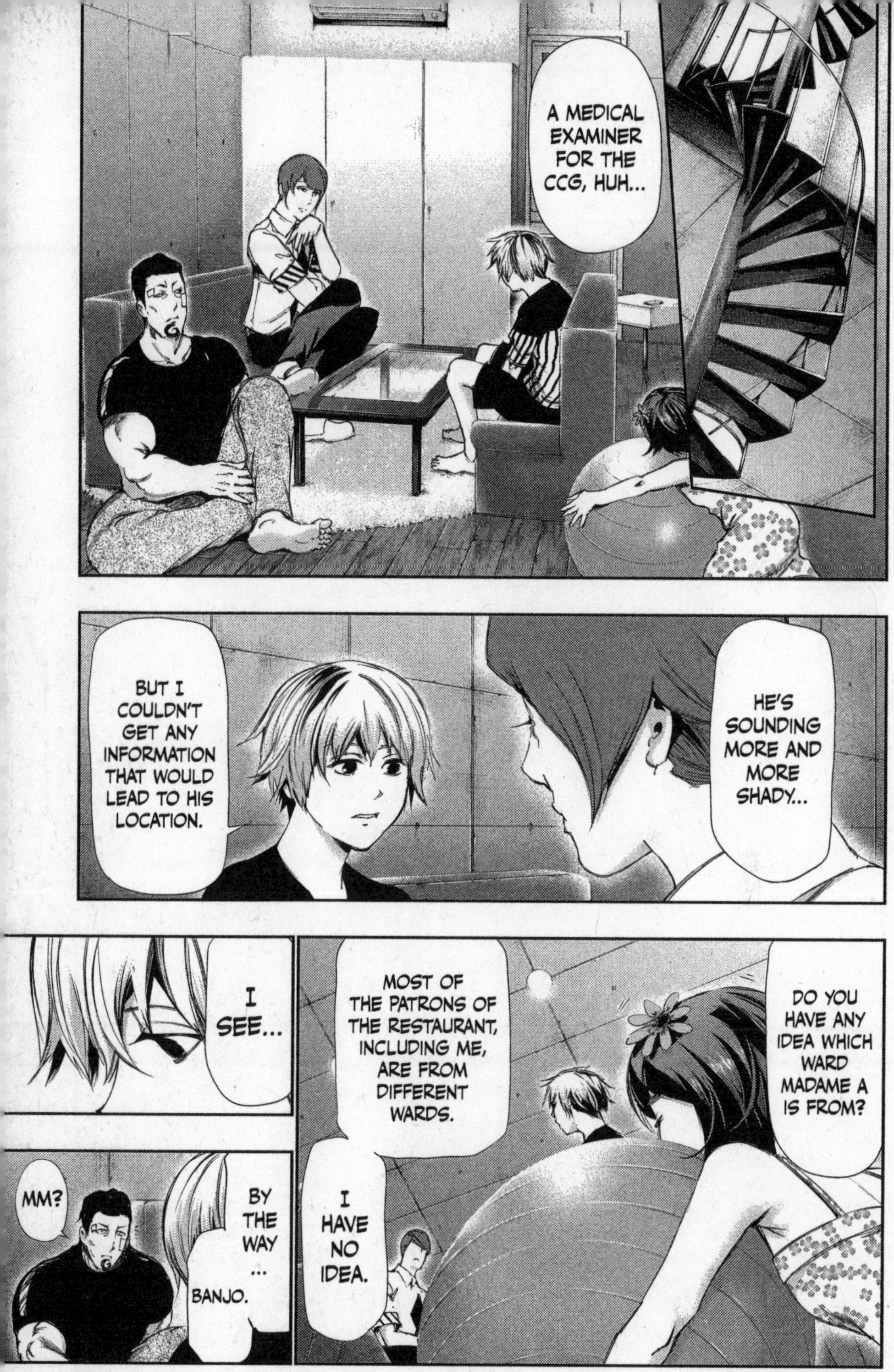
A MEDICAL EXAMINER FOR THE CCG, HUH...
HE'S SOUNDING MORE AND MORE SHADY...
BUT I COULDN'T GET ANY INFORMATION THAT WOULD LEAD TO HIS LOCATION.
DO YOU HAVE ANY IDEA WHICH WARD MADAME A IS FROM?
MOST OF THE PATRONS OF THE RESTAURANT, INCLUDING ME, ARE FROM DIFFERENT WARDS.
I HAVE NO IDEA.
I SEE...
BY THE WAY ...
BANJO.
MM?

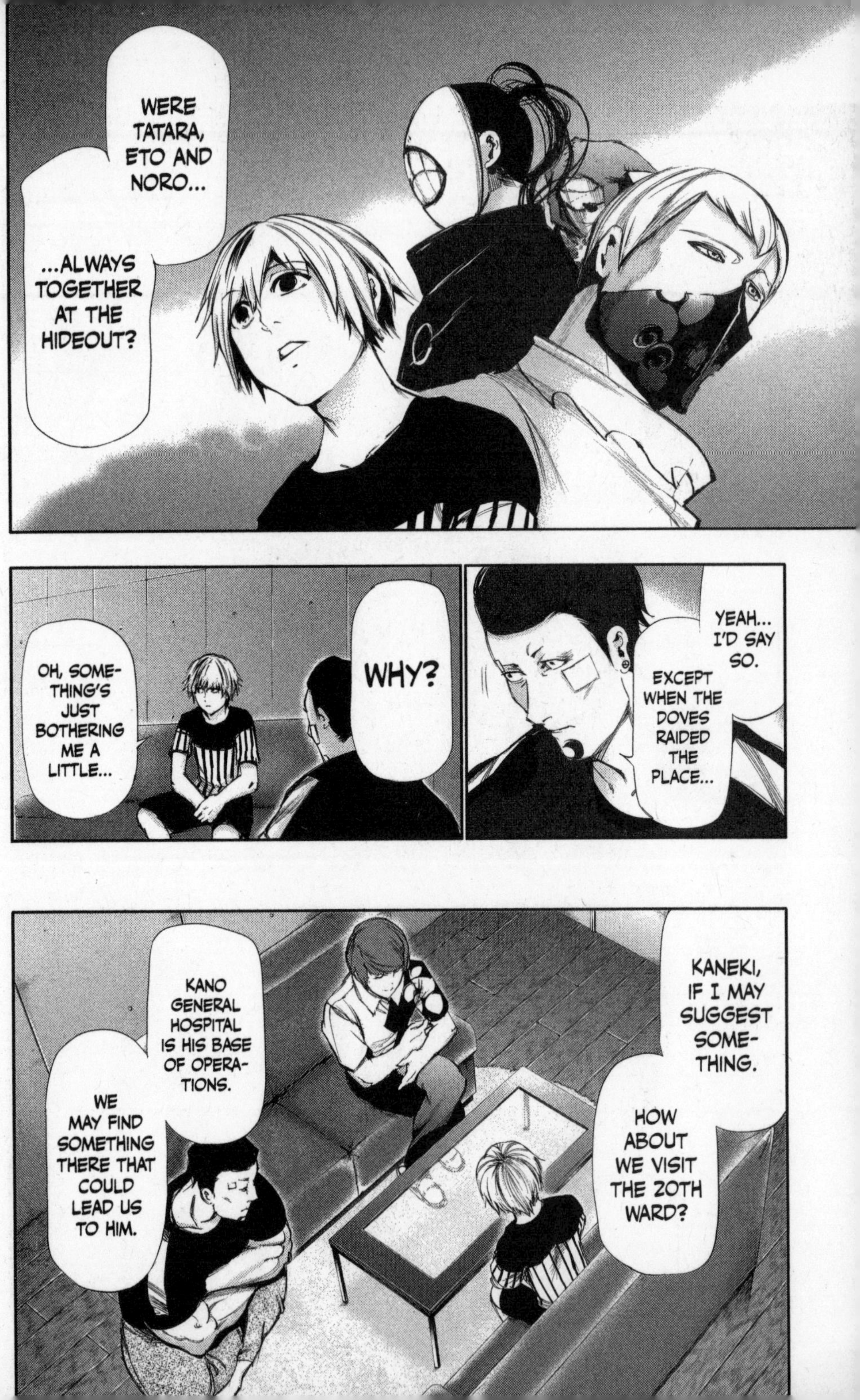
WERE TATARA, ETO AND NORO...
...ALWAYS TOGETHER AT THE HIDEOUT?
YEAH... I'D SAY SO.
EXCEPT WHEN THE DOVES RAIDED THE PLACE...
WHY?
OH, SOME-THING'S JUST BOTHERING ME A LITTLE...
KANEKI, IF I MAY SUGGEST SOME-THING.
HOW ABOUT WE VISIT THE 20TH WARD?
KANO GENERAL HOSPITAL IS HIS BASE OF OPERA-TIONS.
WE MAY FIND SOMETHING THERE THAT COULD LEAD US TO HIM.

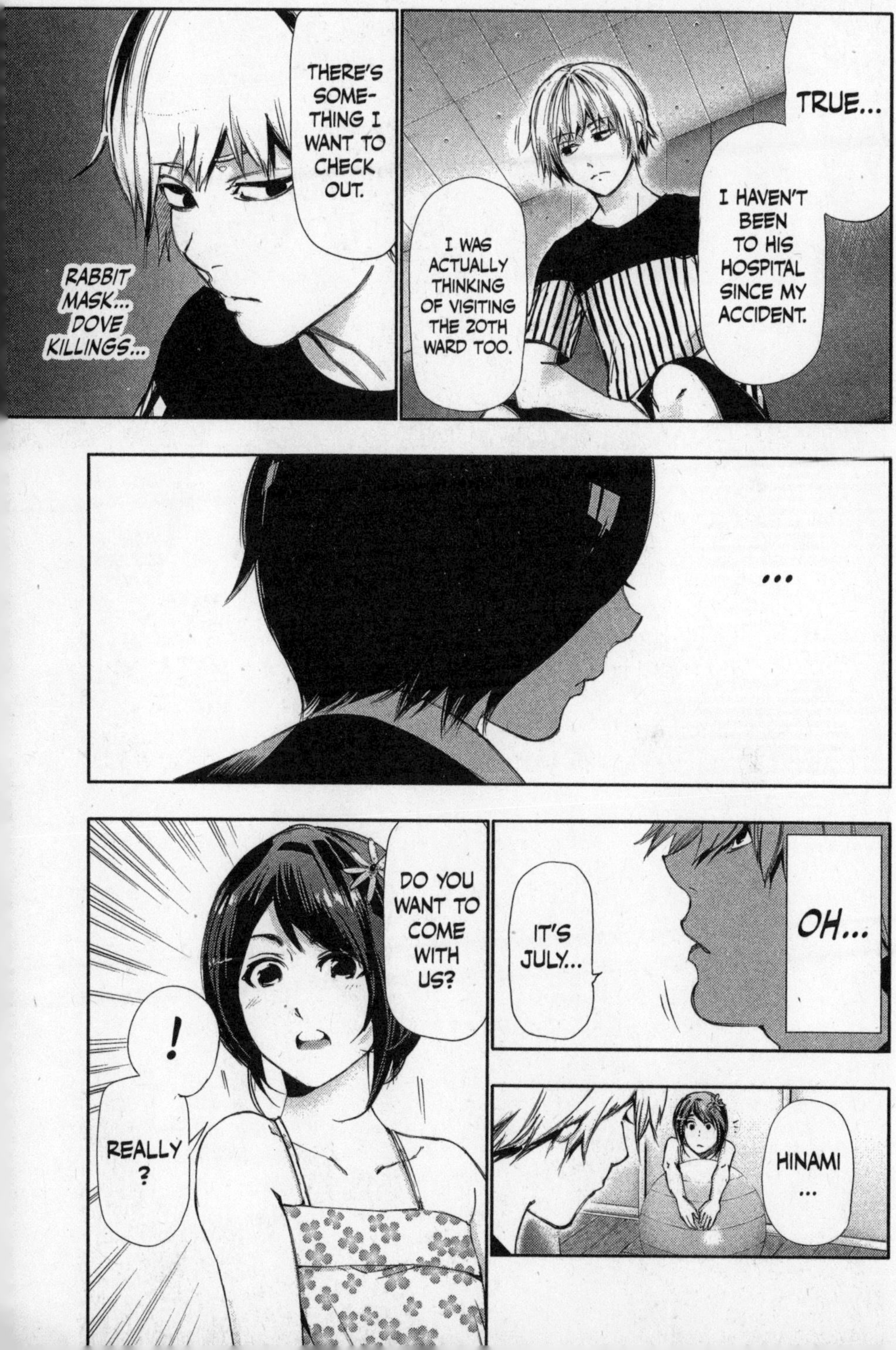
TRUE...
I HAVEN'T BEEN TO HIS HOSPITAL SINCE MY ACCIDENT.
I WAS ACTUALLY THINKING OF VISITING THE 20TH WARD TOO.
THERE'S SOME-THING I WANT TO CHECK OUT.
RABBIT MASK... DOVE KILLINGS...
...
OH...
IT'S JULY...
HINAMI ...
DO YOU WANT TO COME WITH US?
!
REALLY ?

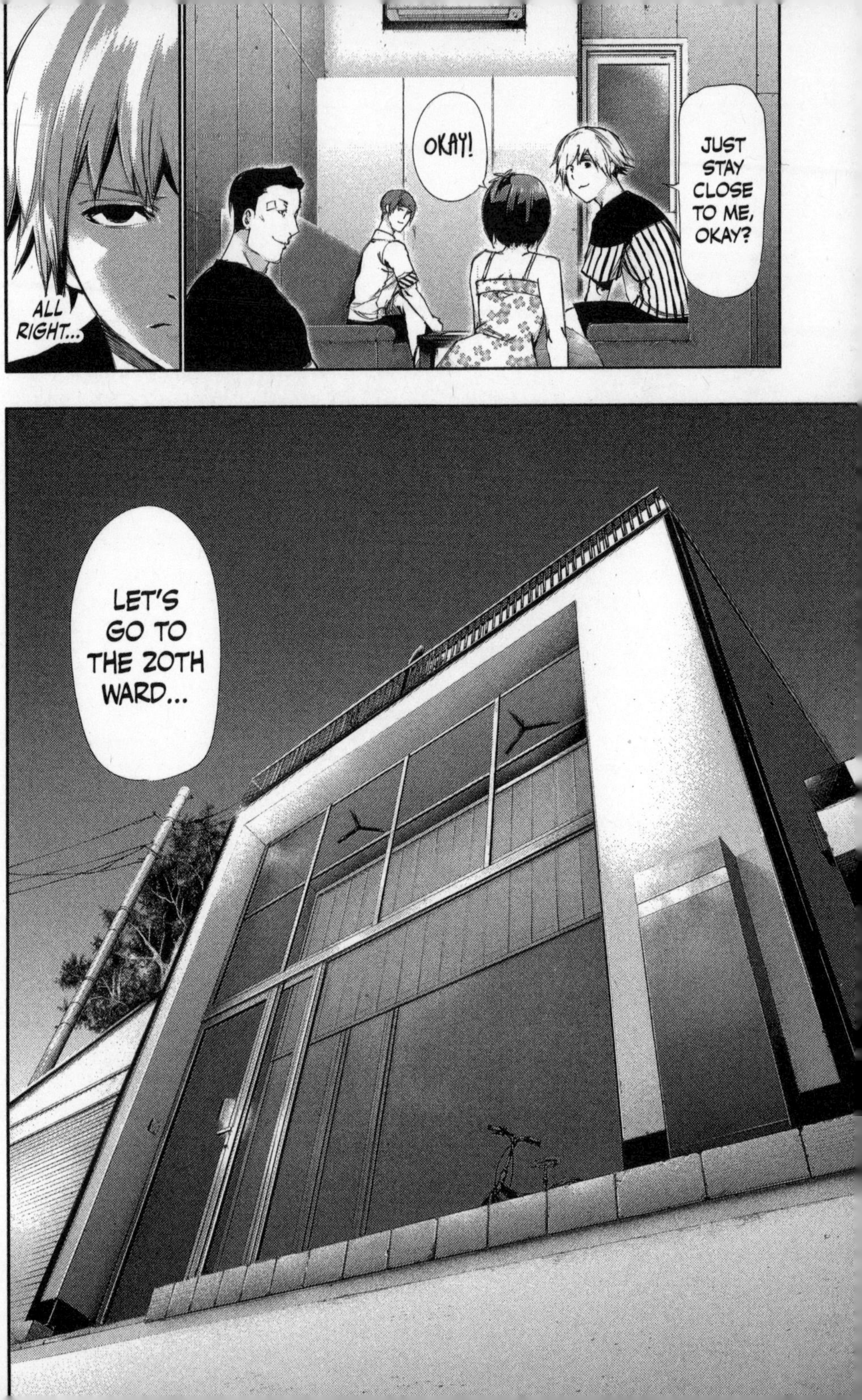
JUST STAY CLOSE TO ME, OKAY?
OKAY!
ALL RIGHT...
LET'S GO TO THE 20TH WARD...

東京喰種
トーキョーグール
喰種
Tokyo
Ghoul

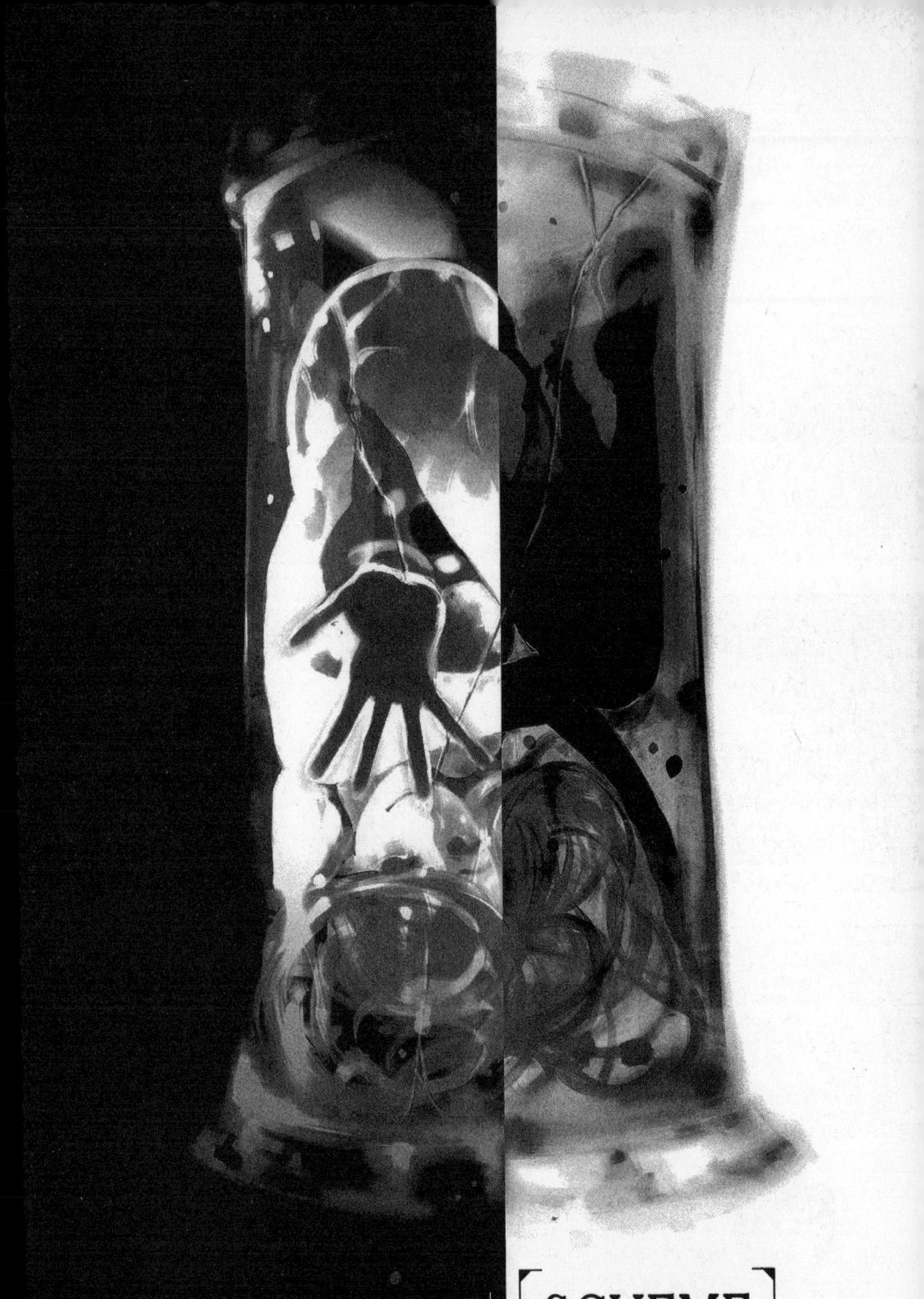

#089 [SCHEME]

TOKYO GHOUL

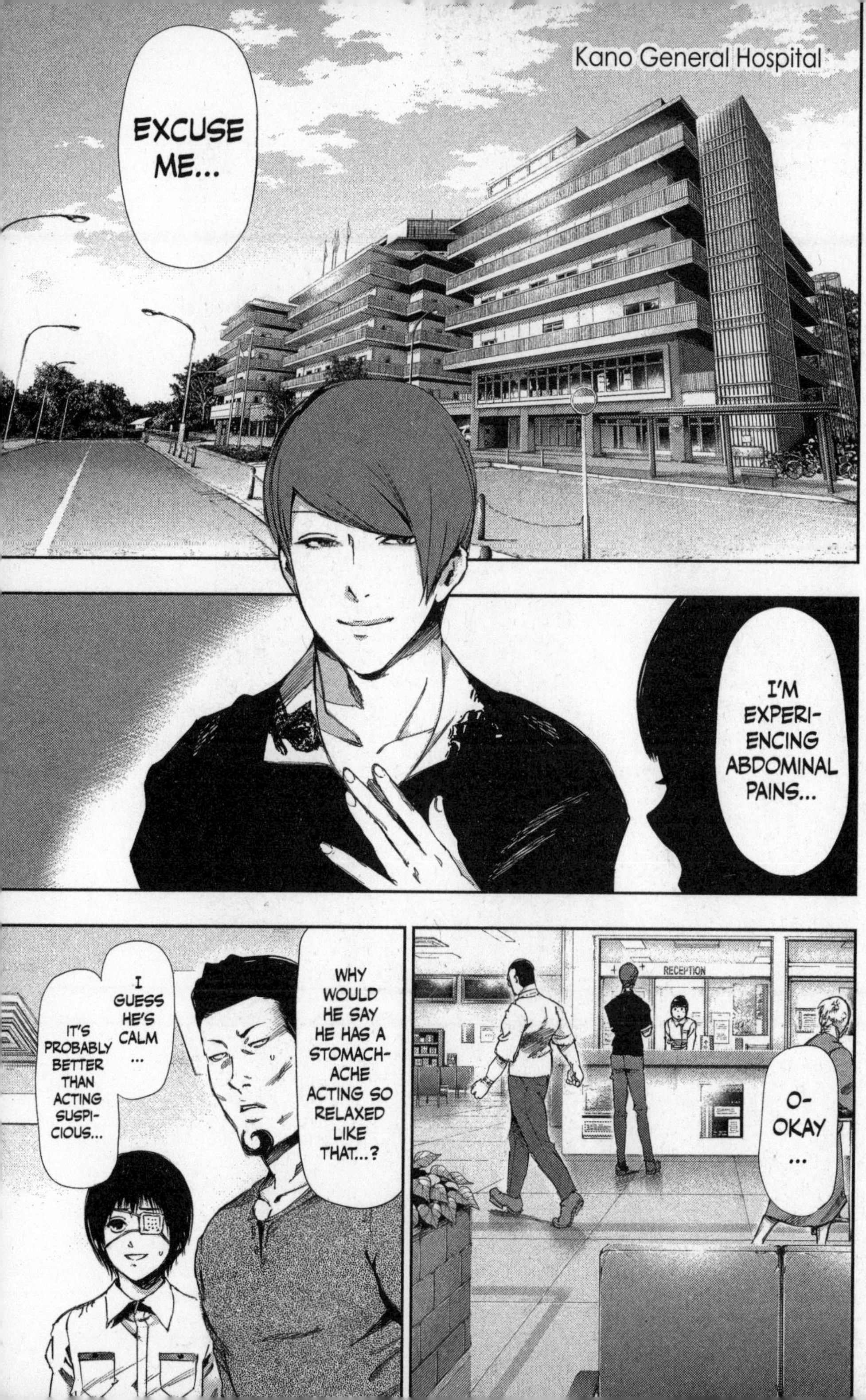
Kano General Hospital
EXCUSE ME...
I'M EXPERIENCING ABDOMINAL PAINS...
O-OKAY...
WHY WOULD HE SAY HE HAS A STOMACHACHE ACTING SO RELAXED LIKE THAT...?
I GUESS HE'S CALM...
IT'S PROBABLY BETTER THAN ACTING SUSPICIOUS...

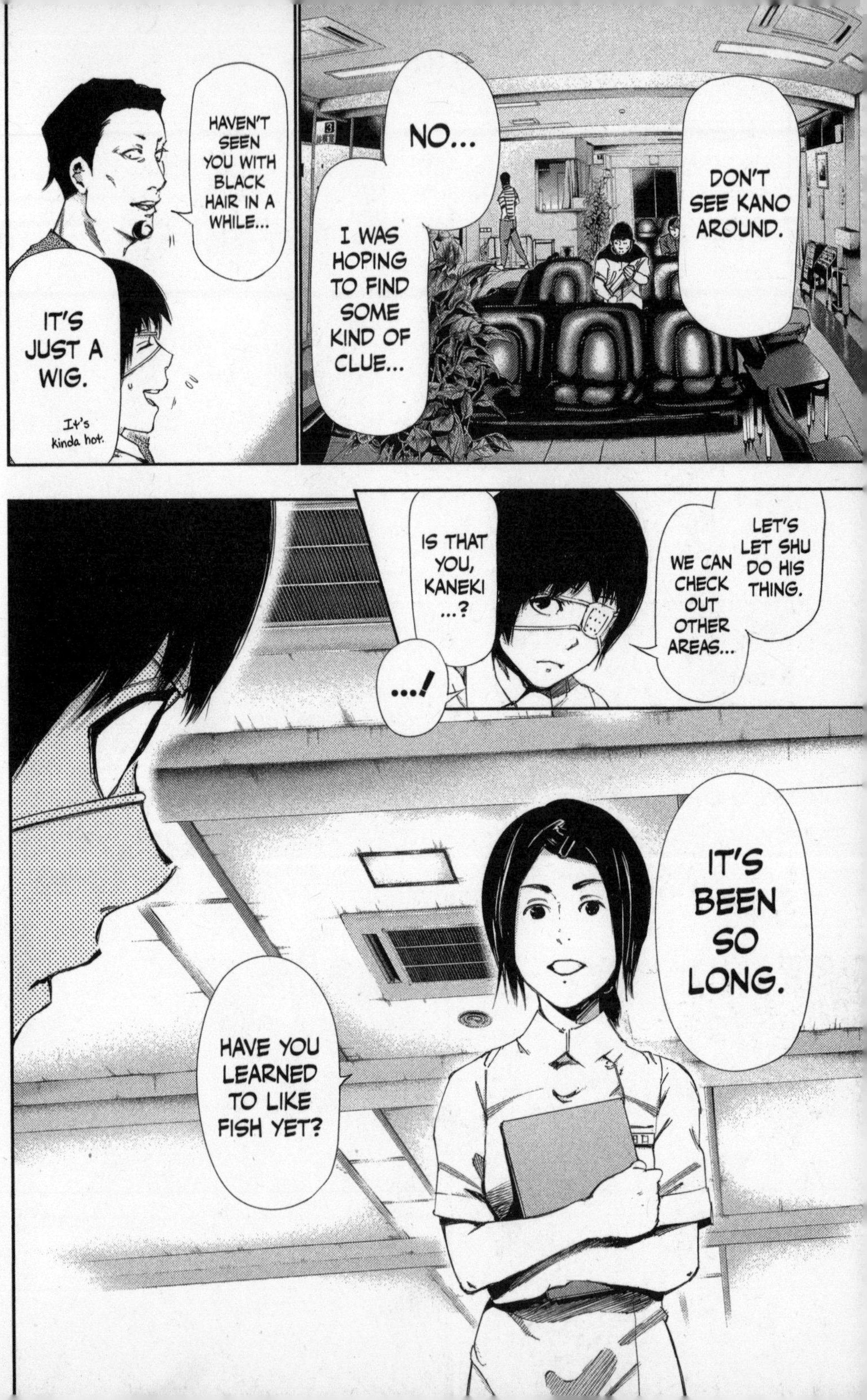
DON'T SEE KANO AROUND.
NO...
I WAS HOPING TO FIND SOME KIND OF CLUE...
HAVEN'T SEEN YOU WITH BLACK HAIR IN A WHILE...
IT'S JUST A WIG.
It's kinda hot.
LET'S LET SHU DO HIS THING.
WE CAN CHECK OUT OTHER AREAS...
IS THAT YOU, KANEKI...?
...!
IT'S BEEN SO LONG.
HAVE YOU LEARNED TO LIKE FISH YET?

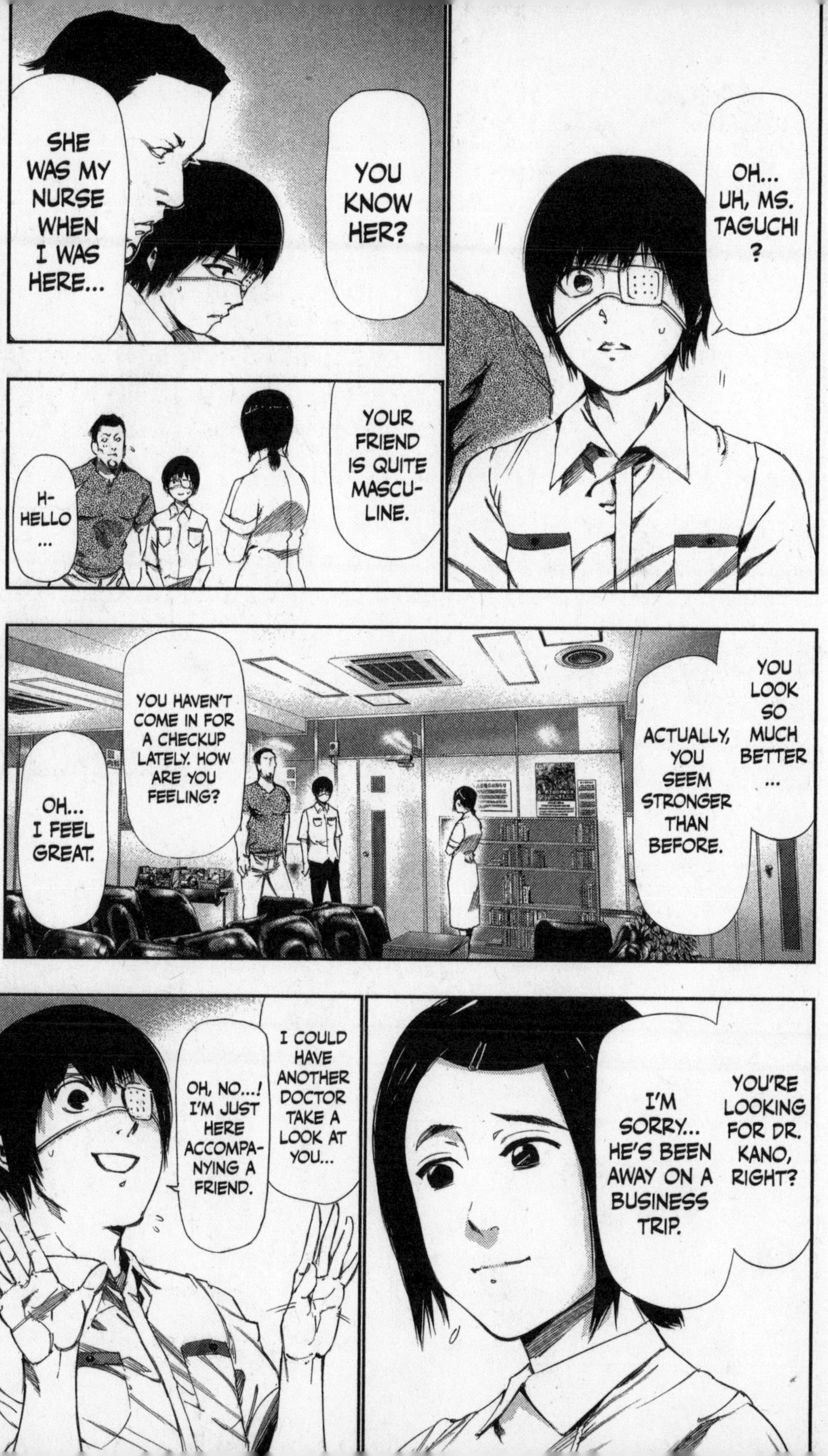
OH... UH, MS. TAGUCHI?
YOU KNOW HER?
SHE WAS MY NURSE WHEN I WAS HERE...
YOUR FRIEND IS QUITE MASCULINE.
H-HELLO...
YOU LOOK SO MUCH BETTER...
ACTUALLY, YOU SEEM STRONGER THAN BEFORE.
YOU HAVEN'T COME IN FOR A CHECKUP LATELY. HOW ARE YOU FEELING?
OH... I FEEL GREAT.
YOU'RE LOOKING FOR DR. KANO, RIGHT?
I'M SORRY... HE'S BEEN AWAY ON A BUSINESS TRIP.
I COULD HAVE ANOTHER DOCTOR TAKE A LOOK AT YOU...
OH, NO...! I'M JUST HERE ACCOMPANYING A FRIEND.

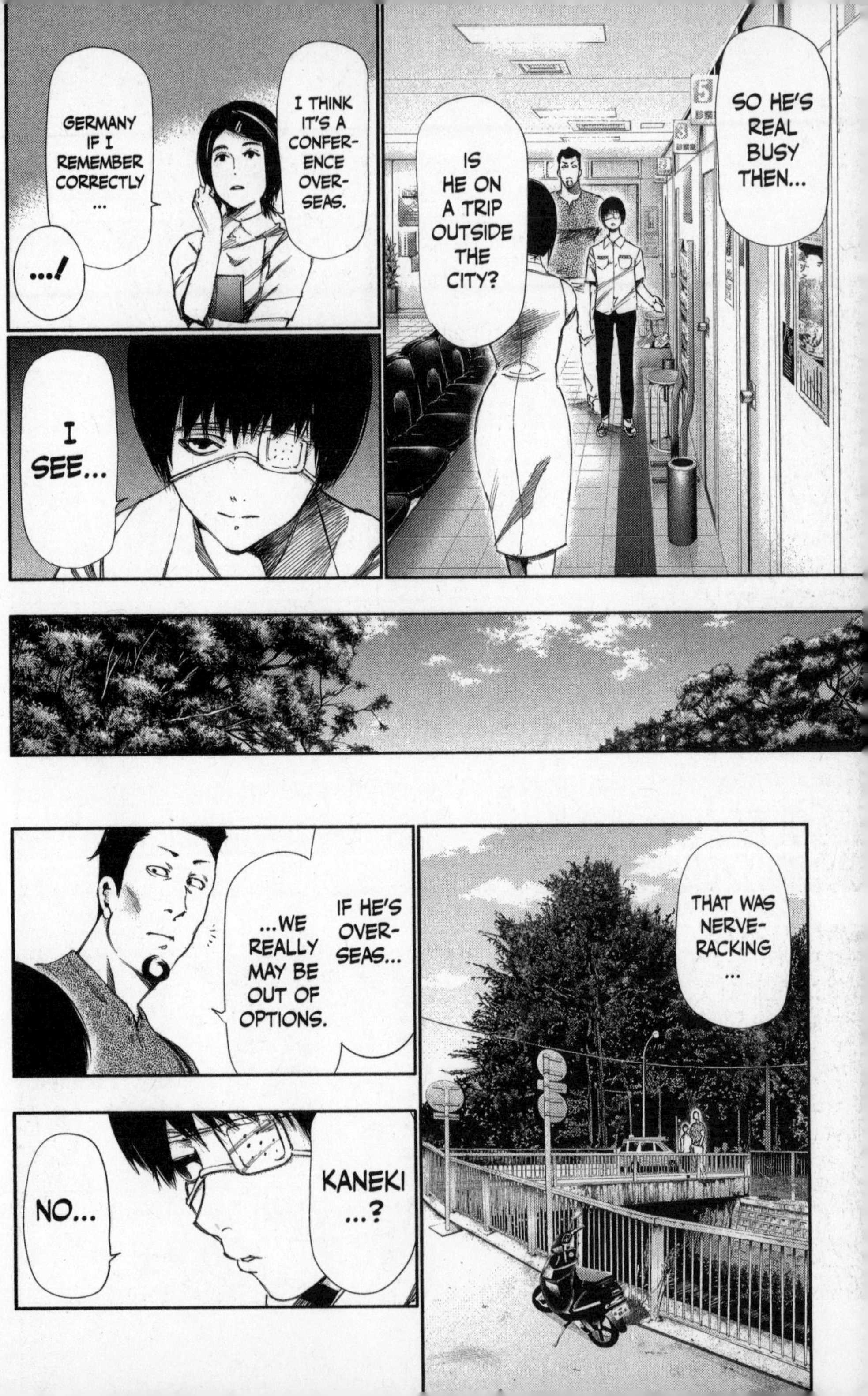
SO HE'S REAL BUSY THEN...
IS HE ON A TRIP OUTSIDE THE CITY?
I THINK IT'S A CONFERENCE OVERSEAS.
GERMANY IF I REMEMBER CORRECTLY...
...!
I SEE...
THAT WAS NERVE-RACKING...
IF HE'S OVERSEAS...
...WE REALLY MAY BE OUT OF OPTIONS.
KANEKI...?
NO...

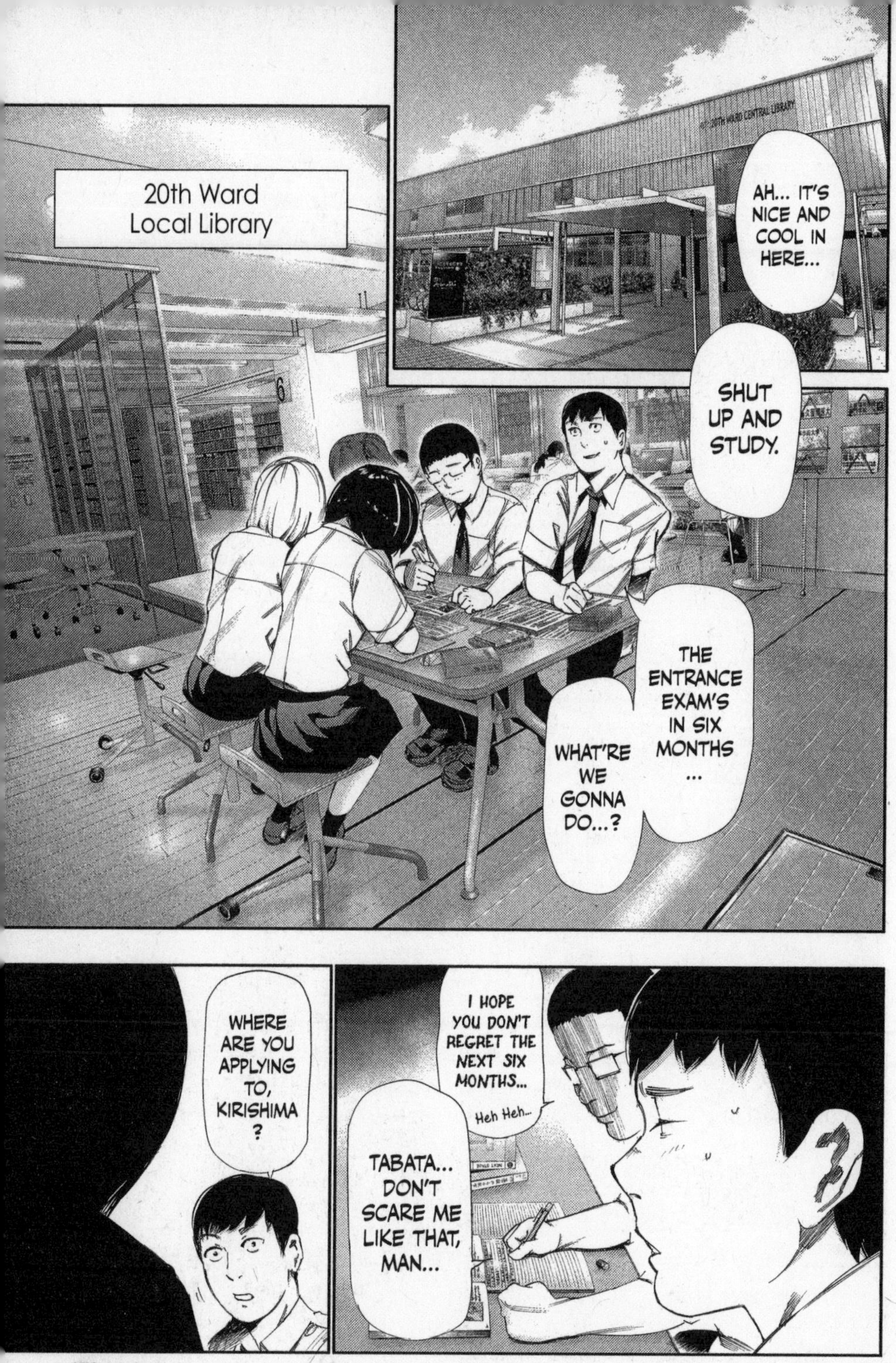
20TH WARD CENTRAL LIBRARY
AH... IT'S NICE AND COOL IN HERE...
20th Ward Local Library
SHUT UP AND STUDY.
THE ENTRANCE EXAM'S IN SIX MONTHS...
WHAT'RE WE GONNA DO...?
I HOPE YOU DON'T REGRET THE NEXT SIX MONTHS...
Heh Heh...
TABATA... DON'T SCARE ME LIKE THAT, MAN...
WHERE ARE YOU APPLYING TO, KIRISHIMA?

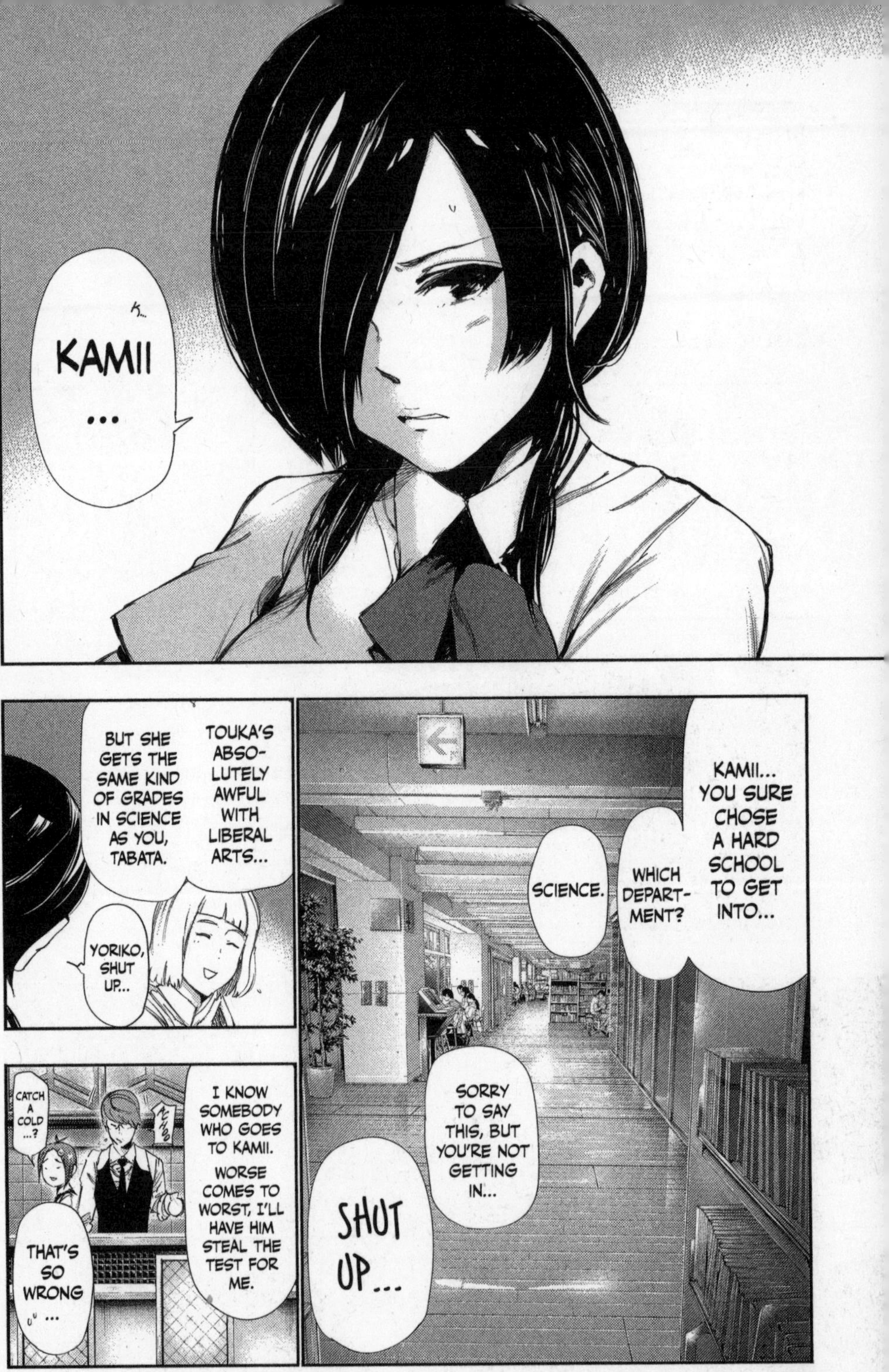
K...
KAMII ...
KAMII... YOU SURE CHOSE A HARD SCHOOL TO GET INTO...
WHICH DEPARTMENT?
SCIENCE.
SORRY TO SAY THIS, BUT YOU'RE NOT GETTING IN...
SHUT UP...
TOUKA'S ABSOLUTELY AWFUL WITH LIBERAL ARTS...
BUT SHE GETS THE SAME KIND OF GRADES IN SCIENCE AS YOU, TABATA.
YORIKO, SHUT UP...
I KNOW SOMEBODY WHO GOES TO KAMII.
WORSE COMES TO WORST, I'LL HAVE HIM STEAL THE TEST FOR ME.
CATCH A COLD ...?
THAT'S SO WRONG ...

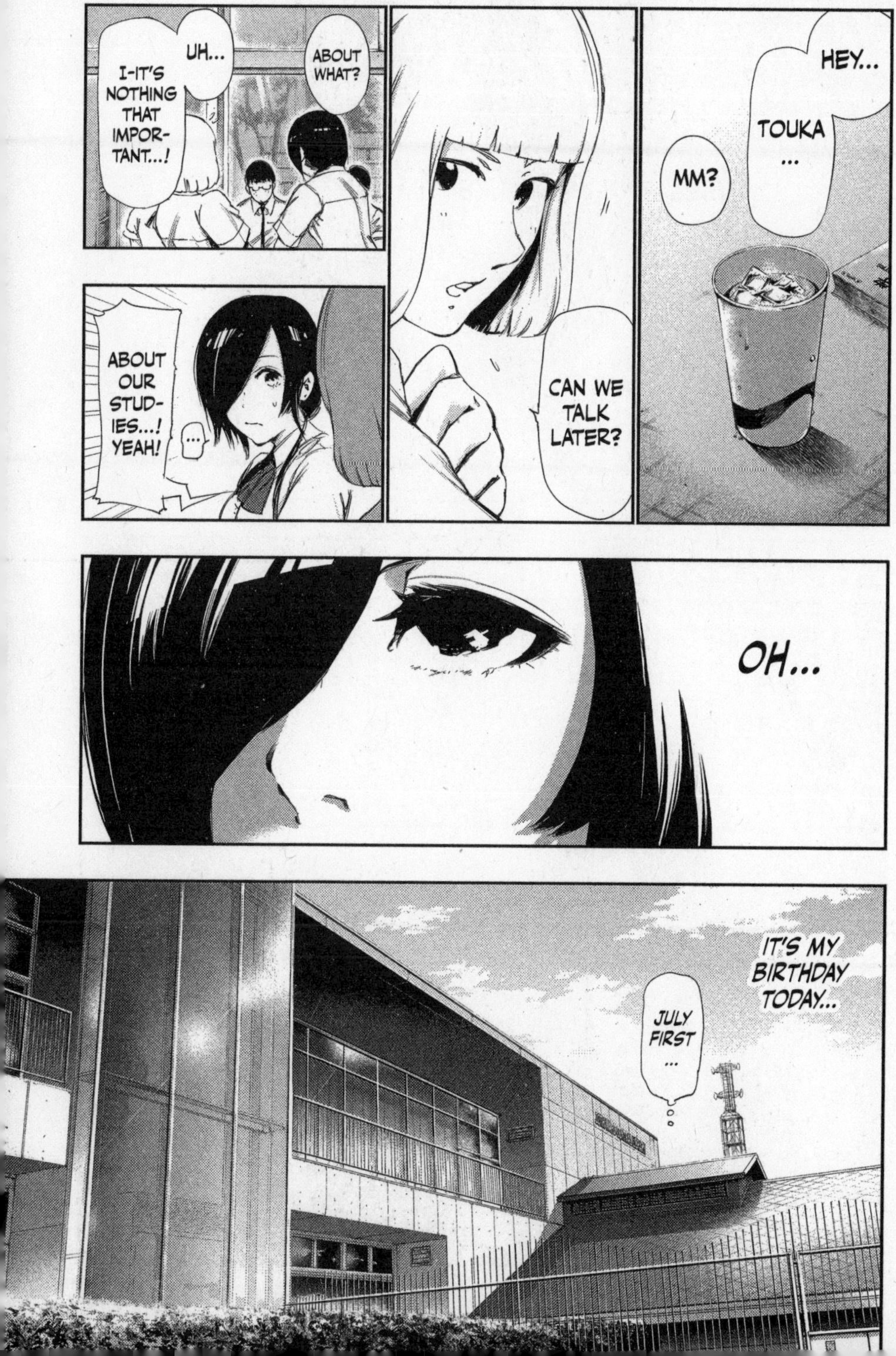
HEY...
TOUKA...
MM?
CAN WE TALK LATER?
ABOUT WHAT?
UH...
I-IT'S NOTHING THAT IMPORTANT...!
ABOUT OUR STUDIES...! YEAH!
...
OH...
IT'S MY BIRTHDAY TODAY...
JULY FIRST...

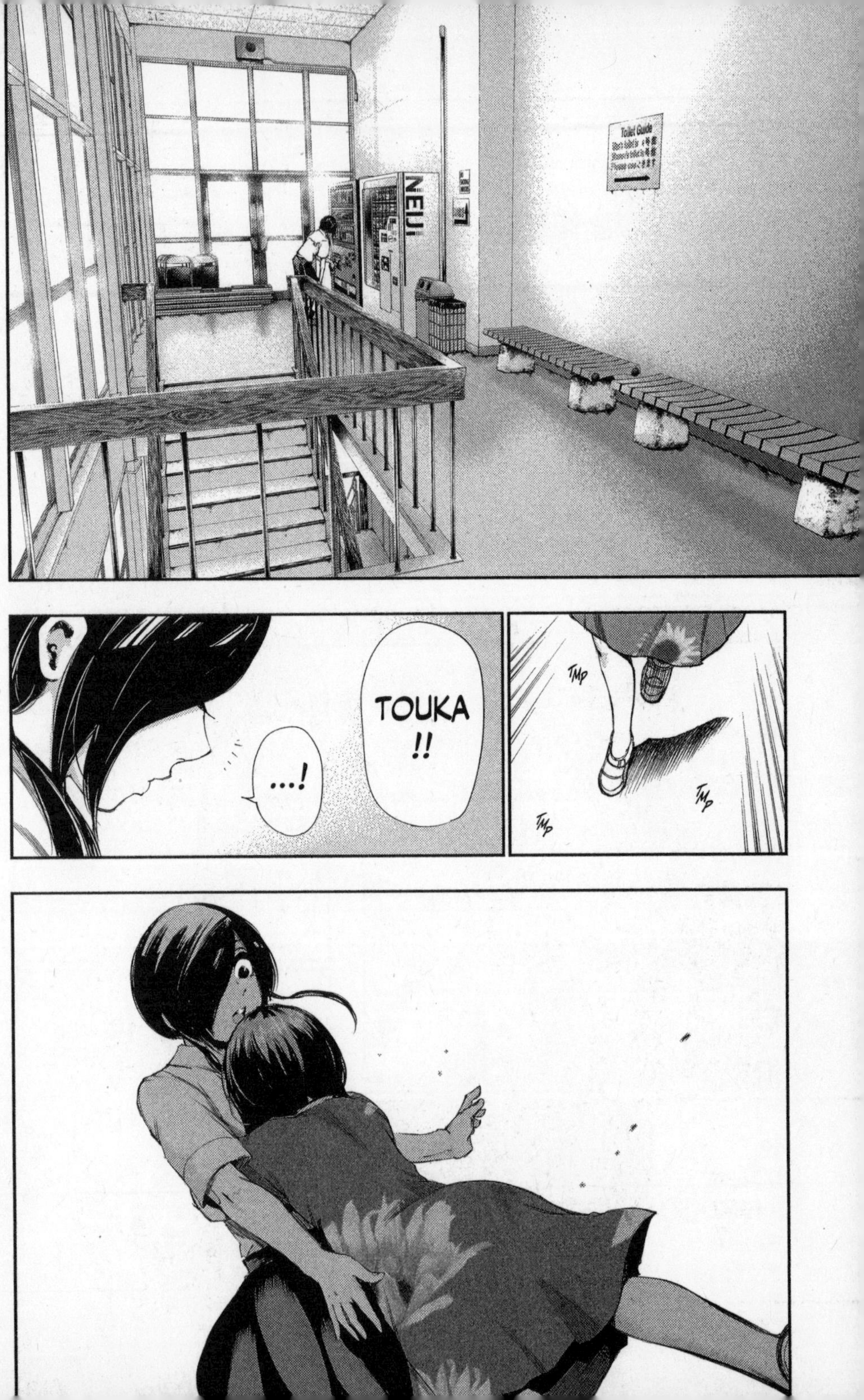
Toilet Guide
TMP
TMP
TMP
TOUKA!!
...!

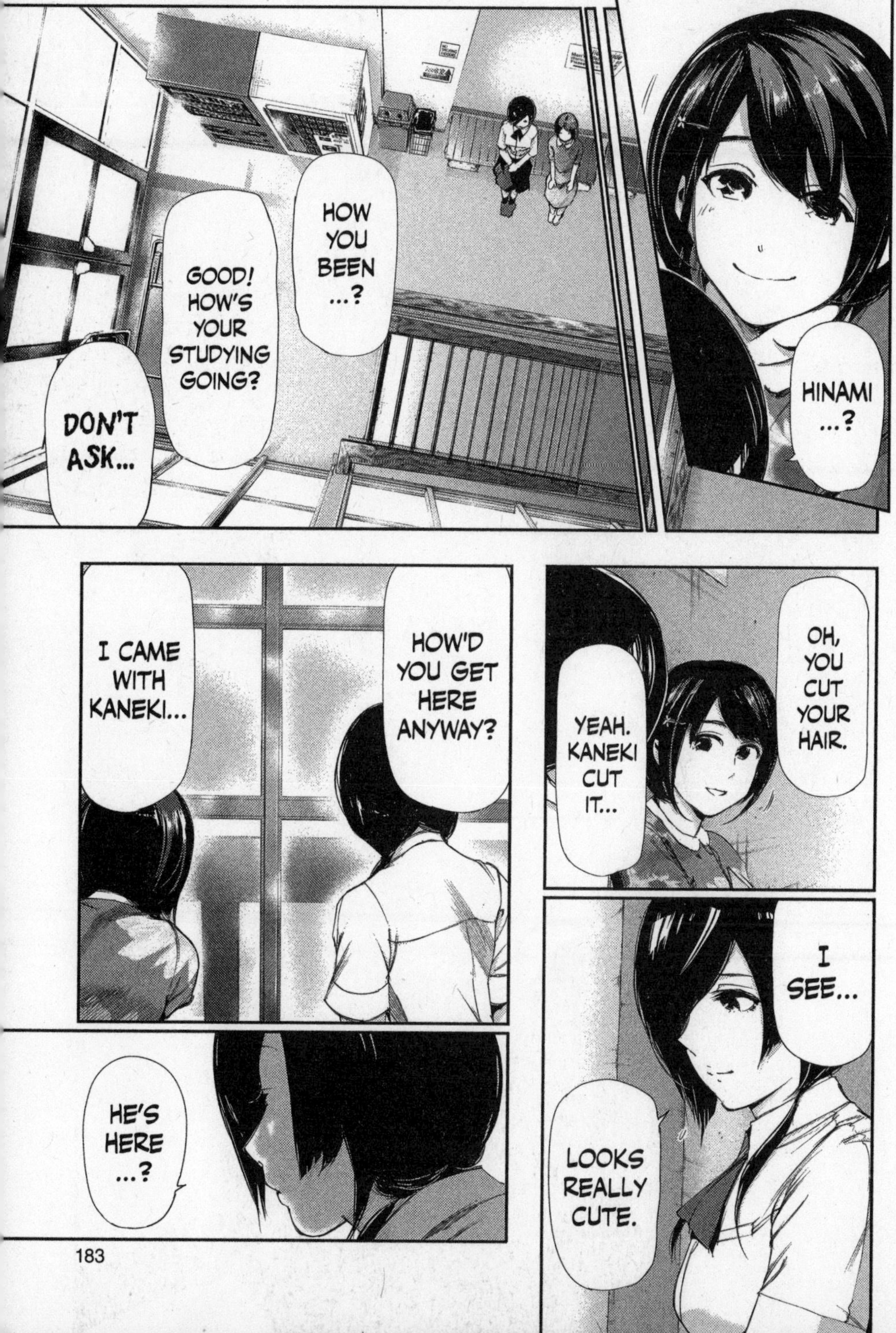
HINAMI ...?
HOW YOU BEEN ...?
GOOD! HOW'S YOUR STUDYING GOING?
DON'T ASK...
OH, YOU CUT YOUR HAIR.
YEAH. KANEKI CUT IT...
HOW'D YOU GET HERE ANYWAY?
I CAME WITH KANEKI...
I SEE...
LOOKS REALLY CUTE.
HE'S HERE ...?

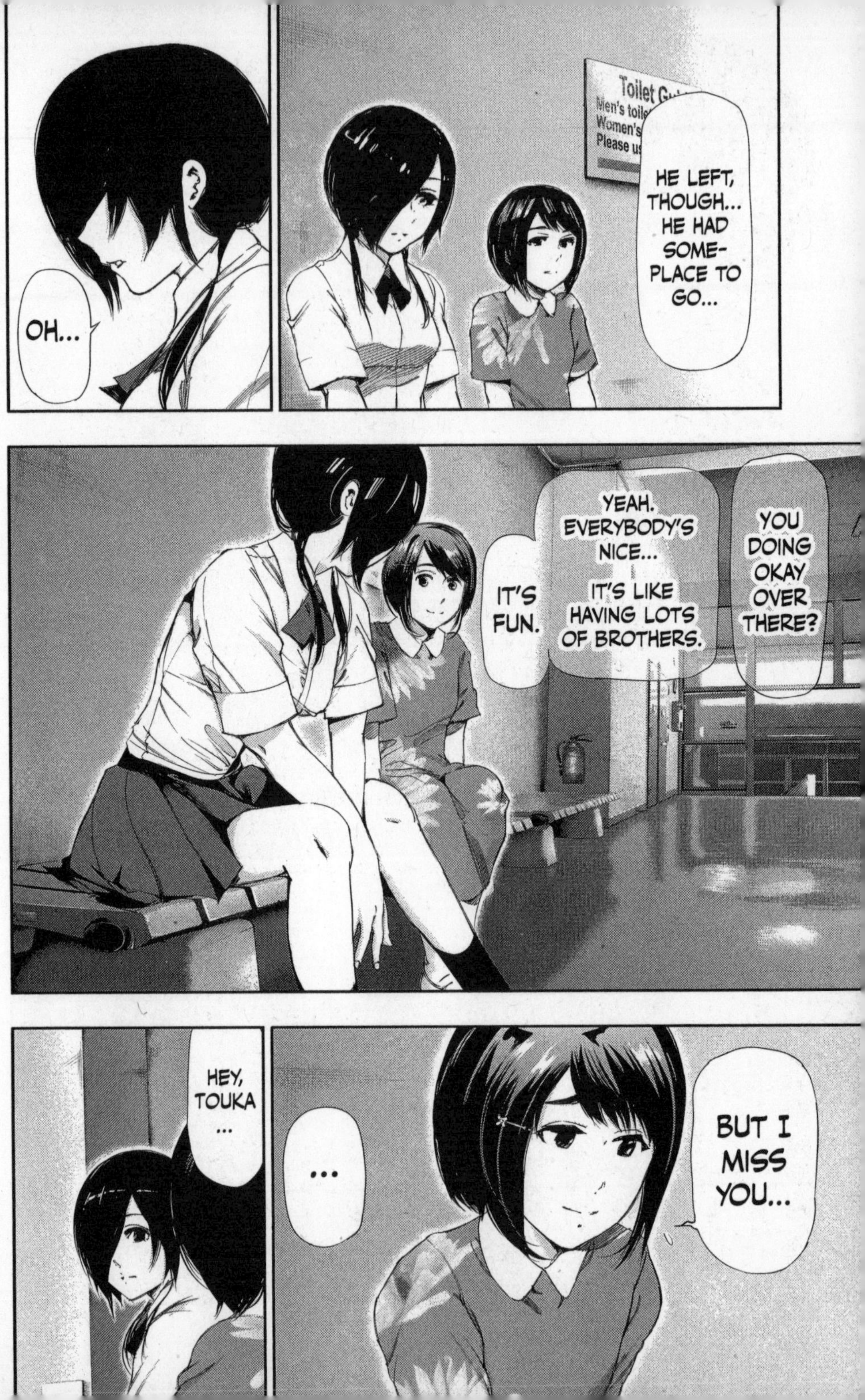
HE LEFT, THOUGH... HE HAD SOME-PLACE TO GO...
OH...
YOU DOING OKAY OVER THERE?
YEAH. EVERYBODY'S NICE...
IT'S LIKE HAVING LOTS OF BROTHERS.
IT'S FUN.
BUT I MISS YOU...
...
HEY, TOUKA ...

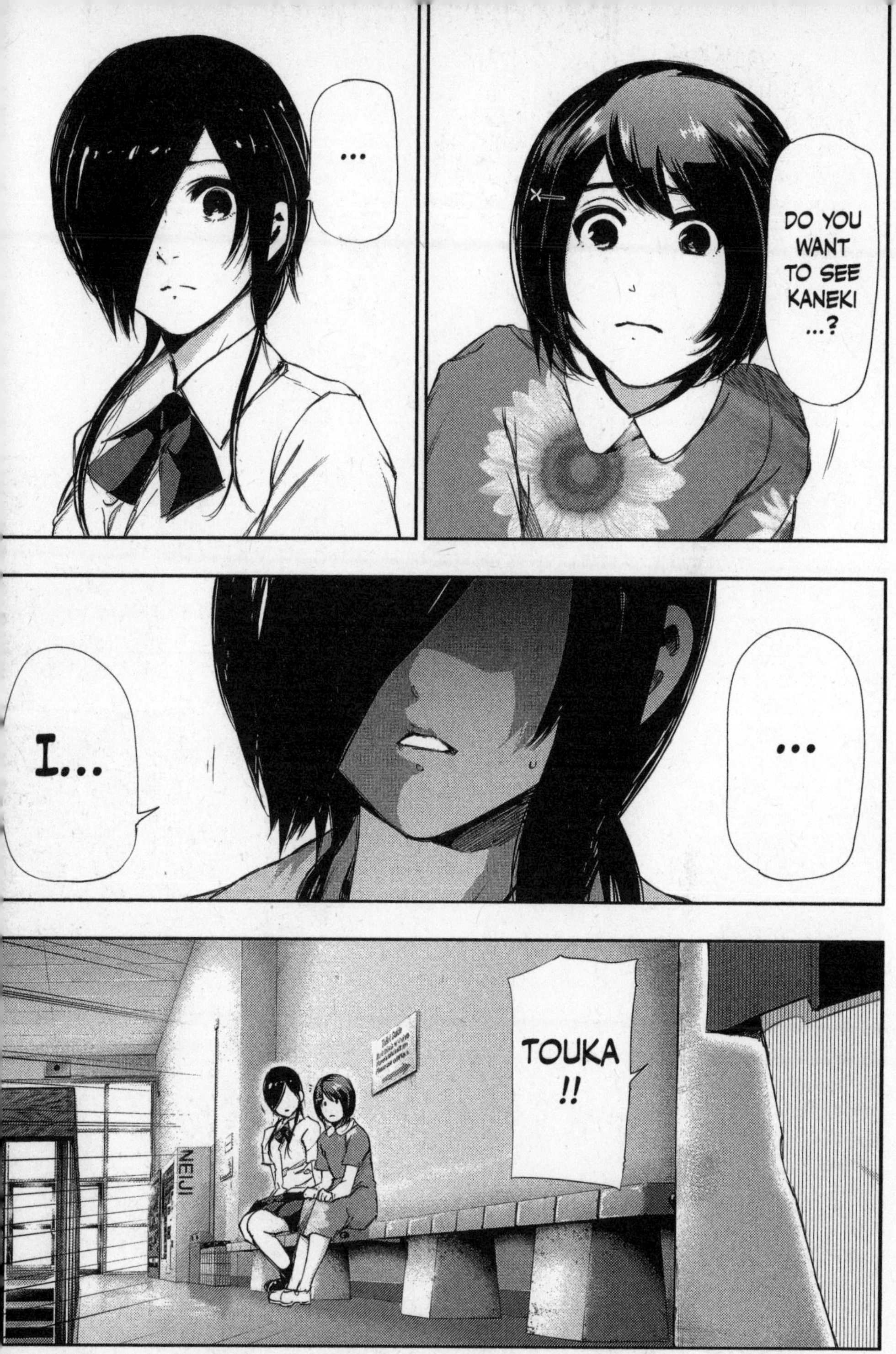
DO YOU WANT TO SEE KANEKI ...?
...
...
I...
TOUKA !!

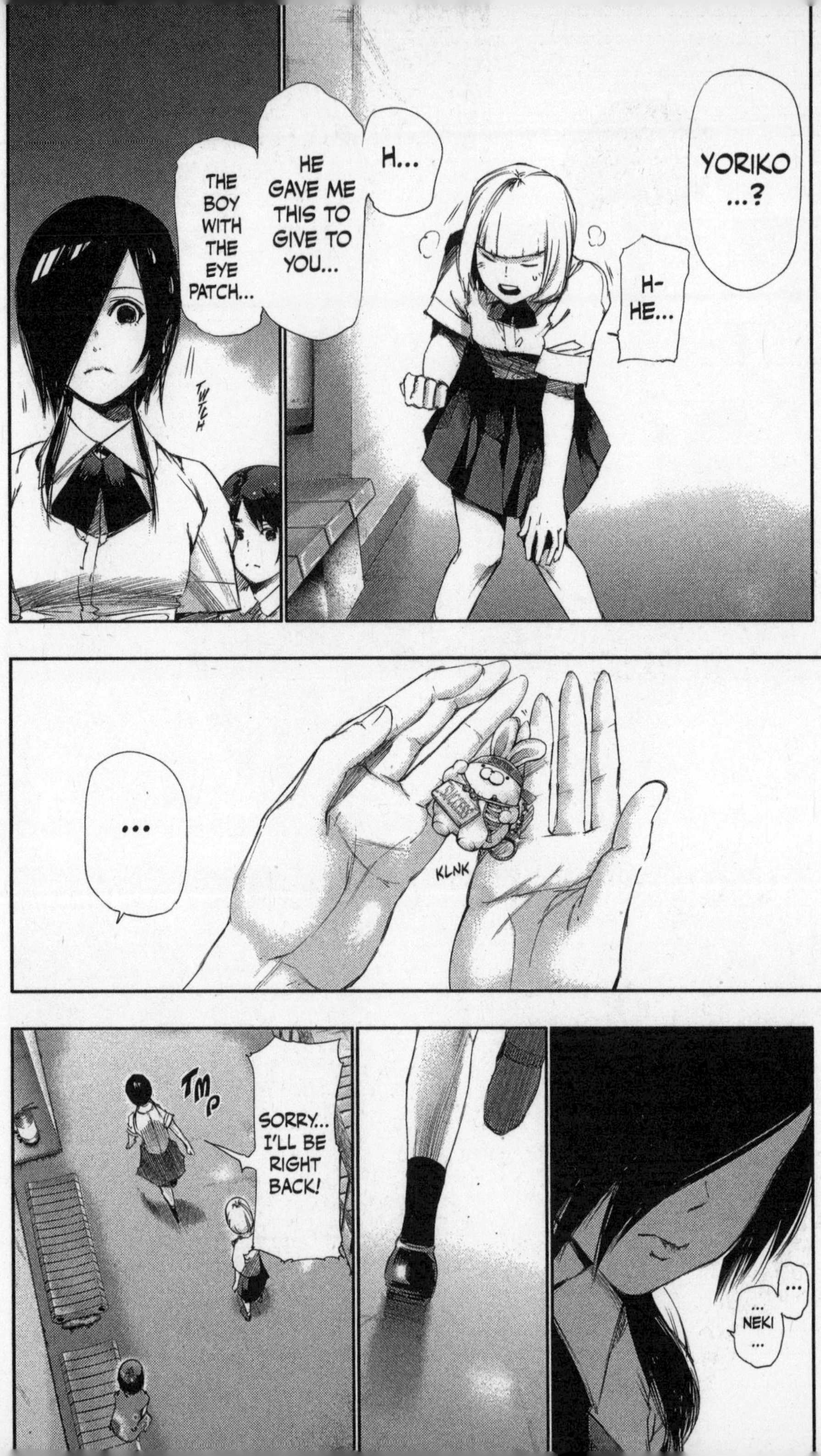
YORIKO ...?
H- HE...
H...
HE GAVE ME THIS TO GIVE TO YOU...
THE BOY WITH THE EYE PATCH...
TWITCH
...
KLNK
... ... NEKI ...
SORRY... I'LL BE RIGHT BACK!
TMP

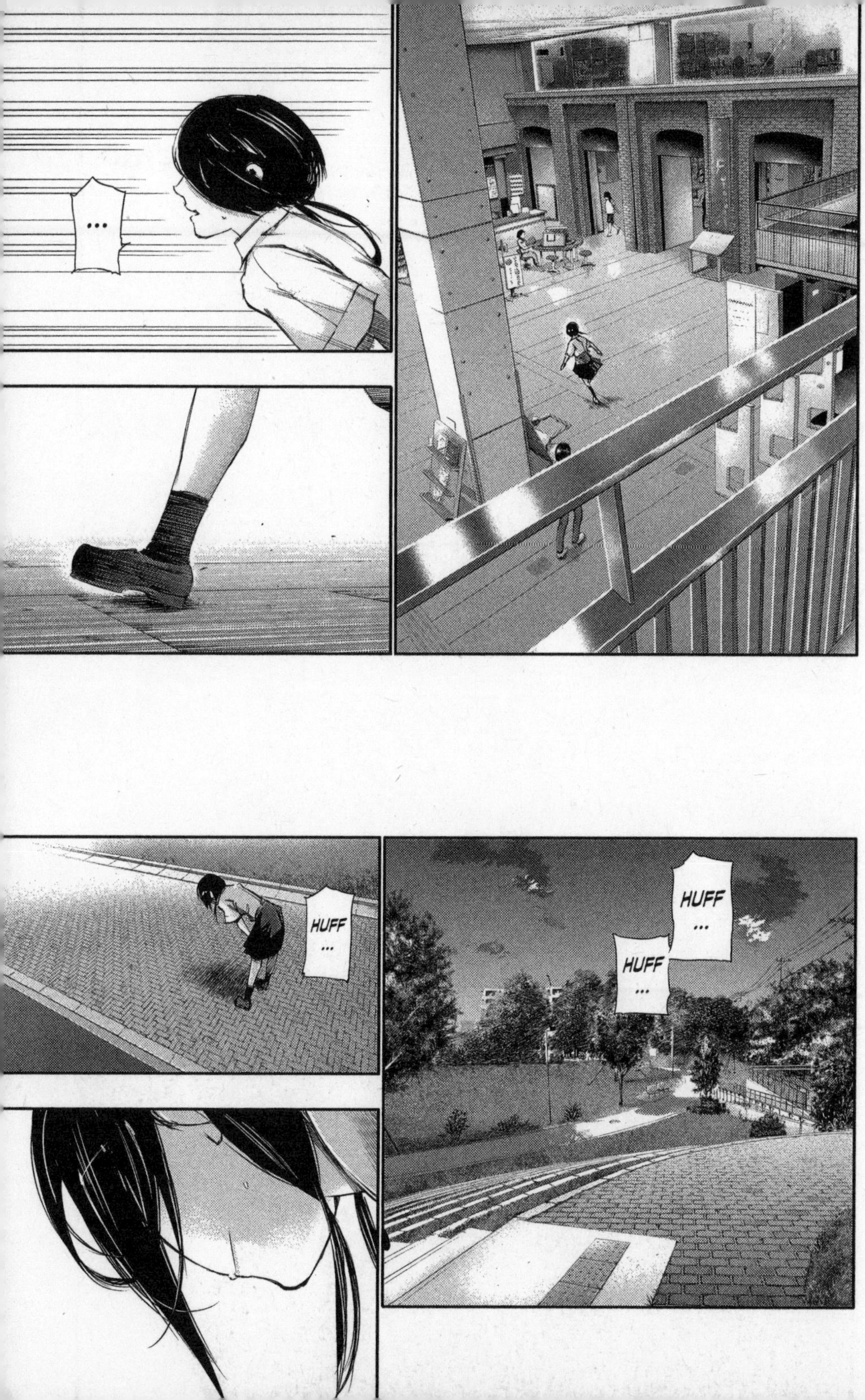
...
HUFF...
HUFF...
HUFF...

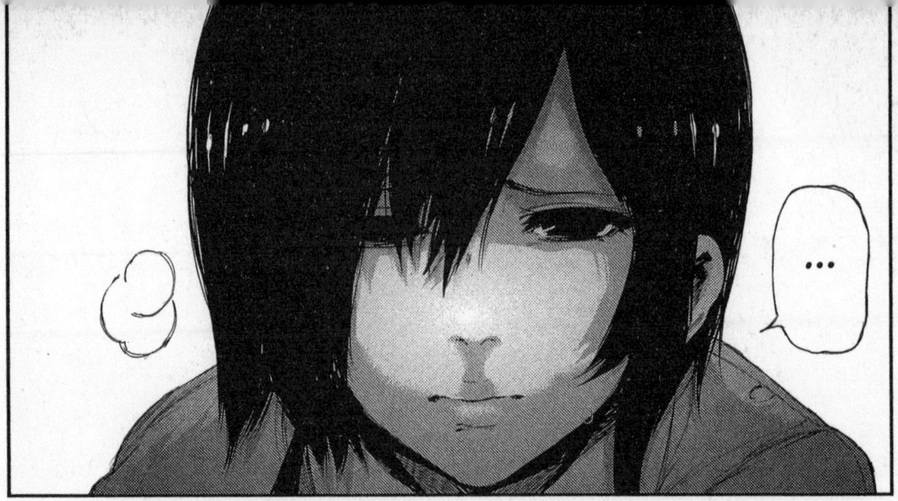
...

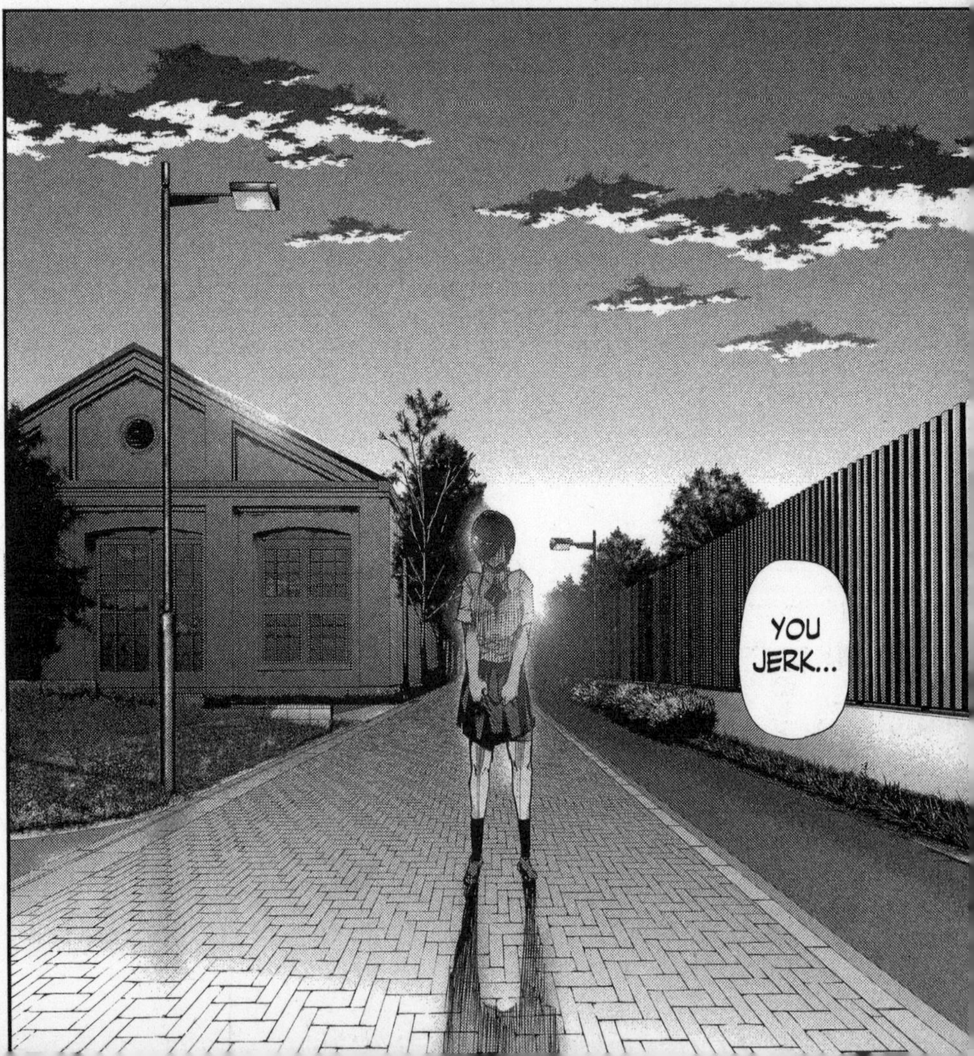
YOU JERK...

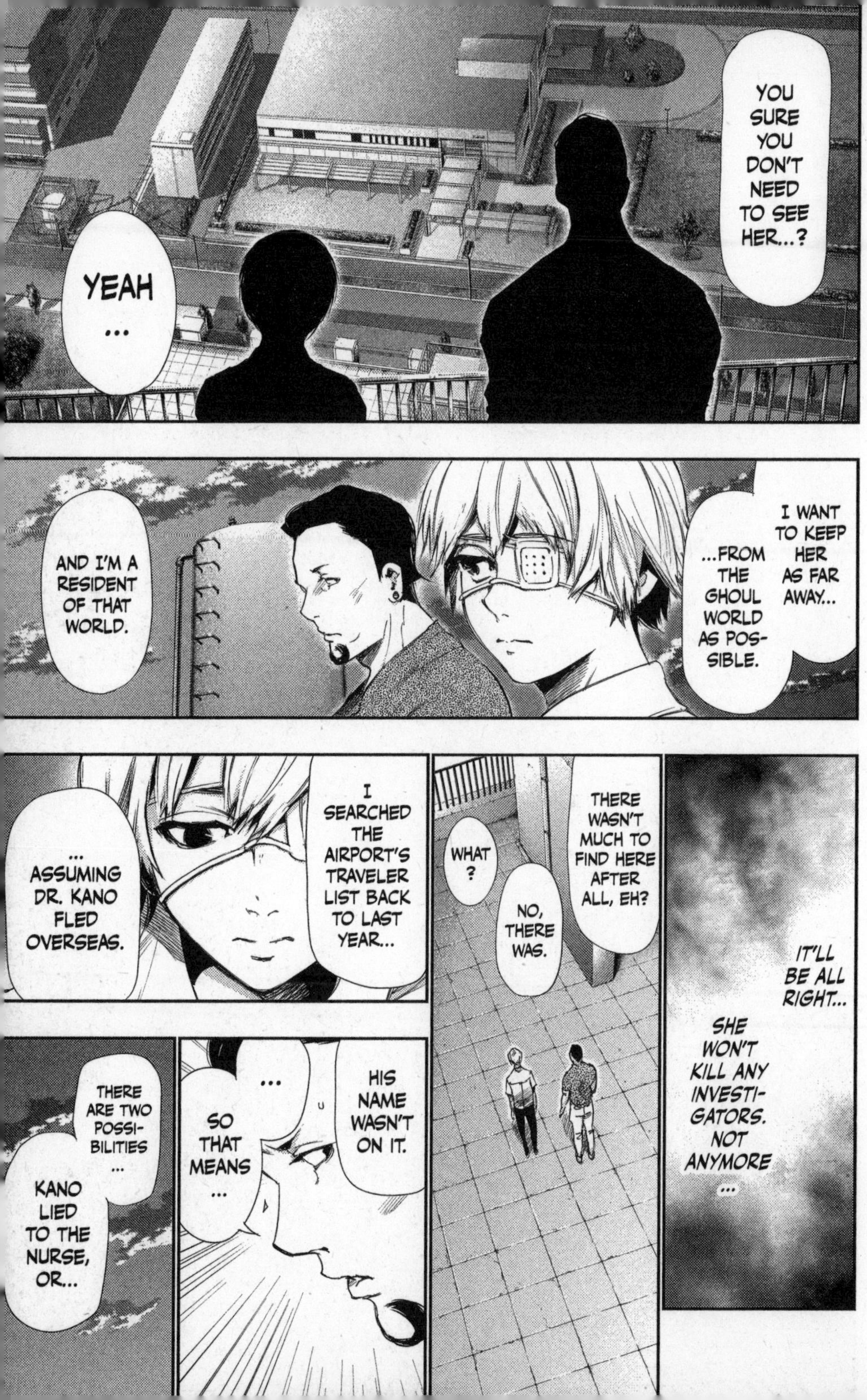

YOU SURE YOU DON'T NEED TO SEE HER...?
YEAH ...
I WANT TO KEEP HER AS FAR AWAY...
...FROM THE GHOUL WORLD AS POSSIBLE.
AND I'M A RESIDENT OF THAT WORLD.
IT'LL BE ALL RIGHT...
SHE WON'T KILL ANY INVESTIGATORS. NOT ANYMORE ...
THERE WASN'T MUCH TO FIND HERE AFTER ALL, EH?
NO, THERE WAS.
WHAT?
I SEARCHED THE AIRPORT'S TRAVELER LIST BACK TO LAST YEAR...
... ASSUMING DR. KANO FLED OVERSEAS.
HIS NAME WASN'T ON IT.
...
SO THAT MEANS ...
THERE ARE TWO POSSIBILITIES ...
KANO LIED TO THE NURSE, OR...

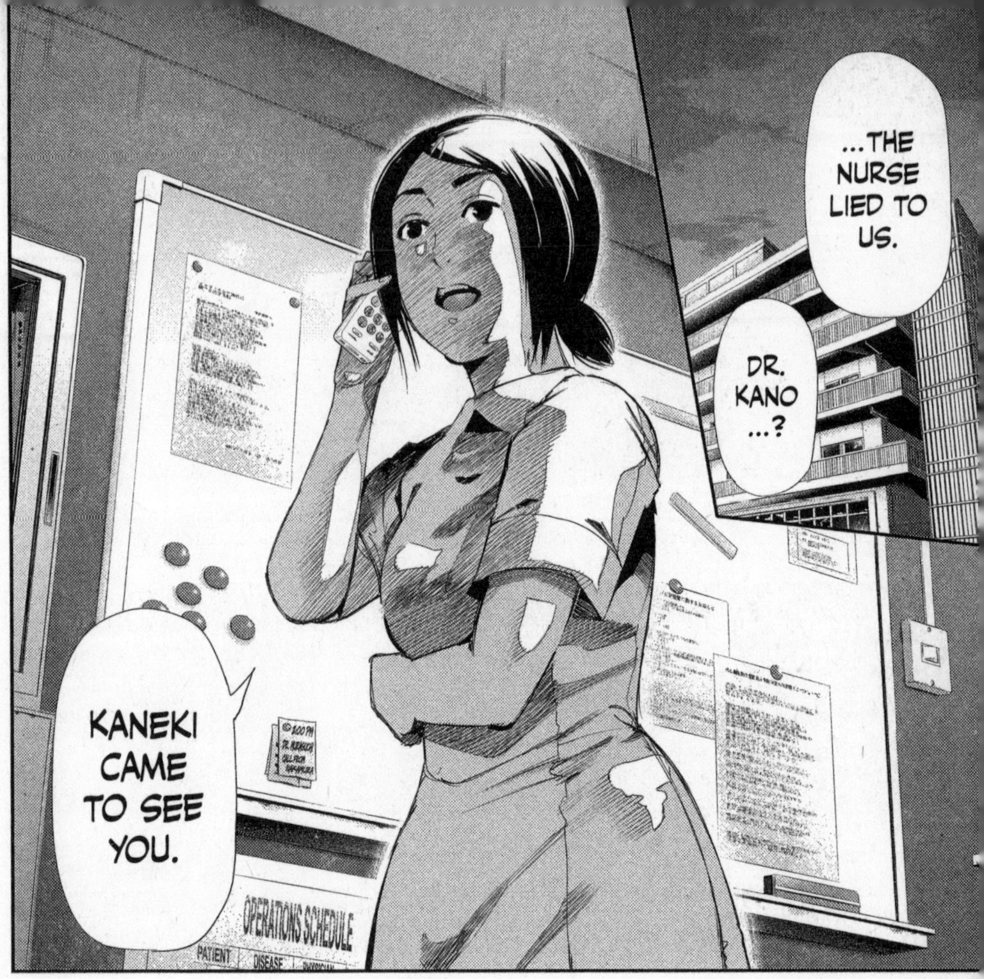
...THE NURSE LIED TO US.
DR. KANO ...?
KANEKI CAME TO SEE YOU.
OPERATIONS SCHEDULE
PATIENT
DISEASE

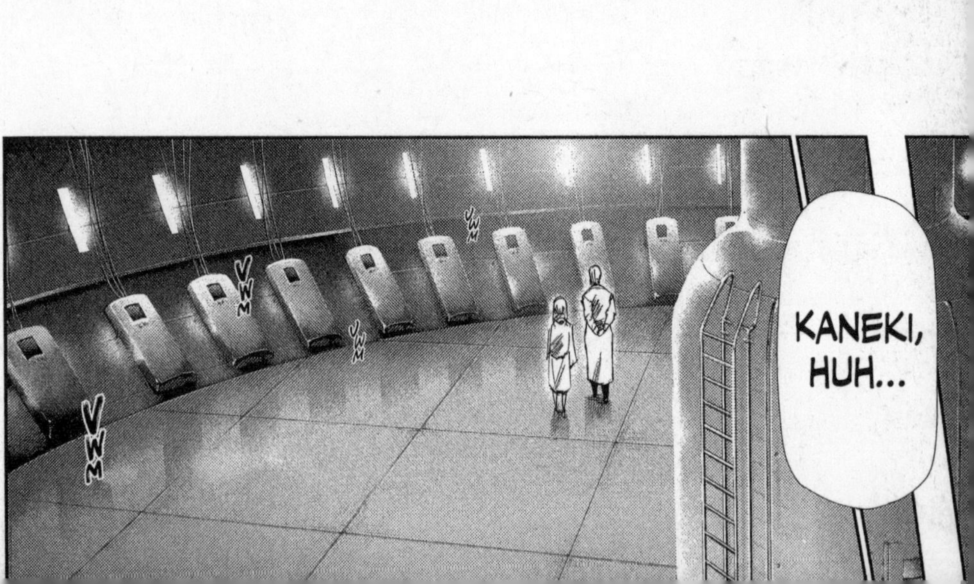
KANEKI, HUH...
VWM
VWM
VWM
VWM

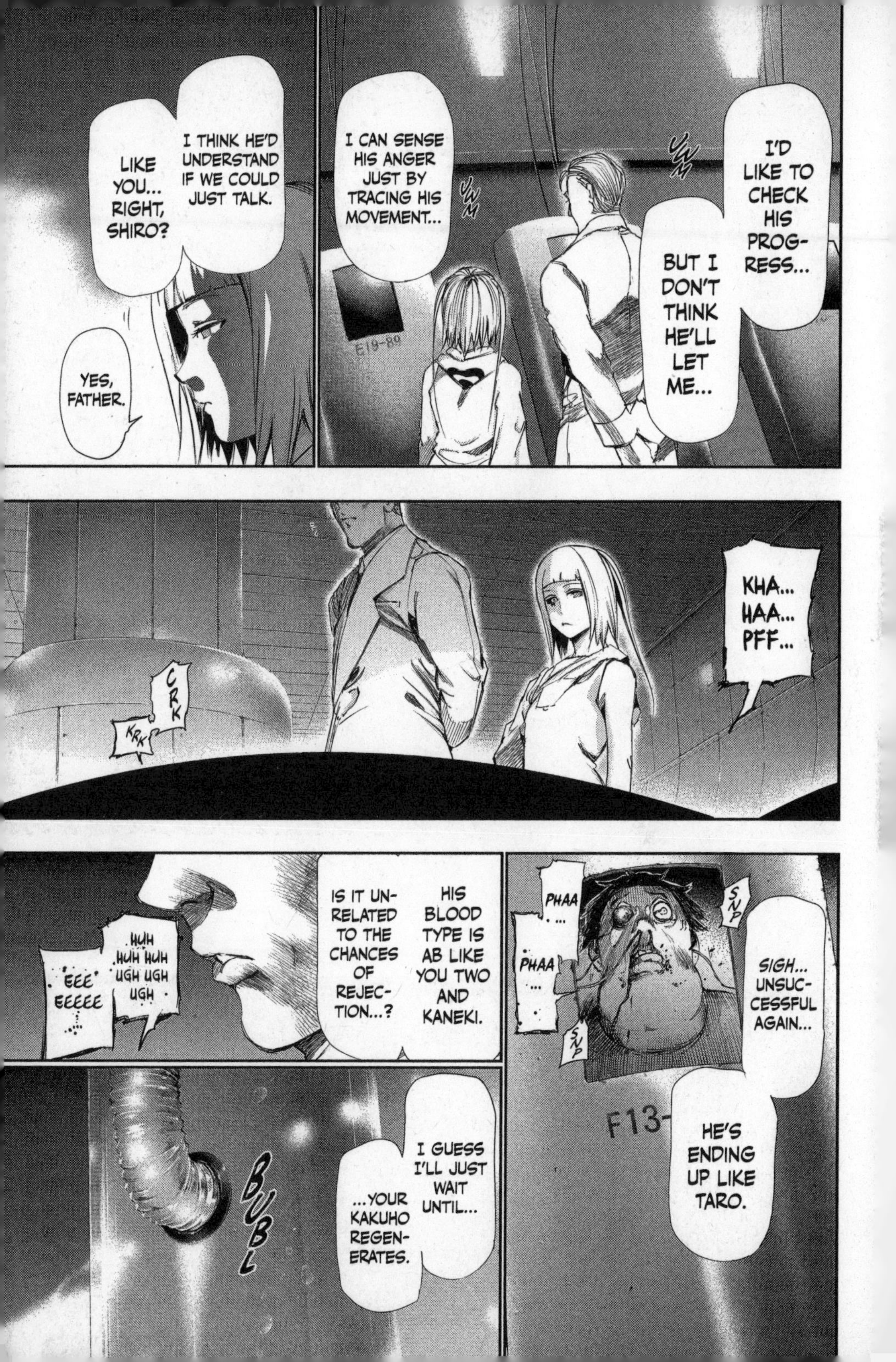
I'D LIKE TO CHECK HIS PROGRESS...
BUT I DON'T THINK HE'LL LET ME...
UWM
I CAN SENSE HIS ANGER JUST BY TRACING HIS MOVEMENT...
UWM
E19-89
I THINK HE'D UNDERSTAND IF WE COULD JUST TALK.
LIKE YOU... RIGHT, SHIRO?
YES, FATHER.
KHA... HAA... PFF...
CRK
KRK
SNP
PHAA...
PHAA...
SNP
SIGH... UNSUCCESSFUL AGAIN...
F13-
HE'S ENDING UP LIKE TARO.
HIS BLOOD TYPE IS AB LIKE YOU TWO AND KANEKI.
IS IT UNRELATED TO THE CHANCES OF REJECTION...?
HUH HUH HUH UGH UGH UGH
EEE EEEEE
I GUESS I'LL JUST WAIT UNTIL...
...YOUR KAKUHO REGENERATES.
BUBL

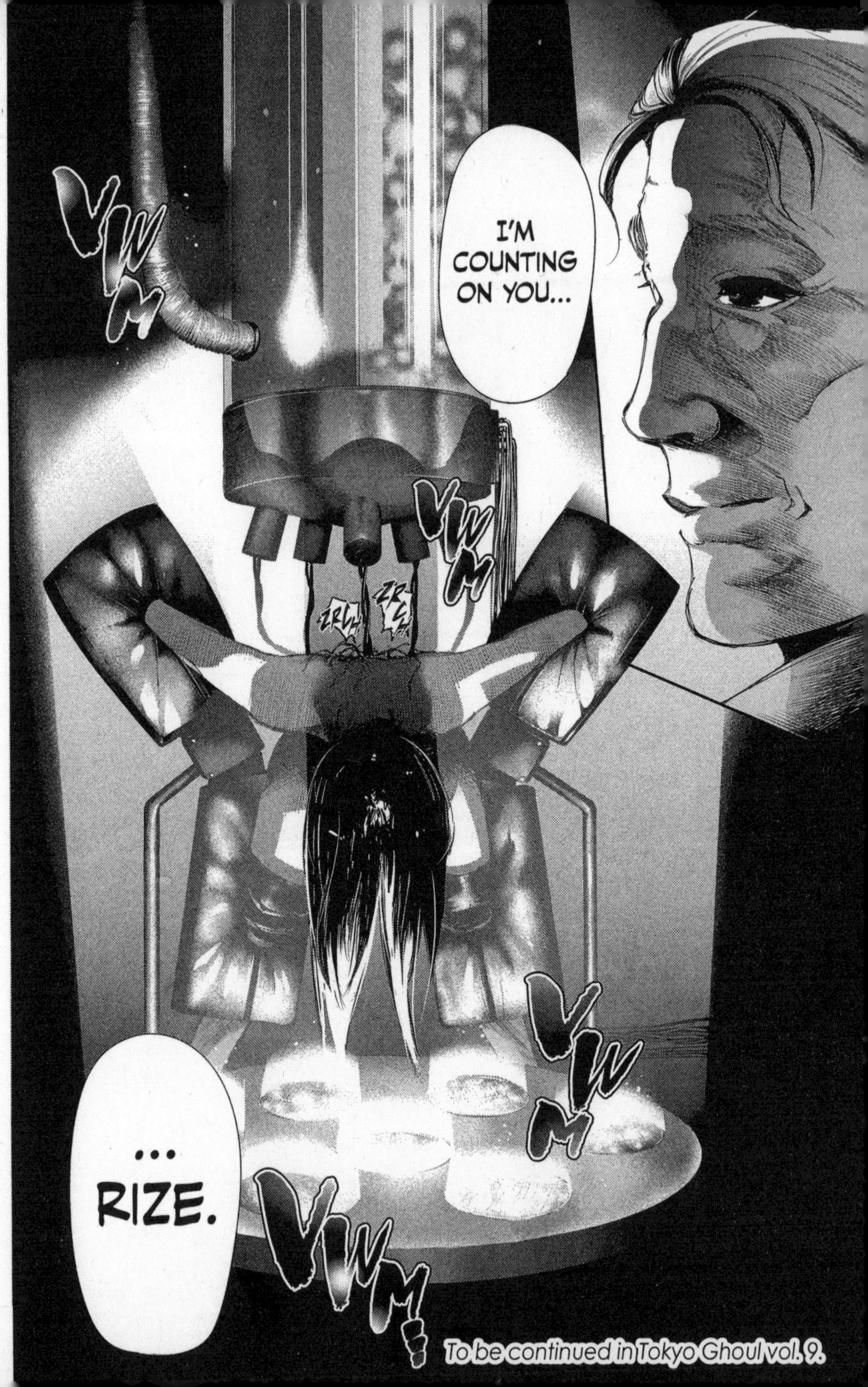
I'M COUNTING ON YOU...
VWM
VWM
ZRCH
ZRCH
VWM
... RIZE.
VWM!
To be continued in Tokyo Ghoul vol. 9.

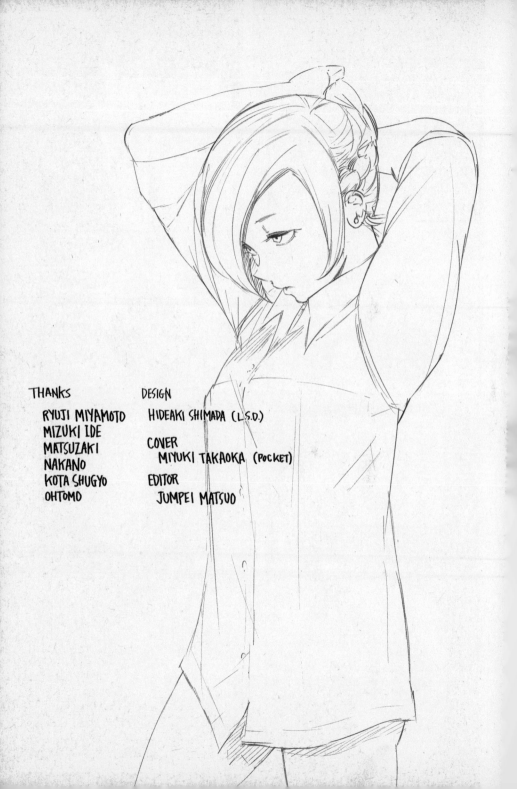

THANKS

RYUJI MIYAMOTO
MIZUKI IDE
MATSUZAKI
NAKANO
KOTA SHUGYO
OHTOMO

DESIGN

HIDEAKI SHIMADA (L.S.D.)

COVER

MIYUKI TAKAOKA (POCKET)

EDITOR

JUMPEI MATSUO

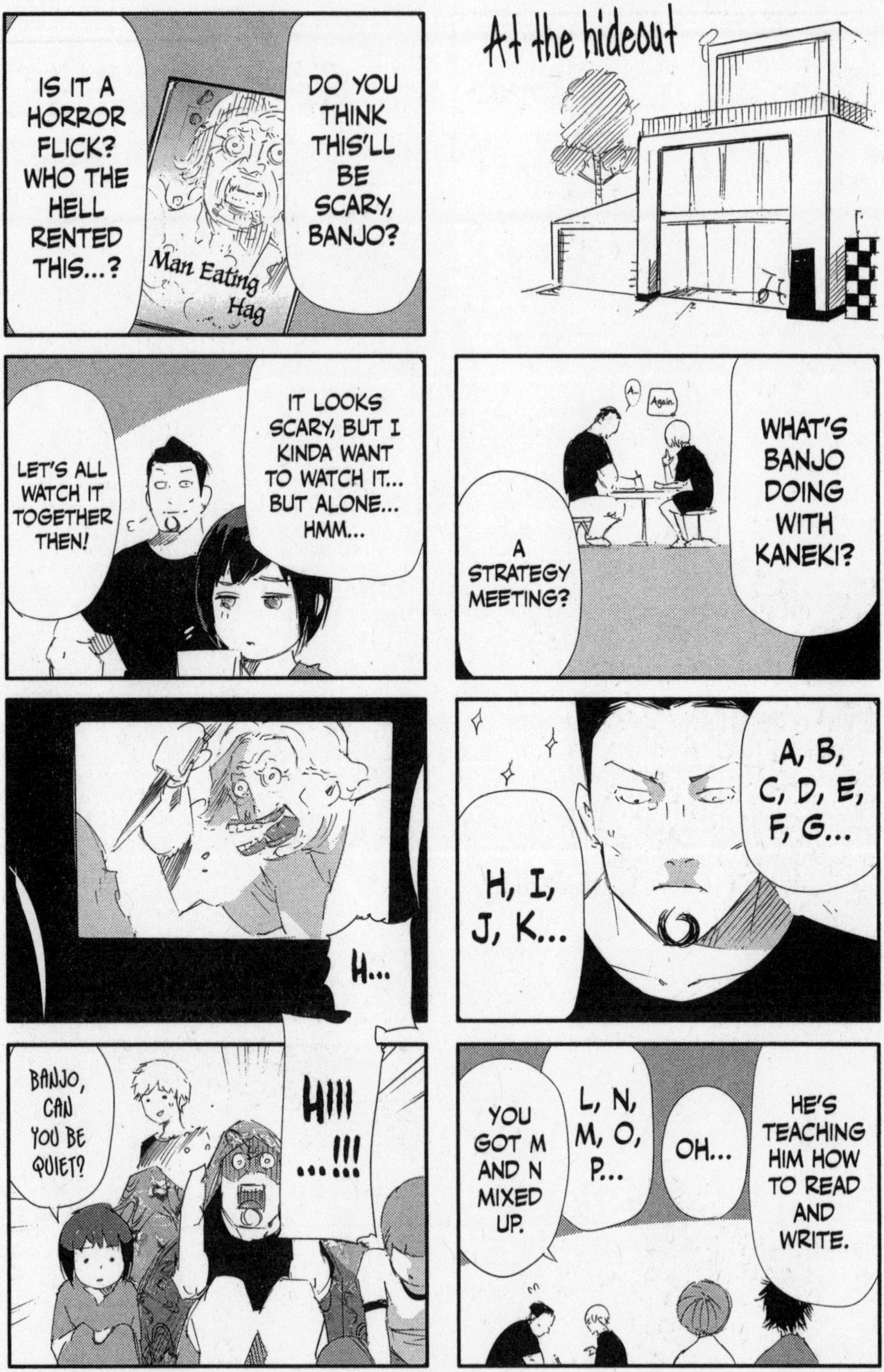
At the hideout
WHAT'S BANJO DOING WITH KANEKI?
A...
Again.
A STRATEGY MEETING?
A, B, C, D, E, F, G...
H, I, J, K...
HE'S TEACHING HIM HOW TO READ AND WRITE.
OH...
L, N, M, O, P...
YOU GOT M AND N MIXED UP.
DO YOU THINK THIS'LL BE SCARY, BANJO?
IS IT A HORROR FLICK? WHO THE HELL RENTED THIS...?
Man Eating Hag
IT LOOKS SCARY, BUT I KINDA WANT TO WATCH IT... BUT ALONE... HMM...
LET'S ALL WATCH IT TOGETHER THEN!
H...
H!!! ...!!!
BANJO, CAN YOU BE QUIET?

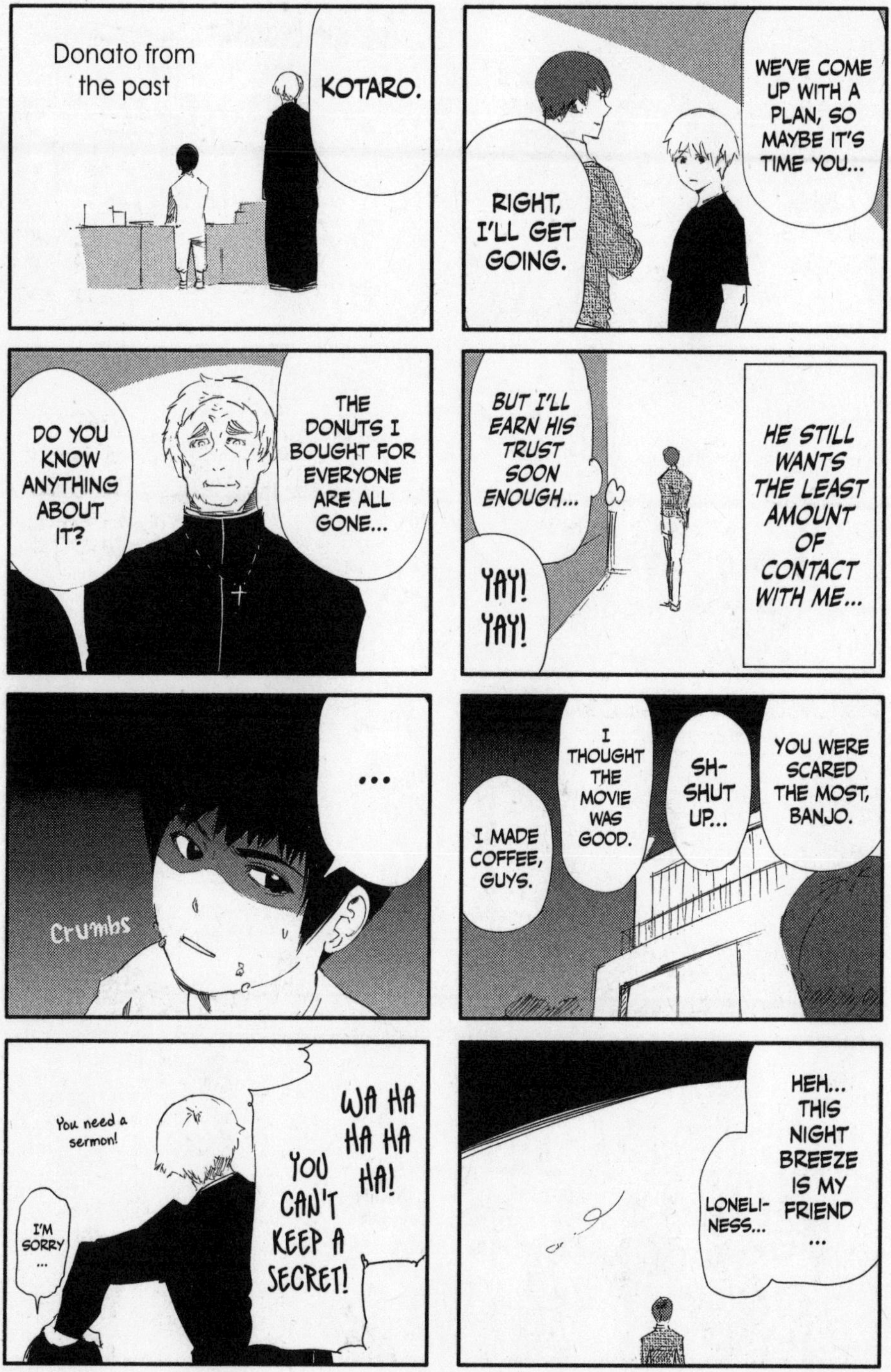
WE'VE COME UP WITH A PLAN, SO MAYBE IT'S TIME YOU...
RIGHT, I'LL GET GOING.
Donato from the past
KOTARO.
HE STILL WANTS THE LEAST AMOUNT OF CONTACT WITH ME...
BUT I'LL EARN HIS TRUST SOON ENOUGH...
YAY! YAY!
THE DONUTS I BOUGHT FOR EVERYONE ARE ALL GONE...
DO YOU KNOW ANYTHING ABOUT IT?
YOU WERE SCARED THE MOST, BANJO.
SH-SHUT UP...
I THOUGHT THE MOVIE WAS GOOD.
I MADE COFFEE, GUYS.
...
Crumbs
HEH... THIS NIGHT BREEZE IS MY FRIEND...
LONELINESS...
WA HA HA HA HA!
YOU CAN'T KEEP A SECRET!
You need a sermon!
I'M SORRY...

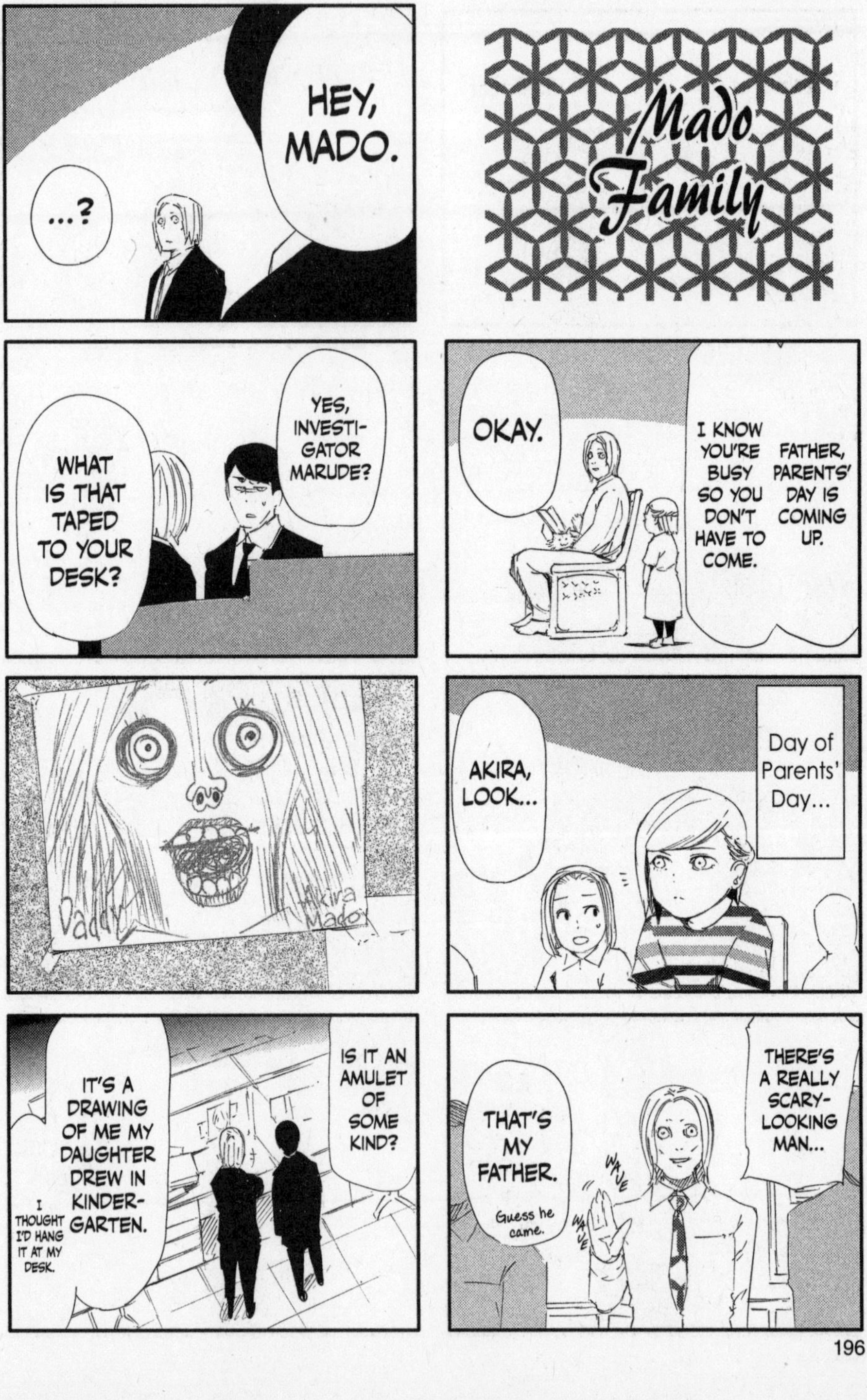
Mado Family
FATHER, PARENTS' DAY IS COMING UP.
I KNOW YOU'RE BUSY SO YOU DON'T HAVE TO COME.
OKAY.
Day of Parents' Day...
AKIRA, LOOK...
THERE'S A REALLY SCARY-LOOKING MAN...
THAT'S MY FATHER.
Guess he came.
WAVE
WAVE
HEY, MADO.
...?
YES, INVESTIGATOR MARUDE?
WHAT IS THAT TAPED TO YOUR DESK?
Daddy
Akira Mado
IS IT AN AMULET OF SOME KIND?
IT'S A DRAWING OF ME MY DAUGHTER DREW IN KINDERGARTEN.
I THOUGHT I'D HANG IT AT MY DESK.

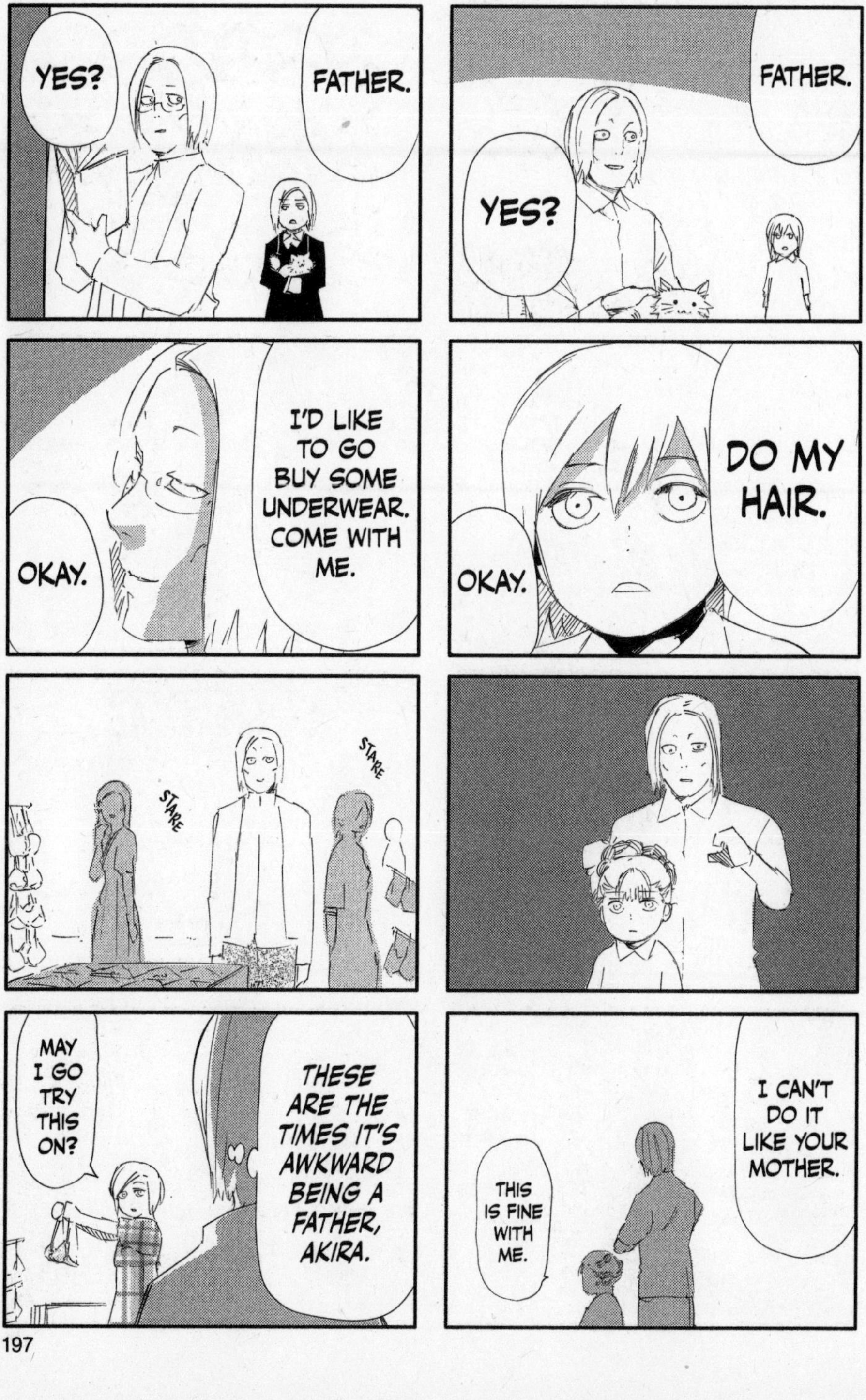
FATHER.
YES?
FATHER.
YES?
DO MY HAIR.
OKAY.
I'D LIKE TO GO BUY SOME UNDERWEAR. COME WITH ME.
OKAY.
STARE
STARE
I CAN'T DO IT LIKE YOUR MOTHER.
THIS IS FINE WITH ME.
THESE ARE THE TIMES IT'S AWKWARD BEING A FATHER, AKIRA.
MAY I GO TRY THIS ON?

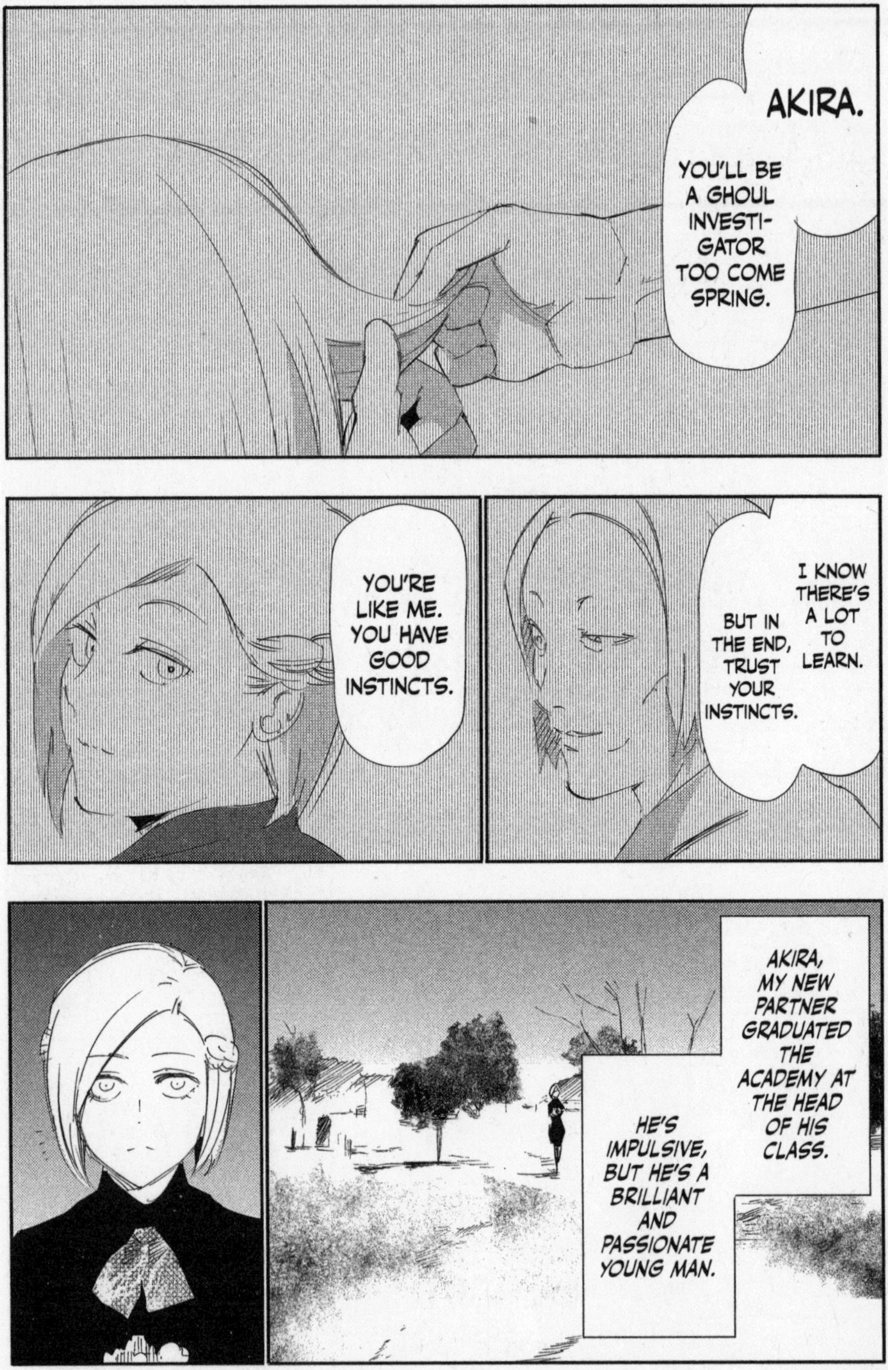
AKIRA.
YOU'LL BE A GHOUL INVESTI-GATOR TOO COME SPRING.
I KNOW THERE'S A LOT TO LEARN.
BUT IN THE END, TRUST YOUR INSTINCTS.
YOU'RE LIKE ME. YOU HAVE GOOD INSTINCTS.
AKIRA, MY NEW PARTNER GRADUATED THE ACADEMY AT THE HEAD OF HIS CLASS.
HE'S IMPULSIVE, BUT HE'S A BRILLIANT AND PASSIONATE YOUNG MAN.

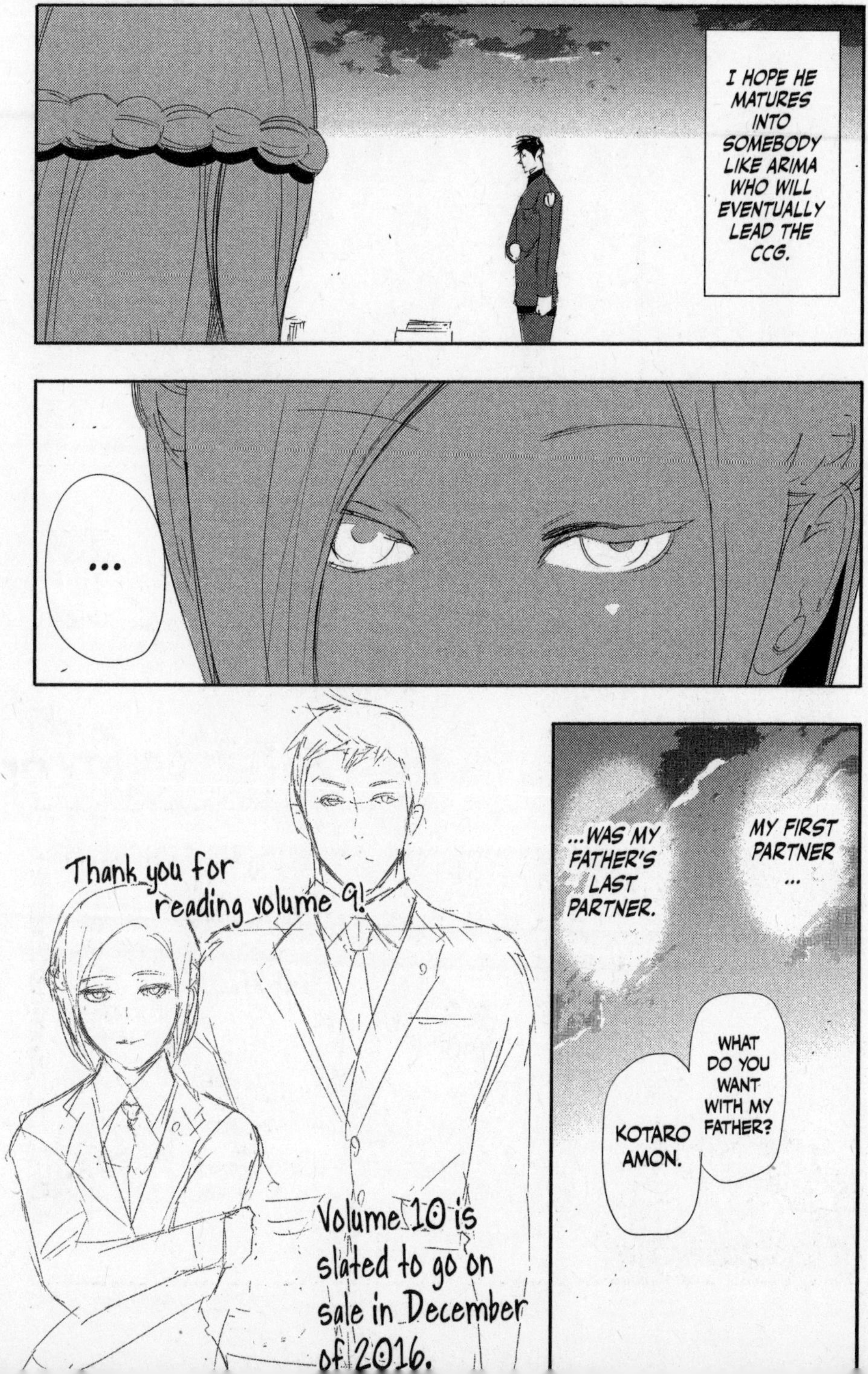
I HOPE HE MATURES INTO SOMEBODY LIKE ARIMA WHO WILL EVENTUALLY LEAD THE CCG.
...
MY FIRST PARTNER ...
...WAS MY FATHER'S LAST PARTNER.
WHAT DO YOU WANT WITH MY FATHER?
KOTARO AMON.
Thank you for reading volume 9!
Volume 10 is slated to go on sale in December of 2016.

TOKYO GHOUL

[THIS IS THE
LAST PAGE]

TOKYO GHOUL
READS
RIGHT TO LEFT

TOKYO GHOUL

東京喰種

VOLUME 9
VIZ Signature Edition

Story and art by
SUI ISHIDA

TOKYO GHOUL © 2011 by Sui Ishida
All rights reserved.
First published in Japan in 2011 by
SHUEISHA Inc., Tokyo.
English translation rights arranged by
SHUEISHA Inc.

TRANSLATION. Joe Yamazaki

TOUCH-UP ART AND LETTERING. Vanessa Satone

DESIGN. Fawn Lau

EDITOR. Joel Enos

Printed in the U.S.A.

Published by VIZ Media, LLC
P.O. Box 77010
San Francisco, CA 94107

10 9 8 7 6 5 4 3 2 1
First printing, October 2016

www.viz.com

PARENTAL ADVISORY
TOKYO GHOUL is rated T+ for Older Teen
and is recommended for ages 16 and up.
This volume contains violence and gore.
ratings.viz.com

VIZ SIGNATURE